Ending

Reviewing the Process
Final Evaluating
Sharing Ending Feelings and Saying Goodbye
Recording the Closing Summary

Working and Evaluating

Rehearsing Action Steps
Reviewing Action Steps
Evaluating
Educating
Advising
Representing
Responding with Immediacy
Reframing
Confronting
Pointing Out Endings
Progress Recording

Contracting

Reflecting a Problem
Sharing Your View of a Problem
Specifying Problems for Work
Establishing Goals
Developing an Approach
Identifying Action Steps
Planning for Evaluation
Summarizing the Contract

GENERIC SOCIAL WORK SKILLS
(apply throughout all phases and processes)

Self-Understanding

Family of Origin
Current Situational Factors
Self-Esteem
Acceptance of Others
Responsible Assertiveness
Self-Control
Readiness for Social Work Practice

Ethical Decision Making

Understanding the Legal Duties of Professional Helpers
Understanding the Fundamental Values and Ethics of Social Work
Identifying Ethical and Legal Implications
Ethical Decision Making

Talking and Listening—The Basic Interpersonal Skills

Voice, Speech, and Language
Body Language
Listening: Hearing, Observing, Encouraging, and Remembering
Active Listening

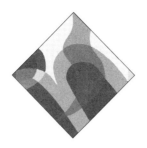

THE SOCIAL WORK SKILLS WORKBOOK

Second Edition

Barry Cournoyer
Indiana University

Brooks/Cole Publishing Company
I⟨T⟩P™ An International Thomson Publishing Company

Pacific Grove • Albany • Bonn • Boston • Cincinnati • Detroit • London • Madrid • Melbourne
Mexico City • New York • Paris • San Francisco • Singapore • Tokyo • Toronto • Washington

Sponsoring Editor: *Lisa Gebo*
Marketing Team: *Nancy Kernal, Margaret Parks*
Editorial Assistant: *Jodi Hermans*
Production Editor: *Marjorie Z. Sanders*
Manuscript Editor: *David Hoyt*

Permissions Editor: *May Clark*
Interior Design & Typesetting: *Patricia K. Bonn*
Cover Design: *Lisa Berman*
Art Editor: *Lisa Torri*
Printing and Binding: *Malloy Lithographing, Inc.*

For more information, contact:

BROOKS/COLE PUBLISHING COMPANY
511 Forest Lodge Road
Pacific Grove, CA 93950
USA

International Thomson Editores
Campos Eliseos 385, Piso 7
Col. Polanco
11560 México D. F. México

International Thomson Publishing Europe
Berkshire House 168-173
High Holborn
London WC1V 7AA
England

International Thomson Publishing GmbH
Königswinterer Strasse 418
53227 Bonn
Germany

Thomas Nelson Australia
102 Dodds Street
South Melbourne, 3205
Victoria, Australia

International Thomson Publishing Asia
221 Henderson Road
#05-10 Henderson Building
Singapore 0315

Nelson Canada
1120 Birchmount Road
Scarborough, Ontario
Canada M1K 5G4

International Thomson Publishing Japan
Hirakawacho Kyowa Building, 3F
2-2-1 Hirakawacho
Chiyoda-ku, Tokyo 102
Japan

Printed in the United States of America
10 9 8 7 6 5 4 3 2

Library of Congress Cataloging-in-Publication Data
Cournoyer, Barry.
    The social work skills workbook / Barry Cournoyer.
        p.   cm.
    "2nd ed."—Pref.
    Includes bibliographical references.
    ISBN 0-534-33875-5
    1. Social work education.   2. Social service.   I. Title.
HV11.C786 1996
361.3'2'076—dc20   95-12973
                                                        CIP

Contents

CHAPTER 6 *Beginning*   *131*

CHAPTER 7 *Exploring*   *159*

CHAPTER 8 Assessing   214

CHAPTER 9 Contracting   246

CHAPTER 10 Working and Evaluating   296

CHAPTER 11   *Ending*   360

Preface

The impetus for developing this workbook originated with observations and, yes, complaints from students. According to them, social work professors and their textbooks tend to "talk *about* practice" rather than helping students learn "what to do and how to do it." A typical comment was: "In the classroom, the professors talk at such abstract levels that when I'm with a client, I don't know what I'm really supposed to do." Clearly, there was a need for a workbook in which students could actually practice the fundamental social work skills through the use of exercises and simulated case situations.

This workbook is designed for use in the following contexts: (1) as the primary text or source book for social work skills laboratory courses (which might be entitled "interviewing skills," "interpersonal skills," "interactional skills," or "helping skills" labs); (2) as a secondary text and workbook for social work practice courses; (3) as a workbook for use by social work students and field instructors during practicum experiences; and (4) by professional social workers interested in refreshing their proficiency in basic social work skills. Social workers and social work students who are currently providing service to actual clients may alter some of the workbook exercises, particularly the summary exercises, for use in agency settings. If so, however, they should carefully consider the implications for social work values and ethics so as to ensure that clients' rights are securely protected.

The workbook provides beginning social workers and social work students with a means to understand and practice the essential skills of direct social work practice. This workbook does not present an exhaustive collection of all skills that have relevance for social workers; there are other skills of great significance. However, the workbook does address those skills most applicable to and congruent with (1) the phases or processes of social work practice (Compton & Galaway, 1994; Perlman, 1957) and (2) eight essential qualities that characterize effective social workers.

The social work skills are presented so as to coincide with the phases or processes of social work practice. Of course, such a phase-to-phase approach runs the risk of suggesting that work with every client follows a similar pattern and that the characteristics and skills relevant to one phase are distinctly different from those of another. This is not the case. Many of the dynamics, tasks, functions, and skills applicable to one phase may, in work with a particular client, be evident in other phases as well. Indeed, some skills may be used over and over again in the course of a social worker's efforts with and for a client.

This second edition of the workbook maintains the original organizational structure, but a number of changes have been made to help students understand and practice the social work skills. The book is arranged in the following manner.

An introductory chapter provides overall perspective on the range of psychosocial problems social workers help to address and the kinds of settings where service occurs. Chapter 1 contributes a working definition of *social work skill* and outlines the conceptual framework used for selecting the skills included in the book. Also discussed are eight essential qualities that effective social workers should show in their professional service with and on behalf of clients.

Building on the introductory chapter, Chapter 2 presents a series of self-assessment exercises. These are designed to assess several of the essential qualities, to initiate a process of self-understanding and self-awareness, and to consider one's general readiness for the profession of social work. Included in this chapter are exercises to further the self-understanding of factors such as family of origin, ecological context or situation, and personal dimensions such as self-esteem, acceptance of others, and assertiveness. New for this edition are more extensive exercises for becoming aware of one's personal prejudices and discriminatory behavior. In addition, self-control has been added as an essential characteristic of effective social workers, and exercises for assessing it are incorporated in Chapter 2.

Chapter 3 introduces the student to the process of ethical decision making in social work practice. Included in this chapter are discussions of the fundamental legal duties and obligations that apply to all helping professionals and the core values and ethical principles that social workers in particular must follow. This edition reflects the central social work values identified in the most recent *Curriculum Policy Statement* (1992) of the Council on Social Work Education. Chapter 3 covers the major principles of the codes of ethics of both the National Association of Social Workers (NASW) and the Canadian Association of Social Workers (CASW). (Both codes are reprinted in their entirety in the appendix, for ready reference.) The issue of malpractice is introduced and the implications of recent court decisions considered. Finally, the conceptual scheme by which ethical dilemmas may be resolved has been updated in accordance with Loewenberg and Dolgoff's Ethical Principles Screen (1992).

Chapter 4 addresses the fundamental interpersonal skills of talking and listening. Included in this chapter are talking skills associated with voice, speech, and language; body language; and listening skills related to hearing, observing, encouraging, and remembering. The talking and listening skills are then combined in the form of active listening—through which the social worker invites, listens, and reflects what other people, including clients, express. Because of the great cultural diversity of North

America, this edition pays greater attention to the significance of language and the social worker's choice of words.

Chapters 5 through 11 address the skills associated with the following phases or process of social work practice: preparing, beginning, exploring, assessing, contracting, working and evaluating, and ending. Each chapter includes a general introduction to the purpose and tasks associated with the work of that particular phase. After the introduction, the social work skills commonly used during the phase are identified and illustrated. Exercises intended to help students learn to apply each skill are provided after each section and at the end of the chapter. For this edition, each of these chapters has been revised to facilitate understanding. Many of the social work skills have been described more completely, and case examples have been clarified, expanded, or updated. For example, the discussion of open-ended and closed-ended probes has been expanded to include the issue of leading questions, which is significant for numerous legal, ethical, and practical reasons. Similarly, exercises for practicing the exploring skill of reflecting feelings have been refined to allow students to generate feeling word vocabularies for various cultural groups whom they might serve.

Cases and situations selected as illustrative examples and for use in the exercise sections have been drawn from a variety of agency settings and circumstances. Most of the case vignettes involve interaction with individuals, but there are some examples of other types of clients (e.g., dyads, families, groups) and nonclient systems (e.g., referral sources, community resources, or related social systems). The cases have been selected with a view to diversity in terms of age, socioeconomic and ethnic status, gender, and sexual orientation.

Instructors who employ the workbook in their social work courses may use the exercises in a variety of ways. As part of a homework assignment, students may be asked to respond to selected exercises. During the classroom session, a professor may then call on students to share their responses. Students may role-play them, to demonstrate the nonverbal as well as the verbal dimensions of their communications. Then class members could share observations and discuss the characteristics that account for superior and inferior applications of the skills. Alternately, an instructor may assign certain exercises as written homework to be submitted for evaluation. The pages of the workbook are perforated to allow for easy removal. During classroom meetings, students may be asked to form pairs, triads, or small groups in order to carry out selected exercises. Role-plays in which students alternately assume the part of client and social worker can be powerful learning experiences, particularly when there is constructive feedback from other students and the instructor. In general, instructors should recognize that the social work skills are ultimately used in the context of helping clients. Therefore, it is preferable to use teaching-learning processes that approximate the actual *doing* with opportunities for constructive feedback.

This edition contains six appendixes to support students' learning. Appendix 1 is a practice test that students may use as a pretest, as a posttest, or as an overall gauge of their knowledge and proficiency in a wide range of social work skills. Appendixes 2 and 3 present the codes of ethics of, respectively, the National Association of Social Workers and the Canadian Association of Social Workers. Appendix 4 is an alphabetized vocabulary of standard English feeling words that students may find useful for developing their empathic reflection skills. Appendix 5 provides students with an opportunity to conduct a summary self-evaluation of their proficiency in the social work skills. Appendix 6 consists of a rating form that should be of use to students in assessing their application of the social work skills during actual interviews with clients.

Acknowledgments

The second edition of *The Social Work Skills Workbook* reflects the experience of practicing social work for more than 20 years and teaching courses to beginning social work students for more than 15 years. Over the years, clients have always been my most important teachers. Time and time again, they forgave my mistakes and guided me toward more fruitful paths. I have learned more from them than from any other source. I am forever indebted to those clients who allowed me a glimpse into their worlds. Their life stories are remarkable, and I feel privileged to have participated with them on their heroic journeys. Likewise, students in the social work skills laboratory course and in various practice courses have been my educators. They have taught me a great deal. If they have learned half of what I have learned from them, I will feel satisfied. Without their teachings, this workbook would not have been possible.

I would also like to recognize those social workers whose teachings and writings have affected me professionally and contributed to the approach taken in this workbook. Dr. Eldon Marshall, my former professor and now colleague, was the first to introduce me to the interpersonal helping skills. I shall never forget his class or the impact of my first videotaped interview. During my doctoral program, Dr. Dean Hepworth, both through his teaching and his writing, furthered the skills emphasis begun during my master's education. Even now, I recall the competence with which he prepared course syllabi. My former colleague, Dr. Beulah Compton, deserves much credit. Her clear conception of fundamental social work processes has served me well indeed. I shall long remember our sometimes heated but always stimulating conversations about social work practice. I also offer profound thanks to my colleague Dr. Gayle Cox, whose professionalism and support have been constant through the years.

Thanks are due to the manuscript reviewers, who offered valuable suggestions: Eric Albert, University of Nevada; Gloria Carpenter, University of Texas; Penny Smith Ramsdell, University of Texas at Arlington; and Delores B. Sykes, Ohio State University.

Much credit is due the extraordinary editorial staff at Brooks/Cole. David Hoyt's editorial work has been masterful. Lisa Gebo has been delightful! Her dedication, enthusiasm, and understanding suggests that she may have a future in social work.

I also wish to thank my parents, Chub, Marjorie, Grant, and Karma for their unflagging support. Finally, to my loving partner, Catherine Hughes Cournoyer, and our children, John Paul and Michael, I express enormous gratitude. Catherine is the most generous person I have ever met and, without question, the best social worker. We serve as supervisors and consultants to one another in our professional as well as our personal lives. This book is as much hers as mine. Each day, she and the boys continue to make me more and better than I could possibly be without them.

Barry Cournoyer

Chapter 1

Introduction

Welcome to the exciting and challenging profession of social work! As a social worker, you will provide helping services to people in all walks of life and in all kinds of situations. The range of settings in which you might serve is wide and varied. At some point in your career, you could serve in a child-protection capacity, responding to indications that a child may be at risk of abuse or neglect and helping families to improve their child-caring capabilities. You may serve in the emergency room of a hospital, intervening with persons and families in crisis situations. You may lead therapy groups for children who have been sexually victimized or provide education and counseling to abusive adults. As a social worker, you may aid couples whose relationships are faltering or help single parents who seek guidance and support in rearing their children. You may serve persons who abuse alcohol and drugs or help family members who have been affected by the substance abuse of a parent, child, spouse, or sibling. You might work in a residential setting for youthful offenders, a prison for adults, or a psychiatric institution. You might serve in a university counseling center, working with college students and faculty members. You could help people who are in some way physically or mentally challenged. You might serve in a school system or perhaps as a consultant to a police department. You could work in a mayor's office, serve on the staff of a state legislator, or perhaps even become a member of Congress yourself. You may function in a crisis intervention capacity for a suicide prevention service. You could work for a health maintenance organization (HMO), a managed health care system, or an employee assistance program (EAP). As a social worker, you might act as an advocate for persons who have experienced discrimination, oppression, or exploitation, perhaps due to racism, sexism, or ageism. You might work with people victimized by crime, or perhaps with people charged with criminal actions. You might serve in a domestic-violence program, providing social services to people affected by spouse abuse, child abuse, or elder abuse. You could provide psychosocial services to persons dealing with a physical illness, such as cancer, kidney failure, Alzheimer's disease, or AIDS, and help their families cope with the myriad psychosocial effects of such an illness. You might work in a hospice, helping people prepare for their own death from a terminal illness or that of a family member. You could help persons locate needed services or resources by providing information and arranging referrals. You might counsel individuals suffering from a mental illness, such as schizophrenia, obsessive-compulsive disorder, or manic depression, and provide support and education to their families. You could work in a nursing home for aged persons, leading groups or counseling family members. You might serve in a halfway house, work with foster parents, or perhaps provide information and support to teenage parents. Or, as an increasing number of social workers do, you might serve in industry, consulting with employers and employees about problems that affect their well-being and productivity.

The range of settings in which you could practice your profession and the variety of functions that you could serve as a social worker are immense indeed. Such diversity can be overwhelming. You may ask yourself, "Can I possibly learn what I need to in order to serve competently as a social worker in all those places, serving such different people, and helping them to address such complex problems?" The answer to that question is certainly No; you could never become truly competent in all the arenas in which social workers practice, since it would require a greater breadth of knowledge and expertise than any one person could ever acquire. Indeed, there is a specialized body of knowledge and expertise needed for each practice setting, each special population group, and each psychosocial problem. You cannot know everything, do everything, or be competent in helping people struggling with all of the many social problems. However, you can acquire expertise in those skills that are common to social work practice in all settings, all population groups, and all psychosocial problems. These common social work skills serve to bring coherence to the profession, despite its extraordinary diversity and breadth.

In addition to using certain skills in common, social workers tend to approach clients from a similar perspective—one that is reflected in a distinct professional language. For example, most social workers prefer the term *client*, rather than *patient*, *subject*, or *case*, in referring to people served. Social workers also lean toward the use of the word *assessment*, as opposed to *diagnosis*, *study*, *examination*, or *investigation*. Furthermore, they tend to look for *strengths* and *competencies* rather than attending exclusively to *deficiencies* or *pathology*. This common perspective and distinctive use of professional language are characteristic of most contemporary social workers, regardless of their particular practice settings.

All professional social workers have earned a baccalaureate, master's, or doctoral degree in social work. They adopt certain common professional values that pervade all aspects of their helping activities, and they pledge to follow a code of ethics for social work. Additionally, social workers, regardless of setting or function, tend to view the *person-and-situation* (PAS) or *person-in-environment* (PIE) as the basic unit of attention and the enhancement of social functioning as the overriding purpose of practice.

Social workers tend to conceive of people and situations as continually changing and as having the potential for planned change. They view professional practice as predominantly for the client, for the community, and for society. Whatever personal benefits accrue to the social worker are secondary; the notion of service to others comes first. The primacy of service in social work is reflected through a special sensitivity to at-risk individuals and oppressed groups—people often overlooked by other professions. These common elements distinguish social work from other helping professions and bring a sense of identity to all social workers. They may also help you individually to maintain a focus as you encounter a variety of people, problems, and settings during your social work career.

Social workers recognize that serving people often involves powerful interpersonal processes that have considerable potential for harm as well as for good. Social workers realize that professional practice requires a highly developed understanding of oneself and extraordinary personal discipline and self-control. A great deal more than admirable personal qualities and compassionate feelings are required. Social workers' words and actions must be based on professional knowledge and guided by social work values, ethics, and obligations. Social workers generally view helping as a mutual and interactive process, following a fairly predictable sequence of phases. Each of these phases requires competence in certain essential *social work skills*.

Social Work Skills

The term *skill* has become extremely popular in social work and other helping professions during the past few decades. Several widely used social work textbooks incorporate *skill* or *skills* in their titles (Henry, 1981; 1992; Hepworth & Larsen, 1986; 1990; Middleman & Wood, 1990; Shulman, 1982; 1984; 1992). The term *skill*, however, is not always used in the same way; it means different things to different authors. For example, Barker (1991, p. 216) defines *skill* as

> proficiency in the use of one's hands, knowledge, talents, personality, or resources. A social worker's skills include being proficient in communication, assessing problems and client workability, matching *needs* with *resources*, developing resources, and changing social structures.

Johnson (1995, p. 55) defines *skill* as "the practice component that brings knowledge and values together and converts them to action as a response to concern and need." Johnson also defines *skill* as "a complex organization of behavior directed toward a particular goal or activity" (1995, p. 431).

Morales and Sheafor (1992, p. 248) define *social work skill* as

> the social worker's capacity to set in motion, in a relationship with the client (individual, group, community), guided psychosocial interventive processes of change based on social work values and knowledge in a specific situation relevant to the client. The change that begins to occur as the result of this

skilled intervention is effected with the greatest degree of consideration for the client and by the use of the strengths and capacity of the client.

According to Smalley (1967, p. 17), "*Skill* . . . refers to the social worker's capacity to *use* a method in order to *further* a process directed toward the accomplishment of a social work purpose as that purpose finds expression in a specific program or service." Middleman and Wood (1990, p. 12) use the term *skill* to refer to "the production of specific behaviors under the precise conditions designated for their use" and refer to four skill categories (p. 14):

> *Inner skills* affect the internal decision making processes that affect the worker's mental preparedness to act. *Interactional skills* occur between the worker and other(s). *Group skills* are needed, in addition to those in the first two categories, when more than one other person is involved. *Strategic skills* are used in special situations.

Henry (1981, p. vii) suggests that skills are "finite and discrete sets of behaviors or tasks employed by a worker at a given time, for a given purpose, in a given manner." Henry (1992, p. 20) also cites Phillips (1957), who characterizes skill as "knowledge in action." Barker (1991, p. 63) defines *direct practice skills* as "the ability to put social work knowledge into effective intervention activities with individuals, families, groups, and communities." Specifically, in this workbook, a *social work skill* is defined as follows.

DEFINITION OF SOCIAL WORK SKILLS

A set of discrete cognitive and behavioral actions that (1) derive from social work knowledge and from social work values, ethics, and obligations, (2) are consistent with the essential facilitative qualities, and (3) comport with a social work purpose within the context of a phase of practice.

Although they are associated with different phases or processes, social work skills should not be viewed as technical activities to be carried out, robotlike, at the same relative time and in the same way with all clients, all problems, and all situations. Rather, the social worker selects, combines, and adapts specific social work skills to suit the particular needs and characteristics of the person-problem-situation.

The skills chosen for inclusion in this workbook are primarily derived from the tasks associated with commonly identified phases of social work practice, as well as eight essential qualities exhibited by effective professional helpers. In this context, the phases of practice are as follows (see Compton & Galaway, 1994; Johnson, 1995; Kirst-Ashman & Hull, 1993; and Perlman, 1957):

- ◆ preparing
- ◆ beginning

- ◆ exploring
- ◆ assessing
- ◆ contracting
- ◆ working and evaluating
- ◆ ending

The following are among the essential qualities that effective social workers generally exhibit in their work with clients.

- ◆ empathy
- ◆ respect
- ◆ authenticity
- ◆ self-understanding
- ◆ self-control
- ◆ understanding of social work values and ethics
- ◆ professional social work knowledge
- ◆ responsible assertiveness

The tasks associated with each phase are organized into small, manageable units of thought and action, compatible with these eight essential qualities—into *social work skills*.

Essential Qualities

The results of research attempting to identify the characteristics of effective professional helpers remain somewhat confusing. During the 1960s and 1970s, research studies (Lambert, 1982, pp. 31–33) tended to suggest that qualities such as empathy, nonpossessive warmth, and genuineness are modestly related to positive client changes. However, identifying and measuring all the potential factors that affect the outcome of helping processes are enormously complex undertakings. Definite conclusions may never be reached. For social workers, who fulfill disparate professional functions in extremely varied settings with a wide range of populations and psychosocial problems, the picture is even more nebulous. As Kadushin (1983, p. 84) suggests, the roles and skills of social workers in their professional practice are diverse indeed:

> The warm, accepting qualities necessary for interviews whose primary purpose is therapeutic are not those required for the interview whose primary purpose is assessment. The "therapeutic" interviewer in an assessment interview may fail to probe inconsistencies or may make compassionate allowance for interviewee reluctance to discuss essential but difficult areas. The interview whose primary purpose is reliable judgment, diagnostic assessment, may require a reserved, extraceptively oriented person; the therapeutic interview may require a warmer, more spontaneous, intraceptively oriented person. The interviewer engaged in advocacy may need a more aggressive, directive, dominant approach to the interview.

In spite of the diversity inherent in social work and the inconclusive nature of the research findings, certain aspects of the worker-client experience can be considered critical to an effective outcome. Donald F. Krill (1986, p. xi), for example, suggests that the relationship between a social worker and a client is more likely to be productive if, among other things, (1) the participants like and respect each other, (2) the client is clearly told what to expect and how to contribute to the helping process, (3) the worker is warm, genuine and sincere and regularly expresses empathy about the client's experience, (4) the worker and client engage in goal-directed activities such as practice, in-session tasks, or between-session action steps, and (5) the social worker actively seeks to involve in the helping process significant persons in the client's life.

Krill (1986) lists among the characteristics of effective helpers those that have been called the *core conditions* or the *facilitative qualities* (Carkhuff, 1969; Carkhuff & Truax, 1965; Ivey, 1971; Ivey & Authier, 1978; Marshall, Charping, & Bell, 1979; Rogers, 1957; 1961; and Truax & Carkhuff, 1967). These qualities, when consistently demonstrated by social workers, aid in the development and maintenance of a special rapport with their clients. This rapport is sometimes called *the helping relationship*, *the working relationship*, *therapeutic rapport*, or *the therapeutic alliance*. According to Perlman (1979, pp. 48–77), the professional working relationship between social worker and client is distinguished from other relationships by the following characteristics:

- ◆ It is formed for a recognized and agreed-upon purpose.
- ◆ It is time-bound.
- ◆ It is *for* the client.
- ◆ It carries authority.
- ◆ It is a controlled relationship.

It is within the context of this special relationship that the *facilitative qualities* become so essential. When the social worker consistently reflects these qualities, the risk of harming the person-and-situation is usually decreased and the probability of helping is usually increased. However, demonstration of these qualities alone is rarely enough to enable clients to reach their goals. The social worker must nearly always add expert knowledge and skills to help the client progress toward goal attainment. Nonetheless, it is clear that both aspects—the facilitative qualities and professional expertise—are usually necessary to the process of helping clients address problems. One element without the other is usually incomplete and ineffective.

The essential facilitative qualities the social worker should consistently reflect in the helping relationship are *empathy*, *respect*, and *authenticity*.

Empathy

The term *empathy* (Rogers, 1975) is widely used in social work and other helping professions, but it is often misunderstood. Barker (1991) defines *empathy* as "the act of perceiving, understanding, experiencing, and responding to the emotional state and ideas of another person" (p. 73). Derived from the Greek word *empatheia*, empathy may be described as a process of joining in the feelings of another, of feeling how and what another person experiences. Empathy is a process of *feeling with* another person. It is an understanding and appreciation of the thoughts, feelings, experiences, and circumstances of another human being. It is not an expression of *feeling for* or *feeling toward*, as in pity or romantic love. Rather, it is a conscious and intentional joining with others in their subjective experience.

Hammond, Hepworth, and Smith (1977, p. 3) state that "empathy is an understanding *with* the client, rather than a diagnostic or evaluative understanding *of* the client." Of course, there are limits to any human being's ability and willingness to feel with and feel as another does. In fact, as a professional social worker, you must always retain a portion of yourself for your professional responsibilities. You should not overidentify with a client by adopting his or her feelings as your own. You must be able both to feel the client's feelings and then leave those feelings with the client. They remain the client's. They are not yours to be taken or assumed.

Empathy helps you, the social worker, gain an appreciation for and sensitivity to the people you serve. Through empathic connection with your clients, you increase the probability of developing rapport and maintaining productive working relationships. Also, you are more likely to gain a realistic perspective about the identified problems as experienced by the people actually affected by them.

Respect

The facilitative quality of *respect* (Hammond, Hepworth, & Smith, 1977, pp. 5, 170–203) is a social worker's attitude of noncontrolling, warm, caring acceptance of other persons. It involves the demonstration of *unconditional positive regard* (Rogers, 1957; 1961).

There are very few relationships in which people are truly accepted as unique human beings with full rights, privileges, and responsibilities—without regard to their views, actions, and circumstances. In most social contexts, people tend to spend time with people who live and work in similar circumstances, who hold views similar to their own, and who are friendly toward them. Conversely, people are often less affectionate toward persons who live and work in different circumstances, who espouse views that differ from their own, or who are insulting or demeaning to them.

As a social worker, you are likely to work with many people who differ from you in numerous ways. You may find that you do not especially like some of the people you serve. Some will undoubtedly dislike you. Nonetheless, as a social worker, you should maintain respect for and caring acceptance of all the clients you serve. Social workers view each human being as unique and inherently valuable. As a social worker, you convey that value by respecting the personhood of all clients, regardless of the nature of their views, actions, or circumstances. Although you may personally disagree with and perhaps even disapprove of a particular client's words or actions, you nonetheless continue to care about and accept that person as a unique individual of dignity and worth. Furthermore, you recognize and respect the fundamental right of clients to make decisions for themselves. This ability to respect clients neither because of nor in spite of their attributes, behaviors, or circumstances is an essential facilitative condition in social work practice.

However, caring for clients as valuable human beings and respecting their rights does not preclude you from making professional judgments or from offering suggestions or advice. Respect for clients does not mean that you avoid taking into consideration other persons or groups as you focus on clients. Indeed, as a professional social worker who adopts a *person-in-environment* (PIE) perspective, you must attend to persons and social systems affecting and affected by the clients you serve.

Authenticity

Hammond, Hepworth, and Smith (1977, p. 7) state that "authenticity refers to a sharing of self by behaving in a natural, sincere, spontaneous, real, open, and nondefensive manner. An authentic person relates to others personally, so that expressions do not seem rehearsed or contrived." Genuineness, congruence, transparency, or authenticity (Rogers, 1961) may sometimes seem contrary to the notion of the professional social worker as cool, calm, and collected. However, professionalism in social work does not mean adopting a stiffly formal or overcontrolled attitude. As a social worker, you need not and should not present yourself as an unfeeling, detached, computerlike technician. People seeking social services almost always prefer to talk with a person who, in addition to acting professionally knowledgeable and competent, also comes across as a living, breathing, feeling human being—not as someone playing a canned role, spouting clichés, or repeating the same phrases again and again.

This emphasis on authenticity in the working relationship, however, does not grant you license to say or do whatever you think or feel at the moment. You must always remember that the helping relationship is fundamentally for the client—not primarily for you, the social worker. Expression of your own thoughts and feelings for any purpose other than serving the client and working toward mutually agreed-upon goals is, at best, inefficient and, at worst, harmful.

Additional Essential Qualities

In addition to *empathy*, *respect*, and *authenticity*, five additional qualities are necessary for effective social work practice: *self-understanding, self-control, understanding of social work values and ethics, professional social work knowledge*, and *responsible assertiveness*.

Self-Understanding

In order to use yourself effectively in helping others, you must possess an extremely well-developed understanding of self (see Compton & Galaway, 1994, pp. 263–306). Although self-understanding is, of course, a lifelong process that is never really finished, as a social worker you must know yourself as well as possible so as to minimize the chance of doing damage to clients. Otherwise, even with the best motivation and intention, you may inadvertently express yourself in unhelpful or perhaps even harmful ways (Keith-Lucas, 1972).

As is the case with most worthwhile endeavors, engaging in self-awareness activities involves certain risks. You may discover aspects of yourself that you have long denied or minimized. For example, you may learn that you have a strong need for power, control, and predictability in relationships. You may find that you relate to women with less interest, energy, or attention than you do to men. You may become aware of fixed racial or ethnic stereotypes that interfere with an objective assessment of individual members of certain groups. You might become aware of unmet childhood needs for acceptance and approval that lead you to avoid confrontation or withdraw from conflict. You may find that you experience heightened anxiety when in the presence of authority figures. You may discover that you have an alcohol or drug problem, that you suffer from occasional periods of depression, carry substantial unresolved rage, or even that you are unsuited for a career in the profession of social work.

This process of self-exploration and self-discovery may give rise to disturbing thoughts and feelings. You may even find yourself reconsidering significant life choices that you had previously thought were resolved. Indeed, there are numerous risks inherent in any serious process of self-examination, but the pursuit of self-understanding and self-awareness is generally well worth the costs. If you fail to do so, you may put yourself and the people you serve at considerable risk of being harmed by the very process that is intended to help.

Self-Control

In addition to self-understanding, professional social work practice requires enormous self-control and self-discipline. You must be able to manage your own thoughts, feelings, words, gestures, and behavior. Under conditions where other people might well be overwhelmed by powerful emotions, you must direct your words and actions so that they conform with the values and ethics of the profession, social work's knowledge base, and the purpose for which you and the other person or persons are meeting.

Additionally, you must be able to control any maladaptive patterns of behavior that have a potential for impairing your professional performance. Alcohol or cocaine use, for example, could interfere with your capacity to serve as a social worker. Similarly, other habitual patterns of behavior must be identified and managed. Compulsive patterns of eating, dieting, exercising, TV watching, and, importantly, relating may interfere with effective social work practice. An example of one such relational pattern is *rescuing*. Rescuing in professional practice occurs when a social worker views other people as victims in need of rescue and therefore assumes disproportionate control over clients and responsibility for them. Rather than empowering people, such behavior often has the effect of substantially diminishing clients' competence, autonomy, and personal power. Of course, people actually do need to be rescued on occasion. A child in danger of freezing to death, because she lives under a bridge during wintertime, should be provided with warmth and shelter. This would not be *rescuing* in the compulsive sense, as it would be if you took responsibility for the decisions of fully competent adults.

Self-control is quite simply essential for professional social work practice. There is no alternative. If you find, in your ongoing processes of self-exploration and examination, that you are unable to manage your own habitual patterns of thinking, feeling, and behaving, then you should strongly question your suitability for a career in social work.

Understanding of Social Work Values, Ethics, and Obligations

In addition to self-knowledge and self-control, as a social worker you must also have a thorough understanding of social work values and ethics (Compton & Galaway, 1994, pp. 219–262), as well as the legal obligations of professional helpers as they affect and inform your work. As a social worker, such understanding involves a great deal more than familiarity with an ethical code. You must have a thorough grasp of the meaning and implications of each ethical principle. You should know your code of ethics and be able to identify the principles that apply in specific situations. When principles conflict, you must have the capacity to address the dilemma. Specifically, you should be able to determine which ethical principle or legal obligation takes precedence over others in situations where several competing responsibilities apply.

Clearly, the topic of values and ethics in social work practice is very complex. As a professional social worker, you must pay constant attention to professional ethics and obligations, because they apply to virtually every aspect of your professional life.

Professional Knowledge

Professional knowledge is another characteristic of the effective social worker (see Compton & Galaway, 1994, pp. 85–188). The particular knowledge required varies according to the characteristics of the setting, the problems for work, the populations served, and the roles assumed. However, a common base of knowledge is required of all social workers, including the following:

1. theory and research related to individual, family, small-group, organizational, and community behavior and development
2. theory and research related to social problems such as child neglect; child, spouse, and elder abuse; poverty; discrimination; and violence
3. theory and research related to understanding and intervening with health, mental-health, and substance-use phenomena
4. theory and research related to various groups and cultures
5. understanding of the differential use of social work theory and principles with diverse and at-risk populations
6. knowledge of preparing, beginning, assessing, contracting, intervening, evaluating, and ending processes in social work practice
7. knowledge of processes associated with clear and accurate communication

8. knowledge of scientific methods and research processes, and
9. knowledge of relevant social policies that affect potential clients and understanding of the processes by which such policies are developed and influenced

The breadth and depth of knowledge that you will need in your social work career is enormous. The knowledge base itself is growing and changing at a speed never before known in human history. Some of what was taken as fact ten years ago has since been disproved, and new knowledge is emerging continually. You will find it difficult indeed to stay abreast of the newest developments. In your efforts to help other human beings, you will soon become aware that you personally, and social workers collectively, will probably never know all that is needed to truly understand and help such complex beings in such complicated circumstances. In your ongoing search for more and better information upon which to base your helping efforts, adopt an attitude of insatiable curiosity and fundamental humility. Keep reading and studying, but maintain the realization that you will never ever know enough!

Responsible Assertiveness

Responsible assertiveness is yet another essential characteristic of effective social workers (Cournoyer, 1983). The term *responsible assertiveness* refers to the expression of one's thoughts and feelings in a manner that does not violate the rights and dignity of others. Such self-expression is, of course, reflected within many of the skills presented in the workbook. In fact, you must be able to express yourself assertively in order to fulfill nearly all social work roles and functions. Responsible assertiveness is a reflection of your personal and professional power, authority, and responsibility. In this workbook, the concept of responsible assertiveness includes the ability and the manner in which you, as a professional social worker, express your knowledge and opinions.

Summary

Empathy, respect, and authenticity are essential characteristics of effective professional social workers. To these, we have added self-understanding, self-control, understanding of professional values and ethics, professional knowledge, and responsible assertiveness. You should exhibit these qualities throughout the entire social work process—from preparing for and beginning with clients on through the conclusion of work. However, their implementation will vary according to the phase of social work practice, the agency mission, programmatic objectives, and the characteristics of the person, problem, and situation.

Chapter 2

Self-Understanding

Social work practice involves the conscious and deliberate use of yourself. *You* are the medium through which knowledge, attitudes, and skill are conveyed. Because you use your self in your work as a professional social worker, you must have an extraordinarily well-developed self-understanding. Without a sophisticated understanding of yourself, you would be likely to act out your own issues with clients or colleagues. You might have nothing but the best motives, intending only to serve others. Nonetheless, if you lacked self-awareness, you could unwittingly follow emotional or behavioral patterns that harm the very people you hope to help.

Self-understanding is not a product or outcome that can be completed and then set aside. Rather, it is an ongoing process through which you grow personally and professionally. Self-understanding reduces the risk of harm to others that can occur if social workers are unaware of their own dynamic patterns, issues, and themes.

To be effective professionally, you must know yourself. You need a sophisticated understanding of who you are, how you present yourself, how you appear to others, the mannerisms you commonly exhibit, the issues that cause you anxiety or uneasiness, the topics that trigger emotional responses, the kinds of people or events that elicit fear or anger, and the patterns of personal interaction you tend to prefer. Of course, such a level of self-understanding does not occur as a result of one set of exercises, one course, or even a complete program of university study. It is certainly not awarded along with a BSW, an MSW, or even a doctoral degree.

Self-understanding is a lifelong process. It is frequently furthered by personal counseling, individual or group psychotherapy, consultation with and supervision by experienced social workers, and participation in professional workshops and training institutes. If you are open to it, self-understanding can also improve as a natural outgrowth of interaction with peers, clients, friends, and family members. This chapter contains a series of exercises intended to help you develop a greater awareness and understanding of yourself—the self that you use to help others.

The Family: Context for Development of Self

Social workers (Hartman & Laird, 1983) have long recognized that a person's family of origin powerfully influences his or her social, psychological, and even biological development. Family and childhood experiences significantly affect people's attitudes, beliefs, values, personality characteristics, and behavioral patterns. Unless you, as a social worker, are keenly aware of the way in which your family of origin has influenced you, you may inadvertently or unconsciously play out a family role or pattern in your work with clients and colleagues. Among the common family roles (see Satir, 1972; Wegscheider-Cruse, 1985) that occur in the backgrounds of social workers are *rescuer*, *peacemaker*, *hero*, and *parental child*. Of course, sometimes it is entirely proper for you to use a part of your family-based self in social work practice. In all such cases, however, it should be for a clearly identified social work purpose, and you should be fully aware that you are doing so.

One means through which people become more aware of the ways their family of origin[1] has influenced them is the use of a genogram. A family genogram is a graphic representation of one's family tree. It provides a picture of the parties involved and a chronology of significant events or themes. Additionally, a genogram may be used as "a subjective interpretive tool" (McGoldrick & Gerson, 1985, p. 2), to develop hypotheses about a person's psychosocial characteristics or a family's interactional patterns.

Certain symbols are commonly used in the preparation of a family genogram (McGoldrick & Gerson, 1985). Males are usually characterized by squares and females by circles. Spousal relationships are represented by bracket lines. A solid bracket line (⌊___⌋) reflects a married couple; a dotted bracket line (⌊_ _⌋) reflects an unmarried relationship. A line extended downward from a relationship bracket line indicates a pregnancy or offspring from that relationship. Separations and divorces are indicated by one and two slash marks (/ and //) respectively, cutting across the relationship line. Pregnancies and births from each relationship are placed in order from earliest to latest, proceeding from left to right. Deaths are indicated by an X symbol placed within the circle or square. Names of persons and dates, if known, for birth, marriage, separation, divorce, and death are written alongside the symbols. For example, just above or beneath a bracket line indicating a marriage relationship might be written "m. 3/18/67." This reflects the date of marriage as March 18, 1967. If this same relationship later results in separation, that event could be indicated by "s. 4/23/74." A subsequent divorce could be shown by "div. 5/7/75."

---

[1]Not all people have traditional, biological families of origin. Many children grow up in foster care settings, children's institutions, or hospitals. In such circumstances, some adaptation of the genogram may be necessary in order to identify significant persons in the individual's childhood. In some circumstances, an eco-map (see next section) may be more applicable than a genogram.

In addition, you may describe characteristics of individual persons and relationships with brief notations. For example, one family member may have served in the military during a war, and perhaps another suffered from diabetes. Significant events, such as major accidents, injuries, crimes, and changes in residence or occupation, may also be recorded. Additional symbols or notations may be used to characterize the nature of selected relationships (McGoldrick & Gerson, 1985). Very close relationships, those that are emotionally cool, those that are strained, and those that involve conflict may be identified. Toward the bottom of the genogram are placed the date and the person or persons who provided the information upon which it was based, as well as the name and title of the person who prepared the genogram.

A family genogram may be as brief or as extensive as the person organizing the information desires. Some people pursue its creation with great zeal, spending hours interviewing parents, aunts and uncles, and grandparents. They may even contact distant relatives and former neighbors. However, others base their genogram solely upon information they personally recall. Usually, the amount of energy expended in collecting data and preparing genograms varies according to the purposes for which they are created. In addition, genograms may be prepared in the present tense—the family as it is now—or on the basis of how it existed at some point in the past. Many people find it useful to take genogrammatic snapshots of the family as they remember it at significant points in their development (e.g., beginning and graduating from school, leaving home, entering military service or college, marrying, or giving birth to or adopting children).

As an illustrative example, consider the case of Mrs. Lynn Chase. Later, additional information about her situation will be presented, but at this point we are primarily concerned with presenting a typical genogram, as shown in Figure 2.1. Susan Holder, the social worker who prepared the genogram from Mrs. Chase's perspective, put together a considerable amount of information in readily accessible form. There are concise notes regarding some major intergenerational family themes and patterns. This genogram will be an important reference in Susan's service to Mrs. Chase.

◆ EXERCISE 2-1: FAMILY GENOGRAM

As a part of an effort to enhance your understanding of self, prepare a genogram of three generations of your own family. Use a large piece of paper. If possible, include your grandparents and parents as well as yourself and your siblings. If you have children, you may include them as the fourth generation. For this exercise, use primarily your own memory, rather than seeking a lot of information from other family members. Try to include the approximate dates and categories of significant family events such as births, deaths, marriages, divorces, separations, graduations, military service, hospitalizations, changes in place of residence, injuries, and traumatic experiences. If you do not remember details, enter question marks instead of facts. Develop a succinct synopsis of the personal characteristics of each of the most significant family members in your experience. In addition, briefly characterize the nature of the various relationships within your family.

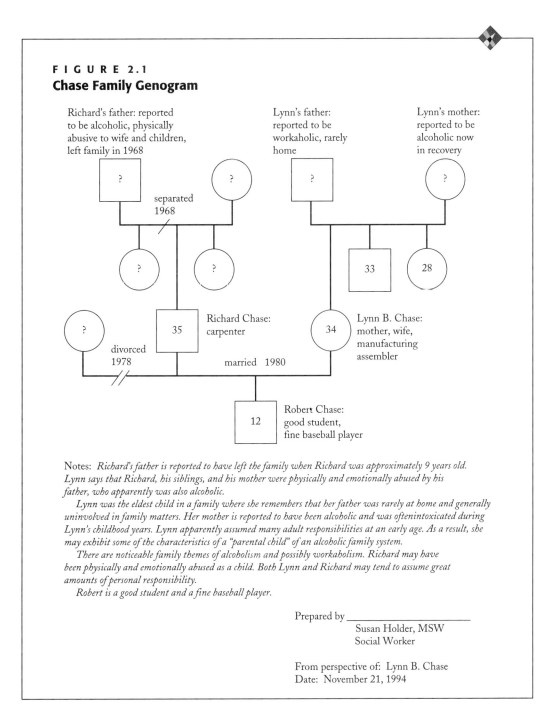

FIGURE 2.1
Chase Family Genogram

Richard's father: reported to be alcoholic, physically abusive to wife and children, left family in 1968

Lynn's father: reported to be workaholic, rarely home

Lynn's mother: reported to be alcoholic now in recovery

separated 1968

Richard Chase: carpenter

Lynn B. Chase: mother, wife, manufacturing assembler

divorced 1978

married 1980

Robert Chase: good student, fine baseball player

Notes: *Richard's father is reported to have left the family when Richard was approximately 9 years old. Lynn says that Richard, his siblings, and his mother were physically and emotionally abused by his father, who apparently was also alcoholic.*

Lynn was the eldest child in a family where she remembers that her father was rarely at home and generally uninvolved in family matters. Her mother is reported to have been alcoholic and was oftenintoxicated during Lynn's childhood years. Lynn apparently assumed many adult responsibilities at an early age. As a result, she may exhibit some of the characteristics of a "parental child" of an alcoholic family system.

There are noticeable family themes of alcoholism and possibly workaholism. Richard may have been physically and emotionally abused as a child. Both Lynn and Richard may tend to assume great amounts of personal responsibility.

Robert is a good student and a fine baseball player.

Prepared by _____
Susan Holder, MSW
Social Worker

From perspective of: Lynn B. Chase
Date: November 21, 1994

When you have completed the genogram, reflect on your childhood and family experience by addressing the following questions. Record your responses in the spaces provided.

1. What role or roles did each family member assume in your family (e.g., family hero, scapegoat, peacemaker, rescuer, parental child)? At the present time, what role or roles do you tend to play in family or familylike relationships?

2. How was affection expressed by each member of your family? At the present time, how do you tend to express affection?

3. How did family members seek help and support in your family? From whom? Today, when you need help and support, how do you seek it? From whom?

4. How was anger expressed by each member of your family? How were other feelings expressed? Sadness? Fear? Joy? At this point in your life, how do you express each of these feelings?

5. How were people (especially children) educated, guided, and disciplined in your family? Who performed these socialization functions? Today, how do you attempt to influence others?

6. Describe the patterns and characteristics of your family that reflect its ethnic or cultural affiliation. How did your family reflect its cultural identity? How do you?

7. Identify five of the more important (positive or negative) things you learned from your family experience. How do these affect you today? Which, if any, of these might you now wish to unlearn? What new learnings might you put in their place?

8. What is your conception of the ideal family? How does it compare with your actual family experience?

9. How are your childhood and family experiences likely to affect your performance as a social worker?

Situational Assessment

In addition to their family experiences, people are also affected by the broader social context in which they live. The social environment influences people's beliefs, feelings, and actions. As a social worker, you too are affected by your past and present circumstances. They affect not only various aspects of your personal life, but also your experience and performance as a social worker.

An eco-map (Hartman, 1978) is an extremely useful tool for portraying the social context, because it provides a diagrammatic representation of a person's social world. In addition to presenting an overview of a person, family, or household in context, the eco-map readily identifies the energy-enhancing and energy-depleting relationships between members of a primary social system (e.g., family or household) and the outside world. The graphic nature of the eco-map highlights social strengths and social deficiencies and helps identify areas of conflict and compatibility. It often indicates areas where change may be needed. The eco-map is a natural adjunct to the genogram.

As in genograms, squares or circles are used to represent members of the primary social system (e.g., household). These are drawn in the middle of a sheet of paper and placed in a large circle. Other significant social systems with which the person, family, or household members interact are also identified and encircled. The nature of the relationships between the identified social systems are characterized by lines. A solid line (———) reflects a strong (generally positive) relationship; a dotted line (- - - - -) reflects a tenuous relationship; and a hatched line (+++++) reflects a stressful or conflicted relationship. Arrows (→) are used to indicate the direction of the flow of energy or resources between systems. These relationship lines may also be used to characterize the exchange of energy among family members. Plus (+), minus (-), and plus-minus (±) signs may be placed adjacent to relationship lines as a supplement, indicating that the relationship is energy-enhancing, energy-depleting, or evenly balanced in terms of energy investment and return.

As an illustrative example, an eco-map of the family of Lynn Chase is shown in Figure 2.2. The social worker preparing the eco-map, using information provided by Mrs. Chase, has identified important social systems with which the Chase family members interact. The relationships among the systems are characterized. When used in the context of providing social work services, the eco-map provides the worker and client with a great deal of information in graphic form. As you can easily observe, Mrs. Chase appears to expend a great deal more energy than she receives from most of her interactions with other people and social systems.

◆ **EXERCISE 2-2: THE ECO-MAP**

On a large piece of paper, prepare an eco-map of your current social situation. Using the guidelines described above, identify and characterize the significant social systems with which you interact. Identify sources of stress or conflict as well as sources of support and nurturance. Indicate the direction of energy or resource flow between yourself and

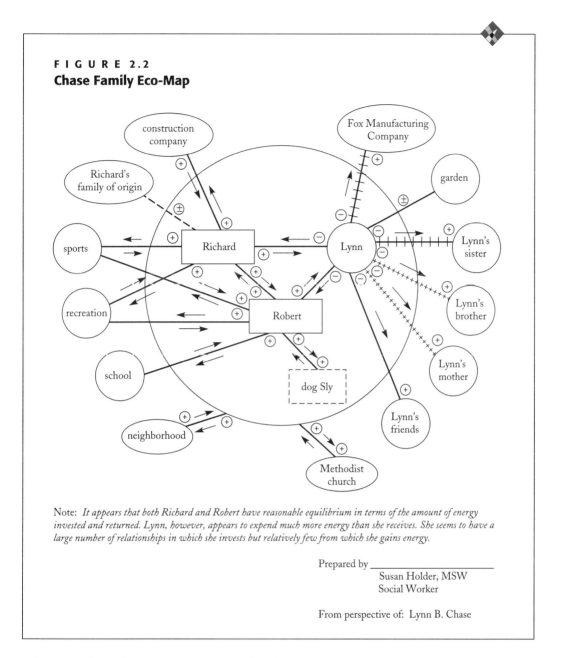

FIGURE 2.2
Chase Family Eco-Map

Note: *It appears that both Richard and Robert have reasonable equilibrium in terms of the amount of energy invested and returned. Lynn, however, appears to expend much more energy than she receives. She seems to have a large number of relationships in which she invests but relatively few from which she gains energy.*

Prepared by _____
Susan Holder, MSW
Social Worker

From perspective of: Lynn B. Chase

other people and systems; use plus (+), minus (-), or plus-minus (±) signs to indicate energy use.

When you have completed the eco-map, reflect on your current social situation and address the following questions. Record your responses in the spaces provided.

1. Which interactional relationships in your current situation enhance your energy level? Which deplete energy?

2. How does your social situation affect the physical, intellectual, and emotional energy you have available for use in your school work, your service to clients, and for investment in other aspects of your social work roles?

3. What is your conception of the ideal social situation? How does it compare with your current situation?

4. Given the nature of your present social situation, what kinds of clients would be likely to elicit strong emotional reactions? What sorts of problems or issues would do the same?

5. What changes in your current social situation might enhance the psychological, emotional, physical, cultural, spiritual, and social resources needed to provide professionally competent social work services to clients?

Self-Esteem

Self-esteem is an extremely important concept in social work practice. Recognized by virtually all social workers, it is frequently used in efforts to understand the inner world of another person.

Self-esteem is defined in various ways. Most definitions involve the nature of a person's view of and feelings toward oneself. For example, Barker (1991) defines *self-esteem* as "an individual's sense of personal worth that is derived more from inner thoughts and values than from praise and recognition from others" (p. 210). Thus, self-esteem is intrinsically related to *inner speech* (the words and pictures one communicates to oneself). Positive, strong, or high self-esteem tends to be associated with inner speech that is realistic, favorable, approving, accepting, and supportive of oneself. High self-esteem and positive inner speech generally serve people well in buffering various stresses that occur continually in everyday life. Negative, weak, or low self-esteem tends to be associated with inner speech that is unrealistic or distorted, unfavorable, disapproving, nonaccepting, and unsupportive of oneself. Low self-esteem and negative inner speech typically add to the deleterious effects of internal and external stresses.

Sometimes, social work practice is directed toward the enhancement of clients' self-esteem and positive inner speech. At other times, social workers help clients enhance other aspects of their social functioning. At all times, however, social work practice involves processes in which the social worker's own self-esteem and inner speech are relevant. Since professional practice involves considerable emotional stress and strain, social workers with strong self-esteem are better prepared to cope in an effective manner than are those whose self-esteem is weak. What's more, social workers' low self-esteem and negative inner speech may indirectly increase the risk of harm to clients. For example, suppose you as a social worker routinely negate your own value as a person through inner speech such as, "I am so stupid!" In times of stress, words that you frequently apply to yourself may inadvertently be applied to clients or colleagues. For numerous reasons, you should strive to maintain positive inner speech and high self-esteem.

◆ EXERCISE 2-3: SELF-ESTEEM RATING SCALE[2]

Complete the following measure of self-esteem. This questionnaire is designed to measure how you feel about yourself. It is not a test, so there are no right or wrong answers. Please answer each item as carefully and accurately as you can by placing a number by each one as follows:

1 = Never
2 = Rarely
3 = A little of the time
4 = Some of the time
5 = A good part of the time
6 = Most of the time
7 = Always

Please begin.

_____ 1. I feel that people would not like me if they really knew me well.
_____ 2. I feel that others do things much better than I do.
_____ 3. I feel that I am an attractive person.
_____ 4. I feel confident in my ability to deal with other people.
_____ 5. I feel that I am likely to fail at things I do.
_____ 6. I feel that people really like to talk with me.
_____ 7. I feel that I am a very competent person.
_____ 8. When I am with other people I feel that they are glad I am with them.

[2]From "Validation of a Clinical Measure of Self-Esteem," by W. R. Nugent and J. W. Thomas, 1993, *Research on Social Work Practice*, 3(2), 191–207. Copyright © 1992 William R. Nugent, Ph.D. Reprinted by permission.

_____ 9. I feel that I make a good impression on others.
_____ 10. I feel confident that I can begin new relationships if I want to.
_____ 11. I feel that I am ugly.
_____ 12. I feel that I am a boring person.
_____ 13. I feel very nervous when I am with strangers.
_____ 14. I feel confident in my ability to learn new things.
_____ 15. I feel good about myself.
_____ 16. I feel ashamed about myself.
_____ 17. I feel inferior to other people.
_____ 18. I feel that my friends find me interesting.
_____ 19. I feel that I have a good sense of humor.
_____ 20. I get angry at myself over the way I am.
_____ 21. I feel relaxed meeting new people.
_____ 22. I feel that other people are smarter than I am.
_____ 23. I do not like myself.
_____ 24. I feel confident in my ability to cope with difficult situations.
_____ 25. I feel that I am not very likable.
_____ 26. My friends value me a lot.
_____ 27. I am afraid I will appear stupid to others.
_____ 28. I feel that I am an OK person.
_____ 29. I feel that I can count on myself to manage things well.
_____ 30. I wish I could just disappear when I am around other people.
_____ 31. I feel embarrassed to let others hear my ideas.
_____ 32. I feel that I am a nice person.
_____ 33. I feel that if I could be more like other people then I would feel better about myself.
_____ 34. I feel that I get pushed around more than others.
_____ 35. I feel that people like me.
_____ 36. I feel that people have a good time when they are with me.
_____ 37. I feel confident that I can do well in whatever I do.
_____ 38. I trust the competence of others more than I trust my own abilities.
_____ 39. I feel that I mess things up.
_____ 40. I wish that I were someone else.

_____ **Self-Esteem Rating Score**

To determine your self-esteem rating (SER), first place a plus (+) sign in front of items 3, 4, 6, 7, 8, 9, 10, 14, 15, 18, 19, 21, 24, 26, 28, 29, 32, 35, 36, and 37. Then, place a minus (-) sign in front of items 1, 2, 5, 11, 12, 13, 16, 17, 20, 22, 23, 25, 27, 30, 31, 33, 34, 38, 39, and 40. Subtract the total of the negative numbers from the total of the positive to find your SER score. The sum of the positive and negative numbers should yield a score somewhere between -120 and +120. Self-esteem is an abstract concept. It is hard to define and difficult to measure accurately. Whatever it is, however, it does change! It changes both as a consequence of changing circumstances and as a result of a person's consciously planned efforts. In assessing the results of the self-esteem rating scale, be aware that your score may be affected by various temporary factors. Your mood and physical health, along with your current social situation, may influence your results. In addition, as is the case in most scales, there is an error factor. Your actual score may be a certain number of points (plus or minus) from the score reflected here. Therefore, please consider the results as hypotheses that should be examined further in light of other forms of information.

In evaluating your own results, please consider that this particular scale (Nugent & Thomas, 1993) reflects two dimensions of self-esteem: *positive self-esteem* and *negative self-esteem*. Positive scores indicate positive self-esteem; the higher the number, the greater your positive self-esteem. Negative scores suggest negative self-esteem; the larger the negative number, the greater the negative self-esteem. Although normative data for this questionnaire are still being collected, the mean score for one sample (Cournoyer, 1994a) of 24 beginning MSW students is +69.62 (SD=12.18). The scores range from +53 to +113. Compare your score to these and recognize that most of us would benefit from an increase in positive self-esteem.

When you have completed and scored the self-esteem rating scale, reflect upon its implications by addressing the following questions. Record your responses in the spaces provided.

1. How do you define self-esteem?

2. What characteristics indicate to you that a person has positive self-esteem?

3. What forms of inner speech do you think are associated with positive self-esteem?

4. How do you think people develop positive or negative self-esteem? In your opinion, what part do gender, age, ethnicity, appearance, skin color, religion, and cultural identity play in the development and maintenance of self-esteem?

5. How do you respond to people who show positive self-esteem? How about those who show negative self-esteem?

6. How might positive self-esteem help you in serving as a professional social worker? How might negative self-esteem hinder your social work performance?

7. In what professional areas and situations is your current level of self-esteem likely to be an asset? In what contexts might it be a liability?

8. In what ways would you like to change your self-esteem and inner speech? Develop the outline of a plan to do so.

Acceptance of Others

In a highly competitive and evaluative society, it is exceedingly difficult to develop genuine tolerance for and acceptance of others. Nonetheless, for the practice of social work, acceptance of others is crucial. The capacity for such acceptance, however, is inevitably affected by the nature of one's prejudices. Barker (1991) defines *prejudice* as "an opinion about an individual, group, or phenomenon that is developed without proof or systematic evidence. This prejudgment may be favorable but is more often unfavorable and may become institutionalized in the form of a society's laws or customs" (p. 179). *Discrimination* is, of course, closely related to prejudice. It may be defined as "the prejudgment and negative treatment of people based on identifiable characteristics such as race, gender, religion, or ethnicity" (Barker, 1991, p. 64). As a social worker, you must learn to transcend the powerful psychological and social forces that maintain prejudiced attitudes and discriminatory behaviors. This is necessary so that you can genuinely accept others who are different in appearance, background, attitudes, and behavior. You must be able to tolerate and value both similarity and diversity and to accept others on their own terms.

Such acceptance does not come easily in a heterogeneous society in which people are highly diverse in terms of economic resources, race and ethnicity, religion, culture, and education. If you are similar to most North Americans who aspire to become professional social workers, you have been exposed to prejudiced attitudes and to both covert and overt forms of discrimination. In all likelihood, you have thought prejudiced thoughts and discriminated against (or for) others; you have probably experienced some of the effects of others' prejudiced attitudes and discriminatory behaviors against (or for) you.

You may even have experienced prejudice for or against yourself and those similar to yourself. Some persons of color and other members of minority groups, for example, have negative prejudices about themselves, judging themselves critically on the basis of a perceived majority standard. Conversely, some white males show positive prejudices about themselves, considering themselves deserving or entitled because of their sex and skin color. This "tendency to consider one's own group, usually national or ethnic, superior to other groups using one's own group or groups as the frame of reference against which other groups are judged" (Wolman, 1973, p. 129) is called *ethnocentrism*. Of course, such prejudices can also occur in reverse. For example, a few white males hold negative prejudiced attitudes about themselves, and some minority group members view themselves as entitled. The forms of prejudice and discrimination are myriad and insidious. As a member of North American society, you have probably adopted some prejudiced attitudes and discriminatory behaviors in your own life. As a step toward transcending these and genuinely accepting other human beings, please undertake the following exercise.

◆ EXERCISE 2-4: IDENTIFICATION OF PREJUDICED ATTITUDES AND DISCRIMINATORY BEHAVIOR

Examine your own personal background and socialization experiences. Explore the psychological and social factors associated with the development of your own prejudiced attitudes and discriminatory behaviors. Consider how you personally manifest aspects of racism, sexism, ageism, xenophobia, homophobia, lookism, and classism. Also, consider the phenomenon of ideological chauvinism—prejudice based upon a difference in beliefs—as it might occur in your relations with others.

1. Make note of at least one occasion when you personally experienced a prejudiced attitude or engaged in discriminatory behavior toward:

   a. *someone of the other sex*

   b. *someone of your own sex*

   c. *someone of another ethnic group*

   d. *someone of your own ethnic group*

   e. *someone older than yourself*

   f. *someone younger than yourself*

   g. *someone about your own age*

   h. *someone of a homosexual orientation*

i. *someone of a heterosexual orientation*

j. *someone of a "higher" economic group*

k. *someone of a "lower" economic group*

l. *someone of your own economic group*

m. *someone you think is better educated*

n. *someone you think is less well educated*

o. *someone who looks different from you in terms of height, weight, skin color, facial characteristics, or attractiveness*

p. *someone who looks similar to you*

q. *someone more physically able-bodied than yourself*

r. *someone less physically able-bodied that yourself*

s. *someone you consider more intelligent than you*

t. *someone you consider not as intelligent as yourself*

u. *someone who has a different belief system (e.g., religious, philosophical, or political)*

v. *someone who has a similar belief system*

2. In the space provided, please discuss how prejudiced attitudes and discriminatory behavior might influence your personal life. How might such attitudes and behavior affect your practice effectiveness as a social worker?

If you can transcend the powerful forces of prejudice and discrimination and come to accept others, you are more likely to conform to the values and ethics of the profession and to be effective in your practice. If you are unable to develop the capacity for sincere acceptance of other people, regardless of their similarities or differences, you are probably incapable of fulfilling the tasks, functions, and obligations of professional social work practice.

To help you further the process of self-understanding in this area, please complete the following instrument.

◆ EXERCISE 2-5: ACCEPTANCE OF OTHERS SCALE[3]

Complete the following measure. This questionnaire is designed to measure your relative acceptance of others. It is not a test, so there are no right or wrong answers. Please answer each item as carefully and accurately as you can by placing a number by each one as follows:

1 = Almost always true
2 = Usually true
3 = True half of the time
4 = Only occasionally true
5 = Very rarely true

---

[3]From "Acceptance by Others and Its Relation to Acceptance of Self and Others: A Revaluation," by W. F. Fey, 1955, *Journal of Abnormal and Social Psychology, 30*, 274–276. Copyright © 1955 American Psychological Association.

Please begin.

Score	Statement of Present Condition or Action
_____	1. People are too easily led.
_____	2. I like people I get to know.
_____	3. People these days have pretty low moral standards.
_____	4. Most people are pretty smug about themselves, never really facing their bad points.
_____	5. I can be comfortable with nearly all kinds of people.
_____	6. All people can talk about these days, it seems, is movies, TV, and foolishness like that.
_____	7. People get ahead by using "pull," and not because of what they know.
_____	8. Once you start doing favors for people, they'll just walk all over you.
_____	9. People are too self-centered.
_____	10. People are always dissatisfied and hunting for something new.
_____	11. With many people you don't know how you stand.
_____	12. You've probably got to hurt someone if you're going to make something out of yourself.
_____	13. People really need a strong, smart leader.
_____	14. I enjoy myself most when I am alone, away from people.
_____	15. I wish people would be more honest with me.
_____	16. I enjoy going with a crowd.
_____	17. In my experience, people are pretty stubborn and unreasonable.
_____	18. I can enjoy being with people whose values are very different from mine.
_____	19. Everybody tries to be nice.
_____	20. The average person is not very well satisfied with himself (or herself).

_____ **Acceptance of Others Score**

The Acceptance of Others Scale is scored in the following manner: First, reverse score items 2, 5, 16, 18, and 19. (*Reverse score* means to change an answer of 1 to 5; 2 to 4; 3 remains 3; 4 to 2; and 5 to 1.) Now add the answers for all 20 items to find your total score.

As in the case of the Self-Esteem Rating Scale in Exercise 2-3, interpret the results of this questionnaire with some caution. Use the results to formulate hypotheses to test by examining evidence from other sources. The guidelines that follow will help you evaluate your results (Fey, 1955).

Persons who score in the 85–100 range generally tend to accept other people, to experience others as accepting of them, and to be accepted by others. The 66–84 range is the average range of scores of the majority of people. Approximately two-thirds of all people taking the scale score in this medium range. For a sample (Cournoyer, 1994a) of 20 beginning MSW students, the average score was 78.4 (SD=7.61) on the Acceptance of Others Scale. Such midrange scores show a mixture of caution about and acceptance of people. Although less accepting of certain persons, individuals scoring in this range clearly have the capacity to accept others fully. Persons scoring in the 0–65 range may be very cautious about and intolerant of others. This hesitancy about other people could be a consequence of significant social, emotional, or physical pain caused by others at some point in the past.

When you have completed and scored the scale, consider its implications by addressing the following questions. Record your responses in the spaces provided.

1. How do you define the *acceptance of others*?

2. Have you ever been truly and completely accepted by someone else? If so, what did it feel like? How did it affect your behavior? If you have never been full accepted by another person, what do you think it might feel like? How might it affect your behavior?

3. Have you ever truly and completely accepted someone else? If so, what do you think enabled you to do so? If not, what prevented you?

4. What characteristics indicate to you that a person is accepting of others? What characteristics reflect intolerance?

5. How do you think people develop the capacity to accept others? How do you think people acquire intolerant attitudes about other people? Discuss the functions served by prejudice, intolerance, and discrimination. (For example, what are the personal benefits of such attitudes and behavior?)

6. How do you personally react to people that you consider intolerant of others? How might you respond if a client expresses intolerance of other people? Is there a difference between your personal and your professional responses to intolerance? If so, discuss the implications of such a difference.

7. In what way is your current level of acceptance of others likely to represent a positive influence on your performance as a social worker? In what ways is it a negative?

8. Finally, outline the specific steps of a plan to strengthen your capacity to accept others and transcend those powerful internal and external forces that tend to perpetuate prejudice, intolerance, and discrimination.

Responsible Assertiveness

Positive self-esteem and a capacity for genuinely accepting other people help you serve clients and interact effectively with others on behalf of clients. In addition to liking yourself and accepting others, however, you must also be able to express yourself in an assertive fashion. Responsible assertiveness involves the capacity to express knowledge, opinions, and, where appropriate, feelings in a manner that respects both your own and others' rights and preferences as unique and valuable human beings. Responsible assertive expression is not indirect or passive—which would violate your own rights and preferences—nor is it aggressive—which would violate the rights and preferences of others. Rather, assertive expression in social work involves active, direct communication that shows respect for both your own dignity and that of the other people involved.

◆ **EXERCISE 2-6: PERSONAL ASSERTION ANALYSIS**[4]

Please read the following statements. Each one describes a situation and a response. Try to imagine a situation in your life that is as close to the one described as possible,

---

[4]From "The Development of an Inventory for Distinguishing Among Passive, Aggressive, and Assertive Behavior," by B. L. Hedlund and C. U. Lindquist, 1984, *Behavioral Assessment, 6*, 379–390. Copyright © 1984 Pergamon Press, Inc. Reproduced with permission of Bonnie L. Hedlund, Ph.D.

then rate the response according to its similarity with what you *might* do in the actual situation.

1 = Just like me
2 = Sometimes like me
3 = Not usually like me
4 = Not at all like me

_____ 1. You'd like a raise, so you make an appointment with your boss to explain the reasons you feel you should receive one.

_____ 2. You usually take the lead when you are in a group of people.

_____ 3. Because of a high-pressure salesperson, you buy a camera that meets most but not all of your requirements.

_____ 4. You're working on a project with a friend but you seem to be doing all the work. You say, "I'd like to see if we could find a different way to divide the responsibility. I feel I'm doing most of the work."

_____ 5. After waiting in a restaurant for 20 minutes, you loudly tell the host of your dissatisfaction and leave.

_____ 6. A very important person you have long admired comes to speak in your town. Afterwards you are too hesitant to go and meet him/her.

_____ 7. Your parents have been after you to spend more time with them. You tell them to stop nagging you.

_____ 8. Your neighbor's stereo is disturbing you. You call and ask if he/she would please turn it down.

_____ 9. A repairman overcharges you. You explain that you feel the charges are excessive and ask for the bill to be adjusted.

_____ 10. A person cuts in front of you in line, so you push him/her out of line.

_____ 11. When you're feeling warm toward your parent/spouse, it is difficult for you to express this to him/her.

_____ 12. You are delayed getting home because you stayed at a friend's too long. When your parent/spouse is angry, you tell him/her it's none of his/her business.

_____ 13. When trying to talk to someone of the opposite sex, you get nervous.

_____ 14. In a job interview you are able to state your positive points as well as your negative points.

_____ 15. You are driving to an appointment with a friend and she/he has a flat tire. While she/he is changing the tire, you tell her/him how dumb it was to let the tires get worn.

_____ 16. You accept your boss's opinion about your lack of ability to handle responsibility, but later complain to some friends about his/her unfairness.

_____ 17. You are arguing with a person and she/he pushes you, so you push her/him back.

_____ 18. In a discussion with a small group of people, you state your position and are willing to discuss it, but you don't feel that you have to win.

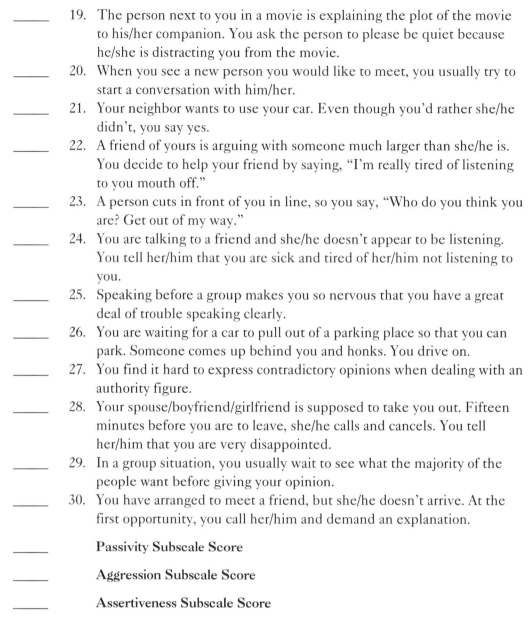

_____ 19. The person next to you in a movie is explaining the plot of the movie to his/her companion. You ask the person to please be quiet because he/she is distracting you from the movie.

_____ 20. When you see a new person you would like to meet, you usually try to start a conversation with him/her.

_____ 21. Your neighbor wants to use your car. Even though you'd rather she/he didn't, you say yes.

_____ 22. A friend of yours is arguing with someone much larger than she/he is. You decide to help your friend by saying, "I'm really tired of listening to you mouth off."

_____ 23. A person cuts in front of you in line, so you say, "Who do you think you are? Get out of my way."

_____ 24. You are talking to a friend and she/he doesn't appear to be listening. You tell her/him that you are sick and tired of her/him not listening to you.

_____ 25. Speaking before a group makes you so nervous that you have a great deal of trouble speaking clearly.

_____ 26. You are waiting for a car to pull out of a parking place so that you can park. Someone comes up behind you and honks. You drive on.

_____ 27. You find it hard to express contradictory opinions when dealing with an authority figure.

_____ 28. Your spouse/boyfriend/girlfriend is supposed to take you out. Fifteen minutes before you are to leave, she/he calls and cancels. You tell her/him that you are very disappointed.

_____ 29. In a group situation, you usually wait to see what the majority of the people want before giving your opinion.

_____ 30. You have arranged to meet a friend, but she/he doesn't arrive. At the first opportunity, you call her/him and demand an explanation.

_____ **Passivity Subscale Score**

_____ **Aggression Subscale Score**

_____ **Assertiveness Subscale Score**

The Personal Assertion Analysis inventory is scored in the following manner. First, add the ratings for items 3, 6, 11, 13, 16, 21, 25, 26, 27, and 29. The total represents your score on the passivity subscale. Second, add your ratings for items 5, 7, 10, 12, 15, 17, 22, 23, 24, and 30. This total is your score on the aggression subscale. Finally, sum your ratings of items 1, 2, 4, 8, 9, 14, 18, 19, 20, and 28. The total represents your score on the assertiveness subscale.

As in the case of other self-report measures, approach the results of this inventory with some caution. Consider the findings in light of information about your style of self-expression from other sources, including people who know you well. In reviewing your results, realize that the possible range for each subscale is 0–40 and that a lower score indicates a greater amount of that kind of behavior. For example, a person scoring 10 on the assertiveness subscale shows more assertiveness than a person who scores 35.

Compare your own scores on the three subscales to the scores of a sample of undergraduate students (average age of 23.39) whose mean scores were 21.20 for passivity, 23.45 for aggression, and 18.97 for assertiveness. (Hedlund & Lindquist, 1984) A sample (Cournoyer, 1994a) of 24 beginning MSW students had average scores of 28.58 (SD = 4.2) for passivity, 33.96 (SD = 3.99) for aggression, and 18.29 (SD = 3.34) for assertiveness. If your scores are lower than these average scores for passivity or aggressiveness (a lower score indicates a greater degree of passivity and aggression) and higher for assertiveness (a higher score reflects a lesser degree of assertiveness), you may wish to explore the issue of assertiveness more fully. Identify specific areas where you tend to express yourself passively or aggressively and develop a plan to express yourself more directly and more assertively in those areas. You may find enrollment in an assertiveness training course or program helpful for developing responsible, self-expressive communication skills.

Reflect on the implications of your scores on the Personal Assertion Analysis inventory by addressing the following questions. Record your responses in the spaces provided.

1. How do you define *passivity*, *aggression*, and *assertiveness?*

2. What do you think and feel when you are responsibly assertive? When you are inappropriately aggressive? When you are nonassertive or passive in a situation where assertiveness is appropriate?

3. What characteristics indicate to you that a person is capable of responsible assertive behavior with others?

4. How do you think people develop the capacity to be responsibly assertive? Aggressive? Passive?

5. How do your gender, ethnicity, and cultural affiliation influence the nature and degree to which you express yourself assertively?

6. How do you react to people who are responsibly assertive with you? Aggressive? Passive?

7. In what ways are your current levels of assertiveness, passivity, and aggression likely to influence your performance as a social worker?

8. In what ways would you like to change your capacity for assertiveness? Develop the outline of a plan by which you might do so.

Self-Control

In addition to self-understanding, positive self-esteem, assertiveness, and the ability to accept others, social workers also need a truly remarkable capacity for self-control. As a social worker, you must be able to manage your emotions and "restrict impulses or behaviors to appropriate circumstances in the environment" (Barker, 1991, p. 210). In work with and on behalf of clients, you must control your verbal and nonverbal expressions as well as your overt behavior. Self-control is one of the true hallmarks of a professional person. It distinguishes a professional social worker from a friendly person with good intentions.

In interacting with others, you must manage your opinions, consciously select the words you say, monitor your body movements and gestures, and control your facial

[5]From "A Schedule for Assessing Self-Control Behaviors: Preliminary Findings," by M. Rosenbaum, 1980, *Behavior Therapy, 11*, 109–121. Copyright © 1980 by the Association for Advancement of Behavior Therapy. Reprinted by permission of the publisher and the author.

expressions and your vocal tone. To do so requires an extraordinary level of self-control. The following instrument is provided to help you assess your current level of self-control.

◆ EXERCISE 2-7: SELF-CONTROL SCHEDULE[5]

Please read the following statements. Indicate how characteristic or descriptive each of the following statements is by using the code given below.

+3 = Very characteristic of me
+2 = Rather characteristic of me
+1 = Somewhat characteristic of me
-1 = Somewhat uncharacteristic of me
-2 = Rather uncharacteristic of me
-3 = Very uncharacteristic of me

Thank you for your cooperation.

_____ 1. When I do a boring job, I think about the less boring parts of the job and about the reward I will receive when I finish.

_____ 2. When I have to do something that makes me anxious, I try to visualize how I will overcome my anxiety while doing it.

_____ 3. By changing my way of thinking, I am often able to change my feelings about almost anything.

_____ 4. I often find it difficult to overcome my feelings of nervousness and tension without outside help.

_____ 5. When I am feeling depressed, I try to think about pleasant events.

_____ 6. I cannot help thinking about mistakes I made.

_____ 7. When I am faced with a difficult problem, I try to approach it in a systematic way.

_____ 8. I usually do what I am supposed to do more quickly when someone is pressuring me.

_____ 9. When I am faced with a difficult decision, I prefer to postpone it even if I have all the facts.

_____ 10. When I have difficulty concentrating on my reading, I look for ways to increase my concentration.

_____ 11. When I plan to work, I remove everything that is not relevant to my work.

_____ 12. When I try to get rid of a bad habit, I first try to find out all the reasons why I have the habit.

_____ 13. When an unpleasant thought is bothering me, I try to think about something pleasant.

_____ 14. If I smoked two packs of cigarettes a day, I would need outside help to stop smoking.

_____ 15. When I feel down, I try to act cheerful so that my mood will change.

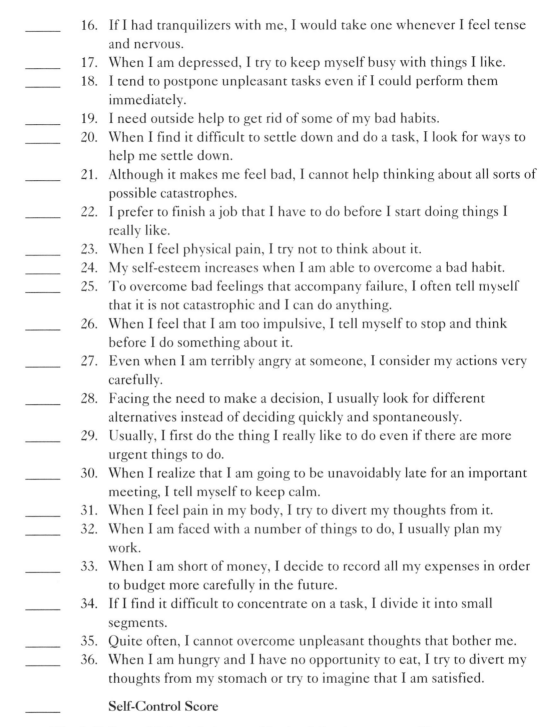

_____ 16. If I had tranquilizers with me, I would take one whenever I feel tense and nervous.

_____ 17. When I am depressed, I try to keep myself busy with things I like.

_____ 18. I tend to postpone unpleasant tasks even if I could perform them immediately.

_____ 19. I need outside help to get rid of some of my bad habits.

_____ 20. When I find it difficult to settle down and do a task, I look for ways to help me settle down.

_____ 21. Although it makes me feel bad, I cannot help thinking about all sorts of possible catastrophes.

_____ 22. I prefer to finish a job that I have to do before I start doing things I really like.

_____ 23. When I feel physical pain, I try not to think about it.

_____ 24. My self-esteem increases when I am able to overcome a bad habit.

_____ 25. To overcome bad feelings that accompany failure, I often tell myself that it is not catastrophic and I can do anything.

_____ 26. When I feel that I am too impulsive, I tell myself to stop and think before I do something about it.

_____ 27. Even when I am terribly angry at someone, I consider my actions very carefully.

_____ 28. Facing the need to make a decision, I usually look for different alternatives instead of deciding quickly and spontaneously.

_____ 29. Usually, I first do the thing I really like to do even if there are more urgent things to do.

_____ 30. When I realize that I am going to be unavoidably late for an important meeting, I tell myself to keep calm.

_____ 31. When I feel pain in my body, I try to divert my thoughts from it.

_____ 32. When I am faced with a number of things to do, I usually plan my work.

_____ 33. When I am short of money, I decide to record all my expenses in order to budget more carefully in the future.

_____ 34. If I find it difficult to concentrate on a task, I divide it into small segments.

_____ 35. Quite often, I cannot overcome unpleasant thoughts that bother me.

_____ 36. When I am hungry and I have no opportunity to eat, I try to divert my thoughts from my stomach or try to imagine that I am satisfied.

_____ **Self-Control Score**

The Self-Control Schedule is scored in the following manner. First, reverse score items 4, 6, 8, 9, 14, 16, 18, 19, 21, 29, and 35. On this scale, reverse score means to change a positive number to its negative or a negative number to its positive (e.g., a +3 would become -3; +2 would become -2; +1 would become -1). Then, sum the ratings for the 36 items. The total represents your self-control score.

As with other self-report measures, view the results of this inventory with a degree of caution. In assessing your capacity for self-control, consider information from other sources as well. In reviewing your score on the Self-Control Schedule, recognize that the scores could possibly range from -108 to +108. Most samples taking this schedule yield mean scores in the 23 to 27 range. The average score of nonclinical populations tends to be approximately 25 (SD = 20) (Rosenbaum, 1980). A sample (Cournoyer, 1994a) of 24 beginning MSW students scored an average of 36.46 (SD = 20.60) on the Self-Control Schedule. A higher score represents a greater degree or level of self-control. If your score is substantially less than these average scores, it may be helpful to institute a program designed to increase your level of self-control. If your score is +5 or lower, you should probably seek consultation concerning how best to do this. Such a low level of self-control could be problematic in your role as a professional social worker.

When you have completed and scored the Self-Control Schedule, reflect on its implications by addressing the following questions. Record your responses in the spaces provided.

1. How do you define *self-control?*

2. In what life-areas have you exhibited strong self-control? In what areas have you shown insufficient self-control?

3. Maladaptive repetitive patterns of behavior, sometimes called *bad habits*, *compulsions*, or *addictive behaviors*, can significantly interfere with your degree of self-control and the quality of your social work service to others. Identify any maladaptive and repetitive behaviors in your own life that could impair your functioning as a social worker.

4. Discuss those aspects of social work practice that are likely to require you to exercise the greatest amount of self-control.

5. Outline a specific plan to strengthen your self-control in those areas that might adversely affect your performance as a professional social worker.

Readiness for Professional Social Work

Social workers come from all sorts of backgrounds and have diverse personality profiles. They are attracted to the profession for many different reasons. Some social workers have a strong sense of altruism—a desire to give of themselves to others. Others have a philosophical commitment to social justice or to a better world. Some are proponents of a particular cause they can appropriately pursue through their professional practice. Others follow in the footsteps of a relative or other significant person who is or was a social worker. Some see social work as a way to continue in a family role, such as caretaker, with which they are personally familiar, while others see social work as an efficient route to becoming a psychotherapist. A few select social work as a second choice, having been denied admission to a clinical psychology program or a law school. Others choose social work because they believe that the course work is less difficult and the grading less rigorous than in some other schools or departments. Still others have personal or social problems that they believe might be resolved through schooling in social work and through service to others, or perhaps they have been clients themselves and identified with the social workers who served them.

Of all the various forms of self-understanding that you as a social worker must pursue, none is more important than your readiness for the profession. At some point, you must honestly address the question, "Am I personally ready and suited for this profession and for the nature of the work it entails?" As a way to move toward an answer, please complete the following exercise. It will help you explore your motives for selecting social work and evaluate your overall readiness to pursue it as a profession.

◆ EXERCISE 2-8: SOCIAL WORK READINESS ASSESSMENT

Now that you have completed several exercises intended to increase your self-awareness and self-understanding, integrate the results through a summary assessment of your overall readiness for professional social work. Toward this end, address each of the following items. Record your responses in the spaces provided.

1. Look ahead to the professional social work career to which you aspire after graduation. Describe the setting, the nature of the problems, and the kinds of people with whom you would prefer to work. Identify and describe the personal qualities and attributes that you think will be required of you in order to practice social work effectively in such a context.

2. Identify those settings, problems, and people with whom you would prefer *not* to work. Discuss the reasons for these preferences. What are the implications of those reasons for your personal and professional development?

3. Identify three major factors or incidents in your personal, familial, or situational experience that contributed to your choice of social work as a career. How do these three affect your current readiness for professional social work practice?

4. What do you anticipate will be the single most rewarding or satisfying part of being a professional social worker? What will be the single most difficult?

5. Consider your family genogram, eco-map, the results of the questionnaires, and your responses to the exercises. In your best judgment, ask yourself, "Do I possess or can I develop the personal capacities necessary to function effectively as a professional social worker?" If your answer is No, check out your conclusion by meeting with an adviser, a social work professor, or a guidance counselor. If your negative answer is confirmed through discussions with others, proceed to identify other careers for which you may be better suited. If your answer is Yes, identify the personal areas requiring further

exploration and indicate those capacities you need to strengthen. Outline a specific plan to do so.

6. Finally, based on your current level of self-awareness and self-understanding, what are the three issues most significant to you that you would want to explore with an outstanding, experienced social worker? Identify three specific questions that you would ask.

Chapter 3

Ethical Decision Making

In serving clients, social workers use information from a variety of sources: theoretical knowledge; knowledge from research studies; wisdom gained from life experience and service to clients; the expertise of colleagues and supervisors; agency policies and procedures; and their own intuition. One source of information, however, must serve as a screen for all others. The values, ethics, and obligations of the profession are preeminent. Every aspect of practice, every decision, every assessment, every intervention, and virtually every action you undertake as a social worker must be considered from the perspective of your professional ethics and obligations. This dimension supersedes all others. Ethical responsibilities take precedence over theoretical knowledge, research findings, practice wisdom, agency policies, and, of course, your own personal values, preferences, and beliefs.

Assumption of the role of professional social worker entails considerable personal sacrifice, enormous intellectual effort, and extraordinary self-discipline. Because you affect, for better or worse, the lives of the people you serve and because you pledge to follow the ethical code of the social work profession, you assume substantial responsibilities and obligations. You must consistently use ethical decision-making skills in every aspect of your service to others.

Ethical decision making involves several dimensions. First, you must understand those legal duties that apply to all professional helpers. Second, you must thoroughly comprehend the core social work values and the social work code of ethics. Third, you must be able to identify those ethical principles and legal duties that pertain to specific social work practice situations. Finally, when several competing obligations apply, you must be able to determine which take precedence. When there is no conflict among the ethical and legal responsibilities relevant to a particular case, making a decision and taking appropriate action is fairly straightforward. You merely conform to the appropriate ethical obligations. Much of the time, however, the applicable principles and duties conflict with one another. Deciding which obligation takes precedence is the most complex and challenging aspect of ethical decision making.

Understanding Your Legal Obligations

Along with psychiatrists, psychologists, marriage and family counselors, and nurses, social workers are sanctioned by society as members of the professional helping community. As a social worker, therefore, you are subject to certain legally determined obligations or duties. These derive from common law, legislation, regulations, and various court decisions. Some legal obligations coincide with the responsibilities suggested by social work values and the code of ethics; others do not. You are responsible for understanding both the legal duties applicable to all professional helpers and those ethical obligations that apply specifically to social workers.

Unfortunately, the legal duties of professional helpers are not always clear. They are certainly not permanent. New laws and regulations are continually enacted by various professional and governmental bodies. Thousands of court cases are processed every year. As new laws and regulatory policies emerge, they change the nature and extent of the legal duties of professional helpers, including social workers. As a professional social worker, you are subject to these evolving responsibilities.

Malpractice may be defined as "a form of negligence that occurs when a practitioner acts in a manner inconsistent with the profession's standard of care—the way an ordinary, reasonable, and prudent professional would act under the same or similar circumstances" (Reamer, 1994, p. 9). Barker (1991, p. 137) defines malpractice as

> wilful or negligent *behavior* by a professional person that violates the relevant *code of ethics* and professional standards of care that proves harmful to the client. Among a social worker's actions most likely to result in malpractice are inappropriately divulging confidential information; unnecessarily prolonged services; improper termination of needed services; misrepresentation of one's knowledge or skills; providing social work treatment as a replacement for needed medical treatment; providing information to others that is libelous or that results in improper *incarceration*; financial exploitation of the client; and physical injury to the client that may occur in the course of certain treatments (such as group encounters).

Malpractice by professional social workers is, in legal terminology, a form of *tort*. A person or group may file a lawsuit in civil court because of injury or suffering resulting from the "wrongful actions or inactions" (Saltzman & Proch, 1990, p. 412) of the professional person. The plaintiff, often a client and sometimes a member of a client's family, typically seeks monetary damages to compensate for injuries or suffering. Occasionally, additional *punitive damages* are imposed in order to punish the professional person guilty of malpractice.

Consider the example of a California court case. A father whose adult daughter accused him of childhood sexual abuse was awarded monetary damages from a psychiatrist and a family therapist who had treated the daughter. Based upon his daughter's allegations that he had molested her when she was a child, the man was fired from his high-paying job, and his wife divorced him. Both his daughter and his former spouse have, since the time of the allegations, refused to have contact with him. Because memory is known to be affected by the leading questions and suggestions of authorities, the court concluded that the helping professionals involved had acted unprofessionally in suggesting that the client's emerging recollections of previously repressed memories were necessarily true and valid. Interestingly, the court did not assert that the daughter's memories were false—only that the validity of the retrieved memories could not be determined because of the undue influence of the suggestive words of the helping professionals. The court awarded the accused father several hundred thousand dollars as compensation for the damage caused him by the unprofessional conduct.

The precise number of lawsuits filed against social workers is unknown. Besharov and Besharov (1987) and Reamer (1994) provide estimates that range from a few hundred to several thousand. Whatever the figure is, it will undoubtedly increase substantially as the years pass. Of course, the filing of a lawsuit against you does not mean that you are, in fact, guilty of malpractice; some lawsuits are unwarranted, frivolous, and even harassing. In case of litigation, the best defense is undoubtedly ethical, competent, and well-documented social work practice, but it does not guarantee you freedom from legal action. You may still have to defend the quality of your professional practice in a court of law.

Although the increasing frequency of litigation against social workers and other professional helpers is cause for concern, it should not unduly frighten you. The probability of being sued is still extremely low. Social work service remains a personally and professionally satisfying endeavor. However, the possibility of a lawsuit serves to underscore the importance of understanding the legal duties that apply to all social workers and other helping professionals.

Several common categories of lawsuits have been filed against social workers and other service professionals (Besharov & Besharov, 1987, pp. 519–520; Myers, 1992; Saltzman & Proch, 1990; and VandeCreek & Knapp, 1993):

- treatment without consent (a client may allege that professional treatment procedures were undertaken without informed consent; the parents of a minor child may assert that their child was given treatment without their awareness or consent)
- professional malpractice (a client may assert that a social worker did not provide competent professional services, as indicated by the use of inappropriate, inadequate, or unconventional assessment procedures or interventions)
- failure to report suspected abuse or neglect (a client, a client's family, or a state agency may assert that a social worker who had information of possible child endangerment failed to report suspicions that a child was being abused or neglected)

- reporting suspected abuse or neglect (a client or a client's family may assert that a social worker who reported to state authorities suspicions that a child was being abused or neglected did so without adequate evidence and, as a result, caused severe and irreparable damage to the affected parties)
- failure to consult or refer to other professionals or specialists (a client or client's family may allege that a social worker should have consulted with a medical doctor when it became apparent that the problems and symptoms revealed by the client suggested the real possibility of a medical condition)
- failure to prevent a client's suicide (the family of a client who committed suicide may assert that a social worker knew or should have known that the client was suicidal, yet failed to take action necessary to protect the client from his or her own suicidal impulses)
- causing a client's suicide (the family of a client who committed suicide may allege that a social worker's words or actions provoked the client to take his or her own life)
- failure to protect third parties (a person injured by a client may assert that a social worker knew or should have known that the client was potentially dangerous and intended to harm the person in question, yet failed to take action to notify the targeted individual and protect her or him from the client's violent actions)
- inappropriate release of a client (a client or a client's family may allege that the social worker and other professionals were negligent in permitting a client to leave a facility while the client was in a state of acute distress or incapacity)
- false imprisonment (a client may claim that his or her commitment to a facility such as a psychiatric institution or a drug treatment center constituted wrongful detention or incarceration)
- failure to provide adequate care for a client in residential settings (a client or a client's family may assert that the client was injured due to the neglectful and inadequate care provided by a social worker and other staff members in a hospital or other facility)
- assault or battery (a client may allege that a social worker was threatening or engaged in improper or inappropriate physical contact)
- intentional infliction of emotional distress (a client may assert that a social worker's actions, such as a counseling procedure or perhaps the removal of a child from the home of a biological parent, so traumatized the client as to cause significant mental or emotional distress)
- sexual involvement with a client (a client may allege that a social worker used professional authority and expertise for the purposes of sexual seduction and exploitation)
- breach of confidentiality (a client may allege that a social worker inappropriately communicated confidential information to an unauthorized party)
- breach of contract (a client may believe that a social worker indicated that his or her marriage would be saved through the process of marriage counseling—in effect, providing a guarantee; when the marriage ends in divorce, the client may assert that the social worker did not fulfill the terms of the agreement)

- invasion of privacy (a client may assert that a child abuse investigation was overreaching or harassing in nature)
- defamation of character (a client may believe that a social worker, orally or in writing, made an untrue and derogatory statement about the client that harmed the client's reputation)
- violation of a client's civil rights (a client in a residential facility may allege that his or her civil rights were violated when personal property was confiscated by a social worker)
- failure to be available when needed (a client may assert that a social worker was inaccessible or unavailable when he or she was in desperate need of service)
- inappropriate termination of treatment (a client may allege that a social worker concluded treatment abruptly or unprofessionally)
- malicious prosecution or abuse of process (a client may allege that a legal action initiated by a social worker, for instance in a child protection case, was undertaken with full knowledge that the case would be dismissed by the court and therefore was maliciously intended)
- inappropriate bill collection methods (a client may assert that the social worker used invasive and improper means in an attempt to collect on bills that were outstanding)
- statutory violations (a social worker might be sued for violating requirements of the state law under which social workers are legally certified or licensed)
- inadequately protecting a child (a client, the client's family, or a state agency may assert that a child was injured due to the neglectful and inadequate care provided by a social worker)
- violating parental rights (the parents of a child may assert that their rights were violated by a social worker who provided professional services to their child without their informed consent)
- inadequate foster care services (a client, the biological parents of a child, or a state agency may assert that a social worker placed a child in a foster care setting that provided inadequate or injurious care)

Certain forms of practice and certain settings constitute a greater risk for litigation against social workers. For example, because child welfare work often involves the provision of *involuntary* services, there is a greater likelihood of both civil and criminal legal action against social workers who work in such settings.

Although most malpractice litigation occurs in civil court, social workers may occasionally be subject to criminal action related to the nature and extent of their professional services. Saltzman & Proch (1990, p. 428) describe such a case.

In Colorado, for example, a case worker and her supervisor were criminally prosecuted when a child with whom the case worker was working was killed by her parents. The parents had been reported to the worker as abusive but the worker had chosen to keep the child in the home. The worker and her supervisor were convicted.

The criminal convictions in the Colorado case were later overturned on technical grounds by an appellate court. Nonetheless, the case illustrates the enormous responsibilities associated with professional social work practice as well as the litigious nature of contemporary society.

Undoubtedly, as time passes, there will be changes in the nature and extent of the legal responsibilities that apply to social workers, but the general legal duties or obligations listed in Box 3.1 are likely to remain in effect for the next several years (see Everstine and Everstine, 1983, pp. 227–251).

Duty of Care

As a professional social worker, you are legally obligated to provide a *reasonable standard of care* in delivering social work services. Clients have a right to expect that you will be competent in discharging your professional responsibilities. There is an implied contract to that effect. Services provided must meet at least an adequate standard of care—as determined in part by the social work profession and in part by common expectations of helping professionals.

The National Association of Social Workers has published numerous booklets related to basic standards in various forms of social work practice (see, for example, *NASW Standards for Social Work Services in Schools*, 1978; *NASW Standards for Social Work Practice in Child Protection*, 1981; *NASW Standards for Social Work Services in Long-Term Care Facilities*, 1981; *NASW Standards and Guidelines for Social Work Case Management for the Functionally Impaired*, 1984; *NASW Standards for Social Work in Health Care Settings*, 1987; *NASW Standards for the Practice of Clinical Social Work*, 1989; *NASW Standards for Social Work Case Management*, 1992; and *NASW Standards for the Practice of Social Work with Adolescents*, 1993). You are also expected to be knowledgeable about information presented in scholarly books and professional journals related to social work practice generally. Additionally, you should be familiar with the knowledge available in books and journals related to those specific populations you serve and those problems you address in your professional setting. The assessments, diagnoses, treatments, and interventions that you choose must have theoretical or empirical support. Unusual interventions, activities, or procedures that do not have a sound professional rationale may not meet the "duty of care" obligation; they may place you at increased risk of liability.

BOX 3.1
Legal Obligations of Helping Professionals

- ◆ duty of care
- ◆ duty to respect privacy
- ◆ duty to maintain confidentiality
- ◆ duty to inform
- ◆ duty to report
- ◆ duty to warn

Several additional responsibilities may be included under the general duty of care. For example, as a professional social worker you must be available to the clients you serve. Clients should be educated about whom to contact and what to do in case of an emergency situation. Similarly, before going on vacation, you must inform clients well in advance and arrange for equivalent, substitute professional coverage. You must also take action to ensure the physical protection of clients you determine to be (1) dangerous to other persons, (2) dangerous to themselves, or (3) so gravely disabled as to be unable to provide minimal self-care (Everstine and Everstine, 1983, p. 232). Often, you would seek to arrange for the supervision or hospitalization of such clients.

Professional recordkeeping is also related to the "standard of care" obligation. Complete, accurate, timely documentation of your professional activities is considered reasonable and usual professional behavior. The keeping of records suggests at least a modicum of professionalism. Of course, records may also support the quality of your professional service. Accurate, descriptive records are your single most important defense in the event of a malpractice lawsuit. If professional records are absent, notations are sparse, or records seem to have been altered after the fact, many judges see evidence of an inadequate standard of care.

Duty to Respect Privacy

As a professional social worker, you have a duty to respect the privacy of people with whom you interact during the course of your practice. Under most circumstances, you are not entitled to intrude on the privacy of prospective or actual clients. Privacy includes an individual's physical space (home or residence, locker, automobile, wallet or purse, or clothing) as well as those aspects of personal life that constitute a *symbolic region* (Everstine et al., 1980), which is that person's alone to share or reveal as he or she sees fit. You should have a sound professional reason for entry into these private physical or symbolic regions.

Duty to Maintain Confidentiality

Professional social workers have a duty to maintain the confidentiality of what is said by clients. This obligation applies, in general, to all helping professionals. The laws that certify or license social workers require that information shared by clients remain confidential. Indeed, some laws use the term *privileged communication* in describing this legal obligation. "*Confidentiality* refers to the professional norm that information shared by or pertaining to clients will not be shared with third parties. *Privilege* refers to the disclosure of confidential information in court proceedings" (Reamer, 1994, p. 47). When laws specify that your communications with clients are privileged, then you must meet an even higher standard of confidentiality. When information is privileged, it becomes much more difficult, even for a judge, to force social workers to reveal confidential information without their clients' consent.

Generally speaking, material shared by clients is their property. It is not yours, even though you may remember it or record it in a case record. You are merely using the knowledge in order to serve them. It does not become your property simply because you have heard and recorded it. Under most circumstances, clients must give *informed consent* before you may legally and ethically share information with another person or organization.

Duty to Inform

As a professional social worker, you have an obligation to educate clients and prospective clients concerning the nature and extent of the services you and your agency offer. You must inform clients about matters such as cost, length, probability of success, risks, and alternate services that may be appropriate. You should also give clients information concerning relevant policies and laws that could affect them during the provision of social services. For example, early in the process, you should notify clients about your legal obligation to report indications of possible child abuse and neglect or elder abuse. Also, you should inform clients that, should a person's life be in danger, you will take action to protect that person even if it means violating confidentiality. Typically, you should also give clients information about your qualifications, fields of expertise, and, when relevant, areas in which you have limited knowledge or experience. Under most circumstances, you must give clients an opportunity to provide informed consent before professional intervention may begin. Similarly, you must inform clients well in advance before you discontinue services or transfer them to another helping professional.

Duty to Report

Professional social workers have a legal obligation to report to designated governmental authorities indications of certain "outrages against humanity" (Everstine and Everstine, 1983, p. 240). Although the specific process of reporting varies according to what law applies, as a social worker you must report knowledge of certain criminal behavior, including "child abuse, child neglect, child molestation, and incest" (Everstine and Everstine, 1983, p. 240). Increasingly, laws are enacted to expand the kinds of behavior that must be reported. These include abuse, neglect, and exploitation of persons who are elderly, physically or mentally challenged, or developmentally disabled.

Duty to Warn

If, during an interview with you, a client reveals an intent to harm another person, and you determine that the client might act upon that intent in such a way as to endanger another person, then you must (1) try to arrange for protective supervision of the client (for example, through temporary hospitalization), (2) warn the intended victim or victims of the threat, and (3) notify legal authorities of this danger. Of course, because such actions violate some aspects of the client's right to confidentiality and perhaps to privacy, you should clearly document the reasons you have taken this course of action. In such instances, it is useful to quote the words, cite the gestures, and provide related evidence to support your conclusion that the client is potentially dangerous to another person.

Understanding the Fundamental Values and Ethics of Social Work

In addition to the legal obligations to which all helping professionals are subject, social workers must also conform to the fundamental values and code of ethics of the social work profession. Social workers and social work educators have energetically discussed the topic of social work values since the emergence of the profession around the beginning of the 20th century. The discussion continues today and will undoubtedly continue well into the 21st century. Although there is some divergence of opinion regarding the *application* of fundamental social work values, there is considerable consensus concerning the values themselves. For example, in 1992 the board of directors of the Council on Social Work Education (CSWE), the accrediting body for schools of social work in the United States, adopted, as part of the revised Curriculum Policy Statement, the social work values outlined in Box 3.2.

BOX 3.2
Council on Social Work Education
Curriculum Policy Statement
Social Work Values and Ethics[1]

Among the values and principles that must be infused throughout every social work curriculum are the following:

◆ Social workers' professional relationships are built on regard for individual worth and dignity and are furthered by mutual participation, acceptance, confidentiality, honesty, and responsible handling of conflict.

◆ Social workers respect people's right to make independent decisions and to participate actively in the helping process.

◆ Social workers are committed to assisting client systems to obtain needed resources.

◆ Social workers strive to make social institutions more humane and responsive to human needs.

◆ Social workers demonstrate respect for and acceptance of the unique characteristics of diverse populations.

◆ Social workers are responsible for their own ethical conduct, for the quality of their practice, and seeking continuous growth in the knowledge and skills of their profession.

---

[1]From *Curriculum Policy Statement for Master's Degree Programs in Social Work Education*, by the Council on Social Work Education, 1992. Reprinted by permission.

The National Association of Social Workers (NASW) in its *NASW Standards for the Classification of Social Work Practice* (NASW, 1981, p. 18) identifies the values for social work practice outlined in Box 3.3.

These fundamental social work values serve as an extremely useful foundation for the process of ethical decision making. They are invaluable in helping social workers define a professional identity and establish a social work frame of reference. Such abstract concepts, however, are not sufficient for making ethically sound practice decisions. That function is served by codes of ethics, derived from the fundamental social work values but presented in more concrete and prescriptive terms. Reference to a social work code of ethics should help you to make practice decisions that are ethical and congruent with the fundamental social work values.

In order to practice ethically, you must have a thorough understanding of both the fundamental social work values and the principles that guide social workers in making ethical decisions. In the United States, the *Code of Ethics of the National Association of Social Workers* (1994) serves as the primary guide to which social workers must adhere. In Canada, the *Social Work Code of Ethics* of the Canadian Association of Social Workers (1994) is the predominant guide. These codes of ethics tend to be used in court proceedings even for social workers who are not members of the National Association of Social Workers or the Canadian Association of Social Workers.

The NASW code reflects the relationship between values and ethics. The preamble (NASW, 1994, p. v.) states: "This code is based on fundamental values of the social

BOX 3.3
National Association of Social Workers
Standards for the Classification of Social Work Practice
Social Work Values[2]

Commitment to the primary importance of the individual in society.
Respect for the confidentiality of relationships with clients.
Commitment to social change to meet socially recognized needs.
Willingness to keep personal feelings and needs separate from professional relationships.
Willingness to transmit knowledge and skills to others.
Respect and appreciation for individual and group differences.
Commitment to developing clients' ability to help themselves.
Willingness to persist in efforts on behalf of clients despite frustration.
Commitment to social justice and the economic, physical, and mental well-being of all in society.
Commitment to a high standard of personal and professional conduct.

---

[2]From *NASW Standards for the Classification of Social Work Practice*, National Association of Social Workers, 1981, p. 18. Copyright 1981, National Association of Social Workers, Inc. Reprinted by permission.

work profession that include the worth, dignity, and uniqueness of all persons as well as their rights and opportunities. It is also based on the nature of social work, which fosters conditions that promote these values."

In order to practice ethically, therefore, you must be thoroughly familiar with your social work code of ethics. You should carry a copy with you; during your professional activities, you will frequently need to refer to it. The Summary of Major Principles of the NASW's code is reproduced in Box 3.4. A summary of the major ethical responsibilities contained in the CASW's code is shown in Box 3.5. The NASW code is reproduced in its entirety in Appendix 2. The complete CASW code is presented in Appendix 3.

BOX 3.4
National Association of Social Workers
Code of Ethics
Summary of Major Principles[3]

I. The Social Worker's Conduct and Comportment as a Social Worker
  A. Propriety—The social worker should maintain high standards of personal conduct in the capacity or identity as social worker.
  B. Competence and Professional Development—The social worker should strive to become and remain proficient in professional practice and the performance of professional functions.
  C. Service—The social worker should regard as primary the service obligation of the social work profession.
  D. Integrity—The social worker should act in accordance with the highest standards of professional integrity and impartiality.
  E. Scholarship and Research—The social worker engaged in study and research should be guided by the conventions of scholarly inquiry.

II. The Social Worker's Ethical Responsibility to Clients
  F. Primacy of Clients' Interests—The social worker's primary responsibility is to clients.
  G. Rights and Prerogatives of Clients—The social worker should make every effort to foster maximum self-determination on the part of clients.
  H. Confidentiality and Privacy—The social worker should respect the privacy of clients and hold in confidence all information obtained in the course of professional service.
  I. Fees—When setting fees, the social worker should ensure that they are fair, reasonable, considerate, and commensurate with the

continued

---

[3]From *The Code of Ethics of the National Association of Social Workers*, National Association of Social Workers, 1994. Copyright 1994, National Association of Social Workers, Inc. Reprinted by permission.

B O X 3.4 *continued*

service performed and with due regard for the clients' ability to pay.

III. The Social Worker's Ethical Responsibility to Colleagues
  J. Respect, Fairness, and Courtesy—The social worker should treat colleagues with respect courtesy, fairness, and good faith.
  K. Dealing with Colleagues' Clients—The social worker has the responsibility to relate to the clients of colleagues with full professional consideration.

IV. The Social Worker's Ethical Responsibility to Employers and Employing Organizations
  L. Commitments to Employing Organization—The social worker should adhere to commitments made to the employing organization.

V. The Social Worker's Ethical Responsibility to the Social Work Profession
  M. Maintaining the Integrity of the Profession—The social worker should uphold and advance the values, ethics, knowledge, and mission of the profession.
  N. Community Service—The social worker should assist the profession in making social services available to the general public.
  O. Development of Knowledge—The social worker should take responsibility for identifying, developing, and fully utilizing knowledge for professional practice.

VI. The Social Worker's Ethical Responsibility to Society
  P. Promoting the General Welfare—The social worker should promote the general welfare of society.

Identifying Ethical and Legal Implications

In addition to understanding the legal duties of all professional helpers and knowing the code of ethics, you must be able to identify those principles and duties that might apply in a given practice situation. This requires inductive thinking skills as you consider a specific situation and determine which ethical principles and legal obligations are relevant.

For example, imagine that you are a social worker in an agency that provides crisis intervention services. One day, while sitting at your desk catching up on paperwork, a former client whom you had served some eight months earlier telephones to say, "I have locked myself in my basement. I have a gun, and I am going to shoot myself today. I wanted to let you know that you did not help me at all! Goodbye."

BOX 3.5
Canadian Association of Social Workers
Code of Ethics
Summary of Major Principles[4]

Ethical Duties and Obligations

1. A social worker shall maintain the best interest of the client as the primary professional obligation.
2. A social worker shall carry out her or his professional duties and obligations with integrity and objectivity.
3. A social worker shall have and maintain competence in the provision of a social work service to a client.
4. A social worker shall not exploit the relationship with a client for personal benefit, gain or gratification.
5. A social worker shall protect the confidentiality of all information acquired from the client or others regarding the client and the client's family during the professional relationship unless
   (a) the client authorizes in writing the release of specified information
   (b) the information is released under the authority of a statute or an order of a court of competent jurisdiction, or
   (c) otherwise authorized by this Code.
6. A social worker who engages in another profession, occupation, affiliation or calling shall not allow these outside interests to affect the social work relationship with the client.
7. A social worker in private practice shall not conduct the business of provision of social work services for a fee in a manner that discredits the profession or diminishes the public's trust in the profession.

Ethical Responsibilities

8. A social worker shall advocate for workplace conditions and policies that are consistent with the Code.
9. A social worker shall promote excellence in the social work profession.
10. A social worker shall advocate change
    (a) in the best interest of the client, and
    (b) for the overall benefit of society, the environment and the global community.

---

[4]This *Social Work Code of Ethics*, adopted by the Board of Directors of the Canadian Association of Social Workers (CASW), is effective on January 1, 1994 and replaces *The CASW Code of Ethics* (1983). The Code is reprinted here with the permission of CASW. The copyright in the document has been registered with the Consumer and Corporate Affairs Canada, registration No. 427837.

In addition to managing the various emotions you would undoubtedly experience, you would also have to consider several ethical and legal obligations in responding to this situation. The following elements from the National Association of Social Workers' code probably apply:

- ◆ II.F.1. The social worker should serve clients with devotion, loyalty, determination, and the maximum application of professional skill and competence.
- ◆ II.F.8. The social worker should seek advice and counsel of colleagues and supervisors whenever such consultation is in the best interest of clients.
- ◆ II.G. Rights and Prerogatives of Clients—The social worker should make every effort to foster maximum self-determination on the part of clients.
- ◆ II.G.3. The social worker should not engage in any action that violates or diminishes the civil or legal rights of clients.
- ◆ II.H. Confidentiality and Privacy—The social worker should respect the privacy of clients and hold in confidence all information obtained in the course of professional service.
- ◆ II.H.1. The social worker should share with others confidences revealed by clients, without their consent, only for compelling reasons.

The following principles from the Canadian Association of Social Workers' code appear to be relevant:

- ◆ 1. A social worker shall maintain the best interest of the client as the primary professional obligation.
- ◆ 2. A social worker shall carry out his or her professional duties and obligations with integrity and objectivity.
- ◆ 3. A social worker shall have and maintain competence in the provision of a social work service to a client.
- ◆ 4.1 The social worker shall respect the client and act so that the dignity, individuality and rights of the person are protected.
- ◆ 4.2 The social worker shall assess and consider a client's motivation and physical and mental capacity in arranging for the provision of an appropriate service.
- ◆ 5. A social worker shall protect the confidentiality of all information required from the client or others regarding the client and the client's family during the professional relationship. . . .
- ◆ 5.3 The social worker may disclose confidential information to other persons in the workplace who, by virtue of their responsibilities, have an identified need to know as determined by the social worker.
- ◆ 5.4 Clients shall be the initial or primary source of information about themselves and their problems unless the client is incapable or unwilling to give information or when corroborative reporting is required.
- ◆ 5.6 Where information is required by law, the social worker shall explain to the client the consequences of refusing to provide the requested information.

- 5.10 The social worker shall record all relevant information, and keep all relevant documents in the file.
- 5.18 The obligation to maintain confidentiality continues indefinitely after the social worker has ceased contact with the client.
- 5.25 A social worker shall disclose information acquired from a client to a member of the client's family where

  (a) the information involves a threat of harm to self or others. . . .
- 5.26 A social worker shall disclose information acquired from a client to a person or a police officer where the information involves a threat of harm to that person.
- 5.28 When disclosure is required by order of a court, the social worker shall not divulge more information than is reasonably required and shall where possible notify the client of this requirement.

The legal obligations that deserve consideration in this situation are (1) the *duty of care*, including the responsibility to try to prevent suicidal action, (2) the *duty to inform*, (3) the *duty of confidentiality*, and (4) the *duty to respect privacy*.

In spite of the fact that this is, nominally, a *former* client who expresses anger toward you, the codes suggest that you should maintain your professional role and continue to serve him enthusiastically. His best interest continues to be your primary obligation. Because the client shows disappointment in you and may not respond to your attempts to contact him, it is probably in the client's best interest that you seek advice from your supervisor or colleagues. According to the codes, you should also respect the client's civil and legal rights. Additionally, you should maintain the confidentiality of information that the client reveals or share such information with others only for compelling reasons, such as when it involves a threat to harm himself or others. These last three principles apply if or when you consider contacting the caller's family members, a medical doctor, an ambulance service, paramedics, or the police in your determined efforts to protect his life.

As a professional social worker, you should attempt to prevent the client from taking his own life. This is consistent with the legal duty of care under which you are obligated to be available, to try to prevent suicidal action, to avoid causing suicidal action, and to ensure the physical protection of clients who are dangerous to themselves. You also have a duty to inform the client concerning actions you intend to take. Finally, you have a legal, as well as ethical, duty to maintain confidentiality and respect the person's right to privacy.

When you consider the relevance of these various ethical principles and legal obligations, it becomes clear that you cannot possibly meet all of them. If you attempt to serve the client with devotion, determination, and meet your legal duty to try to prevent his suicide by telephoning family members, a physician, or the police, you violate his right to confidentiality and, potentially, his privacy. His right to privacy would obviously be lost at the point that police or emergency medical personnel entered his home. If you maintain his right to confidentiality and privacy, you neglect your legal duty to attempt to prevent his suicide. This is indeed an ethical dilemma. How do you decide what to do?

Ethical Decision Making

Identifying the various ethical principles and legal obligations pertaining to a particular case is the first step in the process of ethical decision making. However, it is often insufficient, since numerous principles and legal duties may apply and sometimes conflict. When they do conflict, you are caught between them.

To help you decide which principles or legal obligations take precedence over others in situations where ethical obligations conflict, Loewenberg and Dolgoff (1992) have developed the Ethical Principles Screen outlined in Box 3.6.

Loewenberg and Dolgoff's Ethical Principles Screen

In their Ethical Principles Screen, Loewenberg and Dolgoff (1992, pp. 60–62) identify and rank-order professional social work's fundamental ethical principles in the form of a hierarchical screen. Ethical Principle 1 is superior to Principles 2 through 7; Principle 2 is of higher rank than Principles 3 through 7, and so on. In any given practice situation, you first identify the relevant ethical principles and legal obligations that apply. If conflicts emerge, you then classify them into the categories suggested by Loewenberg and Dolgoff's Ethical Principles Screen. Finally, you assign priority to the higher principle and take action accordingly.

The first ethical principle indicates that the protection of human life, whether that of a client or other persons, is the paramount obligation, taking precedence over all others. Therefore, a social worker who learns that a client intends to kill a former lover would take action to protect the potential victim, even if other ethical or legal duties are abridged in the process. The second ethical principle suggests that persons of equal

BOX 3.6
Loewenberg and Dolgoff's Ethical Principles Screen[5]

Ethical Principle 1	Principle of the protection of life
Ethical Principle 2	Principle of equality and inequality
Ethical Principle 3	Principle of autonomy and freedom
Ethical Principle 4	Principle of least harm
Ethical Principle 5	Principle of quality of life
Ethical Principle 6	Principle of privacy and confidentiality
Ethical Principle 7	Principle of truthfulness and full disclosure

[5]Reproduced by permission of the publisher, F. E. Peacock Publishers, Inc., Itasca, Illinois. From F. Loewenberg & R. Dolgoff, *Ethical Decisions for Social Work Practice* (4th ed.), 1992, p. 60.

status or power have the right to be treated equally, while those of unequal status or power "have the right to be treated differently if the inequality is relevant to the issue in question" (1992, p. 61). Competent adults therefore have the right to engage in consensual sex. However, because of unequal status and power, an adult does not have the right to engage in sexual activities with a child, even with the child's apparent consent. The third ethical principle guides a social worker to "make practice decisions that foster a person's autonomy, independence, and freedom" (1992, p. 61). Of course, a client's right to independent action is not unlimited. A person does not have the autonomous right to kill him- or herself, or someone else; abuse or exploit a child; or yell "fire" in a crowded theater. The fourth ethical principle suggests that a "social worker should always choose the option that will cause the least harm, the least permanent harm, and/or the most easily reversible harm," (1992, p. 62). The fifth principle holds that a "social worker should choose the option that promotes a better quality of life for all people, for the individual as well as for the community" (1992, p. 62). The sixth principle indicates that a "social worker should make practice decisions that strengthen every person's right to privacy" (1992, p. 62). Therefore, social workers must maintain confidentiality in their service to clients. The seventh principle holds that social workers should be honest and truthful, and "fully disclose all relevant information" (1992, p. 62) to clients and, where applicable, to others as well.

Return now to the case of the man who has locked himself in his basement and is threatening suicide. You have already identified the ethical principles and legal duties that apply in this situation. You may now use Loewenberg and Dolgoff's method to determine which of these several, conflicting responsibilities take precedence.

As suggested by the screen, your first obligation is to save or protect human life. This is consonant with the ethical responsibility to "serve clients with devotion, loyalty, determination, and the maximum application of professional skill and competence" and to "maintain the best interest of the client as the primary professional obligation." These ethical principles are consistent with the legal duty of care that includes the responsibility to prevent suicidal action. The protection of human life takes precedence over all other principles. Therefore, if you have evidence to suggest that the man who telephoned indeed intends to attempt suicide, you are obligated to take action to protect his life. You must intervene—even if such intervention violates other ethical principles or legal duties. Of course, if at all possible, you would first try to intervene in a manner that does not infringe on other obligations. For example, in this situation, you or preferably your supervisor—since the client has targeted you as a source of dissatisfaction—might return the person's telephone call in an attempt to engage him in conversation and defuse the situation.

An attempt to crisis intervene directly with the client by telephone is congruent with Loewenberg and Dolgoff's third ethical principle, that of autonomy and freedom. Such intervention would also support their sixth principle, the principle of privacy and confidentiality. The man, however, may not answer the telephone—or it may be apparent that further contact by you or your supervisor could exacerbate the situation. If such is the case, you may have to infringe on the client's right to privacy, his right to confidentiality, and perhaps even his right to freedom—should temporary police arrest or involuntary hospitalization become necessary.

In your attempt to save the man's life, you may have to call his relatives to inform them about the situation and request their cooperation. You may have to telephone the local police or paramedics and ask them to go to the house. At some point in the process, you may need to provide evidence to a judge or magistrate, or perhaps to a court-appointed physician, to facilitate hospitalization. Taken by themselves, these actions do infringe on several of the client's fundamental civil rights; they do represent violations of some of your own ethical principles and legal duties. Nonetheless, if a client intends to attempt suicide, you are ethically and legally bound to forgo lower-level ethical principles so as to uphold those at a higher level and try to save the person's life.

Summary

The values, ethics, and legal obligations that guide social workers enter into every aspect of professional practice. Indeed, you should consider ethical principles more important than theoretical knowledge, research findings, agency policies, and, certainly, your personal views.

In order to make sound ethical decisions in social work practice, you need to know and understand the values of the profession, the code of ethics, and the legal obligations affecting social work practice. In addition, you must be able to identify the ethical principles and legal duties that may apply to particular situations. Finally, when several obligations conflict, you must be able to determine which take precedence over the others.

The skill of ethical decision making is fundamental to professional social work practice. Without such skill, you cannot legitimately claim professional status. Indeed, attempting to provide social work services without regard for the ethical principles would be, literally, unconscionable.

◆ EXERCISE 3-1: ETHICAL DECISION MAKING

In the space provided, identify the ethical principles and legal duties that you believe may apply to each of the case examples presented below. Then classify and rank-order each principle or duty according to Loewenberg and Dolgoff's Ethical Principles Screen. Finally, based on your rank ordering, describe the actions you might take as a social worker in each situation.

1. As a social worker in the oncology unit of the general hospital, you frequently work with clients who are dying. An intelligent, articulate 88-year-old woman, Ms. T., who has suffered from intense pain for several months, informs you that she has hoarded powerful analgesic medicines and intends to take her own life during the night. She says that she wants to say goodbye to you and

to thank you for all your help during this time. However, she asks that you please do not interfere with her plans.

2. As a social worker in an elementary school system, you frequently work with young children in small groups. During a meeting with several girls in the 8-to-10-year-old age range, one girl says that almost every night, her father comes into her bedroom, puts his hands under her pajamas, and touches between her legs.

3. A 25-year-old man, father of two children (1 and 3 years old), comes to a first interview with you, a social worker in a family counseling agency. During the course of the interview, he reveals that he and his wife argue a lot. He says that she won't stop arguing once she starts and that when he tries to walk away, she pursues him, yelling. He indicates that in those situations he becomes enraged. He reveals that on several occasions he has pushed her and once he punched her in the face, breaking her nose.

4. You have recently been employed in an agency whose clientele is primarily African American and Latino. All the professional staff are white; several of the secretarial and support staff members are African American. No one employed by the agency is Spanish-speaking.

5. You have been working with a married couple who have indicated a desire to improve the quality of their relationship. Direct, open, and honest communication has been agreed upon as a relationship goal. Each has also expressed that sexual fidelity is an important dimension of their marriage. Between the fifth and sixth meetings, you receive a telephone call from one of the partners who says, "I think it would help you to know that I am involved romantically with another person. My spouse does not know and I know that you will not reveal this information. I want you to know because I respect your expertise. You are doing a wonderful job."

6. Using the rating scales below (where 0 = no proficiency and 10 = complete proficiency), assess your current level of proficiency in the following dimensions of the skill of ethical decision making.

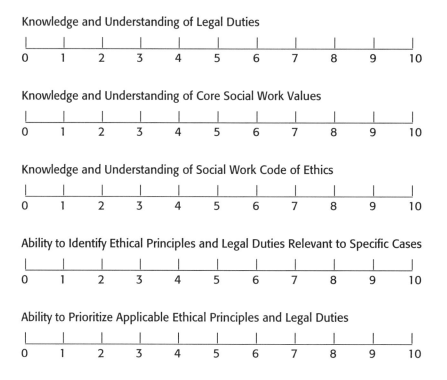

Knowledge and Understanding of Legal Duties

0	1	2	3	4	5	6	7	8	9	10

Knowledge and Understanding of Core Social Work Values

0	1	2	3	4	5	6	7	8	9	10

Knowledge and Understanding of Social Work Code of Ethics

0	1	2	3	4	5	6	7	8	9	10

Ability to Identify Ethical Principles and Legal Duties Relevant to Specific Cases

0	1	2	3	4	5	6	7	8	9	10

Ability to Prioritize Applicable Ethical Principles and Legal Duties

0	1	2	3	4	5	6	7	8	9	10

7. Finally, review your ratings to identify those dimensions of ethical decision making in which you remain less proficient (e.g., a score of 7 or less). Then, outline the steps you might take to improve your skill in those areas.

_____

Chapter 4

Talking and Listening: The Basic Interpersonal Skills

This chapter is intended to help you develop competence in the basic interpersonal skills of talking and listening, which are vital to all phases of social work practice (indeed, to all aspects of human interaction). Inadequate skills in talking and listening can hinder a positive professional relationship and prevent a successful outcome. These basic interpersonal skills facilitate social interaction. Using them enables you to hear, to understand accurately, and to express yourself clearly during exchanges with other people.

In order to interact effectively, you must be skilled in *talking*—using voice, speech, language, and body language—as well as in *listening*—hearing, observing, encouraging, and remembering. Also, you must be able to combine talking and listening into *active listening*, a form of talking by which you demonstrate that you have heard and understood the speaker.

It is extremely difficult for people to communicate accurately with one another—social workers included. Among the common errors social workers make in talking and listening are:

1. interacting in a patronizing or condescending manner
2. interrogating rather than interviewing by asking questions in rapid, staccato fashion
3. attending predominantly to a single dimension of a person's experience (e.g., just thoughts or just feelings; only the personal or only the situational)
4. frequently interrupting with a comment or question
5. failing to listen

6. neglecting to use a person's name or mispronouncing it
7. neglecting to consider the cultural meaning of the interview for a particular person or family
8. failing to demonstrate understanding through active listening
9. using terms that stereotype people or groups
10. offering suggestions or proposing solutions too early in the process (on the basis of incomplete or inaccurate understanding of the person-problem-situation)
11. making statements in absolutist terms (e.g., *always*, *never*, *all*, or *none*)
12. prematurely disclosing one's own personal feelings and opinions or sharing life experiences
13. confronting or challenging a person before establishing a base of accurate understanding and a solid relationship
14. speculating about causes of problems before adequately exploring the person-problem-situation
15. prematurely pushing for action or progress from a person
16. using clichés and jargon
17. making critical or judgmental comments, including pejorative remarks about other persons or groups (e.g., other professionals, agencies, and organizations)
18. displaying inappropriate or disproportionate emotions (e.g., acting extraordinarily happy to meet a new client or sobbing uncontrollably when a person expresses painful feelings)

Voice, Speech, and Language

The words you choose, the quality of your pronunciation, the sound and pitch of your voice, and the rate and delivery of your speech communicate a great deal to clients and others with whom you interact. During a typical first contact—whether face-to-face, by telephone, or even by letter, fax or e-mail—you should use words and phrases that are readily understood by most people. Keep it simple. Save arcane and esoteric language for your professors! Avoid evaluative terms. Even words such as *good* or *right*—intended to convey support and encouragement—may suggest to a client that you regularly make evaluative judgments. A client may think, "If you judge me or my actions positively without knowing much about me, can you really be objective?" Or, perhaps, "At this point, you approve of me. I'd better not say anything that might lead you to disapprove. I guess I'll keep my real problems to myself."

Especially during the early stages of work, you should also be careful about sharing opinions or hypotheses. Use of diagnostic or psychological terminology and legal jargon may suggest to clients that you are reaching conclusions about them or their situation before fully understanding all the intricacies of their circumstances. Labels of all kinds, even positive ones, can significantly affect the tenor of your relationships with clients and the course of your work together. Use of the verb *to be* often results in a labeling effect. Suppose, for example, that you were to say the sentence, "He is a child abuser." Because the word *is* suggests an equivalence between *he* and *child abuser* (i.e., *he* equals *child abuser*), there is a powerful tendency to view that human being through the conceptual screen of "child abuser." You will probably find it difficult to experience the person except through the "child abuser" lens. Rather than a human being who has abused a child, he becomes a child abuser who may have some human qualities.

Of course, child abuse is an offense that should not be tolerated. Perhaps especially among social workers, it is likely to elicit strong emotional reactions. However, even terms that are not so emotionally laden can have deleterious labeling effects. When you think or say, "She is young," "They were foolish," "He was manipulative," "She is seductive," "He is aggressive," "They are poor," "He is white," or "She is unmarried," you draw conclusions that are primarily derived from your own rather than from others' experience of themselves.

The human being convicted of the crime of child abuse may experience himself as a weak, impulsive person guilty of a terrible sin. The person who appears to you to be young may experience herself as old beyond her years. Indeed, she may even question her own sexual identity and wonder if she is really female. The behavior that you consider foolish may have resulted from an excruciating examination of various possibilities. The manipulation that you infer may represent an attempt to maintain a sense of personal control or perhaps salvage some dignity on the part of a person who feels humiliated. What you perceive as seductive may, in that person's family and culture, be a naturally warm and friendly interpersonal gesture. What you consider aggressive may constitute an effort to counter powerful feelings of fear and anxiety. What you see as poverty may be experienced by others as freedom from the petty pursuit of money and material goods. The person you regard as a white male might view himself as Spanish and may have adopted an androgynous philosophy in which the concepts of male and female or masculine and feminine have little relevance. And the person you consider unmarried may have long ago determined for herself that the institution of marriage was anathema to a liberated perspective.

As you can see, hypotheses, inferences, speculation, labels, and other abstractions are risky at all times, especially during the early phases of a relationship. As you interact with people, try to adopt the frame of reference of the person who is communicating. Be careful in your use of the verb *to be*. Try to use words that are descriptive and observational rather than inferential.

Use of inferences involves a serious risk of stereotyping people, perhaps because of their perceived membership in a certain class or group (e.g., male, female, poor, rich, black, white, Italian, Catholic). As a social worker, you should, of course, be aware of sociological theory and research related to different groups, especially cultural groups common in your particular community, and populations generally at risk of oppression, exploitation, and discrimination. For example, in talking and listening with clients, you should be aware of research suggesting that men and women tend to adopt different conversational styles (Tannen, 1990; 1994); that Native American clients may find a social worker's personal questions to be intrusive (Good Tracks, 1973); and that Latino clients may prefer a longer, more informal process of beginning (Aguilar, 1972). However, in using such knowledge, you must be alert to the danger of stereotyping. Many men use conversational styles quite different from many women, but *some* men adopt conversational styles that are quite similar to that of many women; *some* Native

Americans experience personal questions from a social worker as an expression of interest and concern; and *some* Latino clients prefer a direct, businesslike approach as they begin with a social worker. All women are not the same; nor are all men, all people of color, all children, all gay and lesbian persons, or even all politicians! Therefore, be sensitive to and carefully consider the person's sex, class, ethnicity, sexual orientation, religion, and cultural affiliation, but recognize that each individual client is unique. Each person will probably differ, at least to some extent, from the common characteristics of most members of his or her class or group.

As an interview proceeds, you may attempt to match the client's language mode. Some people favor words associated with *hearing*; others prefer those identified with *seeing*; still others like words that indicate *touching*. For example, if you use words such as *hear*, *sound*, *noise*, *loud*, or *soft* with people who favor an auditory language mode, you increase the probability of being understood and valued by them. A similarly favorable reaction is likely if you were to use *see*, *view*, and *perceive* with people who prefer a visual language mode, or *feel*, *sense*, and *touch* with those who favor tactile language (Bandler & Grinder, 1979, pp. 5–78).

Tone of voice affects others. If you communicate in a voice that is monotonous, dramatic, high pitched, loud, or soft, you may distract the other person from the substance of your message and thereby interfere with the communication process. If you speak rapidly, slowly, or haltingly, or punctuate your speech with frequent use of *uhhs* and *you knows*, you may also impede understanding. Similarly, if your verbal responses are not consistent with the topic under consideration or are incongruent with your own nonverbal presentation, your listener may become confused about the true meaning of your message.

In general, try to adopt a speaking style that is moderate in vocal tone, volume, and speed of delivery. Through your voice, speech, and language, convey that you are truly interested in what the client has to say (Ivey, 1988, p. 22). Sometimes, however, you may deliberately increase or decrease your rate of speech in order to match the pace of the client. On other occasions, you may purposely slow your pace in order to lead a fast-speaking client into a slower speaking mode. In some circumstances (for example, when working with a moderately hearing-impaired client), you may need to lower the pitch of your voice in order to be more easily heard. Generally, when you speak or write, active voice is preferable to passive voice, and each unit of speech should not be so long or complex as to impede understanding.

◆ EXERCISE 4-1: VOICE, SPEECH, AND LANGUAGE

Complete the following exercises to become more aware of the sound of your voice and the nature of your speech patterns.

1. Tape-record your voice for five minutes at four periods during the day. First, record your voice upon awakening, again at a point around midday, once more late in the afternoon, and finally just prior to bedtime. Make these recordings when you are alone. Speak approximately the same statement on each occasion

(but do not read from a script). You might, for example, imagine that you are introducing yourself to new client.

How does your voice sound at these different times? Are the samples similar or different? In general, how would you characterize the sound of your voice? Do you like it? How clear is your pronunciation? Is your speech modulated, or does it tend to be monotonous? How would you characterize the pitch or tone of your speech (high or low)? How about the rate of speech (fast or slow)? When you listen to the sound of your voice, what do you feel? Does it remind you of anything or anyone? If so, what or who?

In the space provided, indicate what you have learned about your voice and speech through this exercise, and what, if anything, you would want to change.

2. Tape-record your voice as you express, with emotion, the following statements:

Anger	I am angry. I deserved an A but I got a B!
	I hate your guts!
Fear	I am scared when I go alone into the public housing project.
	I'm frightened that you are going to leave me.
Caring	I care a great deal about you.
	You are very important to me.
Sadness	I am so sad and depressed that I cannot even get out of bed.
	I just can't go on anymore.

Request	I need help. My car has broken down and I need a ride to get to work tomorrow. Would you drive me to work in the morning? Would you please give me an extension for this paper?
Demand	You must pick up your room before you go out to play. Get that report in to me by the end of the workday today.

Replay the tape. As you listen to these different expressions of your voice and speech, what do you notice? Do you seem equally capable of expressing each of these emotions? Which, if any, appear to involve discomfort? With which do you seem at ease? In your everyday life, which emotions do you tend to express in your interactions with others? Are there any that you only rarely express?

In the space provided, briefly discuss what you have learned through this exercise that may relate to your various roles and functions as a professional social worker.

3. Imagine that you work in an agency that provides a wide range of social services. You are about to meet for the first time with a prospective client who is dramatically different from you. If you are female, pretend the client is male. If you are Caucasian, imagine that the client is a person of color. If you are tall, assume that the client is of shorter stature. If you are well educated, consider

the client to be poorly educated. If you are middle-class, pretend that the client is virtually penniless. If you have a residence, presume that the client is homeless. Now tape-record yourself as you speak the words you would say as you begin work with this prospective client. Introduce yourself, describe something about the kinds of services your agency might be able to provide, and ask this imaginary person some of the questions you would like to ask. Continue this imaginary conversation for approximately five minutes.

Now replay the tape and review your language usage. Examine the words you said and consider them from the point of view of the imaginary person you have created for this exercise. How would your prospective client be likely to experience the words and language you have chosen to use?

In the space provided, indicate what you have learned through this exercise that may relate to your roles and functions as a professional social worker. In particular, consider how your use of language is likely to be experienced by persons different from yourself in terms of age, sex, skin color, sexual orientation, educational background, socioeconomic status, ethnicity, physical appearance and ability, and other factors that distinguish human beings from one another.

Body Language

Because a great deal of communication is nonverbal, you must appreciate the power of body language. Factors such as posture, facial expression, eye contact, gait, and body positioning represent powerful forms of communication (Ivey, 1988, pp. 26–27; Kadushin, 1990, pp. 270–299). In social work practice, your body language should generally be congruent with your verbal language. All people, perhaps especially clients, notice discrepancies and incongruities between what you say verbally and what you express nonverbally. When you present yourself in an incongruent fashion, others may be confused about you and your message. When you express yourself congruently, people are more likely to understand your communications and to experience you as genuine and sincere.

In addition to verbal and nonverbal congruence, your body language should communicate attention and interest in the other person, as well as caring, concern, respect, and authenticity. On many occasions, you will need to express your message in an assertive manner that conveys power and authority. In order to emphasize one element or another, changes in body language are necessary.

As a general rule, when beginning interviews with prospective clients, you should typically adopt an open or accessible body position (Egan, 1982a, pp. 60–62): If standing, arms and hands are held loosely along your sides; if seated, the hands are placed on your lap. Arms held across the chest, behind the head, or draped over an adjoining chair may reflect inattention or nonreceptiveness. Tightly clasped hands, swinging legs or feet, pacing, looking at a watch or clock, or drumming fingers tend to communicate nervousness or impatience. Slouching in a chair may suggest fatigue or disinterest. Sometimes, however, you may need to assume an informal body position so as to increase the comfort and decrease the threat experienced by another person. For example, in working with children, you might sit on the floor and talk while playing a game. With teenage clients, significant encounters may occur while sharing a soft drink, shooting pool, or leaning against a fence or wall. Important exchanges may take place while you transport a client to a doctor's office or a food pantry, while you help a parent change a baby's diaper, or while you enjoy a snack together.

The frequency and intensity of eye contact varies depending upon the people involved, the purpose of the meeting, the topic under discussion, and a host of other factors. In general, you should adopt seating or standing arrangements that allow for but do not force eye contact between the participants. Although it is common for social workers to attempt rather frequent eye contact, especially when clients are talking, the degree and intensity should vary according to the individual and cultural characteristics of the person, the problems of concern, and the context of the meeting. In many cultures, regular eye contact is experienced as positive, but in several others it is not. "Some cultural groups (for instance, certain Native American, Eskimo, or aboriginal Australian groups) generally avoid eye contact, especially when talking about serious subjects" (Ivey, 1988, p. 27). Dropping one's eyes to avoid direct eye contact, in certain cultures, conveys respect, while steady, direct eye contact signifies disapproval. For some groups, eye contact is more likely when talking than when listening, while the exact opposite is true in other cultures.

In all cases, however, you should not stare. Staring almost universally constitutes a violation of the other's territorial space and may be experienced as a challenge. It may also suggest a power differential: Many persons of majority status and those affiliated with groups in power feel entitled to look at, peruse, and even stare at people of minority status and those of less power. For example, many men believe it quite acceptable to stare at women. In North America, many Caucasians find it quite permissible to carefully watch or monitor people of color. There are numerous other examples. However, as a social worker interested in relationships characterized by equality, mutual respect, and joint participation, your eye contact should never be so intense or continuous as to constitute an intrusion, a reflection of a greater status or power, or a form of intimidation.

Attending (Carkhuff & Anthony, 1979, pp. 31–60) is a term frequently used to describe the process of nonverbally communicating to others that you are open, nonjudgmental, accepting of them as people, and interested in what they say. A general purpose of attending is, in fact, to encourage others to express themselves as fully and as freely as possible. During the beginning phase especially, your nonverbal presentation is at least as important as any other factor in influencing clients' responses to you.

There is a substantial literature regarding the skill of attending. For example, Carkhuff & Anthony (1979, pp. 39–42) suggest that counselors face their clients squarely, at a distance of three to four feet, without tables or other potential obstacles between the participants. They further recommend regular eye contact, facial expressions showing interest and concern, and a slight lean or incline toward the other person.

Many of these guidelines are useful, but they may tend to reflect nonverbal characteristics common among adult, majority-member, middle- and upper-class North Americans. Many children, members of ethnic minority groups, and people of lower socioeconomic status commonly demonstrate quite different nonverbal characteristics in their interactions with others. Facing some people too directly, too squarely, and too closely may infringe upon personal territory and privacy. For others, a distance of four feet would be much too far for an intimate conversation. Therefore, you must be flexible in your attending and physical positioning. Closely observe the nonverbal expressions of the other person and respect them. Also, within the general guidelines suggested above, assume a comfortable body position. Trying to understand another person requires energy and concentration. If you are distracted by an uncomfortable position, you are less likely to be attentive. Do not, however, become so comfortable that you lose interest. Dozing off during an interview does not convey attention and concern!

When seated positions are desirable and available (e.g., when interviewing an adult in an office setting), place the chairs so that they create an angle of between 90 and 135 degrees. This allows other people to direct their eyes and bodies toward or away from you as desired, and it affords you the same opportunity. Matching, movable chairs are preferred for their flexibility and in order to avoid symbolic distinction between your chair and clients'. Physically leaning toward clients at points when they are sharing emotionally charged material usually demonstrates concern and compassion. However, carefully observe their reactions. Some clients may find the added closeness too intimate or even intrusive, especially during the early stages of the working relationship.

Of course, many times you have limited control over the placement of chairs or even the interview setting. Often an exchange occurs during a walk or an automobile drive, in a kitchen during mealtime, while someone cares for children, and sometimes even while a person watches television. As a relationship develops and you begin to understand the meaning of various gestures to the client, you may find it appropriate to ask to move a chair closer or to lower the volume on the television. These are frequently messages of great significance to clients who realize that you actually do want to hear what they say!

◆ **EXERCISE 4-2: BODY LANGUAGE**

Recruit a friend or colleague to join you in a few nonverbal experiments.

1. Maintaining eye contact, slowly walk toward your partner (who remains standing in position) until it becomes uncomfortable for you. Then stop. Observe the approximate distance between you. Describe your thoughts and feelings as you moved closer and closer to your partner. Ask your partner to express what he or she experienced as you approached. Make note of your experience as well as your partner's.

2. Stand face-to-face with your partner at a distance of approximately four feet. Look directly into his or her eyes until you become uncomfortable. When that occurs, simply avert your eyes. Now, move to three feet, then to two feet, each time looking directly into your partner's eyes until you experience discomfort. Then turn away. Share your reactions with each other. Now, experiment with different kinds and degrees of eye contact within a two-to-four-foot range. For example, try looking at your partner's cheekbone or mouth instead of directly into her or his eyes. Share your reactions. Experiment further by looking into your partner's eyes for several seconds and then slightly change your focus so that you look at a cheekbone for a few seconds, and then return your gaze to

the eyes. Follow that by looking at your partner's mouth for a few seconds, and then return to the eyes. Share your responses to this manner of eye contact. Make note of the form of eye contact you and your partner seem to prefer as well as those that you dislike.

3. Place two chairs squarely facing one another (front to front) approximately two feet apart. Be seated. Share your thoughts and feelings as you sit face-to-face and knee-to-knee. Is it comfortable for both of you, for only one, for neither? If it is uncomfortable, alter the distance until it becomes comfortable. Ask your partner to do the same. Finally, compromising if necessary, move the chairs until they are placed at a mutually comfortable distance. Make note of your partner's remarks as well as your own experiences in this exercise.

4. Change the placement of the chairs so that instead of directly facing each other, they now are side by side in parallel position, approximately six inches apart. As you and your partner take your seats, share your respective thoughts and feelings. Now increase the angle so that the chairs form a 90-degree angle. Share with one another your reactions to this arrangement. Now increase the angle an additional 45 degrees. Describe your reactions to this position. Which arrangement does your partner prefer? Which do you?

5. Based on the results of your experimentation, place the chairs in the position and at the angle that is reasonably comfortable for both you and your partner. Some compromise may be necessary. Now, maintaining a more or less neutral facial expression and without saying a word, try to show through your body language, but without changing your facial expression, that you care about your partner and are interested in his or her thoughts and feelings. Continue to experiment with three or four different body positions, attempting to demonstrate concern and interest, for approximately one minute each. Following each position, seek verbal feedback from your partner concerning her or his reactions. Make note of your partner's comments as well as your own reactions.

6. Based on what you have learned through your experimentation with various body positions, assume a position that your partner indicates reflects caring and interest. Now begin to experiment with different facial expressions. First, let your face become relaxed in its more or less usual state. Retain this facial expression for about one minute while your partner experiences the effect. After a minute, seek feedback from your partner about his or her observations and reactions. Then experiment with other facial expressions through which you hope to express silently, in turn, affection, compassion, joy, sadness, disappointment, disapproval, fear, and anger. Hold each facial expression for a minute or so while your partner tries to determine the feeling you are trying to express. Note your respective thoughts and feelings about this exercise.

7. In the following space, summarize what you discovered from these nonverbal experiments that may help you to become a more effective social worker.

Listening

Listening (Kadushin, 1983, pp. 276–286) refers to the processes of attentively *hearing* others' words and speech, *observing* (Carkhuff & Anthony, 1979, pp. 42–47) their nonverbal gestures and positions, *encouraging* (Ivey, 1988, pp. 93–95) them to express themselves fully, and *remembering* what they communicate. Most people are rather poor listeners, tending to pay more attention to their own thoughts and feelings than to the messages others are trying to convey. Competent listening rarely comes naturally. Yet listening, perhaps more than any other skill, is essential for effective social work practice. It requires two actions. First, you must minimize attention to your own experiences (e.g., thoughts, feelings, and sensations). Then, you must energetically concentrate on the client with a determination to understand—not to evaluate—what the client is experiencing and expressing.

For most people, being truly heard and understood by another person is one of the genuinely humanizing events in life. It conveys respect. It demonstrates that you value them and are interested in what they have to say. In a real sense, careful listening is a gesture of love. Because of this, listening is a dynamic factor in social work practice. It has several purposes. First, effective listening enables you to gather information essential for assessment and planning. Second, it helps clients feel better—often reducing tension or anxiety, heightening feelings of personal safety and well-being, and encouraging greater hope and optimism. Third, attentive listening encourages clients to express themselves freely and fully. Fourth, effective listening usually enhances your value to clients. Finally, attentive listening often contributes significantly to positive change in clients' self-understanding, self-esteem, and problem-solving capacities.

In order to listen effectively, you must be able to manage your own impulses. Containing self (Shulman, 1984, p. 61; 1992, pp. 115–116) is essentially a matter of restraint, self-control, and self-discipline. You hold back from fully experiencing and freely expressing your own reactions, ideas, or opinions. Containing self involves temporarily suspending judgment and action in order to better hear and understand other people. As a social worker, you are probably highly motivated to help people who are troubled. In your desire to serve, you may sometimes be tempted to rush to conclusions and solutions. Although immediate intervention is certainly warranted in life-threatening situations, engaging in premature assessment, advice, or action interferes with effective listening. Frequently, it also has unintended adverse consequences. In most circumstances, you would be wise to listen carefully and fully before assessing or intervening. As Shulman (1984, p. 61) says, "Workers who attempt to find simple solutions often discover that if the solutions were indeed that simple, then the client could have found them alone without the help of the worker."

Containing self is related to the use of silence. Social workers "frequently perceive silence as a hindrance and a hazard to the progress of the interview. . . . The professional assumption is that talking is better" (Kadushin, 1983, p. 286). This is certainly not always the case. Periods of silence, pauses in the exchange, are vital elements in effective communication. Of course, you should not let silence continue so long that it becomes a test to see "who will speak first" (Shulman, 1984, p. 63). However, do recognize that with some clients, at certain moments, silence can be a powerfully helpful experience. "Instead of a threat, silence should be seen and utilized as an opportunity" (Kadushin, 1983, p. 294).

Hearing refers to the process of listening that involves attending to the voice, speech, and language of other people. Hearing can be prevented or impeded by numerous factors. A room might be noisy, or another person might speak in a soft or mumbled fashion, a foreign language, or an unfamiliar dialect. Another person might use words you do not understand or in ways that differ from your understanding of those words. Effective hearing involves diminishing the obstacles and focusing entirely on the words and sounds of the other person. It also involves reducing any tendencies to hear selectively as a result of judging, comparing, criticizing, or evaluating the words and sounds of the other person. In attempting to hear clearly, you hope to take in and remember the messages sent by the speaker. In listening, *process* is as important as content. Therefore, try to hear more than the words themselves. Listen as well to the person's voice and manner of speaking. Try to hear the meaning and feeling just beyond or beneath the words that are actually said.

Another vital element in the listening process is the skill of observation. *Observing* (Carkhuff & Anthony, 1979, pp. 42–47) may be thought of as listening with your eyes. It occurs when you pay attention to the client's physical characteristics, gestures, and other nonverbal behavior. Nonverbal communications are at least as informative as verbal expression, and sometimes more. As a social worker, try to observe nonverbal manifestations of energy level, mood, and emotions. Quite often, clients do not directly express their feelings through verbal speech. Without staring, try to observe carefully in order to notice nonverbal expression of feelings.

The purpose of observing is to gain a better and more complete understanding of the ways in which the client experiences the world. During interviews, look for subtle or indirect communications. These may relate to themes of power or authority, ambivalence about seeking or receiving help, difficulties in discussing topics that involve a stigma or taboo, and inhibitions concerning the direct and full expression of powerful feelings (Shulman, 1984, pp. 20–22, 85–91). Since you are often more likely to pick up indirect communications from nonverbal rather than verbal expressions, you must observe closely. Be careful, however, to avoid the tempting conceptual trap of reaching conclusions. The most you can do is formulate a tentative hypothesis about a theme based on the words and the nonverbal gestures a client used. Such tentative hypotheses are not, in any sense, true or valid. They represent, rather, preliminary hunches!

Among the specific aspects to observe are (1) facial expression, (2) eye contact, and (3) body language, position, and movement. When observing, look for predominant facial expressions, head and body positions, physical gestures, and patterns of eye contact during communication exchanges. Also look for the nature and timing of changes in these nonverbal indicators. These may suggest feeling states such as contentment, calmness, acceptance, joy, sadness, fear or anxiety, and anger. Based on these observations, ask yourself what these expressions, gestures, and behaviors might suggest about how this person experiences her- or himself and the problem of concern. Also, consider what the person might think and feel about you and this meeting.

Encouraging (Ivey, 1988, pp. 93–94) is an element of listening that very closely approaches talking. You can encourage other people to continue expressing themselves by making very brief responses in the form of single words, short phrases, or sounds and gestures that invite them to continue their expression. Some examples of brief verbal encouragers are *Please go on; and?; Uh huh; Mmmm; Yes; Please continue.* Nonverbally, you may further communication by nodding, making attentive eye contact or certain hand motions, and leaning or inclining slightly toward the client.

Repeating a portion of a phrase or a key word that a client uses may also constitute encouragement. Such brief responses enable you to demonstrate that you want to hear more, without interrupting with a lengthy statement of your own. You must be careful, however, to avoid using the same encouragers over and over again. After a while, their repeated use may suggest a lack of sincerity. Also be aware that encouraging is not sufficient in itself to demonstrate empathic understanding. More complete communications in the form of *active listening* are necessary for that.

The final dimension of listening involves *remembering* what the client communicates. Hearing and observing are skills without much inherent value unless you can retain the information received. Remembering is the process of temporarily storing information in order that it may later be used, for example, to communicate understanding, make thematic connections between messages expressed at different times, prepare a written record, or develop an assessment.

◆ EXERCISE 4-3: LISTENING

Recruit a friend or colleague to join you in a listening exercise. Indicate that the purpose of this exercise is to determine how well you can understand and remember what is said. Tell your partner that you would like to tape-record a conversation between the two of you and, following the conversation but before replaying it, you will attempt to write down what was said. Then you will compare what you remember with what was tape-recorded. Ask your partner to identify a topic of interest that the two of you might discuss for approximately ten minutes. As the listener, your tasks are to *encourage* your partner to discuss the subject, *hear, observe,* and *comprehend* what she or he communicated, and *remember* what was said and done. Keep in mind that your partner's perspective is paramount. Withhold your own opinions. It is your partner's time. Let the discussion proceed in whatever way and direction your partner wishes. Encourage him or her to communicate freely and fully, and try not to interfere with the flow of expression. As your partner talks, listen attentively and observe carefully. At the end of the ten-minute period, thank your partner and proceed with the following.

1. Ask your partner to rate on a scale of 0 to 10 (where 0 = did not listen at all and 10 = listened extremely well) how well she or he thinks you listened to what was said. Explore with your partner the reasons for the rating.

    Thank your partner again and say goodbye. Record your partner's rating and make note of other evaluative comments.

Did Not Listen at All   Listened Extremely Well

| 0 | 1 | 2 | 3 | 4 | 5 | 6 | 7 | 8 | 9 | 10 |

2. Now, before listening to the tape recording, get a notebook and (a) try to reconstruct from memory the words your partner said during the discussion; (b) describe your partner's speaking voice, speech, and language in terms of modulation, volume, rate or pace, pitch, and common patterns (e.g., blockages, stammering, and frequent use of fillers); (c) prepare a physical description of your partner's clothing, hair and eye color, approximate height and weight, body build, and apparent physical condition; (d) describe your partner's predominant facial expression and body positions as well as any significant changes or gestures that occurred during the course of the conversation; and (e) based on the above, tentatively hypothesize about your partner's overall mood and the primary emotions that she or he might have experienced during the exchange.

3. Now play the tape recording of the conversation. As you listen, compare it to the written account that you reconstructed from memory. Approximately what percentage of your partner's comments did you recall? Record your rating below.

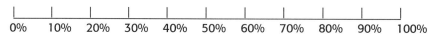

| 0% | 10% | 20% | 30% | 40% | 50% | 60% | 70% | 80% | 90% | 100% |

Identify factors that helped you to remember and those that impeded your ability to retain what was said. If your recall rating is less than 75%, develop a plan and a schedule for practicing the listening skills. Outline the major elements of your plan in the following space.

Active Listening

Active listening combines the talking and listening skills in such a way that clients feel understood and encouraged toward further self-expression. It is a form of feedback. You listen carefully and communicate your understanding of a speaker's messages by reflecting or mirroring them back. In essence, you paraphrase the client's message. Ideally, your words should be equivalent to those of the client. They should be essentially synonymous. If factual information is expressed, your active listening response should convey that factual information. If feelings are communicated, your active listening response should reflect those feelings and should be of equivalent intensity.

Active listening represents a clear and tangible demonstration that you have understood, or at least are trying to understand what a client has expressed. It indicates that you want to comprehend fully and accurately the messages communicated. Active listening shows that you are interested in the client's views, feelings, and experiences. Because it conveys empathy and furthers understanding, there is simply no substitute for active listening. It constitutes a major element of the vital feedback loop between you and your client. If you do not listen actively, you are more likely to miss part of a client's message and thereby misunderstand, distort, or misrepresent it. Furthermore, if you do not listen actively (or if you do so in a consistently inaccurate fashion), you discourage the client from free and full expression. You also significantly diminish your own value in the relationship. Clients look forward to being understood. If you do not accurately communicate understanding, clients may feel unheard, disappointed, and alienated. Experiences of oppression, discrimination, abuse, or exploitation have left many clients feeling profoundly misunderstood throughout the course of their lives. When you, as a professional social worker, communicate sincere and accurate understanding, the effect can be positive indeed. However, if the clients feel that you too, like so many before, also misunderstand, a powerfully adverse effect may result. Experiencing yet another repetition of alienation, such clients may wish they had never sought the very services they hoped would help.

Active listening combines the talking and listening skills into three steps:

Step One: Inviting. By your body position, facial expression, voice, and speech, you indicate that you are prepared to listen. Often, you can invite the other person to express himself or herself by asking a question such as "What happened?" or "How did this all come about?" It is not always necessary, however, to ask a specific question. Many clients begin to talk about themselves and their concerns as soon as you begin to attend to them with your eyes, face, and body.

Step Two: Listening. When a client responds to your invitation to speak and begins to talk, you listen carefully by attempting to *hear, observe, encourage,* and *remember.* In this step, you essentially use your ears and brain to receive and retain the messages sent by the other person.

Step Three: Reflecting. Periodically, as the client pauses at the conclusion of a message segment, paraphrase his or her statement. For example, a client might say, "I'm really frustrated with my boss. He says he wants production, production, production! But then he comes down to my shop and spends hours shooting the breeze." In active listening, you could say in response, "You're annoyed with him because he tells you he wants you to work harder and harder but then he interferes with you when you're trying to do so." Here is another example. Suppose a client says, "Ever since I was seven years old, I felt fat and ugly." You might say in active listening, "From the time of your childhood up through the present time you've thought of yourself as overweight and unattractive." By communicating an equivalent message, you demonstrate empathic understanding.

Active listening is, of course, most useful when you have accurately heard and paraphrased the client's message, but it can be helpful even when you have not. Sometimes a message is misunderstood or part of it is missed as your attention wanders; or the client may misspeak and send an incomplete or confusing message. In such cases, your sincere attempt to understand by active listening almost always elicits further expression from the client.

When your response accurately reflects the client's message, he or she may spontaneously confirm that fact by saying something such as, "Yeah, that's right." Then the client often simply continues to talk. On those occasions when your response is not entirely accurate but is close enough to demonstrate that you have heard some of the message and are genuinely trying to understand, the client may say, "Well, no. What I meant was. . . ." He or she may then try to restate the message so that you can understand. However, when you are extremely inaccurate, perhaps due to your own lack of interest or attention, the client may very well respond with an emphatic "No!" and then become much less expressive. A similar phenomenon may occur when you do not actively listen frequently enough. If you only talk or only listen but do not actively listen, you will probably discourage clients from free and full expression.

There are several common errors social workers tend to make when first developing skill in active listening:

1. using so many of the client's words that your paraphrased reflections sound like mimicry
2. repeatedly using the same lead-in phrases (e.g., "I hear you saying . . . " "It sounds like . . . ")
3. trying to be clever, profound, or interpretive—playing psychoanalyst tends to indicate that you are listening more to your own thoughts and speculations than to the client's message

4. responding only to facts and thoughts or only to feelings and emotions rather than active listening to all dimensions of the client's expression
5. frequently interrupting in order to reflect the client's message
6. active listening following each and every short phrase or statement

◆ EXERCISE 4-4: ACTIVE LISTENING

In the spaces provided, write the words you might say in active listening to the following statements:

1. *CLIENT:* My life is in shambles. My wife is divorcing me and she's going to take me to the cleaners.

2. *SUPERVISOR:* I am disappointed that you did not follow up on the Sanchez case. You know that those children are at risk.

3. *PROFESSOR:* I wonder if the match between your personal values and those of the social work profession is a good one. It appears to me that your attitudes are quite different from those required of social workers.

4. *CLIENT:* My husband thinks I'm an alcoholic. I'm here because he made me come. Sure, I drink. I drink a lot. But he's the reason I drink.

5. *CLASSMATE:* I've missed the last three classes and don't know what's going on in here. Today is the day of the midterm exam and I know I'm going to flunk. I'm so uptight, I can't think straight.

6. *COLLEAGUE:* I am working with a family that is driving me up the wall. I know I have a problem here. I get so angry at this family for not trying to help themselves. I work so damn hard and they don't do a thing!

7. *CHILD:* Sometimes my mommy's boyfriend is mean to her. He hits her and she ends up crying a lot. I don't like him at all.

Summary

The basic interpersonal skills of talking and listening are fundamental to all aspects of human interaction, including the phases and processes of social work practice. In order to talk and listen effectively as a social worker, you must be able to use your voice, speech, language, and body language skillfully in talking. You also must be able to hear, observe, encourage, and remember in listening. Additionally, you must be able to combine the talking and listening skills in the form of active listening. Active listening conveys empathy by overtly demonstrating that you are making a genuine effort to understand.

◆ **EXERCISE 4-5: SUMMARY**

The following exercises are intended to aid you in refining the talking, listening, and active listening skills.

1. With the consent of a friend or colleague, make a videotape (audiotape will suffice) recording of a 15-minute conversation. Indicate that you are trying to practice your interviewing skills and would like to conduct an interview about his or her choice of career. Inform your partner that she or he will not have to answer any questions about which there is discomfort. Also, be sure to tell your partner that your professor and perhaps some of your classmates may review the tape in order to provide feedback about the quality of your interviewing skills. During the interview, explore with your partner how she or he came to make the career choice. Explore influential and motivational factors. Ask about your partner's hopes and aspirations as well as issues and concerns regarding the chosen career.

    During the conversation, encourage your partner to share as much as possible about the career decision. Use the skills of talking, listening, and active listening. At the conclusion of the interview, ask your partner for feedback concerning the experience. Make note of his or her responses. Also, ask your partner to rate on a scale of 0 to 10 (where 0 = completely misunderstood and

10 = completely understood) how well you listened and understood what was said. Ask your partner to identify those factors that contributed to the rating. Thank your partner again and say goodbye. Record your partner's rating and make note of other comments.

Completely Misunderstood   Completely Understood

0   1   2   3   4   5   6   7   8   9   10

2. Consider your own reactions to the interview. How did you feel about the exchange? What did you like and what did you dislike about your part in the conversation? What would you do differently if you were to engage in the conversation again? Summarize your reactions in the space below.

3. Next, play the tape. In a notebook, prepare a transcript so that it accurately reflects what was said by whom. Identify the talking and listening skills you used during the conversation. For example, identify as talking a statement you made or a question you asked that came from your frame of reference. Identify as active listening your attempts to communicate your understanding of your partner's expressions. Use the following format:

	Transcript	Skill Used
Interviewer	Record here the words you said.	Identify the talking and listening skill used, if any.
Interviewee	Record here what your partner said.	

4. At the conclusion of the transcript, evaluate your use of the talking and active listening skills. How would you characterize this sample of your voice, speech, and language? When you listen to the sound of your voice, what do you think and feel? How clear is your pronunciation? Is your speech modulated? What is the rate of speech? How about the pitch? Evaluate your choice of words and your language usage, particularly as it relates to the individual and cultural characteristics of the person you interviewed.

In this conversation, do you speak more or less than your partner? Do you tend to interrupt or to be interrupted? What proportion of your words are factual, descriptive, or informational? What proportion suggest feelings or emotions? What percentage reveal your opinions or assumptions? Do you tend to use extraneous fillers such as *uhh* or *you know*? Are there vocal indications of nervousness or tension? If so, what are they? Do your voice, speech, and language reflect interest in what your partner says? Does your colleague seem interested in what you have to say? What sources of evidence do you use in order to determine his or her degree of interest? If you would change anything about your voice, speech, and language, what would it be?

How often do you engage in active listening? Do you do so too often or not often enough? How accurate are you in your attempts to communicate understanding through active listening? As you paraphrase, are your words equivalent to your partner's? Are there indications that your partner feels understood? Does your partner communicate fully and freely, or does she or he pause or hesitate at points during the interview? How does your partner's sex, age, class, ethnicity, and cultural affiliation influence the communication process? How does yours? In the space provided, summarize the major elements of your self-evaluation.

5. Consider your body position, body language, and facial expressions as shown on the videotape (or as you recall from memory). It may be particularly enlightening to view the videotape with the sound turned off. Evaluate the nonverbal dimensions of your communication during this interview. How well do you physically attend to your partner? What do you think your body position and body language communicate to your partner? What emotions do your facial expressions convey? What is the nature and extent of your eye contact? How comfortable and confident do you appear? How do factors such as your sex, age, class, ethnicity, and cultural affiliation affect your nonverbal style? Summarize your assessment in the space provided.

6. Observe your partner's nonverbal expressions as displayed on the videotape (or as you recall from memory). Make note of facial expressions, eye contact, body position and body language, gestures and movements, and the rate and nature of speech. Indicate what you think are your partner's overall mood, predominant feelings, and energy level. What is your impression of your partner's general attitude about you, this meeting, and the topic of conversation? Would you say your partner is involved and interested in the exchange? Active? Cooperative? Responsive? How do your partner's sex, age, class, ethnicity, and cultural affiliation affect your impressions? Summarize your observations and conclusions in the space below.

7. Ask a colleague or instructor from the school of social work to evaluate your talking, listening, and active listening skills as reflected on the tape recording you made. Summarize his or her feedback in the space provided. With which points do you agree or disagree?

8. Using the following rating scales (where 0 = no proficiency and 10 = complete proficiency), assess your current level of proficiency in the talking and listening skills.

The Talking Skills

Voice, Speech, and Language

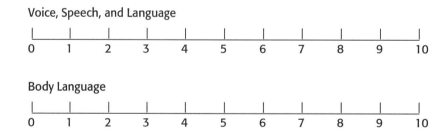

Body Language

The Listening Skills

Hearing

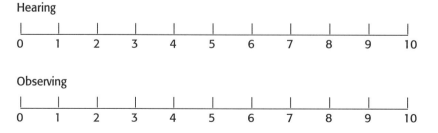

Observing

Encouraging

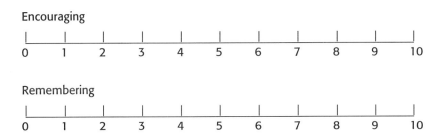

Remembering

Active Listening

9. Finally, review your ratings to identify those aspects of talking, listening, and active listening in which you remain less proficient (e.g., a score of 7 or less). Then, in the space below, outline specific steps you might take to improve your skill in those areas.

Chapter 5

Preparing

This chapter is intended to help you learn the skills relevant to the preparing phase of social work practice. First meetings set the tone and can influence the general direction of subsequent interactions. In fact, the nature of your initial contacts with prospective clients often determines whether they return and actually become clients. For example, in a study of nearly 14,000 persons served in 17 mental health centers, Sue (1977) discovered that approximately 50% of minority applicants did not return following an initial visit, a drop-out rate significantly greater than that for Caucasian clients. Although several factors are undoubtedly involved, insufficient and ineffective preparation for first meetings is certainly part of the problem. Effective preparation can make the difference in whether a client finds the first visit helpful or not (Kadushin, 1983, pp. 123–141).

You need to be personally and professionally ready to perform competently from the first moment of contact. You should use the preparing skills before the first meetings with clients and other persons with whom you interact as part of your professional responsibilities. Then continue to use them in advance of each subsequent encounter. The preparing skills include: (1) preparatory reviewing, (2) preparatory exploring, (3) preparatory consulting, (4) preparatory arranging, (5) preparatory empathy, (6) preparatory self-exploration, (7) centering, and (8) preliminary planning and recording.

Preparatory Reviewing

Preparatory reviewing is a skill in which you examine and consider information that is available to you and your agency prior to an initial contact with another person

(Kadushin, 1983, pp. 136–137). For example, if a prospective client has received service at the agency before, you would look over relevant records the agency has on file. When a telephone contact has preceded the first visit, examine any notes concerning the nature and substance of that interaction. In the case of first meetings with other persons, such as an agency director, a client's medical doctor, or a new supervisee, thoughtfully review relevant materials concerning the general purpose for the meeting and any topics likely to be addressed.

Preparatory reviewing helps you grasp significant factual information. This reduces the possibility that the applicant, client, or other persons will have to repeat information they have previously provided. It allows for more efficient use of time and helps people feel that what they say is heard and remembered. In some instances, failure to review available materials could constitute professional negligence. For example, suppose a teenage boy contacts the agency. He has a history of making serious suicide attempts following conflicts in romantic relationships. Your agency has served him off and on over the past several years, and the pattern of previous suicide attempts is clearly recorded in his case file. He requests an appointment for some time later that day, indicating that he needs help because his girlfriend recently "dumped" him, deciding that she wanted to date another boy. If you fail to review the case record, you may decide to give the teenager an appointment several days from now, not realizing that he is currently at serious risk of ending his own life.

There are also numerous practical reasons for engaging in a review of information before a first visit. You may learn, for example, that a prospective client does not speak English or any other language spoken in your agency, so an interpreter will be required. You might find out that a client uses a wheelchair or will be accompanied by a seeing-eye dog, so that a chair must be removed from your office to allow enough open space.

Of course, in addition to the benefits of reviewing materials, there are some potential disadvantages as well. For example, some records contain hearsay information or opinions that are expressed as if they were undisputed facts. You may inadvertently accept at face value invalid information contained in an agency record. In addition, some records contain personality profiles or psychiatric diagnoses that can lead you to form a stereotypical conception of a person before your first meeting. Such profiles and diagnoses may have been inaccurate when initially recorded, or they may since have become so. The person, the problem, or the situation may have changed, sometimes dramatically, since the first contact. In preparatory reviewing, you must recognize that information contained in case records or other forms of written material may be incomplete or mistaken. It is vital that you maintain an open mind during the preparatory reviewing phase.

◆ EXERCISE 5-1: PREPARATORY REVIEWING

CASE EXAMPLE: At 10:13 A.M. on Tuesday, an agency intake worker received a telephone call from a woman identifying herself as Mrs. Nancy Cannon. The intake worker jotted a few notes concerning the call on a form entitled Telephone Intake Report. The intake worker later gave the report to you, the social worker assigned to conduct the initial face-to-face interview and, if appropriate, provide needed professional services.

Telephone Intake Report

November 29, 1994, 10:13 A.M. Mrs. Nancy Cannon telephoned from her place of work (the Capital Insurance Company—phone 234-6213). She sounded concerned. She said that on the previous Saturday night, her 14-year-old daughter Amy had come home after her 9 P.M. curfew, smelling of alcohol. She says that she "grounded" her daughter but now wants to talk with a social worker about the situation. Mrs. Cannon requested an appointment for herself alone, indicating that she wanted to sort things out with someone before she dealt further with her daughter.

Mrs. C. reported that this was the first such incident. She said, "I've never had any trouble from Amy before." She stated that she had never sought professional help before and that this was her first contact with any social service or mental health agency. She indicated that her husband, Amy's father, had recently filed for divorce and had left the home approximately six weeks ago. Mrs. C. wondered whether that might be connected with Amy's misbehavior over the weekend.

Disposition: An appointment was scheduled with an agency social worker Wednesday, November 30 at 12:00 noon. Mrs. C. requested a lunch-hour appointment, if at all possible, in order to reduce the amount of time away from her job.

Demonstrate your use of the preparatory reviewing skill by examining the telephone intake report above. Using a pen or marker, highlight the information contained in the report which you, as the social worker, would want to remember for a first meeting with Mrs. Cannon.

Preparatory Exploring

The skill of *preparatory exploring* involves asking questions of receptionists, intake workers, or referring persons about the prospective client and the situation. This is an important but often neglected skill. Physicians, judges, teachers, ministers, and, of course, family members often contact social service agencies on behalf of someone else. They may possess important information concerning the client, the presenting problem and situation, and sometimes even the nature of the service needs. Take advantage of opportunities to learn about the person, problem, and situation (as long as such exploration does not infringe upon the rights and preferences of the person to privacy and confidentiality). Also realize that what you hear from others is communicated from their own perspective. The client may view things in quite a different way, and you may too.

Preparatory exploring is also applicable if a prospective client has previously been served by a colleague in your agency. For example, by reviewing agency files, you may learn that a prospective client had previously been served by Ms. Castillo, another social worker in the agency, some two years before. You should ask Ms. Castillo about her recollections of the case.

The use of the preparatory exploring skill can result in a more positive and productive first meeting. However, information gained through the preparatory exploring process must not lead you to stereotype people or formulate inaccurate hypotheses concerning the nature of a problem situation. You can resist such temptations by consciously distinguishing fact from opinion and recognizing that the views of one person are likely to differ from those of another.

In preparatory exploring, you seek information that may help you be a more effective service provider. Names and approximate ages of the persons involved are often noted; so are phone numbers, addresses, and other demographic data. Details concerning the nature, severity, and urgency of the problem are extremely important, as are indications of the strengths and resources available to the client.

◆ **EXERCISE 5-2: PREPARATORY EXPLORING**

CASE EXAMPLE: At 3:15 P.M. on Wednesday, you receive a telephone call from Father Julio Sanchez, a Catholic priest in a largely Mexican parish. He indicates that a family of seven needs help. He says that the parents and older children are migrant workers. He reports that the family had been traveling to a new work site when their automobile broke down.

In the space provided, write the questions you would ask and identify the information you would seek as you use the skill of preparatory exploring with Father Sanchez.

Preparatory Consulting

The skill of *preparatory consulting* involves seeking advice from a social work supervisor or colleagues concerning an upcoming first visit with a prospective client or other person. Commonly, you would seek such consultation in order to identify tentative objectives for an interview or to discuss other related practice considerations. The specific nature of the consultation, however, varies from situation to situation. On one occasion, you might discuss possible locations for the interview. In another, you might seek advice concerning how best to ensure your own safety when you are about to interview a person who has previously been physically violent toward people in positions of authority. In still another, you might focus on the agency policies or legal obligations that could apply in a particularly case. By engaging in preparatory consultation, you can enhance the quality of initial meetings. The usually modest investment of time it takes to consult with a colleague or supervisor can pay significant dividends in effectiveness.

◆ **EXERCISE 5-3: PREPARATORY CONSULTING**

CASE EXAMPLE: You work in an agency serving an elderly population in the community. On Tuesday morning, a woman telephoned the agency and talked with you about her neighbor, Mrs. Anderson. According to the caller, Mrs. Anderson is 82 years old and lives by herself in an apartment. The caller reported that Mrs. Anderson has not left her apartment in three days and would not answer her door or telephone. The neighbor did say, however, that she could hear movement in the apartment.

Immediately following the phone call, you examined agency files and discovered that Mrs. Anderson had not previously received agency services.

In the space provided below, please identify the information you would seek and the issues you would address as you consult with your supervisor before taking any action concerning Mrs. Anderson.

Preparatory Arranging

The skill of *preparatory arranging* is the logistical preparation for a first meeting. It includes scheduling an appointment, ensuring that there is adequate time and privacy, and organizing the physical environment. It may involve securing an interview room, locating an interpreter, or rearranging furniture. It includes considering the appropriateness of your apparel, appearance, and perhaps even hygiene. Some clients are offended by a social worker's noticeable body odors; other people are allergic to perfumes or colognes and react adversely to such scents. Preparatory arranging could involve any number of considerations: locating transportation for a client, or perhaps organizing temporary child care so that you can meet separately with a parent. When making visits outside your agency, consider the environment in terms of its significance for the client (Kadushin, 1983, pp. 141–148). Many people assign special meaning to their home and might feel ill at ease should you arrive before adequate preparations could be made. Food may also have significance to a client, or certain chairs in a home may be reserved for specific persons. Therefore, always pay close attention in order to convey respect for these special familial and cultural meanings.

In agency settings, preparatory arranging includes considering the potential effects of the physical environment. Do clients have a comfortable place to sit upon their arrival at the agency? Are interviewing rooms sufficiently soundproofed that privacy may be maintained? When you have office space assigned to you, arranging involves selecting and displaying pictures, posters, and other items such as college degrees and professional certificates. It may also include the selection of paints or wallpapers and the placement of furniture. The office environment can have a powerful impact on clients. For example, suppose you provide social services in an area where firearms are widely prized. You would be unwise to decorate your office wall with a poster that says "Ban handguns." You would needlessly alienate many clients. Personal or political messages may interfere with clients' ability to experience you as an objective professional who genuinely respects them.

In sum, preparatory arranging should facilitate communication and diminish, to the extent possible, interference and distraction.

◆ EXERCISE 5-4: PREPARATORY ARRANGING

CASE EXAMPLE: Assume that you are a social worker in a high-security men's prison. You have been assigned an office, which you share with another worker. The office contains two desks, chairs behind and next to each desk, two bookcases, two telephones, and two file cabinets. In addition, there is a small area containing a sofa, two comfortable chairs, and a coffee table. You have a 10:00 A.M. appointment scheduled with a prisoner, Mr. Somes. The topic for conversation is the serious illness of his wife of 23 years. According to a report you have just received from her physician, it appears that Mrs. Somes will die sometime within the next few days.

As the appointment time approaches, you notice that your social work colleague remains at his desk, actively engaged in paperwork. You had expected him to be out of the office, as he usually is during this time of day.

In the following space, discuss how you would use the skill of arranging in preparation for the meeting with Mr. Somes.

Preparatory Empathy

Preparatory empathy involves "putting oneself in the client's shoes and trying to view the world through the client's eyes" (Shulman, 1984, p. 22). You try to "get in touch with the feelings and concerns that the client may bring to the helping encounter" (Shulman, 1992, p. 56). Even before the initial face-to-face meeting, you should engage in preparatory empathy in order to heighten your sensitivity to the prospective client's possible agenda, thoughts, feelings about him- or herself, the presenting concern, and the situation. You tune in to possible dynamics related to seeking or receiving social service, to the nature of the client's motivation for the contact, to the client's thoughts and feelings about engaging an unknown authority figure, and to potential issues related to the client's sex, stage of life, culture, ethnic background, and socioeconomic status.

Preparatory empathy in regard to cultural aspects is especially important. Members of some cultural groups are often conflicted about visiting a social worker. Certain people may prefer a slow and informal beginning. Others might find it difficult to share personal information about their families. Some may be concerned that their culturally traditional sex and family roles might be challenged. For many people, visiting an agency is not a simple request for service. The meaning of this event can be extraordinarily complicated for members of many cultural groups. Therefore, as part of preparatory empathy for each new client, be sensitive to the potential cultural implications of the upcoming interview.

Preparatory empathy involves trying to experience, on the basis of whatever limited information is available to you, what the client may be thinking and feeling as this initial interview begins. Because preparatory empathy is done in advance of face-to-face contact, realize that much of the time you will be off target. Preparatory empathy is therefore always tentative, always preliminary, and always subject to immediate change based on the client's actual communications. Even when your preparatory empathy proves to be inaccurate, however, it is a productive activity, because it helps you be sensitive to actual expressions of the client when you finally do meet in person.

Returning to the new client Mrs. Nancy Cannon, a social worker engaging in preparatory empathy might review the telephone intake report and then go through a mental process like the following.

If I were in Mrs. Cannon's shoes, I might feel anxious for, concerned about, and disappointed in my daughter. I would also love her a great deal. I might feel responsible and perhaps even guilty about my parenting behavior. I might feel uncertain about how to proceed. I could very well feel inadequate and maybe frightened. I would be concerned about what the future might hold for Amy and for me. I am aware that my husband's divorce petition and his recent departure from the home may have adversely affected my daughter, and I might feel angry at him—both on my own behalf as well as my daughter's. If I believed I could have been a better spouse or taken actions to prevent his departure, I might also feel guilty about the separation and upcoming divorce proceedings. I might perceive the divorce as the result of some misbehavior of my own. Alternately, I may have initiated the divorce process and experience conflicted feelings about the decision to do so.

However the separation and divorce process began, I would feel a great deal of stress during this period. I would probably feel confused about the present and fearful about the future. I might be concerned about finances; about after-school supervision of Amy; about my ability to guide and discipline Amy; about whether there is another person in my husband's life; about whether there is now or ever will be someone else in my life; about my capacity to assume the roles of a single person and a single parent; about my ability to deal with my husband around parental issues concerning Amy; and about dozens of other issues provoked by my husband's departure and Amy's recent behavior. I would probably feel enormously burdened and perhaps over- whelmed by the events of recent weeks. If sadness and grieving have not yet occurred, I might begin to experience them soon. It is also possible that I may have begun to anticipate that not only has my husband left the household, but eventually Amy will also leave. After all, she is already 14.

Mrs. Cannon seems to be of a different ethnic background than my own and I am at least 10 years younger. I have never been married and do not have children of my own (Mrs. Cannon may ask about my marital and parental status.) As a result of these cultural and status differences, she may experience me as less likely to understand and appreciate her situation. She may even see me as less able to help her, since I have not gone through some of these same difficulties.

Engaging in the skill of preparatory empathy sensitizes you to some of what another person may experience as the first meeting gets underway. By empathizing in advance, you increase the likelihood that you will approach the prospective client as a unique human being with all of the complexity that entails. A major challenge in this form of anticipatory empathy, however, is resisting the temptation to narrow your view of the person so that it becomes more of a fixed stereotype than an open set of possibilities.

CASE EXAMPLE: Assume that you are a social worker in a general hospital. This morning, a physician contacts you and asks that you accompany her while she informs the mother and father of a 23-year-old man that their son has AIDS. The physician wants you to provide support and social services to the family after she informs them of the diagnosis and prognosis.

Engage in the skill of preparatory empathy as if you were about to meet the parents of the AIDS patient in this situation. Record your thoughts and feelings in the space provided below.

Preparatory Self-Exploration

In addition to engaging in preparatory empathy, you should also engage briefly in *preparatory self-exploration* before meeting with clients or prospective clients. Preparatory self-exploration is a form of self-analysis in which you, a human being who happens to be a social worker, identify how you might be affected by your interaction with this particular person, these specific problem areas, and this unique situation. In self-exploring, you would ask yourself questions such as "How am I likely to feel about this individual or family? How are the cultural and demographic similarities or differences between us likely to affect me? Given what I know about the problem and situation, what personal reactions might I expect to experience?"

The purpose of this skill is to identify the potential impact on the client of your own personal history, characteristics, needs, biases, emotional tender spots, and behavioral patterns. Self-exploration helps you to bring into conscious focus those aspects of your personal self that might affect the nature and quality of your social work services to a particular client.

Preparatory self-exploration also involves identifying other personal factors that may affect your readiness to provide service. For example, there may be extraneous factors, unrelated to the particular client, that might influence you personally. If you have a splitting headache, are dealing with the breakup of a significant relationship, are in the process of repairing your furnace, have just lost out on an opportunity for promotion, did not sleep last night, or are worried about a family member of your own, the quality of your service might be affected. Identifying these factors and their effect on you constitutes the first step toward managing them so that they do not interfere with the professional quality service that all clients deserve.

◆ **EXERCISE 5-6: PREPARATORY SELF-EXPLORATION**

CASE SITUATION: Assume that you are a social worker in an agency that provides psychosocial counseling services to children who have been sexually abused. You have recently begun to work with Cathy, a 7-year-old who had been molested for a period of four years by her biological father. Approximately one month ago, Cathy's father forced her to perform fellatio. That incident led to his arrest and departure from the family home while awaiting further legal developments. You are about to interview Cathy's father for the first time. The general purpose for the interview is to gather information upon which to base a tentative assessment of his potential to benefit from a counseling program.

In the space provided below, please write what you discover about yourself as you engage in self-exploration before meeting Cathy's father.

Centering

When, through preparatory self-exploration, you have identified personal factors that might affect your ability to provide high-quality service to a prospective client, you must attempt to manage or contain them. As part of this centering process, you ask yourself, "What can I do to ready myself personally before the meeting begins?" *Centering* involves organizing your personal thoughts, feelings, and physical sensations so that they do not interfere with the performance of your professional obligations and delivery of social services. Depending upon the personal factors involved, centering might include various kinds of activities. Among the more common are brief stress-management exercises, intended to reduce emotional reactivity and gain executive control. Among the useful stress-reducing activities are positive self-talk, visualization, muscular relaxation, journal writing, and brief meditation.

For example, suppose that years ago when you were a teenager, you had been a victim of date rape. At that time you had simply put the issue away and have not addressed it since. Recently, you became aware that you do indeed have rather strong feelings about that sexual victimization and have decided to seek out a social worker in order to address the issue. As you look at the intake form of the new client you are scheduled to meet later today, you realize that the presenting concern is that she was raped two weeks ago by a man she had dated once before.

Through preparatory self-exploration, you might recognize that you remain unresolved about your own rape experience, even though it happened years before. You also realize that you would probably not serve this client well if you remain caught up in the emotions of your own experience. Therefore, you might center yourself by taking a few deep breaths, engaging in a brief relaxation exercise, and compartmentalizing (temporarily putting into an enclosed area of yourself) your personal experience in order to provide full attention to the client. As part of the process, you say to yourself, "I'm still tender about being raped but I'm able to manage my feelings of rage and guilt and fear so that they don't get in the way of my service to this client. Since it is obvious, however, that I still have some unresolved issues, I hereby commit myself to arrange for an appointment for myself with that social worker I've heard about. I promise that I will telephone her agency office at 11 o'clock when I have a free hour."

In centering, please do not deny or minimize your personal issues and strong feelings. Rather, manage them temporarily and develop a specific plan to address them at another time in a more appropriate context.

◆ EXERCISE 5-7: CENTERING

CASE SITUATION: Assume that you are scheduled to meet with a client in approximately ten minutes. While finishing a brief coffee break with a colleague, you learn that everyone else in the agency received a pay raise of 7%. In spite of the fact that you have earned outstanding evaluations and were recently promoted, you know that you received only a 3% raise.

In the space provided below, please describe the activities you would undertake in order to center yourself before meeting with the client.

Preliminary Planning and Recording

As a social worker, you should engage in the skill of *preliminary planning* before meetings, contacts, and interviews with clients and other people with whom you interact as part of your professional duties. Begin the process of formulating a preliminary plan by asking and answering questions such as "Why is this meeting occurring? What is its overall purpose? What do I hope to accomplish through this meeting? What is my tentative agenda? What might be the other person's agenda? What would I consider to be desired outcomes? What are my functions or roles in this meeting? How do I wish to begin? What things do I definitely want to say? What questions do I definitely want to ask? What kind of interactional process would I like to see? How would I like the meeting to conclude?"

Alfred Kadushin (1983, p. 21) states that the "general purposes of most social work interviews can be described as informational (to make a social study), diagnostic (to arrive at an appraisal), and therapeutic (to effect change). These are discrete categories only for the purpose of analysis; the same interview can, and often does, serve more than one purpose."

In *information-gathering interviews*, you encourage people to discuss their views and feelings about themselves, their preferences and strengths, problems and goals, and the situation. Basically, you gather data that may help you and your client reach a better understanding of the circumstances. In *information-giving interviews*, you share needed or useful knowledge. You might offer information about a program, policy, or resource in your attempt to respond to a request or address a perceived need. In *assessment-forming interviews*, your overall purpose is to arrive at an assessment, diagnosis, evaluation, or conclusion. Often, such an interview is followed by the preparation of a recommendation. In *change-making interviews*, you effect or help to effect movement or change somewhere within a targeted system. Change might occur within an individual person (e.g., thoughts, feelings, or actions), within a group of people (e.g., a family, organization, or community), or in the interactional processes that occur between persons and other social systems (e.g., communication practices or feedback mechanisms).

Most of the time, you should be able to identify, at least tentatively, a general purpose for a given interview. Sometimes, of course, a meeting serves more than one purpose. Once the purpose or purposes are identified, you may sketch out a preliminary plan for the meeting.

Many first meetings have as their primary purpose the gathering of information. In such cases, you might formulate a general but flexible plan concerning what data to seek and from whom. For example, in planning for a first meeting with a family, you may have to decide whether to see all family members together or to see some of them separately. If you plan to see members individually or in the form of smaller subsystems (e.g., mother-daughter dyad or parental dyad), you must determine whom to interview first, second, and so forth.

Take the case of a client who has telephoned expressing an interest in resolving a family problem. Your tentative plan might be as follows:

1. engage in introductions
2. identify a general purpose and direction for the meeting
3. establish the ground rules for the process
4. address any questions or uncertainties concerning the agency, you as the social worker, the purpose, the process, or the ground rules
5. determine the identities and characteristics of the family or household members
6. explore the presenting problem that stimulated the phone contact
7. explore the history and development as well as the consequences of that problem
8. examine how the family has attempted to address this and other problems, and determine the effects of those efforts
9. explore strengths within the family systems and identify available resources that might contribute to problem resolution
10. conclude the interview with some sense of what will happen next in the process.

Preliminary planning enables you to begin the interview in a coherent fashion and helps you formulate a tentative purpose to share with the client. The process leaves the impression of flexible structure, which can help you come across as organized and competent in your first meetings with other people.

The written recording that results from preparation in advance of meetings may take several forms and include various components. Many agencies use a telephone *intake form* to make relevant notations: the caller, the reason for the call, the substance of the conversation, and any plans that have been made. A more extensive *face sheet* allows for recording identifying characteristics of a person-problem-situation (e.g., name, sex, age, reason for contact, preliminary description of concern or problem, occupation, family role, address, and phone numbers). The face sheet may be used instead of or in addition to the intake form. Notes that are the result of telephone conversations must be considered tentative in nature. Nonetheless, they provide valuable information to the social worker who subsequently engages a person or family in a face-to-face meeting. Many workers also develop, often in outline form, a summary of their preliminary plan for the meeting.

For example, Ruth Hernandez, the social worker assigned to interview Mrs. Cannon (see Exercise 5.1) might write the following notes in advance of her first meeting. Notice how useful these brief notes could be in helping her to be prepared from the very first moment of contact.

Preliminary Notes
December 2, 1994

Mrs. Nancy Cannon—seems to prefer "Mrs."—presenting concern: 14-year-old daughter Amy alleged to have drunk alcohol and come home after her 9:00 P.M. curfew. First such incident; may be related to separation and filing for divorce by Mrs. C.'s husband (Amy's father). He left the home about six weeks ago—uncertain who initiated the separation and divorce process. Mrs. C. wants a noontime appointment to avoid time away from work. Could there be financial constraints or concerns about keeping her job?

Preliminary Plan

1. Introduce myself, my profession, and affiliation with the agency; use "Mrs. Cannon" as initial reference to her and ask how she would prefer to be addressed.
2. General purpose for the meeting appears to be information gathering. Collect relevant information related to Mrs. C., her daughter, estranged husband, the problem areas, and the situation.
3. Make sure that Mrs. C. understands limits of confidentiality including duty to report indications of child abuse or neglect, and the slight future possibility of a subpoena regarding child custody issues. Indicate the mutual nature of this working relationship and invite her to participate actively.
4. Explore the apparent presenting problem (Amy's drinking), as well as the related concern of the separation and divorce. Explore history, development, and current status of drinking and marital conflict.
5. Clarify Mrs. C. and Amy's current household situation; inquire about Mr. C's circumstances as well. Identify significant others who are involved with the three family members.
6. Explore strengths of Mrs. C., Amy, and perhaps Mr. C. Identify available resources that might relate to problem resolution.
7. Explore in detail how Mrs. C., Amy, and Mr. C. have attempted to deal with the separation and divorce processes, and with the issue of drinking or other "misbehavior" by Amy. Identify approaches have been helpful and those that have been ineffective.
8. Conclude the interview with a specific next step. Consider the possibility of a second appointment, perhaps with Amy and Mrs. C. together, Amy alone, Mr. C. separately, or possibly Mr. and Mrs. C. together.

Rose Hernandez, B.S.W.
Certified Social Worker

◆ EXERCISE 5-8: PRELIMINARY PLANNING AND RECORDING

CASE SITUATION: Assume that you are a social worker who works in conjunction with a court that handles child custody disputes. You have been assigned the responsibility of collecting information and formulating a recommendation as to the placement of a 12 year old boy whose parents are divorcing. Each parent wants custody of the child.

1. Develop and record in the space below a preliminary plan for the meeting or meetings you would have with the various parties involved in this situation.

CASE SITUATION: Assume that you are a social worker in a Vietnam veterans' center. You receive a telephone message from Ms. Francine Rivera concerning her brother Hector. Ms. Rivera indicates that Hector is 47 years old and completed two tours of combat duty in Vietnam. She reports that he has had trouble keeping jobs, drinks alcohol (beer) every day, has nightmares at night, and occasionally has violent outbursts. She has become especially concerned lately because he has talked about ending "his own miserable life." She says that he won't go to an agency but he might be willing to talk with someone if a counselor came to the house. You agree to go for a first visit at 5:30 P.M. on the next afternoon.

2. In the following space, develop and record a preliminary plan for the meeting or meetings you would have with the various parties involved in this situation.

Summary

The preparing skills enable you to provide professional social work services effectively from the earliest person-to-person contact. The preparing skills are used extensively prior to initial interviews and are also commonly used in advance of later meetings.

The preparing skills include (1) preparatory reviewing, (2) preparatory exploring, (3) preparatory consulting, (4) preparatory arranging, (5) preparatory empathy, (6) preparatory self-exploration, (7) centering, and (8) preliminary planning and recording.

◆ **EXERCISE 5-9: SUMMARY**

Assume that you are a social worker with an agency that offers a broad range of social services. Using the skills requested, prepare for a first meeting with each of the following clients.

CASE SITUATION: A family of seven (two parents and five children, ranging in age from 1 to 7) have been sleeping in their dilapidated Chevy in a rest area on the highway. En route to another city where they hope to find work, they have run out of money and food and nearly out of gas. A highway patrolman has referred them to your agency.

1. Engage in the process of preparatory empathy as you ready yourself to meet with this family. Describe the results below.

2. Through preparatory self-exploration, identify those personal factors that might affect you as you provide social services to the family. Then describe how you might center yourself in order to diminish any potentially adverse responses.

3. In the space below, record a preliminary plan that reflects the results of your preparation activities before meeting with the family.

CASE SITUATION: A 33-year-old man is accused of molesting his girlfriend's 13-year-old-daughter. He is required to undergo counseling in order to stay out of jail while the judge considers whether to proceed with felony charges. The man was living with his girlfriend but has now been required to leave the house.

4.   Engage in the process of preparatory empathy as you ready yourself to meet with this prospective client. Describe the results below.

5.   Through preparatory self-exploration, identify those personal factors that might get in the way of your helping the man. Then describe how you could center yourself in order to manage your reactions.

6. In the space below, prepare a preliminary plan that reflects the results of your preparation in advance of meeting this man.

CASE SITUATION: You are a social worker with Child Protection Services (CPS), the agency that investigates allegations of child abuse or neglect. You receive a telephone report from a neighbor of the Smith family that the parents have neglected and abused their two children (ages 1 and 3). According to the neighbor, the mother sleeps while the children play in a filthy yard (which contains animal waste, junk, and potentially dangerous materials— glass and sharp metal objects). Also, the neighbor reports that the man in the house drinks heavily and beats both mother and children. Following the telephone call, you prepare to make a home visit to the family in question.

7. Engage in the process of preparatory empathy as you ready yourself to meet with this prospective client system. Describe the results.

8. Through preparatory self-exploration, identify those personal factors that might affect the quality of your professional services. Then describe how you might center yourself in order to diminish any potentially adverse responses.

9. In the following space, prepare a preliminary plan for the meeting.

CASE SITUATION: You serve as a medical social worker on the cancer ward of a children's hospital. You receive a request from a physician that you join her as she informs the parents of an 8-year-old girl that their daughter has terminal leukemia.

10. Engage in the process of preparatory empathy as you ready yourself for this meeting with the physician and the parents. Describe the results below.

11. Through preparatory self-exploration, identify those personal factors that might inhibit your effectiveness in this situation. Then describe how you might center yourself in order to diminish these potentially adverse responses.

12. In the following space, prepare a preliminary plan for the meeting.

13. Using the following rating scales (where 0 = no proficiency and 10 = complete proficiency), assess your current level of proficiency in the preparing skills.

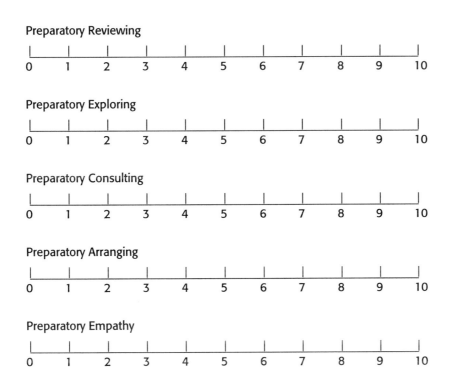

Preparatory Reviewing

0	1	2	3	4	5	6	7	8	9	10

Preparatory Exploring

0	1	2	3	4	5	6	7	8	9	10

Preparatory Consulting

0	1	2	3	4	5	6	7	8	9	10

Preparatory Arranging

0	1	2	3	4	5	6	7	8	9	10

Preparatory Empathy

0	1	2	3	4	5	6	7	8	9	10

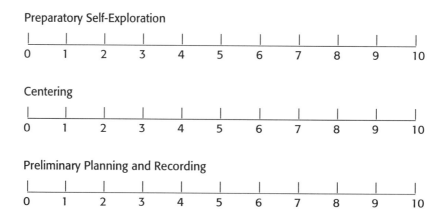

Preparatory Self-Exploration

| | | | | | | | | | | |
0   1   2   3   4   5   6   7   8   9   10

Centering

| | | | | | | | | | | |
0   1   2   3   4   5   6   7   8   9   10

Preliminary Planning and Recording

| | | | | | | | | | | |
0   1   2   3   4   5   6   7   8   9   10

14. Finally, review your ratings to identify those preparing skills in which you remain less proficient (e.g., a score of 7 or less). Then, in the space below, outline the steps you might take to improve your skill in those areas.

Chapter 6

Beginning

The beginning phase of social work practice starts when you and the prospective client or applicant first come together. Because first impressions are so important, the initial face-to-face contact often affects all future encounters. The beginning portion of each subsequent interview tends to influence the course of those sessions as well.

Competent use of the beginning skills helps to ensure that meetings are positive and productive. An effective beginning results when you and the prospective client accomplish the purpose for which you first meet (information gathering, information giving, assessment forming, or change making) and reach some mutual conclusion concerning a next step in the process (conclude your relationship, continue to work together, or make arrangements for service from another professional or agency).

Typically, you make contact with prospective clients in one of two ways (Compton & Galaway, 1994, p. 346): "(1) The individual, family, or group may reach out for help with a problem they have identified as being beyond their means of solution; or (2) a community source may identify an individual, a family, or a group as having a serious problem threatening the welfare of themselves or others (a vulnerable person or group) and request that the social worker intervene to solve that problem."

In general, during the beginning of a first meeting, you hope to facilitate an exchange of introductions, establish a tentative direction or purpose for the meeting, outline the general expectations of clients, describe the policies and ethical principles that might apply during this and future encounters, and ensure that the prospective client understands the parameters within which the interview takes place. This is a crucial part of the beginning process, because it fulfills part of your legal and ethical obligations with respect to informed consent. Generally, at this point in the process, you give the prospective client an overview of relevant agency policies, as well as information about pertinent laws and ethical principles. The prospective client can thus understand the context within which helping endeavors take place. Throughout the beginning phase, you should frequently seek feedback concerning information discussed. Often, prospective clients need further clarification about complex or confusing policies and principles.

The beginning skills are commonly used quite extensively during the first few meetings with clients. They are also extremely useful during initial meetings with other people. It is important to be clear about purposes and roles when meeting with referral sources, colleagues from your own or other agencies, government officials, parents, and others with whom you interact as part of your professional responsibilities. Some of the beginning skills are also used during the early portions of later encounters. The beginning skills include (1) introducing yourself, (2) seeking introductions, (3) describing initial purpose, (4) outlining the client's role, (5) discussing policy and ethical factors, and (6) seeking feedback.

Introducing Yourself

At the beginning of any first interview, you should identify yourself by name and profession and by agency or departmental affiliation. For example, at the beginning of a meeting in the agency where he works, a social worker might say, "Hello Mr. and Mrs. Adabu [offers hand to shake]. I'm Dan Majors. I'm a social worker here at the family service agency. I specialize in helping people who are dealing with family difficulties of one kind or another."

At the start of a visit to the home of a prospective client, another social worker might say, "Hello Ms. White [offers hand to shake]. I'm Joanna Samples. I'm a social worker with the local school system. I specialize in service to families of the students in our school district. Please call me Joanna."

In most circumstances, a friendly facial expression and a warm, firm handshake are helpful in making contact. A few informal comments about such things as the weather may also help some prospective clients feel more at ease with you, but do not overdo it. Spending too much time with chitchat may be frustrating to clients who are grappling with serious concerns and urgently wish to talk about them. Your introduction and informal remarks should always be considered in light of the context. Be especially sensitive to cultural factors. Prospective clients fully realize that you do not yet truly know them as individual people. Therefore, too much informality or effusiveness with some clients may be premature and, in some cultures, quite rude. Sometimes, clients experience exaggerated informality and effusive introductions as disingenuous and affected.

In addition to identifying yourself by name, profession and agency affiliation, you might also want to provide formal identification. For example, as part of her introduction to families, Joanna Samples routinely gives out her business card:

Joanna Samples, B.S.W., M.S.W.

School Social Worker
Center Township School District
902 West New York Street
Indianapolis, IN 46260-5156
Telephone 317-274-6708

In office settings, putting your university degrees and professional certificates on a wall may help in the introductory process. Clients may notice that you have earned a Bachelor of Social Work (BSW) or a Master's of Social Work (MSW) degree and are certified or licensed to practice social work in your state or province. Some social workers also provide a one-page summary of their professional background, training, and expertise.

◆ EXERCISE 6-1: INTRODUCING YOURSELF

The following exercises give you an opportunity to practice the skill of introducing yourself. In the spaces provided, write the words you would say and describe the actions you would take in introducing yourself in the following circumstances.

1. Assume that you are a social worker in a residential nursing facility for elderly persons. You are scheduled to meet with family members concerning the possibility of placing their 85-year-old parent there. What would you say and do in introducing yourself?

2. Assume that you have recently been hired as a social worker in a training center for developmentally disabled children and young adults. Today you are about to lead a group of six or eight teenage residents. The students are already

seated in the room when you arrive. Although a few of them may have seen you walking around campus, none of them actually knows you and you do not know any of them. What would you say and do in introducing yourself?

Seeking Introductions

A person's sense of self is often integrally associated with his or her name. Therefore, early in a first meeting, you should encourage each new client to say her or his name, and then try to pronounce it correctly. Thereafter, periodically throughout the interview, refer to your client by name. For example, after introducing yourself, you might say, "And your name is . . . ?" Or if you already know the person's name, "And you're Mr. Nesbit? Is that right? Am I pronouncing your name correctly?" Then ask how the person prefers to be addressed (Miss, Ms., Mrs., Mr., Reverend, first name, or nickname). Frequently, clients may share additional forms of identification during the exchange of introductions. Suppose a new client introduces herself by saying, "I'm Mrs. Jones. I'm the mother of this mob of children." From her words, you might infer that she prefers to be addressed as "Mrs. Jones" and that a significant part of her personal and social identity is related to her role as parent.

In family and group contexts, you may find it useful to ask members to go around and introduce themselves. Because initial group meetings often provoke anxiety, you could incorporate a stress-reducing, ice-breaking dimension to the introduction process. For example, you might ask group members to introduce themselves and share a few of the thoughts that occurred to them as they anticipated coming to this first meeting.

◆ EXERCISE 6-2: SEEKING INTRODUCTIONS

For these exercises, assume that you are a social worker at a counseling center for families and children. Respond in the spaces provided by writing the words you would say in each situation.

1. You are about to begin an interview with a recently divorced 55-year-old man. As you walk together to your office, you smell a strong odor of alcohol. How would you introduce yourself and seek an introduction from him? What else, if anything, would you say or do? Discuss your rationale for the words you choose and approach you propose.

2. You are about to begin an interview with a 77-year-old widow who has a hearing impairment. She can make out most words if they are spoken clearly, distinctly, and at a low pitch. How would you introduce yourself and seek an introduction from her? What else, if anything, would you say or do? Discuss your rationale for the words you choose and the action you propose.

3. You are about to begin a first interview with a family of seven members. You know that it is a blended family and that not all of the children have the same last name. You do not, however, know which children are from which relationships. How would you introduce yourself and seek introductions from the family members? What else would you say or do? Discuss your rationale for the words you choose and the action you propose.

4. You are about to begin an interview with a prospective client. As you introduce yourself and seek an introduction from her, you realize that she speaks neither English nor Spanish but another language, which you do not understand. What would you do? Discuss your rationale for the approach you have taken.

Describing Initial Purpose

As part of the process of preparing for all meetings (see the section on preliminary planning in Chapter Five), you identify a tentative general purpose (W. Schwartz, 1976, pp. 188–190; Shulman, 1992, pp. 79–101). Especially in initial meetings, new clients tend to look to you, as the professional person in an authority role, for a beginning direction. Therefore, you should clearly and succinctly describe a tentative purpose for the meeting. If you do not know or do not share some such beginning direction, your clients are likely to feel even more uncertain, anxious, and ambivalent about a process that is already stress provoking. If, on the other hand, you share a tentative general purpose, clients usually feel somewhat less anxious. This moderately structured way of beginning also tends to indicate that you do, in fact, know what you are doing.

In some instances, not only is a general purpose for the meeting clear, but so is the professional social work role that you will assume in relation to that purpose. When such a strong degree of clarity exists, you may also appropriately use the skill of *describing your role* (W. Schwartz, 1976, pp. 188–190; Shulman, 1984, pp. 37–49; Shulman, 1992, pp. 79–101). This skill involves expressing to the prospective client your view of the role or roles that you expect to assume as you work toward the general purpose for coming together.

Among the more common social work roles are *advocate, broker, case manager, counselor, educator, evaluator, facilitator, investigator, mediator, therapist,* and *trainer*. With persons who visit you on an involuntary or nonvoluntary basis, both the purpose and your role warrant more complete and lengthy description. This is also the case in situations where clients seek a specific service offered through your agency. For example, your agency may sponsor an educationally oriented six-week group experience for teenagers who are considering marriage. Because it is a structured group that follows a predictable agenda, your social work roles are clear: educator and group facilitator. Therefore, you may appropriately describe to prospective group members both an initial purpose and the professional roles that you expect to fulfill during the group experience.

Frequently, however, the exact nature of your professional role is unclear at the time of the first meeting. This often occurs with voluntary clients who seek service from organizations that have several programs and serve a variety of functions. When this happens, rather than speculating about possible roles, the tentative description of general purpose should suffice.

In the following examples, a social worker tentatively describes an initial purpose for a first meeting.

CASE SITUATION: The client is a woman (age 30) who called the agency a few days previously asking for help with a troubled marriage. The worker and client have already exchanged introductions. The worker begins to describe a tentative general purpose for this initial meeting.

WORKER: When you telephoned the agency the other day, you said that your marriage is on the brink of collapse and that you and your husband argue all the time. Is that correct? Yes? During our meeting today, I'd like to explore in detail with you the nature of your marriage, its history, and how it developed to this point. As we both gain a better understanding of the circumstances, we can decide together what to do next.

CASE SITUATION: The divorcing parents of a 9-year-old boy are involved in a child custody proceeding. The social worker has been employed by the juvenile court to make recommendations to the judge about the placement of the child. The worker has just exchanged introductions with the father and describes a purpose and role as follows.

WORKER: Judge Bloom has asked me to meet with you, your former wife, and your son for the purpose of making a recommendation to the judge about the custody arrangements for Kevin. I'll be meeting with Mrs. Brown [former spouse] this afternoon and with Kevin [son] tomorrow morning. After these three meetings I should have a fairly good understanding of the situation. At that time, should further meetings be needed, I'll let you know.

I certainly recognize that this is a difficult time for you and for everybody involved. You may feel a bit like you're on trial here. It may seem that way. I'll try my best to make it as reasonable a process as possible. You should know, however, that your son Kevin will be fully considered in these processes. My efforts will be geared toward determining what is best for him, for his growth and well-being. I'm sure that you are also concerned about the consequences of the divorce and the upcoming court proceedings on Kevin and want what's best for him too. I hope that we can approach this interview with that in mind and can work together toward finding the best resolution for this difficult situation.

CASE SITUATION: This is the first meeting of an educational group for persons arrested for driving under the influence (DUI). The participants range in age from 16 to 62 and cross gender, ethnic, and socioeconomic class lines. The group experience involves 12 weekly meetings of approximately two hours each. Members participate in order to decrease the chance of a jail sentence. The worker and group members have exchanged introductions and engaged in some small talk. The worker now proceeds to describe an initial purpose and role.

WORKER: I have been asked by the county prosecutor to lead this educational group for the next eight weeks. It's my understanding that each of you is here because you were arrested for driving under the influence of alcohol and that you have chosen to participate in the group in order to reduce the chances of a term in the county jail. I imagine that you all have other places that you would rather be at this time. Some of you are probably pretty annoyed at having to be here. If I were in your shoes, I'd be feeling quite a bit of resentment and perhaps a bit of embarrassment too. It's my hope that, in spite of these feelings, the series of group meetings will increase your knowledge about drinking and driving and will be of use to you in the future.

CASE SITUATION: The interview setting is the front doorstep of the Frankel residence. It is a large home in an upper-middle-class neighborhood. The social worker knocked on the door and it was opened by a woman who appears to live there. Employed by the Child Protection Service (CPS) Division of the Department of Human Services, the worker is visiting the home unannounced because the agency received a complaint that Mrs. Frankel had severely beaten her 4-year-old son. Upon arriving at the home the worker exchanged introductions, learned that the woman is indeed Mrs. Frankel, and gave her a business card along with a brochure about CPS.

WORKER: Child Protection Services is responsible for investigating all allegations of abuse or neglect of minor children in this county. We have received a complaint concerning the treatment of your 4-year-old son. I'd like to discuss this situation with you and meet your son. May I come in?

◆ EXERCISE 6-3: DESCRIBING INITIAL PURPOSE

Use the following case situations to practice the skill of describing a tentative initial purpose for the meeting and, where you think appropriate, describing your social work role. Please respond to each situation in the spaces provided.

1. Assume that you are a social worker with a public housing agency. You are currently in the process of interviewing all residents of a building in an effort to determine their social service needs. You have just knocked on the door of Mrs. Strong's residence. Mrs. Strong is a single mother with five children who range in age from 9 years to 6 months. Write the words you would say to her as you describe an initial purpose for the meeting. If you think your social work role would be clear in this situation, describe that as well.

2. You are a social worker in the emergency room of a general hospital. Paramedics have just brought in an automobile accident victim. Doctors and nurses are providing lifesaving measures. Family members of the patient arrive. It is your function to provide them with a place to wait and to inform them in general terms about what is happening to the patient. You go up to the family, introduce yourself, and guide them to a more private waiting area. Write the words you would say in describing an initial purpose for the meeting. In this case your role is also likely to be fairly clear. Describe your role as well.

3. You are a social worker in a nursing residence for elderly persons. A new resident arrived over the weekend, and you go to her room for a first visit. You intend to introduce yourself and get acquainted. You realize that you will need

to undertake a complete social history and assessment before the week is out. You want to set the stage for that more lengthy interview. Write the words you would say in describing an initial purpose for that upcoming meeting.

4. Along with other professional duties, you lead counseling groups for children who have been sexually abused. You are about to begin a new group, composed of five girls who range in age from 7 to 10. You have met individually with each of the five before and talked with them at length. However, this is the first time they have been in a group, and they have not met each other before. You ask each girl to share her first name with the others. They all do so, although several introduce themselves in soft and tentative voices. You want to begin the group in a warm, safe, and secure manner. Write the words you would say in describing an initial purpose for the meeting. Following that, describe the professional role or roles that might accompany such a purpose.

Outlining the Client's Role

During the beginning phases of a professional helping relationship, clients often experience considerable uncertainty and anxiety about what is expected of them. Prospective clients are certainly concerned about the problems that have led to the contact, but many are also worried that they may not be able to do what is needed to improve the situation or resolve the difficulties. In particular, prospective clients are often uncertain about how they may best help you, the social worker, help them. Ambiguity about what they are "supposed to do" is probably associated with the relatively high discontinuation or dropout rates of clients generally, and particularly members of minority groups (Sue, 1977). You may help to clarify the situation by outlining how the client may cooperate in the helping process (Garvin, 1987, pp. 72–74). For example, in the first meeting of a group for adolescents having school problems, you might outline the role of group member in a manner such as the following:

Outlining the Group Member's Role

We all have problems at some point in our lives. It's part of being human. We've found that talking about such problems with other people who are in similar situations tends to help resolve those problems. This group is intended to provide you with opportunities to share with others your problems and concerns as well as your hopes and dreams. Although you are, of course, not required to say anything that you wish to keep to yourself, we do hope that members will express themselves to one another, listen carefully to what others say, and offer suggestions about how things could be better. All group members are also expected to follow the rule of confidentiality. That means that whatever is said within the group setting stays here. Nothing discussed here should be repeated outside this room.

You might attempt to outline the individual client's role as follows.

Outlining the Individual Client's Role

You can best help in this process by sharing your thoughts and feelings as freely and as fully as you possibly can. Please ask questions when you do not understand, offer suggestions about what might work better, and give feedback about what helps and what doesn't. Finally, you can be helpful in this process by trying as hard as you can to take the steps that we devise together in our efforts to resolve the problems and accomplish the goals we've agreed upon.

In outlining a client's role, recognize that role expectations necessarily vary according to the purpose for which a client is seeking or receiving social work services. Additionally, client role expectations differ somewhat depending on the agency where you work, its programs, and on the makeup of the client system—its size and the ages, capabilities, and motivations of its members. For example, the client role of an adult male client who is about to begin an intensive, three-month psychoeducational group experience for men who batter women is likely to be quite different from the client role of an 8-year-old child who witnessed her father shoot and kill her mother.

◆ EXERCISE 6-4: OUTLINING THE CLIENT'S ROLE

Use the following case situations to practice the skill of outlining the client's role. Please respond to each situation in the spaces provided.

1. Assume that you are a social worker meeting for the first time with a couple who want help with marital difficulties. Mr. and Mrs. Koslow have been married for ten years and have two children (8 and 10 years old). They have an adequate income. You have introduced yourself, secured introductions from Mr. and Mrs. Koslow, and have identified as a purpose for this first meeting to explore the problems and concerns that led the couple to come to the agency. You now want to outline their roles as clients in this process. What would you say?

2. Assume that you are a social worker meeting for the first time with a family of four (a single parent and three children, ages 11, 13, and 16). The eldest child, a daughter, has reportedly begun to use marijuana and to drink beer and wine. The mother is very concerned and has brought the entire family to meet with you. You have introduced yourself, secured introductions from each of the family members, and stated as a purpose for this first meeting to explore the problems and concerns that led the family to come to the agency. You now want to outline their roles as clients in this process. What would you say?

Discussing Policy and Ethical Factors

An extremely important skill applicable to the beginning phase of work involves the discussion of potentially relevant legal, policy, and ethical factors. Understanding the ground rules is a critical element in the development of an authentic, honest, and trusting relationship. It constitutes part of the informed consent process. For example, suppose an adult male client assumes that absolutely everything he says to you will remain confidential. During a meeting, he tells you that he often uses a wire coat hanger to "discipline" his 2-year-old child. Operating on the assumption of "absolute confidentiality," he is likely to feel profoundly betrayed when you report to state child-protection authorities what he told you about the "coat hanger spankings."

As a professional social worker, you are bound by certain guidelines in the performance of your duties (see Chapter 3). Some of these originate with the agency with which you are affiliated (agency policies and procedures), others are promulgated by the profession (The *National Association of Social Workers [NASW] Code of Ethics* or the *Canadian Association of Social Workers [CASW] Code of Ethics*), and still others are formulated by governmental bodies (laws and regulations). Clients have a right to be informed of the policies and ethical principles that may apply to them. Many agencies wisely provide prospective clients with brochures and other publications describing relevant policies. Box 6.1 shows a sample document that social workers might provide to prospective clients and use in guiding the discussion of policy and ethical issues. However, some clients do not or cannot truly understand the full meaning of such written material. You should therefore discuss at least the major policy elements with almost all prospective clients.

Before discussing relevant policy and ethical factors, you must, of course, consider several aspects of the person-problem-situation, including the relative urgency of a situation, timing, and context. Suppose, for example, you serve as a social worker in the emergency room of a hospital. An ambulance has just brought in a young child who has been severely injured in an automobile accident. The child's parents are in a waiting area and are visibly distraught. It should be obvious that you would defer discussion of policy and ethical factors while you provide information and comfort to them. In such instances, their immediate needs take precedence over your obligation to discuss policies. In fact, all the social work skills must be considered within the context of the person-problem-situation. Often, a skill applicable in one circumstance is totally inappropriate in another. Because social work practice is a professional rather than a technical endeavor, you must continually make judgments about how to best use your self and your social work skills.

BOX 6.1
Agency Policies

The agency operates on a *sliding fee* basis. This means that the cost of each individual or family session varies according to clients' ability to pay. The higher the family income, the higher the cost—up to a maximum of $35 per session. Group sessions are generally somewhat less. Reimbursement from insurance companies, where applicable, is the responsibility of the client, but agency staff will help clients to complete the necessary claim forms.

If a scheduled meeting must be canceled, the agency should be notified at least one day prior to the appointment.

As a general rule, whatever clients say during sessions remains confidential among agency personnel. There are, however, a few exceptions. If a client wants us to provide information to another person or agency (for example, to a medical doctor), he or she may sign a *Release of Information* form specifying which information to transfer and to whom. Also, as required by law, indications of possible child abuse or neglect will be reported to child-protection authorities. Similarly, evidence that a person represents a danger to himself or herself or to others will not be considered confidential. Action to protect the lives of the persons involved will be taken. In potentially life-threatening circumstances, the value of human life takes precedence over that of confidentiality. Finally, clients should be aware that occasionally (for example, in child custody disputes), social workers may be subpoenaed to testify in a court of law. Under such circumstances, agency social workers might be required to answer some questions about clients and the services that have been provided.

In this agency, we have a procedure for expressing concerns about the nature and quality of the services clients receive. If, for any reason whatsoever, you are uncertain about or dissatisfied with the services you receive, please discuss it with your social worker. If you do not receive an adequate explanation, if the service remains unsatisfactory, or if you feel uncomfortable talking directly with your social worker about the issue, please contact our agency's client representative, Ms. Sheila Cordula in Room 21 (telephone 789-5432). She will attempt to address your concerns.

◆ **EXERCISE 6-5: DISCUSSING POLICY AND ETHICAL FACTORS**

Use the following case situations to practice the skill of discussing policy and ethical factors. Please respond to each situation in the spaces provided.

1. Assume that you are a social worker in a public housing agency. You are currently in the process of interviewing all residents of a building to determine

their social service needs. You have just introduced yourself and described an initial purpose and role to Mrs. Strong, a single mother with five children who range in age from 6 months to 9 years. Write the words you would say in discussing policy and ethical factors.

2. You are a social worker in a nursing residence for elderly persons. A new resident had arrived during the previous weekend. Earlier in the week you introduced yourself, and now you are about to undertake a complete social history and psychosocial assessment. Following a reintroduction of yourself and a description of purpose and role, you want to outline the ground rules for the working relationship. Write the words you would say in discussing policy and ethical factors with this new resident.

3. You are a social worker for an agency that serves children who have been sexually abused. You are about to begin a new group for girls 7 to 10 years of age. You have introduced yourself, sought introductions from them, described an initial purpose for the group, and outlined your professional roles in the process. You have taken extra time in order to lessen their anxiety and encourage them to view the group experience as a "place of safety." Continue this beginning process by writing the words you would say in discussing policy and ethical factors as they might relate to this group of five girls.

Seeking Feedback

In using the skill of *seeking feedback* (Schwartz, 1976, pp. 188–190; Shulman, 1984, pp. 37–49; Shulman, 1992, pp. 79–80), you encourage clients to comment about the initial purpose, your role, their role, policy or ethical factors, or any other aspects of your introductory remarks. An important part of communicating effectively involves checking whether communications by either party have been accurately heard and understood. Seeking feedback serves this function. As a social worker, you routinely seek feedback throughout the entire course of work with clients, but you should recognize that it is especially important during the beginning phase. By asking for feedback about your initial description of purpose and role and your discussion of policy and ethical factors, you initiate the process of informed consent. You also invite clients to identify areas that are unclear, to elaborate on anything that occurred to them, to introduce a new topic, or to express any disagreement about your comments. By seeking feedback, you effectively send a message that this is a mutual and reciprocal process. You convey that you are genuinely interested in what clients have to say about you and what you have said, and that you hope that they will actively participate in the process.

Among the more common ways to seek feedback about purpose, roles, and policy factors are probes such as "How does that sound to you? What do you think about what we've talked about so far? What questions or comments do you have?" "As we've talked about these ground rules, what thoughts have occurred to you?" Often, clients respond to your efforts to seek feedback by asking for further clarification. This gives you an opportunity to explain in greater detail your views about the initial purpose for the meeting, roles, or policy and ethical factors. In general, clients who clearly understand these ground rules and believe that you sincerely want their feedback are likely to feel both informed and respected.

◆ **EXERCISE 6-6: SEEKING FEEDBACK**

Use the following case situations to practice the skill of seeking feedback. Please respond to each situation in the spaces provided.

1. You, a social worker in an agency that serves children and their families, are meeting for the first time with a 32-year-old mother and her 8-year-old daughter. They have voluntarily sought help regarding some problems with the child's schoolwork. At this time, you do not know anything more about the school or family situation. You have introduced yourself and elicited introductions from them. You have learned that Ms. Pomerantz prefers to be called "Joan" and that her daughter prefers "Emily." You have asked them to call you by your first name. You have also outlined an initial purpose for this first meeting by saying, "In today's meeting I hope that we'll gain a beginning understanding of the concerns that led to this visit. Once we understand better what contributes to the problems, we'll try together to plan some ways to resolve them."

Write the words you would use in seeking feedback regarding purpose from Joan and Emily.

2. As you continue to interact with Joan and Emily, you state: "Everything that you and Emily say during our meetings will be treated as confidential. No one outside the agency will have access to information you share. The only exceptions to this policy of confidentiality are when you specifically and in writing request that we provide information to someone else, or when there are indications of child abuse or neglect. In such instances, we are required by law to report that to authorities responsible for protecting children. Also, if subpoenaed by a court of law (for example, when a divorce and a child custody dispute occur), we might be required to provide information to the court."

Write the words you would use in seeking feedback from Joan regarding policy and ethical factors.

3. You are a social worker in an agency that serves adults and children who have been involved in child abuse. You are meeting for the first time with a 22-year-old man who has been charged with severely beating his 4-year-old son. He has come to this first meeting involuntarily. He is required to receive counseling as part of an adjudicated court agreement that, depending on the results of the counseling, may enable him to avoid incarceration. Thus far you have introduced yourself and elicited an introduction from him. You sense from the nature of his body position that you should address him in a formal manner. You refer to him as "Mr. Battle" and indicate that he may call you by your first name if he prefers. You have also outlined an initial purpose for this first meeting by saying, "In today's meeting I hope that we will be able to gain a beginning understanding of your current situation and identify some preliminary goals for our work together. It is my understanding that you are required by Judge Koopman to participate in counseling sessions at least once per week for a minimum of six months."

Write the words you would use in seeking feedback from Mr. Battle concerning what you have said thus far.

4. As you continue to interact with Mr. Battle, you say, "I hope that we will be able to identify some of the factors that have contributed to incidents of violence and that together we will work toward eliminating any future violent actions. You should know that in situations such as this, where the court is involved, I will be providing regular reports to the judge. I will report to the judge the number of sessions you attend, the degree of your cooperation in the process, my evaluation of progress, and my assessment concerning the risk of further violence."

Write the words you would use in seeking feedback from Mr. Battle concerning what you have said.

Summary

During the beginning phase, you introduce and identify yourself and seek an introduction from the prospective client. Following the exchange of introductions, you describe a tentative initial purpose for the meeting, possibly identify one or more professional roles that you might undertake, outline the role the client might assume to participate actively in the process, and identify relevant policy and ethical factors that might apply. Throughout this beginning process, you regularly seek feedback from clients concerning their understanding of and reactions to your introductory comments. By using the beginning skills, you help to clarify the nature and boundaries or ground rules of the helping process, lessen the initial ambivalence prospective clients often experience, and establish a tentative direction for work.

◆ EXERCISE 6-7: SUMMARY

Assume that you are a social worker with a human service agency that offers a broad range of social services. Prepare for a first meeting with each of the following prospective clients. In the spaces provided, write the words you would say and the actions you would take as you meet for the first time. Among the skills useful for this series of exercises are: introducing yourself, seeking introductions, describing an initial purpose and (sometimes) your professional social work role, outlining the client's role, discussing policy and ethical factors, and seeking feedback. Please label each of the beginning skills you use in each case situation.

1. Earlier in the day, a woman telephoned the agency and said she wanted to talk with someone about an incident that had occurred about one week earlier. A man she had met in a bar drove her home and then raped her. She had thought that she would be able to manage her feelings about the crime, but she now realized that she needed help to cope. She said, "I'm falling apart." An

appointment has been scheduled for the present time. What would you do and say in beginning?

2. The agency receptionist informs you that in the waiting room there is a 55-year-old man who is rapidly pacing back and forth in an agitated fashion, saying "I have to die. I have to die." You are the social worker responsible for interviewing all persons who come to the agency without appointments. You proceed to the reception area and ask him to accompany you back to your office. What would you do and say in beginning?

3. Recently, a 14-year-old African American girl told her school teacher that she is pregnant by her white boyfriend. She also told her that she needs to get an abortion quickly, or "her parents will kill her if they find out she's pregnant." The teacher urged her to talk with you, the school social worker, and secured the girl's permission to tell you about the situation. The teacher has done so and an appointment has been arranged for this time. What would you do and say in beginning?

4. An 8-year-old victim of sexual molestation seems to be in a state of emotional shock. She has not spoken a single word or expressed feelings since the incident was discovered. The child-protection caseworker tried to encourage the child to talk about what happened, but her efforts were unsuccessful. The child has been referred to you, a social worker who specializes in work with victimized children.

    A home visit has been scheduled for the present time. You drive to the girl's home, where she resides with her mother. The alleged perpetrator, a 19-year-old neighbor, has been detained in a juvenile center while awaiting a judicial hearing. The child's mother answers the door. What would you do and say in beginning, first with the mother and then with the 8-year-old girl herself?

5. A 42-year-old woman, beaten nearly to death by her husband several times over the past ten years, wants help in dealing with the situation. After the most recent episode, she sought refuge in a shelter for battered women, where you serve as a social worker. You are about to meet her for the first time. What would you do and say in beginning?

6. Using the following rating scales (where 0 = no proficiency and 10 = complete proficiency), assess your current level of proficiency in the beginning skills.

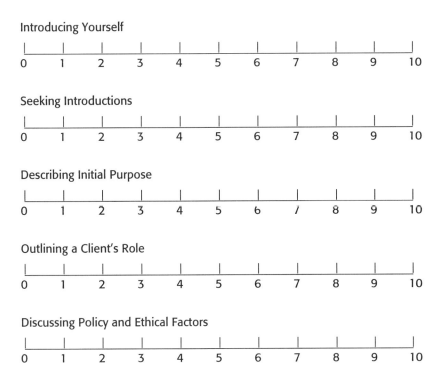

Introducing Yourself

| | | | | | | | | | | |
0 1 2 3 4 5 6 7 8 9 10

Seeking Introductions

| | | | | | | | | | | |
0 1 2 3 4 5 6 7 8 9 10

Describing Initial Purpose

| | | | | | | | | | | |
0 1 2 3 4 5 6 7 8 9 10

Outlining a Client's Role

| | | | | | | | | | | |
0 1 2 3 4 5 6 7 8 9 10

Discussing Policy and Ethical Factors

| | | | | | | | | | | |
0 1 2 3 4 5 6 7 8 9 10

Seeking Feedback

```
|    |    |    |    |    |    |    |    |    |    |
0    1    2    3    4    5    6    7    8    9    10
```

7. Finally, review your ratings to identify those beginning skills in which you remain less proficient (e.g., a score of 7 or less). Then, in the space below, outline the steps you might take to improve your skill in those areas.

Chapter 7

Exploring

Following the beginning phase, you start to explore the person-problem-situation. The exploring skills help you encourage clients to share thoughts and feelings about themselves, the concerns that led to the contact with you, and the situation (the social context and environment). Through this process of exploration, you and the client gather information. You both derive a more complete and realistic understanding of the person-problem-situation. Clients often enhance their own self-understanding as a result of this exploratory process. Indeed, greater self-awareness is a common result of publicly expressing oneself, since talking openly with another person also involves listening to oneself. As clients share their thoughts, ideas, and feelings as well as facts, they not only perceive your reactions; they more fully experience their own. Through the process of exploration, you and the client together consider information regarding the person, the problem, and the situation. This helps both parties understand the factors associated with the origin, development, and maintenance of the problem as well as those strengths, attributes, and resources that may later be useful in working toward problem resolution. Such information, in conjunction with your own professional knowledge, contributes to the development of an assessment and a plan for work.

The skills most applicable to the exploration phase are (1) probing, (2) seeking clarification, (3) reflecting content, (4) reflecting feelings, (5) reflecting feeling and meaning, (6) partializing, and (7) going beyond what is said. Applied to the person-problem-situation, these skills are used for exploring the person, exploring the problem, and exploring the situation.

In undertaking the exploration process with clients, consider the exploration matrix shown in Table 7.1. You may find it useful to first explore with the client the problem as it is now (cell 1), then trace its history and development (cell 2). As you do so, many clients will naturally begin to describe elements of themselves personally as well as dimensions of the situation. As needed, you may next explore clients' present view of themselves (cell 3), followed by a review of their past experiences (cell 4). Then, to the degree that it has not already been discussed, you encourage description of the present situation, including the social context and physical environment (cell 5) and then the situation as it has been in the past (cell 6). Finally, you encourage clients to envision what the future might be like if they, the problem, and the situation were to continue as before (cells 7, 8, and 9). You also explore the possible effects if aspects of themselves, the problem, or the situation should happen to change.

Of course, these nine dimensions overlap. As the problem is discussed, clients may share information about themselves and their situations. While exploring the present, clients may reveal material about the past or hopes and fears concerning the future. It is not necessary to interrupt in order to maintain a particular order or sequence. Clients should generally be encouraged to share information in their own way. Please do not view the exploration matrix as a fixed interview schedule. Instead, consider it as a flexible guide for exploring with clients relevant aspects of the person-problem-situation over time.

TABLE 7.1
Exploration Matrix

	Present	Past	Future
Problem	1	2	7
Person	3	4	8
Situation	5	6	9

Exploring the problem involves examination of the present status of the problem—its intensity, frequency, and duration—and the context in which it tends to happen. As a social worker, you are interested in what happens before, during, and following the occurrence of the problem. Additionally, you should explore the problem as it has been in the past. Trace or track its development from the time of its initial occurrence up to the present. In your exploration of the problem, include a careful examination of clients' attempts to resolve, cope with, or avoid the problem. You would like to learn about those efforts that have been successful, those that were partially successful, and those that were unsuccessful. Be sure to identify strengths and resources that were used in previous problem-solving efforts. As part of this exploration, encourage clients to share any thoughts, feelings, and actions associated with the problem.

Exploring the person involves encouraging clients to talk about themselves as individual human beings. In this dimension, you are especially interested in the *thinking, feeling,* and *doing* aspects of clients' experience. Seek information about personal strengths and assets as well as weaknesses and deficiencies. Within the dimension of thinking, explore both the substance of clients' thoughts—whether they occur as beliefs (the words people say to themselves) or as images (the mental pictures people visualize)—and the thought processes (the cognitive steps people take as they move from one thought or idea to another). Within the dimension of feeling, consider clients' emotions (e.g., anger, fear, or sadness) as well as physical sensations (e.g., energy, fatigue, muscular tension, nausea, or light-headedness). Within the dimension of doing, explore overt behavior (e.g., walking, speaking, hitting, looking) as well as the absence of behavior (e.g., behaviors, such as assertive requests, that clients might have used appropriately in a situation but, for whatever reasons, failed to use).

Exploring the situation involves examining current and, when applicable, past circumstances. Collect information about social, economic, and cultural aspects of situations as they may relate to the person, the identified problems, and resources that might be useful for problem resolution. Elicit information about significant other persons, family systems, communities, ethnic affiliations, religious involvement, housing, education, employment, and finances.

Exploring the future involves an examination of the problem, the person, and the situation as they may be in the future. In particular, you are interested in exploring three scenarios: (1) how the problem, person, and situation are likely to be if things continue along the current developmental trend line, (2) how they might be in a "worst possible case" scenario, and (3) how things might be in a "best possible case," where the problem and its negative effects upon person and situation were completely resolved. The latter process is often extremely revealing, as it serves to help you and clients identify possible directions for work.

Usually, within one or two meetings, you and the client have discussed the more pressing concerns. At this point, you can decide whether you and your agency have the authority, resources, and expertise necessary to help address the identified problems. Often, in large part due to a lack of familiarity with social service and mental health networks, prospective clients contact agencies that are not well prepared to address their particular problems. By exploring the presenting concerns, you may be able to determine that another organization in the community specializes in such problems and would probably be better able to provide help in this instance. Then, if the client concurs, you could contact the other agency to initiate a professional referral. Of course, the referral process should be done with great care, so that the client does not feel rejected by you or your agency. Also, the referral agency's personnel should be treated with professionalism and courtesy. The nature of your relationships with other community professionals often determines whether prospective clients receive a warm or a cool reception. Therefore, relate to your colleagues in other agencies with the same high degree of professionalism you show to clients.

When the presenting problems are congruent with your agency's function and range of services, and fall within your areas of expertise, you and the client may continue with a more complete exploration of the person-problem-situation. This more refined process should yield a fairly clear sense of direction for the work that you will do together.

Probing

When the beginning phase of work is complete, and you and the client substantially agree about the purpose of the meeting, you may then proceed to seek information about the concerns that led to this encounter (Perlman, 1957, p. 88). *Probes* are used to elicit facts, ideas, and feelings concerning the person, the problem, the situation, and potential means for resolving the identified difficulties (Cournoyer, 1994b, pp. 328–335). The process of probing yields information necessary for mutual understanding, assessment, contract formulation, movement toward problem resolution and goal attainment, evaluation, and ending.

The first use of the probing skill typically occurs after you and the client have concluded the beginning phase. By this time, you have introduced yourselves, reached a tentative understanding of the purpose for meeting, and, usually, discussed the policies and ethical principles that may apply. The initial exploratory probe represents the first substantive entry into the realm of the problem that led to the contact. Commonly, the probe is phrased in such a way as to allow clients maximum opportunity to express themselves fully and freely. You may phrase probes as questions or, occasionally, as requests. For example, you might ask, "When you telephoned the other day, you mentioned something about family problems. What's happening within the family that concerns you?" Or "What led you to contact us at this time?" Or you could say, "Please tell me about the difficulties that are troubling you." In the case of an involuntary client, you might say, "I understand that the judge has required you to come here for counseling. I know quite a bit about the situation, but I'd like to hear the full story from you. How did this all come about?" As you might expect, the probing skill is applicable at many points throughout the exploration phase and, of course, all other phases as well. Probes are used to explore relevant aspects of the person-problem-situation, including the circumstances surrounding the origin, development, and current status of the identified problems. Examples of common probes include: "How did these difficulties begin?" "Who was included in your family as you were growing up?" "What were your parents like?" "Who lives with you now?" "What did you feel when she left?" "What were you thinking about when that happened?" "What would you like to be different?" "What did you do then?"

Generally, probes are phrased as questions. The questions derive from your active pursuit of information regarding the person-problem-situation, from the time the problem first occurred up through the present. There are two general types of questions: closed-ended and open-ended. *Closed-ended questions* (Goodman & Esterly, 1988, pp. 123–127) are phrased in such a way as to elicit short responses, sometimes simply yes or no. Closed-ended questions yield a great deal of information in a brief amount of time. They are especially useful in crisis situations where vital information must be gathered quickly.

Here are a few examples of closed-ended questions that you might ask. "What is your phone number?" "What's your address?" "Do you have a car?" "Do you live at home?" "When were you born?" "What grade are you in?" "Where do you work?" "Who is your family doctor?" "When was your last physical exam?" "Does anyone live with you?" "Is there somebody there in the house with you right now?" "Which do you prefer?" "Have you taken some medicine?" "How many pills did you take?"

Usually, answers to such questions are quite brief. This can be advantageous or not, depending on the purpose of meeting and the needs of the situation. Sometimes the rapid collection of specific information is so important that you postpone free and full exploration of other aspects of the person-problem-situation. However, too many closed-ended questions, asked one after another, may make clients feel more like subjects in an investigation than people seeking help. They may feel interrogated rather than interviewed, and the quality of your professional relationship may suffer. Therefore, unless the situation is immediately life-threatening or otherwise urgent, it is usually wise to mix closed-ended with open-ended questions and active listening responses.

Some closed-ended probes constitute, in legal terms, *leading questions*. A leading question is one that is phrased in such a way as to encourage a specific answer—one that the questioner wishes to hear. For example, suppose a social worker were to ask, "Haven't you experienced lots of pain in your pelvic area? Yes? And, haven't you felt that pain since you were a young child? Yes? Aren't these painful symptoms common among people who were sexually abused as children? Yes? So, isn't it likely that you were sexually abused as a child?" Such a series of questions would clearly lead or suggest to a client that a certain conclusion held by the social worker is the right and valid conclusion. During the exploration phase, such leading questions are generally ill-advised, as they tend to narrow a process that should usually be quite open and expansive. In particular, whenever you serve an investigative function in your service as a social worker, be extremely careful in your choice of words and the phrasing of questions. If you frequently ask leading questions in such interviews, your courtroom testimony could be easily challenged and perhaps disallowed. Such leading questions may also be problematic at other times and in other contexts. During the exploring phase especially, try to avoid leading questions.

Open-ended questions (Goodman & Esterly, 1988, pp. 127–137) are phrased in a manner that encourages people to express themselves more extensively. Open-ended questions are designed to further exploration on a deeper level or in a broader way. They are usually not leading questions because they enable the client to respond in any number of ways. Often they are phrased as "what" questions: "What is the nature of your concern?" "What is she like?" "What happened then?" "In what way did you . . . ?" "What did you say then?" "What" questions can be expressed as closed- or open-ended questions. Most of the time, they tend to elicit a factual answer, unless a feeling response is specifically requested. For example, "What feelings did you experience when he left?" encourages clients to share emotions. "How" questions nearly always yield open responses from clients. Probes such as "How did that come to happen?" "How did he react?" "How do you feel right now?" "How did he act in that situation?" also tend to elicit expansive expressions from clients.

Some statements can serve as open or closed probes. For example, "Please tell me more about that," "Please elaborate," "Please continue," "Tell me more about that part of your life," all serve to encourage open responses. "Please spell your name," "Please give me your exact street address," serve as closed probes.

"Why" questions can generate defensiveness. Clients may conclude that you are judging them critically and feel compelled to defend themselves or justify some aspect of their behavior or circumstances. Therefore, be cautious about the use of "why" questions. If you use a gentle tone of voice and an open, accepting facial expression, you may not have to avoid them completely. Also, the way you phrase the question can help. For example, the defensive-eliciting quality of a "why" question can sometimes be moderated by qualifying phrases such as "I wonder why (that is)?" or "Why do you think that happens?" When asking "why" questions, be certain to communicate nonverbally an attitude of warmth and acceptance.

During the exploration process, intersperse your probes with active listening responses. Realize that probes can suggest blame, evaluation, or advice. Probes are not always simply neutral requests for information. For example, "Have you talked with your mother yet?" might imply that you had expected the client to talk with his or her mother. "Have you completed that form?" may convey a similar message. Although it is sometimes useful to express a statement of opinion or preference in the form of a question, be aware that you are doing so. Sharing your personal or professional opinion within the context of a question does not relieve you of responsibility for the substance of the message. Also, try to avoid asking either-or questions, multiple-choice questions, or a string of questions at the same time. For example, "Are you still going with Jackie or have you given up on her and are now dating only Jill? And what about Cathy?" would confuse most clients. They would not know whether to respond to your first, second, third, or fourth question. Instead, ask one at a time.

During the exploration phase, probes can be extremely useful for providing a sense of coherence and continuity to the interview. As clients talk about themselves as people, the problems of concern, and the situational contexts in which they function, they sometimes (quite understandably) focus a great deal on one topic while entirely avoiding or only briefly touching on important related information. When that occurs, you can select probes to guide clients toward an exploration of other pertinent aspects of the person-problem-situation. For example, you might ask, "As you were growing up, how was your relationship with your older sister?" in order to gather information about an aspect of a client's family and social situation that had been neglected. Be aware, however, that clients' psychological and interpersonal defenses should be respected. This is especially important during the exploring phase. When a client is especially fragile concerning a particular topic or theme, you would usually be wise to postpone probing that specific dimension until your working relationship becomes more established. Then, when the client feels more secure, you may return to probe into areas that require further exploration. Possible exceptions occur when a life-threatening emergency exists or, perhaps, when serving in a substance-abuse treatment agency.

Probes are obviously relevant to the exploration phase. Indeed, they are of great utility throughout all phases of practice.

For these exercises, assume that you are a social worker at a counseling center for families and children. In the spaces provided, write the words you would say in each situation.

1. You are in the midst of the first interview with Mr. K., a recently divorced 55-year-old man. You have introduced yourself and have addressed the other aspects of the beginning phase of practice. You are now ready for an initial exploratory probe. At this point, you know only that Mr. K.'s concern relates in some way to the divorce. Therefore, you wish to encourage him to explore that topic in depth. Write the words you would say in making this first probe. After you have written it, indicate whether your probe is open- or closed-ended. Discuss your rationale for choosing this particular probe. How do you think Mr. K. would respond?

2. You have just begun to interview Mrs. O., a 77-year-old widow who lives alone in a small apartment. You have already introduced yourselves, outlined some of the services that might be of interest to Mrs. O. (e.g., transportation, meals on wheels, or in-home medical services), and addressed other dimensions of the beginning phase. Now write the words you would say in making an initial exploratory probe. After you have written your probe, determine whether it is

open- or closed-ended. Discuss your rationale for choosing this particular probe and anticipate how you think Mrs. O. would react to it.

3. You have begun the first interview with the S. family, a seven-member blended family who have sought your help with problems of family tension and conflict. You have gone through the introductions and addressed other aspects of the beginning phase. As your initial probe, you asked, "What do you see as the major problems within the family?" The father responded to this question first, then the mother answered, followed by other family members. Although the specific nature of the responses varied somewhat, there appeared to be considerable agreement that the major problem is the strained relationship between the two teenage boys (biological children of the father) and their father's wife (their stepmother). Their relationship appears to involve a great deal of tension, conflict, and anger. As the social worker, you now wish to probe the origin and development of the difficulties in this relationship. Write the words you would say in doing so. After you have written your probe, determine whether it is open- or closed-ended. To whom is it directed—the boys, the other children, Mrs. S., Mr. S., or the entire group? Discuss your rationale for choosing this probe and for selecting the person or persons you decided to

address. What do you anticipate would be the boys' reaction to this probe? How might Mrs. S. respond?

Assume that you continue to explore the problem, the family, and the situation. Write the words you would say in formulating five additional probes. For each one, determine whether it is open- or closed-ended. Also, identify whether each probe addresses the person, family, problem, or situation aspect of the case. Finally, identify how you think various family members might react to each probe.

4. You have begun to interview a prospective client of Latino background who speaks both Spanish and English fluently. You have completed the introductions, addressed the policy and ethical factors, and established a tentative purpose for the meeting: to explore the concerns Mrs. F. has about her two children, 7 and 9 years old. It appears that they are the only Latino children in their school and have been subject to harassment from some teenage boys. Mrs. F. is worried that her children might be in physical danger and that their attitude toward school might be negatively affected by these experiences.

As the social worker, you are now ready to explore the problem further. Write the words you would say in an initial exploratory probe. Follow that by writing the words you might say in expressing five additional probes concerning the problem, the children, Mrs. F., the family system, or the school situation. Briefly discuss your rationale for the probes you have selected. Determine whether each is closed- or open-ended and predict the reaction that Mrs. F. might have to each question.

Seeking Clarification

Sometimes during an interview, clients may make statements that seem unclear. They may communicate in an apparently contradictory fashion, skim over a relevant issue, or entirely neglect some significant aspect of themselves, the problems, or the circumstances. Such indirect, unclear, or incomplete messages often involve important aspects of the person's experience, so the manner in which you respond may substantially affect the nature of the relationship, the direction for work, and the outcome of the helping endeavor. In such instances, it may be appropriate to respond by *seeking clarification*. That is, you attempt to elicit a more complete expression of the meaning of previous words or gestures. In effect, you ask the client to elaborate on and be more specific about something he or she has just said. During the early portion of an interview, you seek clarification in order to gather more information about particular aspects of the person-problem-situation.

Of course, you will not always completely understand everything that clients say. Sometimes, this is because you are not listening well. At other times, clients do not express themselves clearly because they are uncertain about what they actually do think and feel. After all, one purpose of exploring is to help clients understand themselves better. It is unlikely that they will always have a complete and coherent understanding of all aspects of the person-problem-situation, but sometimes clients may send subtle or indirect messages that they truly hope you will notice. Many people are reluctant to ask directly for help. Such hesitancy is quite common among members of many cultural groups and may be intensified if the social worker happens to be a person of majority status and they are of minority status. In addition, many issues are so embarrassing or emotional in nature that clients find it difficult to talk openly about them. Therefore, subtle communications are common. You must be sensitive to indirect expressions in the form of hints, nonverbal gestures, or incomplete or mixed messages. Be aware that considerable anxiety may be associated with such messages. Because clients may not be fully aware of or comfortable with some aspects of their thinking or feeling, or because they fear that you might disapprove, they may send extremely significant messages in an indirect manner.

In responding to such communications, move carefully toward a greater degree of specificity and clarity by asking for further information concerning the unclear, incomplete, or indirect message. For example, during a first meeting a 50-year-old client says to a 25-year-old social worker, "I've never had much luck with young social workers. You're all so innocent—still wet behind the ears." The worker might respond to such a statement by asking, "When you talk about not having 'much luck' with other young social workers, it sounds like there have been some problems—what kind of difficulties have you had in the past with young social workers?"

The skill of seeking clarification tends to encourage clients to elaborate on and describe more specifically aspects of a thought, feeling, action, or situation (Shulman, 1984, pp. 60–61; Shulman, 1992, pp. 115–123). People often communicate in vague or general terms. Seeking clarification about detailed aspects of an experience or the specific meaning of a term may enable you and the client to gain a more complete and realistic understanding.

Seeking clarification is especially applicable in circumstances where the social worker and client come from different cultural backgrounds. Words, phrases, and gestures commonly used in one culture may be nonexistent in another, or their meaning may differ dramatically. Although the client may know exactly what she or he means by a particular term, it is unlikely that you always could—at least when it is first used. Even when a client uses standard English, a term may have a unique meaning to that person. Also, many clients come from cultural backgrounds different from your own. They may use words that you have never heard before, or they may use a familiar term in a manner that is unusual to you. The skill of seeking clarification can help in these circumstances. In seeking clarification, you seek additional specific information about a particular word or phrase, or some other aspect of a client's verbal or nonverbal communication. To practice using this skill, consider the following formats.

SUGGESTED FORMATS FOR SEEKING CLARIFICATION

What, specifically, do you mean when you say _____?

or

Could you be more specific about _____?

or

Would you please elaborate on _____?

Example

CLIENT: My spouse and I just don't get along. We haven't for years. The relationship stinks.

WORKER: When you say "The relationship stinks," what specifically do you mean?

As is the case with most exploring skills, seeking clarification is applicable throughout the entire helping process. It is especially relevant during the problem-definition and goal-setting phases, the working and evaluating phases, and the ending processes. Often, you can effectively precede your request for clarification with an active listening or reflective response.

◆ EXERCISE 7-2: SEEKING CLARIFICATION

For these exercises, assume that you are a social worker at a counseling center for families and children. Respond in the spaces provided by writing the words you would say to seek clarification in each situation.

1. You are in the midst of the first interview with Mr. K., a recently divorced 55-year-old man. You have introduced yourself and addressed other aspects of beginning. You are in the midst of exploring the person-problem-situation. Mr. K. says, "I hurt so bad. I miss her terribly. I'm not sure I can go on." Write the words you would say in seeking clarification of what he has just said. After you have written your response, discuss your rationale for the words you have chosen. How do you think he might react to this question? Now try preceding your clarification-seeking with an active listening response. What effect does that have?

2. As an outreach worker for elderly persons, you are in the midst of an interview with Mrs. O., a 77-year-old widow who lives alone. At one point in the conversation, Mrs. O. abruptly stops talking and looks blankly away. For perhaps 45 seconds, she does not respond to any of your questions. Then, suddenly, she shakes her head slightly and redirects her attention to you. Write the words you would use to seek clarification in this situation. After you have written your response, discuss your rationale for the words you have chosen. How do you think Mrs. O. might react to this question?

3. You have begun the first interview with the S. family, a seven-member blended family. You are in the midst of exploring the nature and development of the problem when one of the teenage boys (biological children of the father) angrily refers to their father's wife (their stepmother) as a "home wrecker." In reaction, Mrs. S. lowers her eyes and becomes very quiet. Write the words you would say in seeking clarification from the teenager. Discuss your rationale for the words you have chosen. How do you think the teenager who made the remark might react? What about Mrs. S.? Mr. S.? Other members of the family? Now write the words you would say in seeking clarification from Mrs. S. concerning her nonverbal reaction to the term *home wrecker*. How do you think she and the other family members might react to your request for clarification from Mrs. S.?

4. Assume that you are in the midst of exploring problems with Mrs. F., who is of Latino background and speaks both Spanish and English fluently. Mrs. F. is concerned about her two children's safety at school. During the course of the problem exploration, Mrs. F. says angrily, "WASPs control this whole country and don't care about anybody but themselves!" Write the words you might say in seeking clarification. Discuss your rationale for the words you have selected. How do you think Mrs. F. might react to your question? Now write three other ways in which you might seek clarification in this situation.

Reflecting Content

Reflecting content (Carkhuff, 1987, pp. 95–97) is the empathic skill of communicating your understanding of the factual or informational part of a message. As are the other reflecting skills, reflecting content is a more precise form of active listening. Commonly, use of this skill involves paraphrasing the informational aspects of the client's words and expressing them back. By accurately reflecting content, you demonstrate that you have heard and understood the information that the client is trying to convey.

You may use lead-in phrases such as, *You're saying . . . , If I understand you correctly, you mean that . . . , I hear you saying . . . .* However, repeated use of such phrases can begin to sound artificial and mechanical. As much as possible, try to use your own words to reflect or mirror the information the client has conveyed. If you accurately reflect the content of the person's message, such lead-in phrases are usually unnecessary. Here is an example of an exchange in which a social worker responds to a client's message by reflecting content.

Example
Reflecting Content

CLIENT (MR. C): Several years ago, I lost my job. They closed the plant where I had worked for years and years. There was a huge layoff. Most of my buddies and I were let go. Since then, my wife has worked part-time and that keeps some food on the table. My unemployment compensation ran out long ago. We've not been able to pay the mortgage on the house for about the last six months. I think the bank is going to foreclose on us soon.

WORKER: You haven't had an adequate income for a long time and it's beginning to look like you may lose your home.

Although it is extremely likely that Mr. C. is experiencing a lot of emotion while he expresses himself, he has not actually mentioned his feelings. In using the skill of reflecting content, you stay with the factual content of the message. Even when a client does express feelings along with facts or opinions, you might choose to use the skill of reflecting content in order to highlight the informational portion of the message. You might do so when the urgency of a situation requires that *facts, ideas,* or *preferences* be elicited quickly; when you determine that the meaning of a client's message is more relevant at that particular point than feelings; or when you are trying to help a client maintain emotional self-control. In general, during the early stages of the exploration process, you would be wise to respect clients' defensive and coping mechanisms. Follow their lead. If a client is expressing primarily facts and opinions in a nonemotional or even intellectualized fashion, use the skill of reflecting content. At this stage, there is usually no pressing need to reflect feelings that clients have not directly expressed. Mr.

C., for example, may be trying to maintain control of his emotions by expressing himself in a matter-of-fact, businesslike fashion. He may not yet trust the worker enough to risk full and free expression of his true feelings. The worker could further develop the relationship by accurately reflecting the content of Mr. C.'s stated message and then, perhaps later during the interview, return to an exploration and reflection of his feelings.

◆ EXERCISE 7-3: REFLECTING CONTENT

For these exercises, assume that you are a social worker at a counseling center for families and children. Respond in the spaces provided by writing the words you would say in reflecting content in each situation.

1. You are in the midst of problem exploration with Mr. K., a recently divorced 55-year-old man. He says, "The divorce was final about three weeks ago. She said she'd had enough of my constant criticism and sarcastic comments, and that she was leaving me." Write the words you would say in reflecting the content of what he has said. After you have written your response, discuss your rationale for the words you have chosen. How do you think he might react to your reflection?

2. You are in the midst of an interview with Mrs. O., a 77-year-old widow who lives alone. Following an episode in which she appeared to lose awareness of her surroundings, Mrs. O. says, "I do occasionally have these spells. I don't pass out or fall down or anything like that. I just kind of wake up after a while." Write the words you would use in reflecting the content of Mrs. O.'s message. After you have written your response, discuss your rationale for the words you have chosen. How do you think Mrs. O. might react to your content reflection?

3. You are in the midst of an interview with the seven-member blended S. family. During the course of the exploration, Mrs. S. says, "I fell in love with Hank [Mr. S.], and when we married I hoped that his children and mine would come to love one another as brothers and sisters. I also wanted his kids to know that I would love and treat them as if they were my own children." Write the words you would say in reflecting the content of Mrs. S.'s message. Discuss your rationale for the words you have chosen. How do you think Mrs. S. might react? Now write two other ways in which you might reflect the content of her message in this situation.

4. You are interviewing Mrs. F., a Latina mother of two children who have been harassed at school by several boys. During the course of the problem exploration, Mrs. F. says, "I have talked to the teachers and the guidance counselor. They listen politely but they don't care about what this does to my children. They won't do a thing about it." Write the words you might say in reflecting content. Discuss your rationale for the words you have selected. How do you think Mrs. F. might react to your response? Now write two other ways in which you might reflect the content of Mrs. F.'s message in this situation.

Reflecting Feelings

Reflecting feelings (Carkhuff, 1987, pp. 99–110) is another of the empathic, active listening skills. It usually consists of a brief response that communicates your understanding of the feelings expressed by the client. Some of the more effective responses consist of a simple sentence with a single feeling word. For example, phrases such as "You are really hurting" or "You're terrified!" can be powerful empathic reflections of feeling. In spite of its brevity and apparent simplicity, however, reflecting feelings is not a skill that all social workers find easy to use. Reflecting emotions requires that you, at least to some extent, feel those same feelings yourself. Empathy can be uncomfortable, even painful. Partly because of such discomfort, you may be tempted to convert feeling reflections to content reflections by neglecting to use words that convey emotions. For instance, suppose a client says, "I am devastated." You might reflect the feeling by saying, "You're crushed." If, however, you were to respond by saying, "It feels like you've been hit by a freight train," you merely imply the feeling; you do not actually say it. The message conveys an idea rather than a feeling. Although *hit by a freight train* is an apt phrase to amplify the feeling of devastation, it is much more effective when used in conjunction with one or more feeling words. For example, "You feel crushed. It's like you've been hit by a freight train" includes both a feeling word and a powerful idea that amplifies the emotion. Certain lead-in phrases, such as *You feel like* . . . , tend to be followed by ideas, analogies, or metaphors rather than words that connote actual feelings. Therefore, at least for training purposes, try to use a format such as the following.

SUGGESTED FORMAT FOR REFLECTING FEELINGS

You feel (*insert appropriate feeling word*)

The single most important aspect of the skill of reflecting feelings is to capture accurately the primary emotion experienced by the client and mirror it back so that she or he *feels* your empathic understanding. When two feelings are in evidence you may respond to both. For example: "You feel _____ and _____." It is often possible, however, to identify a single word that communicates both feelings. For example, *burdened* and *discouraged* might be reflected as *overwhelmed*. Here are some examples of feeling reflections.

Example
Reflecting Feelings

CLIENT: (His former wife remarried about a year ago. Last month she and her current husband left the area with the client's 5-year-old son. They moved 2,000 miles away. The client tried to stop their relocation by filing a motion with the court, but his former spouse won the right to move with her son.) I just can't stand it. I miss my son terribly, I know that he'll gradually lose interest in me and I can't do a thing about it.

WORKER: You feel sad and powerless.

Example
Reflecting Feelings

CLIENT: (16-year-old girl who wanted desperately to be selected to the school's cheerleading team but was not chosen) It's awful. I can't go back to school. I can't face them. I wanted to be on the team so bad. It hurts. It really hurts.

WORKER: You feel terribly rejected. You're awfully disappointed.

During the early portions of your work with clients, you would usually reflect only the feelings that are expressed verbally. After establishing a base of accurate reflections, or when the nonverbal, emotional message is very clear, you may reflect what you perceive to be the unspoken feeling message. Nonverbal messages in the form of facial expressions, body positions and movements, tone of voice, and so on are important means for communicating emotions. They should not be ignored. When you reflect a feeling suggested by nonverbal behavior, however, recognize that you are taking a modest risk. Your reflection of a feeling expressed nonverbally must be done in a tentative fashion, because the client has not actually used feeling words. Also, a client may not be ready to acknowledge feelings that he or she does experience. Therefore, be cautious when reflecting unspoken emotions, particularly early in the working relationship. When you do so, use a gentle, tentative tone of voice. Be prepared to return to the use of content-reflection or clarification-seeking skills if the client indicates that your feeling reflection is premature or off target.

In order to use feeling reflections effectively, you need a large vocabulary of terms that connote feelings. To convey different kinds of emotions at various levels of intensity, you should be familiar with a wide range of feeling words commonly used by the cultural groups that you are likely to serve in your community. Otherwise, you will have difficulty accurately mirroring the feelings expressed. For example, anger is an emotion everyone experiences to one degree or another. A person who is mildly annoyed or irritated would probably not feel understood if you were to say, "You feel enraged." The words you use should match both the kind as well as the intensity of the feelings expressed by clients.

◆ EXERCISE 7-4: REFLECTING FEELINGS

In order to use competently the skill of reflecting feelings, you need a sophisticated vocabulary of feeling words. Without such a vocabulary, it is extremely difficult to paraphrase the feelings, emotions, and sensations experienced and expressed by clients. In order to begin to develop a feeling vocabulary of your own, please consider the six categories of emotional experiences listed in Table 7.2 (on page 184). Identify at least ten feeling words that connote some degree of the emotion listed for each of the six categories of feelings. For example, under the *happiness* category, you might include the word *satisfied*; under the *anxiety and fear* category, you might list *stress* as an associated term. If you become stuck, review the alphabetized list of feeling words in Appendix 4. That should enable you to easily generate ten standard English feeling words for each category. Once you have listed ten words for each category, rate them in terms of relative intensity (1 = mild; 2 = moderate; 3 = strong). For example, under the *anger* category, you might assign a "3" (strong) rating to the words *enraged* and *furious*. Similarly, you might assign a "2" (moderate) to the terms *irritated* and *annoyed*.

Next, develop feeling vocabularies for several different cultural groups. For example, you might develop separate lists of feeling words for contemporary North American teenagers, persons of African ancestry, Latinos, people of a Jewish culture, gays and lesbians, and so forth. Focus your efforts on the preparation of feeling vocabularies for those cultural groups you would probably serve as a social worker in your community.

Now that you have developed some familiarity with a range of feeling words, begin to practice some feeling reflections. Assume that you are a social worker with a family counseling center. In the spaces provided, write the words you would say to reflect feelings in each situation.

1. During your first interview with Mr. K., a recently divorced 55-year-old man, he says, "I am absolutely lost. There is no reason to go on. I feel like someone reached into my gut and wrenched out my insides." Write the words you would say in reflecting the feelings Mr. K. has expressed. After you have written your response, discuss your rationale for the words you have chosen. How do you think he might react to your reflection? Identify two alternative feeling reflections that might also apply in this situation.

2. In the midst of an interview with Mrs. O., a 77-year-old widow, she says, "I feel just fine. Sure, I have my low points, but everybody does. I still cook my own meals and care for myself. I'm proud of that—but, with these spells, I'm afraid I won't be independent much longer." Write the words you would use to reflect the feelings contained in Mrs. O.'s message. After you have written your response, discuss your rationale for the words you have chosen. How do you think Mrs. O. might react to your reflection? Identify two alternative feeling reflections that might also apply in this situation.

3. You are interviewing the seven-member, blended S. family. Mrs. S. has just said, "I fell in love with Hank [Mr. S.], and when we married I hoped that his children and mine would come to love one another as brothers and sisters. I also wanted his kids to know that I would love and treat them as if they were my own children." Following her statement, she hangs her head as tears fall down her cheeks. Mr. S.'s eyes are also watery. Although specific feeling words were not used, write the words you would say in reflecting the feelings suggested by Mrs. S.'s nonverbal messages. Then do the same for Mr. S. Discuss your rationale for the words you have chosen for each feeling reflection. How do you think Mrs. S. might react to your response? Mr. S.? Identify two additional ways in which you might reflect the feelings suggested by their communications in this situation.

4. You are interviewing Mrs. F., a Latina mother who is concerned about the safety at school of her two children. At one point, Mrs. F. says, "I'm so angry. Talking with the teachers and the guidance counselor does not help at all. It's so frustrating having to fight so hard for fair treatment. My kids deserve to be protected." Write the words you might say in reflecting her feelings. Discuss your rationale for the words you have selected. How do you think Mrs. F. might react to your response? Now write two other ways in which you might reflect the feelings indicated by Mrs. F.'s message in this situation.

T A B L E 7.2 **Standard English Feeling Vocabulary**					
Happiness	*Hurt & Loss*	*Anxiety & Fear*	*Sadness*	*Anger*	*Guilt*

Reflecting Feeling and Meaning

Reflecting feeling and meaning (Carkhuff & Anthony, 1979, pp. 78–82) is one of the more complete forms of active listening and empathic communication. It conveys the emotional as well as the factual elements of a message. Thus, it constitutes the most complex form of reflection. For training purposes, use a format such as the following.

SUGGESTED FORMAT FOR REFLECTING FEELING AND MEANING

You feel _____ because _____.
or
You feel _____ and _____.
or
You feel _____ but/yet/however _____.

Reflecting feeling and meaning mirrors clients' emotions and the facts or thoughts associated with them. As with other reflections, your response should represent an accurate and equivalent form of the message expressed by a client. Do not speculate or interpret. Rather, paraphrase or mirror the feeling and meaning as experienced by the other person. When clients convey their view of the cause of feelings they experience, reflect their perspective even though you might personally believe it to be incomplete or inaccurate. Often the meanings that clients convey suggest external or situational causes for their feelings (e.g., "My mother makes me feel guilty."). At other times, clients refer to aspects of themselves (attitudes, habits, traits, psychological patterns, fears, or physiological conditions) as the reason for their feelings. Whether the meaning associated with the feelings is externalized or internalized, when reflecting feeling and meaning, remain congruent with the client's experience and resist the temptation to modify the meaning of the message. As with other reflections, your response should be essentially equivalent to the message communicated by the client. Here are two examples of a social worker reflecting feeling and meaning.

Example

CLIENT: (60-year-old man who has just lost his job after 35 years of employment)
I have nowhere to turn—no job—no income—no nothing. They just let me go after 35 years of pain and sweat for them. I'm scared and angry.

WORKER: (reflecting feeling and meaning) You feel desperate because the company has turned you out after so many years of hard work, and it doesn't look like you'll be able to find something else.

Example

CLIENT: I'm a wreck. I can't sleep or eat; I can't concentrate. I know my head is really messed up.

WORKER: *(reflecting feeling and meaning)* You feel awful. You're anxious and confused, and you know you're not thinking straight right now.

◆ **EXERCISE 7-5: REFLECTING FEELING AND MEANING**

For these exercises, assume that you are a social worker at a family counseling center. In the spaces provided, write the words you would say in reflecting feeling and meaning in each situation.

1. In the midst of your first interview with Mr. K., a recently divorced 55-year-old man, you are exploring his feelings about his situation. He says, "I was so used to her being there. I needed her but I never told her so. Now that she's gone, I realize just how much she meant to me." Write the words you would say in reflecting the feeling and meaning contained in what Mr. K. has said. After you have written your response, discuss your rationale for the words you have chosen. How do you think Mr. K. might respond? Identify two alternative feeling and meaning reflections that might also apply in this situation.

2. You are in the midst of an interview with Mrs. O., a 77-year-old widow who lives alone and occasionally has blackouts. During the conversation she says,

"I'm afraid of being a burden to somebody. I'd rather be dead than be treated like a small child who cannot care for herself." Write the words you would use to reflect the feeling and meaning contained in Mrs. O.'s statement. After you have written your response, discuss your rationale for the words you have chosen. How do you think Mrs. O. might react to your response? Identify two alternative feeling and meaning reflections that might also apply in this situation.

3. You are interviewing the seven-member, blended S. family. Following a moment when both Mr. and Mrs. S. began to cry, one of the teenage boys (Mr. S.'s biological children) says, "Well, it just seems that she came into the house expecting to be Mom. She'll never be my mother, and I resent it when she tries to be." Write the words you would say in reflecting the feeling and meaning contained in his statement. Discuss your rationale for the words you have chosen. How do you think the teenager might react to your response? Mr. S.? Mrs. S.? Identify two additional ways in which you might reflect the feeling and meaning suggested by the boy's words.

4. You are interviewing Mrs. F. While exploring the problem, Mrs. F. says, "I'm frustrated with the whole system! This society is racist to the core! Money and power are the only things they respect." Write the words you might say in reflecting feeling and meaning. Discuss your rationale for the words you have selected. How do you think Mrs. F. might react to your response? Now write two other ways in which you might reflect the feeling and meaning indicated by Mrs. F.'s words.

Partializing

Partializing (Perlman, 1957, pp. 144–149; Shulman, 1984, pp. 80–81; Shulman, 1992, pp. 141–143) is a skill you can use to help clients break down several problems, issues, or concerns—complex phenomena—into more manageable units in order to address them more easily. It is frequently very helpful during the exploration phase of practice. If you and the client tried to deal with a multitude of concerns simultaneously, one or both of you would probably end up quite confused. Often, there are simply too many to address effectively all at once. Using the partializing skill helps organize the process as workable pieces of the whole are explored one at a time.

Example

CLIENT: *(40-year-old mother and wife)* My whole life is a mess. My husband drinks two six-packs every night and even more on weekends. I think he's an alcoholic. He's out of work—again! My teenage son smokes dope. I've found marijuana in his room. And he's just been expelled from school for stealing money from another kid's locker. So, both of them are at home now. I'm the only one working and I'm falling apart. I'm a nervous wreck. And, I'm angry as hell!"

WORKER: You sure have a lot happening all at once. It sounds like everybody in the family has their own share of problems and you're affected by them all. I wonder, since there are so many issues to address—your husband's behavior, your son's, and your own feelings about it all— could we start by looking at them one at a time? Does that make sense to you? Okay? Which piece of all of this concerns you most right now? Let's start with that one."

◆ EXERCISE 7-6: PARTIALIZING

Assume that you are a social worker at a family counseling center. In the spaces provided, write the words you would say in using the skill of partializing in each situation.

1. You are interviewing Mr. K., a recently divorced 55-year-old man. He says, "I think I'm on the brink of a nervous breakdown. I can't do my work. I can't sleep at night. I don't eat. All I do is think of her. I wonder what she's doing and whether she ever thinks of me. It's affecting my job. I think my boss is getting tired of my mistakes. I've also forgotten to pay some bills. Creditors are calling all the time. My whole life is a mess." First, separate and identify each of the elements in the client's message. List them in outline fashion. Which do you think is most important? Now write the words you would say in attempting to partialize what Mr. K. has said. After you have written your partializing response, discuss your rationale for the words you have chosen. How do you think Mr. K. might react?

2. You are in the midst of an interview with Mrs. O., a 77-year-old widow who lives alone. During the conversation, Mrs. O. says, "Sometimes I get so lonely. All my friends have moved away or died. And my children don't visit me any more. One of them lives in town, but he doesn't even telephone me. I don't get birthday cards from them. It's like I'm already dead. And I'm really worried

about these spells. I don't know what's going to happen to me." First, separate and identify each of the elements in the client's message. List them in outline fashion. Which do you think is most important? Now write the words you would use in attempting to partialize Mrs. O.'s statement. After you have written your response, discuss your rationale for the words you have chosen. How do you think Mrs. O. might react to your words?

3. You are interviewing the seven-member, blended S. family. During the course of the exploration, Mr. S. says, "Since we married, we've had troubles with both my kids and hers. Basically, they dislike each other, they seem to hate us, and lately my wife and I have begun to fight. Finances have become a problem, and there's no time for anything. I don't think I've had a single minute to myself in six months. My wife and I haven't been out of the house on a weekend evening since our wedding." First, separate and identify each of the elements in the client's message. List them in outline fashion. Which do you think is most important? Now write the words you would say to partialize the complex message communicated by Mr. S. Discuss your rationale for the words you have chosen. How do you think Mr. S. might react?

4. You are interviewing Mrs. F. During the conversation, she says, "I've had troubles ever since I moved into this community. The school system is totally insensitive to the Latino population. My kids have begun to disrespect me and berate their own heritage. All the neighbors are WASP and haven't even introduced themselves to us. My mother is seriously ill in Peru, but I don't dare leave the children here while I feel they're in danger." First, separate and identify each of the elements in the client's message. List them in outline fashion. Which do you think is most important? Now write the words you might say in partializing this message. Discuss your rationale for the words you have selected. How do you think Mrs. F. might respond?

Going Beyond What Is Said

Going beyond what is said (Hammond, Hepworth, & Smith, 1977, pp. 137–169) occurs when you use your empathic understanding of the other person to extend slightly what he or she has actually said. Instead of mirroring exactly what clients have said, you use your knowledge, experience, and intuition to add to the feelings or meanings actually communicated. Through a process called *additive empathy*, you take a small leap beyond the spoken words, often bringing into greater awareness or clarity information that a client already knows. As Hammond, Hepworth, and Smith (1977, p. 137) suggest, your responses "go beyond what the client has explicitly expressed to feelings and meanings only implied in the client's statements and, thus, somewhat below the surface of the client's awareness. Consequently, these . . . add implicit material that the counselor infers from the client's message."

Going beyond what is said sometimes involves combining what clients say verbally with what they express nonverbally. In going beyond, however, continue to remain generally congruent with clients' overall direction and perspective. Although departing somewhat from their actual words, stay with their frame of reference. Rather than initiating your own agenda to move in an entirely new direction, build on the agenda your client has previously established.

For example, during the early part of a first meeting, a client who has immigrated from Haiti might say to a white worker, "Do they have any black social workers at your agency?" This may be an indirect communication (Shulman, 1984, pp. 20–28; Shulman, 1992, pp. 67–73) by a client who wonders whether a white worker has the capacity to understand him and to value his culture. He might prefer a black social worker. Perhaps he has had a negative experience with a white social worker at some point in the past. A white worker might respond to this question by saying something such as, "Yes, we have several black social workers [sharing information], although not as many as we should [sharing opinion]. I wish we had more [sharing opinion]. Since you ask that question though, I wonder are you saying that you'd prefer to work with a black social worker if that's possible [going beyond what is said]?"

Example

CLIENT: *(41-year-old mother)* I've been depressed for months. I've been down in the dumps ever since my son died in that terrible motorcycle crash. I feel so ashamed. Just before he drove off that morning I yelled at him for not picking up the dirty clothes in his room. Why did I have to say anything? My last memory is of me pestering him.

WORKER: *(reflecting feeling and meaning; going beyond what is said)* You feel guilty because of the last words you said to your son before he died. Do you sometimes feel that if you hadn't yelled at him about those dirty clothes, he might somehow still be alive?

Going beyond what is said is not a psychoanalytic interpretation, nor is it a wild speculation or guess. Rather, it involves putting into words those thoughts and feelings that a person probably thinks or feels but which have not yet been verbally expressed.

Example

CLIENT: *(12-year-old girl who was sexually molested by her mother's male friend)* My mother loved him very much and now he's gone.

WORKER: *(going beyond what is said)* You sometimes wonder whether you should have said anything. You think that maybe your mom might be happier and still have her boyfriend if you had just kept quiet about what he did to you?

◆ EXERCISE 7-7: GOING BEYOND WHAT IS SAID

For these exercises, assume that you are a social worker with a family counseling center. Respond in the spaces provided by writing the words you would say in using the skill of going beyond what is said.

1. You are interviewing Mr. K., a recently divorced 55-year-old man. You are in the process of problem exploration when he says, "I guess I'm a real wimp! I want so bad for her to come back home. All I do is think of ways to get her back. I make these plans about how to contact her; how to persuade her to change her mind. I constantly wonder what she's doing and whether she ever

thinks of me." Write the words you would say in going beyond what Mr. K. has said. After you have written your response, discuss your rationale for the words you have chosen. How do you think he might react to your response? Identify two other ways you might go beyond what he said.

2. You are in the midst of an outreach interview with Mrs. O., a 77-year-old widow who lives alone. Mrs. O. says, "Oh, I guess all children forget about their parents when they get old. They have so much to do, what with their work and their own children and all. They're busy. I know that. I guess I should be grateful for what I do have." Write the words you would use in attempting to go beyond Mrs. O.'s verbal statement. After you have written your response, discuss your rationale for the words you have chosen. How do you think Mrs. O. might respond? Identify two alternative means for going beyond what she said.

3. You are interviewing the seven-member, blended S. family. During the course of the exploration, Mrs. S. says, "Things are so bad between my kids and his kids that I've begun to wonder whether it's worth trying to continue like this. Maybe my children and I should just leave. We made it on our own before, and we can do it again." Write the words you would say in going beyond what Mrs. S. has said. Discuss your rationale for the words you have chosen. How do you think Mrs. S. might react to your response? Identify two additional ways in which you might go beyond what she said.

4. You are interviewing Mrs. F. At one point, she says, "Maybe it's not worth fighting this racist system. Maybe I should just accept things as they are. I'm just one person—just one woman—what can I do?" Write the words you might say in going beyond her verbal message. Discuss your rationale for the words you have selected. How do you think Mrs. F. might respond? Now write two other ways in which you might go beyond Mrs. F.'s statement.

Summary

During the exploration phase of social work practice, you encourage clients to share thoughts, feelings, and experiences about the problems that led to the contact. Through the process of exploration, you and the client gather and review information regarding the person, the problem, and the situation. This material is used by both parties. Together, they attempt to understand the development, maintenance, and current status of the problem and to identify strengths and resources that may be applied in problem-solving efforts. When combined with your professional knowledge and the client's input, the information collected contributes to the development of an assessment and plan for work.

Some beginning skills, such as seeking feedback, are also relevant in the exploring phase. However, the other social work skills are especially applicable for collecting data regarding the person, problem, and situation: (1) probing, (2) seeking clarification, (3) reflecting content, (4) reflecting feeling, (5) reflecting feeling and meaning, (6) partializing, and (7) going beyond what is said. The exploring skills are functional throughout the entire helping process; they are used again and again as you and the client examine the person-problem-situation.

◆ **EXERCISE 7-8: SUMMARY**

Assume that you are a social worker with a human service agency that offers a broad range of social services. You are actively exploring various aspects of the person-problem-situation. For each of the cases below, write the words you would use and describe the actions you might take in using the requested skills.

> *CASE SITUATION:* You are in the midst of the first interview with a teenage couple (an African American male and white female) who have sought counseling in advance of their forthcoming marriage. She says, "I know there are going to be lots of difficulties, and that's why we're here. We don't want the problems to get in the way of our feelings for each other."

1. Write the words you would say in reflecting the content of her statement.

2. Formulate an open-ended probe to follow her statement.

3. Write the words you would say in seeking clarification of her expression.

Following your response, she says, "One of the biggest problems has to do with my parents. My mom is fit to be tied and my dad is even worse. He's ready to kill Johnnie, and he doesn't even know him. I'm afraid they won't even come to the wedding. That would really hurt."

4. Write the words you would say in reflecting the feeling and meaning contained in her message.

5. Demonstrate how you would use the skill of going beyond what is said in response to her words.

CASE SITUATION: You are interviewing a family of seven (two parents and five children, ranging from 1 to 7 years of age) who had been sleeping in their dilapidated Chevy in a rest area on the highway. En route to another part of the country, where they hoped to find work, they ran out of money and food, and nearly out of gas. A policeman referred them to the agency.

During the interview, Mrs. Z., says, "We don't want charity. We just need enough money and food to make it there."

6. Write the words you would say in seeking clarification following her statement.

7. Write three probes that might yield useful information in your effort to understand and help the family.

Following one of your probes, Mrs. Z. says, "The baby hasn't been eating well. She's sleeping all the time and has a fever. Yesterday she vomited three times."

8. Write how you would seek clarification following her statement.

9. Then write the words you would say in asking three additional probes concerning the baby's health.

CASE SITUATION: You are interviewing for the first time a man, Mr. T., who has been accused of molesting the 13-year-old daughter of his woman friend. Mr. T. is required to receive counseling in order to stay out of jail while the judge considers whether to proceed with felony charges. He had been living with the girl's mother but has been required to leave the house during this period. During the interview, Mr. T. says, "I don't know why she said that I did those things. It really hurts me. I've been good to her and her mother. She's just lying and I don't know why. Maybe she's jealous."

10. First, write the words you would say in seeking clarification concerning his message.

11. Write three probes that might follow his statement.

12. Reflect the content of his statement.

13. Reflect the feeling and meaning contained in his message.

14. Demonstrate how you might use the skill of reflecting feeling in response to his statement.

15. Write three ways in which you might go beyond the words he has said.

CASE SITUATION: You serve as a social work investigator for Child Protection Services. Recently, your agency received a telephone call in which the caller alleged that Mr. and Mrs. D. have neglected and abused their children (ages 1 and 3). According to the caller, the mother sleeps while the children play in a filthy yard that contains animal waste, junk, and potentially dangerous materials—pieces of glass and sharp and rusty metal objects). The caller also reported that Mr. D. drinks heavily and beats both mother and children.

Mrs. D. has permitted you to enter the house, and the two of you have begun to talk. Mrs. D. says, "I know who made the complaint. It's that nosy neighbor from down the street. She's always poking into things that are none of her business."

16. Which of the exploring skills would you use in responding to Mrs. D.'s message? Discuss the rationale for your choice. Write the words you would say in using that skill.

17. Write five probes you would want to ask at some point during this interview with Mrs. D.

◆ EXERCISE 7-9: SUPPLEMENTAL

Now that you have had some beginning practice with the exploring skills, it is time to attempt an actual interview. Recruit a colleague from the school of social work. Inform your peer that you are practicing some social work skills and would like her or him to assume the role of client while you practice in the role of social worker. A classmate in this course or a student who has already completed it might be receptive to your request. Inform your colleague that you would need a few hours of time over the course of the next several weeks. Indicate that he or she would be expected to serve in the role of client and would be asked to behave as if voluntarily seeking help from a social worker. Inform your colleague that she or he would be expected to identify at least one problem or concern for exploration. Be sure to indicate, however, that you will only meet together a few times. Your peer should understand that you will probably not be of any actual help with the identified concerns, except to the extent that talking about them might be beneficial.

You might mention that it is often professionally useful for social workers and social work students to take on a client role. By assuming the role of clients, social workers may become more sensitive to the experience of seeking help. It is not always easy to ask for and receive assistance. Being clients can also significantly heighten social workers' awareness of things to do or not do in their own social work practice. The experience often leads to greater understanding of how to be an effective social worker.

Inform your colleague that the meetings will be audiotaped or possibly videotaped, and that you will prepare a written recording based on the interviews for your instructor to review. Indicate that you might discuss the interviews with your professor but that you will not reveal your colleague's name or other identifying characteristics. Mention that, as the client, he or she may read your written records when they are completed. Assure your colleague that in your notes about the interview, her or his identity will be disguised in order to ensure privacy. Also, ask your peer to use only a first name or nickname while being tape recorded during the interviews. Assure your colleague that you will not reveal his or her identity to anyone, including the instructor, without consent. Indicate that your colleague will not have to discuss any aspect of her or his personal life that would better be kept private. Tell your peer that if you happen to address a topic that he or she does not want to talk about, simply say, "I prefer not to talk about this." Notify your colleague that this is an entirely voluntary exercise. It is perfectly all right to decline this invitation. Finally, advise your colleague that you are still learning about social work and have not perfected the social work skills. You will probably make mistakes. Therefore, your colleague should realize that you may not really be of any actual help. The primary purpose of the exercise is for you to practice the social work skills. The purpose is not to provide actual social work services, nor to help your peer.

Request that the problem or concern identified as the focus of the meetings be a genuine one for which your colleague might conceivably seek service from a social worker. Ask your partner to make sure it is a problem or issue that is reasonably under control—one that has been addressed before and found to be manageable. The problem should not reflect an immediate crisis situation, nor should it be one with a potential to overwhelm your colleague's coping mechanisms. Students who are dealing with pressing concerns or crisis situations should avoid using them as the focus for these exercises, or they should refuse to participate altogether. After all, you are practicing skills here, not actually providing social work services.

If your colleague understands what is requested and provides consent, arrange for a time and place during the next week to meet privately for approximately 30 minutes. Inform your peer that you will assume the role of social worker during that entire period. Remind your partner that you will ask about a problem or concern for which social work services might be sought. Also indicate that your peer should assume the role of client from the moment you come together at the time of the scheduled meeting.

With your partner's consent, tape-record the interview. The overall purpose of the interview should be the exploration of your colleague's problem or concern as well as those aspects of the person and situation that may have relevance to the identified problem. Limit the interview to the preparing, beginning, and exploration phases only. Do not attempt to assess, contract, or in any way try to work toward resolution of the problem. Resist any temptation to speculate about underlying reasons for the problem or to offer theoretical interpretations. Do not give any advice. At the conclusion of the meeting arrange for a second 30-minute meeting in approximately one week.

1. When you have finished the 30-minute interview, leave your respective social worker and client roles. Then ask your partner for feedback concerning his or her thoughts and feelings about the experience. Request completely candid reactions to the following questions. (a) Did you feel comfortable and safe with me? (b) Did you feel that I was sincerely interested in you and in what you had to say? (c) Did you feel that I understood what you were trying to communicate? If so, what suggested to you that I did understand? If not, what indicated that I did not understand? (d) Were there aspects of yourself, the identified problems, or your situation that we should have explored that we did not? If so, what were they? (e) What information would you have liked to share that I did not ask you about? (f) In general, did you enjoy the experience? If so, what made it enjoyable? If not, what contributed to that? (g) What suggestions do you have for me concerning how the interview could have been better or more productive for you? Summarize your partner's feedback in the space below.

2. In the space below, discuss your own reaction to the interview. How did you feel about it? What did you like and what did you dislike about it? Discuss your performance of the social work skills. What would you do differently if you had a chance to conduct the interview again?

3. Play the audiotape or videotape. In a notebook designated for use in this course, prepare a transcript that accurately reflects what was said by whom. As part of the transcript, identify where you used specific skills. For example, if you responded to a statement of your partner by asking a question concerning his or her current situation, identify that response as a probe. If you requested further information about a statement he or she has made, indicate that as seeking clarification.

Use the following format to organize your transcript.

Suggested Format for Transcribed Recording

	Content	Skill Used	Your Gut Reactions	Your Analysis
Worker	Report words you said	Identify social work skill, if any, you used	Describe your subjective (e.g., thoughts, feelings, sensations) reactions to your own words during this exchange	Objectively evaluate your selection of the skill, if any, used and the quality of your performance
Client	Report words client said		Describe your subjective (e.g., thoughts, feelings, sensations) reactions to the client's words and gestures during the exchange	To the degree possible, objectively analyze the client's words and gestures during this exchange

Example

	Content	Skill Used	Your Gut Reactions	Your Analysis
Worker	How are you feeling during this difficult time?	Open probe	I have a hunch that the client wants to and probably needs to talk about her feelings, but I'm scared it might be too much for her—and perhaps for me—to handle.	I think this is an appropriate skill to use at this point. I also believe that I phrased it well. An open probe is more useful here than a closed probe.
Client	I'm just so tired all the time.		I can believe it! I'd be exhausted too. If I were in her shoes, I don't know if I could even get out of bed to face the world.	Client's words appear to represent an accurate description of her feelings at this time. I wonder, might she be depressed enough that she should talk to her medical doctor?
Worker	You're simply exhausted.	Reflecting feelings	She looks and feels terribly fatigued. I feel depleted as I try to feel what she's feeling.	I believe that I'm on target with this feeling reflection. I also think that it's the right skill to use at this time.

4. Using the exploration matrix reproduced below, indicate the degree to which you have explored various dimensions of the person-problem-situation. Use approximate percentages to reflect the extent of exploration within each category. For example, if you believe you have fully discussed the problem as it exists at the present time, write 100% in that box. If you have not talked at all about the origin and development of the problem in the past, place 0% in that category. Identify those aspects of the person-problem-situation that you would like to explore in a subsequent interview.

Exploration Matrix

	Present	Past	Future
Problem			
Person			
Situation			

In the space below, write three probes for each matrix category needing further exploration.

5. Based on your performance in the interview, use the following rating scales (where 0 = no proficiency and 10 = complete proficiency) to assess your current level of proficiency in the exploring skills.

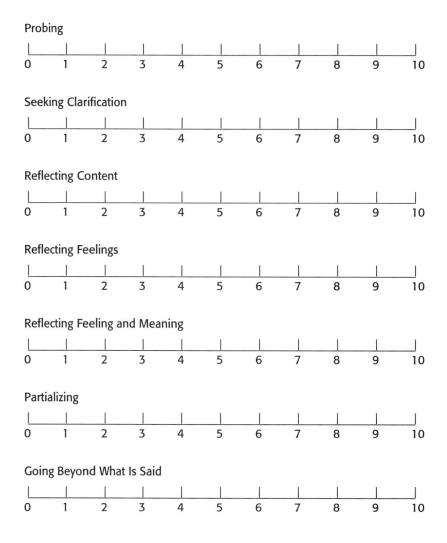

Probing

| | | | | | | | | | | |
|0|1|2|3|4|5|6|7|8|9|10|

Seeking Clarification

| | | | | | | | | | | |
|0|1|2|3|4|5|6|7|8|9|10|

Reflecting Content

| | | | | | | | | | | |
|0|1|2|3|4|5|6|7|8|9|10|

Reflecting Feelings

| | | | | | | | | | | |
|0|1|2|3|4|5|6|7|8|9|10|

Reflecting Feeling and Meaning

| | | | | | | | | | | |
|0|1|2|3|4|5|6|7|8|9|10|

Partializing

| | | | | | | | | | | |
|0|1|2|3|4|5|6|7|8|9|10|

Going Beyond What Is Said

| | | | | | | | | | | |
|0|1|2|3|4|5|6|7|8|9|10|

6. Finally, review your ratings to identify those exploring skills in which you remain less proficient (e.g., a score of 7 or less). Then, in the space below, outline the steps you might take to improve your skill in those areas.

Chapter 8

Assessing

Assessment is a fundamental process in all social work practice (Compton & Galaway, 1994, pp. 370–376; Hepworth & Larsen, 1990, pp. 193–317; Perlman, 1957, pp. 164–203; Richmond, 1944; Ripple, 1955; and Zastrow, 1995, pp. 75–104). When the exploration phase has progressed well, you and the client have gathered a substantial amount of information concerning the person-problem-situation. Together, you can then attempt to understand how the person and situation influence the problem, and vice versa. The understanding gained through assessment usually yields an emerging focus or direction. The assessment represents the base upon which a more detailed contract for work may be established. Two primary social work skills are involved in the assessment process: organizing descriptive information and formulating a tentative assessment.

Although social work assessment is an ongoing process rather than a finished product, the process does typically result in a written recording. However, the assessment frequently changes, sometimes dramatically, during the course of work with a client system. Also, it is a professional activity, not a technical one; social work assessments are not undertaken in exactly the same way with all clients. Rather, the nature of the assessment varies according to the unique characteristics of the person, the problem, and the situation, as well as those of the worker and agency. For example, if you served as a social worker in a crisis intervention and suicide prevention program, your assessment process would undoubtedly differ from that of a colleague who works in a general hospital providing discharge planning services for elderly patients seeking quality nursing care. A social worker who works with couples, whole families, or small groups engages in assessments quite unlike those of a practitioner who serves individual clients. A social worker who specializes in serving children conducts assessments that differ from those of one who serves adults. Similarly, social workers who practice from an ecological perspective conduct assessments that are considerably different from those of workers who adopt a task-centered approach. Because most professional social workers adhere to certain common conceptual premises and practice principles, however, there are similarities as well as differences in the nature of all social work assessment processes.

Through assessment, you and the client reach an understanding of the elements and forces within the person-situation system that affect and maintain the problems of concern. Together, you define the problems, determine who constitutes the primary client system, and identify other persons or systems that may need to be involved in the intervention process. You and the client begin to consider potential targets for change—those aspects that, if altered, might alleviate the problem. You predict probable consequences if things do not change. You also assess risk and determine how urgently intervention must be undertaken. Together, you identify strengths, assets, and resources, as well as probable obstacles to progress. In addition, you jointly explore intervention modalities, strategies, tasks, activities, and techniques that might be applicable to a resolution of the problems of concern. Finally, you develop a means for evaluation and identify a time frame for work.

Assessment is a multidimensional process and serves many purposes. In general, it leads you and the client to an understanding of the factors associated with the origin and maintenance of the identified problems as well as those factors that may aid or hinder their resolution.

There are many ways to structure a social work assessment and record the results. The Description, Assessment, and Contract (DAC) presented in Box 8.1 is only one of

---

BOX 8.1
Description, Assessment, and Contract (DAC)

I. Description
   A. Client Identification
   B. Person System, Family and Household System, and Community System
      1. Person System
      2. Family and Household System
      3. Ecological System
   C. Presenting Problems and Initial Goals
   D. Strengths and Resources
   E. Referral Source and Process; Collateral Information
   F. Social History
      1. Developmental
      2. Personal and Familial
      3. Critical Incidents
      4. Sexual

continued

B O X 8.1 *continued*

    5. Alcohol and/or Drug Use

    6. Medical/Physical

    7. Legal

    8. Educational

    9. Employment

   10. Recreational

   11. Religious/Spiritual

   12. Prior Psychological or Social Service

   13. Other

II. Tentative Assessment

  A. Person

    1. Identity and Structure

    2. Mood and Emotion

    3. Life Cycle Development

    4. Competence

    5. Risk

  B. Family/Household/Primary Social Systems

    1. Identity and Structure

    2. Mood and Emotion

    3. Life Cycle Development

  C. Environment

    1. Resources

    2. Sociocultural

  D. Summary Assessment

III. Contract

  A. Problems

    1. Client-Defined Problems

    2. Worker-Identified Problems

    3. Problems for Work

  B. Final Goals

  C. Plans

    1. Approach

    2. Client's Tasks or Action Steps

    3. Worker's Tasks or Action Steps

    4. In-Session Tasks or Action Steps

    5. Plans to Evaluate Progress

many formats that you might consider for the professional social work roles and functions in your specific practice setting.

As the title suggests, the DAC includes three major sections. First, the information gained through the exploration process is organized into a *description*. Second, ideas and hypotheses concerning the person-problem-situation that you and the client have generated are formulated into a tentative *assessment*. Third, the *contract* for work that you and the client have negotiated is summarized.

The description and assessment parts of the DAC are addressed in this chapter. The contract portion is reviewed in Chapter 9.

Completing the description portion of the DAC helps organize a great deal of information about a client system, the situational context, and the problems of concern. The assessment section yields processed information, which you and the client have generated as a result of analysis, synthesis, and the formulation of questions or hypotheses concerning the descriptive data. At first glance, the DAC may appear exhaustingly inclusive. Although it does cover a great many areas, several of these would obviously be inapplicable for work with many clients, problems, and contexts. Please adapt the DAC format to fit the unique needs and functions of your specific social work setting and function. Realize that there are numerous alternate schemes available to social workers (see, for example, Compton & Galaway, 1994). Ultimately, in consultation with your supervisors and agency colleagues, you must determine the utility of any assessment format for the particular circumstances of your social work practice.

Organizing Descriptive Information

Most social work interviews do not occur in so logical a fashion that a straight transcript of the interaction between worker and client would represent a coherent description of the available information. Therefore, your first step in the assessment process is to organize the information gained through exploration into a form that allows for efficient retrieval and examination. Typically, this involves arranging data according to certain categories that you and agency professionals consider to be significant.

Regardless of what organizational format is used to record information, you should always distinguish clearly between reported and observed information. Also, information that is the result of speculation or inference, deduction or induction, should be stated as opinion or hypothesis and differentiated from factual data. Assertions or opinions are not facts and should never be presented as such.

Descriptive organization allows you to present coherently information that you read, directly observe, or hear. The source of data should be noted. This information may be organized within the description part of the DAC in accordance with the following guidelines.

SUGGESTED FORMAT

Description Section of the
Description, Assessment, and Contract

    I. Description
        A. Client Identification
            In this section, place information that identifies the client and
            other relevant members of the person and situation systems.

Such data as names and ages of household members, birth dates, Social Security numbers, home addresses, places of work, telephone numbers, family doctors, and persons to notify in case of emergency may be included.

B. **Person System, Family and Household System, and Community System**

1. **Person System**

In this section, include information that helps describe the client further. Whenever possible, use information that comes from clients themselves and your direct observations, rather than your inferences. Also, identify the source of the information (e.g., "Client stated that he had 'just had his 32nd birthday,' " or "I observed that the client walked with a limp"). Whenever possible, quote significant words or phrases that the client uses in self-description. Be careful to use language that enhances the description of the person rather than stereotypes. For example, the statement "Mary is a 45-year-old, white, divorced female" tends to emphasize age, race, and marital status in a manner that could unnecessarily narrow the focus. Contrast that with this description, "Mary describes herself as a person with a 'great deal of energy and zest for life.' She describes herself as 'single and happy to be so.' She says she 'just turned 45 years old but feels 30.' "

Information based on your own observations of clients, such as their approximate height and weight, physical appearance, striking or characteristic features, speech patterns, and clothing may be included in this section. Ensure, however, that such information is actually relevant for the purpose of assessment, and note that it is based on your own observation.

2. **Family and Household System**

In this section, describe the client's family and household, or primary social system. If you have not included them elsewhere, include names, ages, and telephone numbers and addresses of significant persons. Family genograms and household eco-maps are useful tools for organizing this information. Cite the source of information and quote significant words and phrases.

3. **Community System**

In this section, describe the community system within which the identified client functions. Indicate the source of the information and include systems such as school, work, medical, recreational, religious, neighborhood, ethnic, cultural, and friendship affiliations whenever appropriate. The eco-map is a valuable tool for presenting this kind of information and can be included within this section.

C. Presenting Problems and Initial Goals

In this section, describe the problems or issues of concern as identified by the client or person who undertakes the reporting process (e.g., parent, teacher, or medical doctor). Clearly identify the source of the information and summarize the origin, development, and current status of the problems. Quote significant words and phrases that help to describe problems or goals. In this section, outline how social services came to be sought or required at this time. Also, if identified, record the initial, desired outcome of the social service as envisioned by the client. Unless the situation is of such an urgent or life-threatening nature that you are required to define the problem immediately, defer your own view of problems and goals until you and the client have undertaken a more thorough exploration and assessment.

D. Strengths and Resources

In this section, record information concerning the strengths, assets, and resources available within the client and situation systems. The kinds of resources indicated might include the involvement of a concerned relative, or sufficient financial assets, or an optimistic attitude, or a high energy level. Identify the source of this information about strengths and resources (the client, a family member, or your own observations or inferences). Where possible, quote significant descriptive words and phrases.

As a social worker, you encourage identification of strengths and resources in order to provide a balanced picture—one not solely characterized by problems, concerns, and deficiencies. Also, the assets identified here often become extremely relevant later, during the planning and intervention phases of work.

E. Referral Source and Process; Collateral Information

Summarize information concerning the source of the referral (who suggested or required that the identified client make contact with you) and the process by which the referral occurred. Information provided by sources other than the identified client or the client system (e.g., family member or a close friend) may be presented here. Cite the source by name, role or position, and phone number. Try to quote specific words and phrases used in describing the person-problem-situation and the events that prompted the referral.

F. Social History

In this section, include summary information about the identified client's social history and current social circumstances. Include data that is relevant to the purpose of your agency's involvement. Do not include information that is clearly irrelevant

to the person-problem-situation. Cite the source of the information (e.g., the client, a family member, or your own observation
or inference) and quote significant words and phrases wherever
possible. Depending on the agency program and the specific circumstances of the case, this section could contain some or all of
the following subsections.

1. **Developmental** You might include a description of a
   client's developmental history. You might provide information such as the nature of the client's birth, infancy, childhood, adolescent, and adult developmental processes.
   Specific information regarding events or experiences might
   be included here.

2. **Personal and Familial** You may summarize here information concerning the significant past and present personal, familial, and cultural relationships. Significant processes and
   events that influenced the client's biopsychosocial development and behavior may be recorded here.

3. **Critical Incidents** Summarize events or situations that might
   have been significant in some way. Identify experiences of
   violence, abuse, rape or molestation, suicides or suicide attempts, victimization, oppression, discrimination, or other
   critical events. Describe how these negative experiences affected the client. Also, summarize processes and incidents
   that were positive, growth-enhancing, empowering, or liberating in nature. Describe their effects on the client as well.

4. **Sexual** You may include here, if relevant to the social work
   purpose, information related to the person's sexual development and history. Avoid such exploration unless it is clearly
   relevant to the person-problem-situation.

5. **Alcohol and/or Drug Use** Because alcohol and/or drug
   abuse is so prevalent in our society, unless this topic is clearly
   irrelevant to the social work purpose, it is frequently useful to
   explore and summarize clients' history in these areas.

6. **Medical/Physical** Summarize here the person's medical and
   physical history. This might include presentation of illnesses,
   injuries, disabilities, and current physical health and well-
   being. Be sure to include the date of the client's most recent
   physical examination. The client's family doctor or source of
   medical care should be identified.

7. **Legal** Include here, as relevant, history of involvement in the
   criminal justice and legal system.

8. **Educational** Summarize the client's educational history.
   Both formal and informal educational experiences should be
   noted. Often educational experiences represent strengths or
   resources.

9. **Employment** Include here the client's employment history, including military and volunteer experiences. These may constitute strengths or resources.

10. **Recreational** Where applicable, summarize recreational activities that the client has undertaken over the years. Often, these endeavors constitute strengths or resources.

11. **Religious/Spiritual** Summarize current and past religious and spiritual affiliations and activities, and their meaning and significance for the client. Often, aspects of this dimension represent strengths or resources.

12. **Prior Psychological or Social Service** Summarize here previous involvement with psychological and social services. Where relevant, identify the names, addresses, and telephone numbers of agencies and service providers.

13. **Other** Include here any additional historical information.

The following example illustrates how you might organize and record information about the case of Mrs. Lynn Chase into the description section of the DAC.

Example
Lynn B. Chase

I. Description
A. Client Identification
Date of Interview: 11-21-94
Person Interviewed: Lynn B. Chase, Date of Birth: 10-05-60
Residence: 1212 Clearview Drive, City
Home phone: 223-1234
Employment: Assembler at Fox Manufacturing Co., phone 567-5678
Household Composition:
  Lynn Chase is married to Richard S. Chase, 35 years old, carpenter with Crass Construction Co.—work phone 789-7890
  Robert L. Chase, 12 years old, son, sixth-grade student at Hope Middle School
Referral Source: Sandra Fowles (former client of this agency and personal friend of Lynn B. Chase)

B. Person System, Family and Household System, and Community System
1. Person System
Lynn B. Chase prefers to be addressed as "Lynn." She described herself as "Irish-American" and said she was "raised

as a Roman Catholic." She indicated that her maiden name was Shaughnessy. She looked to me to be approximately five feet six inches tall and of medium build. On the date of this interview, I noticed that she was attired in slacks and blouse. I noticed what appeared to be dark circles under her eyes and the small muscles in her forehead looked to be tense. She seemed to walk slowly and expressed an audible sigh as she sat in a chair. She spoke in an accent common to this area—although in a slow and apparently deliberate fashion. I noticed that she occasionally interrupted her speech to pause for several seconds, then sighed before resuming her speech.

2. **Family and Household System**

During the interview, Mrs. Chase reported the following. The Chase family household is composed of Lynn, Richard, Robert, and a mongrel dog, "Sly." They have lived on Clearview Drive for five years and "like it there." Their family life is "busy." During the week, Monday through Friday, both Lynn and Richard work from 8:00 A.M. to 5:00 P.M. One parent, usually Lynn, helps Robert ready himself for school and waits with him until the school bus stops at a nearby street corner at about 7:15 A.M. Then she drives herself to work. After school, Robert takes the bus home, arriving at about 3:45 P.M. The parents arrive home at about 5:45 P.M.

Mrs. Chase indicated that Robert and his father have a very positive relationship. They go to sporting events together and both enjoy fishing. Robert was a member of a Little League baseball team this past summer, and his dad went to every game. She described her own relationship with Robert as "currently strained." She also indicated that while she "loves her husband, there is not much joy and romance in the relationship at this time."

3. **Community System**

Mrs. Lynn Chase indicated that the Chase family is involved with several other social systems. [see Figure 2.2 in Chapter 2.] Mrs. Chase reported that the family regularly attends the First Methodist Church, although "not every week." She said that she helps out occasionally with bake sales and other church activities. She indicated that Robert goes to Sunday school almost every week. Mrs. Chase said that her husband Richard is not really involved in many social activities. "He doesn't really have close friends. Robert and I are his friends." She said that Richard attends Robert's sporting events and goes fishing with him. Outside of work and those activities with Robert, Richard spends most of his time working on the house or in the yard. She said that Richard has a workshop in the basement and constructs furniture for the home.

Mrs. Chase reported that Robert has generally been a good student. She said that his teachers tell her that he is shy. When called upon in class, they said, he speaks in a quiet and hesitant voice but usually has thoughtful answers to questions. Mrs. Chase indicated that Robert had played very well on his Little League baseball team this past summer. She said that his coach thought highly of him and believed that he would make the high school team in a few years. Mrs. Chase said that her son has two or three close friends in the neighborhood.

Mrs. Chase reported that the family lives in a middle-class neighborhood. She indicates that, racially, it is minimally integrated and that the rate of crime is low and the neighbors friendly. She indicated that most of the homeowners tend to maintain their property carefully. Mrs. Chase said that their family is friendly with several families in the neighborhood and perhaps once every month or so, two or three of the families get together for dinner or a cookout.

Mrs. Chase reported that her job is "okay." She says she works "primarily because the family needs the income." She indicated that her husband truly loves his work: "Being a carpenter is what he's made for."

C. Presenting Problems and Initial Goals

Mrs. Chase said that she has been concerned lately because she and her son have been getting into arguments "all the time." She said that she does not know what causes the trouble. She reported that she finds herself becoming critical and angry toward Robert at the slightest provocation. She said that Robert is "not misbehaving" and that "it's really my own problem." She indicated that about six months ago she began to become more irritable with Robert and, to some extent, with Richard as well. She reported that she hasn't slept as well as she once did and has lost about ten pounds during that six-month period. She indicated that she took up smoking again after quitting some five years ago and has begun to have terrible headaches several times each week. Mrs. Chase reported that these problems began about the time that she took the job at Fox Manufacturing six months ago. "Before that I stayed at home to care for Robert and the household."

Mrs. Chase indicated that she hoped these services would help her to feel less irritable, sleep better, have fewer headaches, discontinue smoking, and have fewer arguments with her son and husband.

D. Strengths and Resources

Mrs. Chase acknowledged that she has an above-average intellect and a capacity to consider thoughtfully various aspects and dimensions of issues and problems. She reported that she is extremely responsible: "At times, too much so." She said that she is dependable in fulfilling her various roles. Mrs. Chase said that the family has sufficient financial resources and that her job has provided them with a "little bit more than we actually need." She indicated that the family lives in a "nice home in a safe and pleasant neighborhood." She said that her job is secure. She indicated that even though she has worked there only six months, her employer values her work highly, and her colleagues enjoy her company. Mrs. Chase reported that she has several close women friends who provide her with support and understanding. She mentioned, however, that "most of the time I am the one who provides support to them." She said that she feels loved by her husband and indicated that both her husband and son would be willing to do anything for her.

E. Referral Source and Process; Collateral Information

Mrs. Chase was referred to this agency by her friend and neighbor, Sandra Fowles. Ms. Fowles is a former client of this agency. In talking about Mrs. Chase, Ms. Fowles said that she is "an incredibly kind and thoughtful woman who would give you the shirt off her back. She may be too kind for her own good." Ms. Fowles made preliminary contact with the agency on behalf of Mrs. Chase and asked whether agency personnel had time to meet with her. A telephone contact with Mrs. Chase was subsequently made and an appointment scheduled for this date.

F. Social History

1. Developmental

Mrs. Chase reported that she believed that her mother's pregnancy and own her birth and infancy were "normal." She described her childhood as "unhappy" (see personal and familial section below).

2. Personal and Familial

Mrs. Chase reported the following about her personal and family history. She comes from a family of five. [Refer to Figure 2.1 in Chapter 2.] Her mother and father married while in their late teens. Her mother became pregnant with Lynn right away. Mrs. Chase is the eldest sibling. She has a brother one year younger and a sister five years her junior. Her parents are alive and, she says, "somehow still married." Mrs. Chase reported that during her childhood her father "was, and still is, a workaholic" who was rarely home. She described her mother as an "unstable, angry, and critical woman who never praised me for anything and always put me down." Mrs. Chase said that she "raised her younger sister" because, at that time, her mother was drinking all the time. Mrs. Chase indicated that her mother has refrained from drinking alcohol for the past three years and now goes to Alcoholics Anonymous meetings. She described the relationship between her mother and father as "awful—they have hated each other for years." She said, "They don't divorce because they're Catholic." Mrs. Chase said that her mother disapproved of her marriage to Richard because he had been married once before. She said that her mother would not attend her wedding. She said that her mother continues to berate Richard and "frequently criticizes the way I am raising Robert too."

Mrs. Chase reported that she rarely sees her mother, who lives 200 miles away, but does visit her sister about once a month. She said that her sister frequently needs emotional support, advice, and sometimes requires financial assistance. Mrs. Chase said that her sister had formerly abused alcohol and drugs, but the problem is "now under control."

Mrs. Chase said that her husband's family was "even more messed up than mine—if that's possible." She indicated that Richard also came from a family of five. She reported that his father abandoned the family when Richard was 9 and his sisters were 10 and 7. Mrs. Chase said that Richard's father had a serious drinking problem and that Richard remembered his father frequently beating both his mother and himself. Mrs. Chase indicated that Richard grew up in very destitute circumstances and learned to value money. She reported that even today he closely watches how the family's money is spent and worries that "we'll end up broke."

Mrs. Chase reported that her childhood was an unhappy one. She said that she remembers feeling "different" from other children. She indicated that as a child she was very shy, often afraid, and easily intimidated by other children. She reported that she often felt guilty and ashamed when parents or teachers criticized or corrected her. She indicated that she always tried to be "good" and, she continued, "for the most part—at least until my teenage years—I was." She said that she received excellent grades in school, although she remembered that she was sometimes taunted by other children, who called her a "teacher's pet." She said that she was slightly overweight during her childhood years and always thought of herself as "fat." She indicated that she had only a few friends during her younger years. She remembered one or two close childhood friends and described them as "shy and unattractive too." She recalled occasions when other children she had hoped would become friends "rejected" her. She remembered feeling sad and depressed on many occasions throughout her childhood.

3. **Critical Incidents**

She described an incident that occurred when she was about 12 years old. She said that a boy she had liked said she was "fat" in front of a group of her peers. She said that she felt humiliated and "stayed at home and cried for days." She also recalled a time when she was about 14 or 15. She said she had begun to explore her body and to experiment with masturbation. She indicated that she found it pleasurable but believed that such activity was sinful. She said that she discussed it with a priest during a regular confession. Mrs. Chase said that the priest became "very angry" at her and told her in a forceful way to "stop abusing herself in that disgusting way." She said that she felt horribly guilty and ashamed. She reported that it was this experience in particular that led her to later leave the Catholic Church.

Mrs. Chase indicated that she has never been the victim of rape or any other violent crime. She did recall, however, several occasions when a male relative (maternal uncle) attempted to kiss her and fondle her breasts. She said that each time, she pushed him away but she remembered feeling disgusted and dirty anyway. She said she was approximately 12 or 13 years old at the time and never told anyone about what had happened.

4. **Sexual**

Mrs. Chase reported that she did not date until her senior year in high school, when she went out with one boy a few times. She said that she "lost her virginity" in this relationship. She reported that had sex with "lots of boys" after that but that she "never really enjoyed it." She indicated that she met her future husband Richard about two years after graduation from high school and that, she was "pleased to say, has found it pleasurable and satisfying." She said that her marital sex life has been "great throughout our marriage" but she has not had much interest in sex during the last several months.

5. **Alcohol and/or Drug Use**

Mrs. Chase stated that she does not now have an alcohol or drug use problem but recalled drinking heavily as an 18-year-old. She said that after she graduated from high school, she ran around with a crowd that "partied a lot," and she drank a lot of alcohol at that time. She indicated that at that time she sometimes drank in order to "belong" and to feel comfortable in sexual relations with boys.

6. **Medical/Physical**

Mrs. Chase reported that she has not had any major medical or physical problems except for an enlarged cyst which was surgically removed from her uterus approximately eight years ago. She said that since that time she has been "unable to get pregnant again," although "both Richard and I wished we could have another child." She said that she has concluded that "it's not going to happen," and "I guess that's what's meant to be."

Mrs. Chase said that she "gained control of the weight problem" during the early years of her marriage by going to Weight Watchers. She reported that she has maintained her appropriate weight since that time. She indicated that she had recently spoken with her medical doctor about her occasional feelings of extreme fatigue, her change in sleep patterns, the loss of weight, and the periodic headaches. Her doctor could find nothing physically wrong and raised the question of "stress-related symptoms."

7. **Legal**

Mrs. Chase indicated that she and her family have not had any contact with the legal or criminal justice systems.

8. **Educational**

Mrs. Chase reported that she has a high school education and has taken approximately two years of college courses. She said that she had taken a course each semester until about six months ago, when she discontinued an evening course in order to "be at home more."

9. **Employment**

Mrs. Chase reported that she had worked in both secretarial and administrative positions following graduation from high school. She said that when Robert was born, she quit working outside the home in order to care for him. When he went to grammar school, she went back to work part time. She said that about three years ago, she was laid off from that job and was unable to find another part-time job that would enable her to be home at the end of Robert's school day. She indicated that a little more than six months ago, she and Richard decided that Robert was old enough to be at home alone for a couple of hours each day. She therefore applied for and was appointed to the full-time position at Fox Manufacturing.

10. **Recreational**

Mrs. Chase reported that over the years she has found great pleasure in gardening. She also said, however, that during the last year or so she has discontinued that activity. She indicated that she thought she could rekindle that sense of satisfaction if she were to resume gardening again at some point in the future.

11. **Religious/Spiritual**

Mrs. Chase reported that she quit going to the Catholic Church at the age of 18 when she graduated from high school. She said she did not attend any church until the birth of her child. She indicated that she and her husband then decided that they wanted their children to be brought up with some religious involvement. She remembered joining the neighborhood Methodist Church because "it was nearby."

12. **Prior Psychological or Social Service**

Mrs. Chase reported that she had not sought or received social or psychological services before. She reported that her mother has been in "therapy" for approximately four years.

◆ **EXERCISE 8-1: ORGANIZING DESCRIPTIVE INFORMATION**

For this exercise, assume that *you* are your own client. In a separate notebook, draft the description section of a written record as if you had, as a social worker, learned what you know about yourself as a person and about your situation. Identify one or two problems, issues, or goals for which you might conceivably consult a social worker. As do all human beings, social workers also confront obstacles, difficulties, and dilemmas throughout the course of life. Such challenges are inevitable. Therefore, build on the self-awareness exercises that you undertook in Chapter 2 by organizing information about yourself and your situation into a descriptive record. Use the DAC format to prepare the description portion of your own case record. Be sure to include your genogram and eco-map.

Formulating a Tentative Assessment

After recording the available information in an organized fashion, you—with the active participation of the client—begin to formulate a tentative assessment through analysis and synthesis, the primary cognitive skills involved in assessment. *Analysis* involves examining in fine detail various pieces of information about the person-problem-situation. For example, consider a 30-year-old woman who reports that she "feels anxious in the presence of men." Commonly, you and she would analyze how the different dimensions of anxiety interact. After collecting information about what the client thinks, feels, senses, imagines, and does when she experiences anxiety, you might piece together or track the precise sequence of events leading up to and following the feelings of anxiety. Such an analysis might reveal, for example, that the anxious feelings usually occur in the presence of men who are of her own age or older, who are confident and appear successful, and who are eligible for romantic consideration. Further analysis might enable you to uncover that the client does not feel anxious when she interacts with men in business or professional contexts, men who are married or who are gay, or men who are much younger or less successful than she is. Together, you might also discover that the client, when she first notices the early signs of anxiety, immediately begins to say to herself such things as, "I must not become anxious right now; if I become anxious, I will not say what I want to say and I will embarrass myself."

Analysis often leads you and the client to pinpoint critical elements or themes from among the various pieces of information. These become cornerstones in the formulation of a tentative assessment.

Synthesis builds on what is gained from analysis. It involves assembling significant pieces of information into a coherent whole by relating them to one another and to elements of your theory, knowledge, and experience base. For example, you might consider the client's anxiety in the presence of certain men in light of her experience growing up as an only child, attending girls-only grammar and high schools, and later enrolling in a women's college. These associations reflect the synthetic process of selecting various bits of data and configuring them into some form of relationship. Usually, social workers apply theoretical concepts to determine which pieces of information go with others, and to help grasp their relationship within the context of a unifying theme.

There are dozens of theoretical perspectives that you may find useful. For example, social learning theory may lead you to consider prior family and educational experiences in relation to certain concerns. Systems and ecological theories may lead you to consider how change or stress in one subsystem affects other subsystems. Ego-psychology might enable you to consider the defense mechanism of repression when attempting to understand certain behavior (e.g., a client's blocked memory in response to a question about combat experiences during a war). Fundamental concepts within role theory—role ambiguity, role change, and role conflict—may also be considered in relation to signs of frustration and stress. Crisis theory may help during emergencies, such as natural disasters, violent experiences, and other circumstances that involve sudden change. Family systems concepts may lead you to consider the effects of enmeshed boundaries or the absence of feedback processes within a family unit. Understanding of individual, family, and organizational development theories may allow you to identify tasks necessary for further growth and appreciate the possible communication value of a particular behavior pattern. Ecological perspectives may help you to appreciate how a particular phenomenon might represent an understandable adaptation to social and environmental circumstances. A plethora of theories may prove useful as you and your client seek to understand and synthesize significant information about the person-problem-situation.

In the early stages of work with a client, the analysis and synthesis processes of assessment must be considered tentative and speculative, because you and the client will usually not have conclusive support or confirmation for your ideas. In fact, analysis and synthesis typically yield a series of hypotheses or questions that guide the collection of additional information and the conduct of various intervention experiments. Throughout this assessment process, resist the temptation to conclude that you have the key to understanding the person-problem-situation. There are very few situations for which there is one key. Most of the time, there are many plausible hypotheses—your professional challenge is to identify those most likely to be useful for each unique set of circumstances. In addition to helping you formulate pertinent hypotheses and questions, analysis and synthesis usually lead you to highlight critical events and significant themes, patterns, and issues for further consideration.

As you do with descriptive data, organize the results of your analysis and synthesis into a coherent structure. The particular format used varies from agency to agency, program to program, and indeed from worker to worker. Nonetheless, virtually all social work assessment schemes refer in one way or another to various theoretical dimensions and include consideration of the person, problem, and situation. The organizing structure may be derived from a single theoretical perspective or, eclectically, from several.

Guidelines for using the assessment part of the DAC to organize social work assessments are presented below. When prepared in written form, the assessment follows the description portion of the Description, Assessment, and Contract.

SUGGESTED FORMAT

Assessment Section of the
Description, Assessment, and Contract

II. Tentative Assessment
    A. Person
        1. Identity and Structure
            Within this dimension, consider the problem as it relates to the client's identity and view of self. You may include your own, as well as the client's, hypotheses, but identify the source of the opinion. It may be relevant to include an assessment of a client's self-concept (its nature and strength) as well as the degree of positive or negative self-esteem. Note the primary role identities and consider the extent of congruence among them. Observe the client's sociocultural affiliations and personal value systems. Assess the relative flexibility or rigidity of the client's personal boundaries. Note whether the client tends to refer to inner or outer resources when making decisions.

            Note the nature of the person's defensive and coping processes and assess their relative strength and functionality.

Assess the strength of the client's capacities for coping with stress and change, ability to control desires and impulses, and vulnerability to decompensation. Assess how adaptive and congruent the client's personal, interpersonal, and lifestyle characteristics are in relation to the identified problem.

2. **Mood and Emotion**

   In this section, assess the person's mood and emotional state in relation to the identified concerns. Consider whether there might be other strong emotions that are not being expressed. Assess the relative congruence between verbal and nonverbal expressions of emotion.

3. **Life Cycle Development**

   Consider the problem in terms of the person's phase of life cycle development. Identify the developmental tasks and issues with which the client may now or may soon be dealing and, if relevant, assess the congruence between chronological and developmental age.

4. **Competence**

   In this section, consider the problem in relation to the person's relative level of competence to fulfill age- and situation-appropriate roles and tasks. Assess whether the person is currently capable of self-care and self-control, and determine the degree to which the client can participate in the helping process.

5. **Risk**

   Assess, if relevant, the degree of risk to the person's life and well-being, as well as any potential danger to other people. Assess the risk of suicide, homicide, violence, abuse, and neglect as it relates to the particular circumstances of the case.

B. **Family/Household/Primary Social Systems**

1. **Identity and Structure**

   In this section, assess the problem in relation to the family or household system's identity and structure. Consider the relevance of the system's ethnic, religious, and cultural traditions. Review the system's history and generate expectations for its future. Assess the degree of energy, cohesion, and adaptability of the system. Assess how the needs and aspirations of the system's members are addressed. Characterize the system in terms of its operating procedures; the distribution of power and the availability of resources; the assignment of roles; the boundaries between members, subsystems, and other systems; and the processes of decision making.

   Assess the problem in relation to the nature and extent of communication and interaction among members of the system. Determine the form of communication, the degree of understanding, and the quality of relationships among members of the system.

2. **Mood and Emotion**

Assess the problem in relation to the dominant emotional climate within the system. Identify feelings that are disguised or expressed indirectly and assess the degree of affection and support that members give to and receive from one another.

3. **Life Cycle Development**

Consider the system in terms of its life cycle phase. Assess the problem in relation to the issues that might apply to a system in this phase, and identify the system's developmental tasks that may need to be undertaken.

C. **Environment**

1. **Resources**

Assess the problem in relation to the extent and sufficiency of resources within the environment. Determine the relative availability of basic resources such as money, shelter, food, clothing, and social and intellectual stimulation. Characterize the sociopolitical and economic environment. Highlight potential resources and opportunities and identify deficiencies and obstacles within the ecological system.

2. **Sociocultural**

Consider the problem within the context of the sociocultural values and traditions of the environment. Determine their relationship, if any, to the identified concerns and identify how they might be utilized in meeting needs and addressing problems.

D. **Summary Assessment**

Provide a narrative summary of the assessment of the problem in relation to concrete and theoretical aspects of the person, family and household, and ecological systems. Address the legal and ethical implications of the case. Assess the effects of the problem on the person and situation, and generate hypotheses concerning the possible functions the problem may serve for both systems. Formulate projections concerning the potential benefits as well as the risks that could possibly occur should the problem be resolved.

The case of Mrs. Lynn B. Chase can be used to provide an example of a tentative assessment, organized as part of the DAC.

Example
Lynn B. Chase

II. Tentative Assessment
A. Person
1. Identity and Structure

Based on the information learned in the first interview, it appears to me that Mrs. Chase views herself primarily as wife and mother. She also appears to assume the role of "big sister" with her siblings. She seems open to input from others, including this worker, and has a well-established sense of personal identity in relation to family roles. She seems less clear and secure, however, when it comes to roles outside the family system. In these other areas, she appears more uncertain and less inner-directed.

Questions: Who is Lynn Chase when she is not wife, mother, daughter, or sibling? What are her personal life goals apart from raising a family? How does she see herself as an individual person? What does she see as her major personality characteristics?

Mrs. Chase appears to reflect a coherent and integrated personality. Her lifestyle has been stable and congruent. She seems to feel a strong sense of obligation and responsibility toward others, especially her son and husband. She appears to have superior thinking capacities and probably possesses above-average intelligence. She appears less comfortable, however, when it comes to permitting herself time for free and spontaneous play or recreation. In the past, she seems to have enjoyed gardening, but at least since she starting working at Fox Manufacturing, she appears to have become reluctant to allow herself time for "unproductive" leisure and relaxation. I wonder if she may have a tendency to assume disproportionately high levels of personal responsibility. If so, she might feel "stressed and burdened" and, perhaps, "guilty" should she be unable to fulfill those responsibilities in the manner she expects of herself.

Questions: How similar is Mrs. Chase to her father in terms of a workaholic, or compulsive, approach to life? How critical is she of herself? What happens when Mrs. Chase takes time for herself alone? Does she begin to feel anxious or uncomfortable without a specific worthwhile and "productive" goal?

Mrs. Chase appears to have well-developed coping skills and defense mechanisms that have served her well over the years. Presently, however, she experiences sleep loss and heightened anger and irritability; she has frequent arguments with her son and, to a lesser degree, her husband. These may be indications that her coping capacities are diminishing somewhat. The patterns may also be somewhat reminiscent of Mrs. Chase's description of her own mother, whom she described as "unstable, angry, and critical." These problems appear to have first occurred at about the time she went to work outside the home at Fox Manufacturing.

Questions: What does Mrs. Chase think about when she lies awake at night? Might her reactions to working outside the home be in some way related to her view of her father as "a workaholic who was never at home?"

2. **Mood and Emotion**

In my opinion, Mrs. Chase looks sad. She may be depressed. I also notice signs of some anxiety or stress. Over the past several months, she has experienced frequent feelings of anger and irritation. She does not recall having such feelings to this degree of intensity or frequency at any previous time in her life.

Questions: Might Mrs. Chase feel ambivalent—perhaps guilty—about working outside the home and being less available to her son and husband? Does she have feelings of anger of which she is unaware or which she does not directly express? If so, at whom or what is she angry? Is she angry that she's working outside the home? Disappointed or sad that her son is growing up? Resentful that her husband is happy in his work? Does anger associated with mother and father remain unexpressed? Is there any indication that depression may run in the family? Is she sad that she cannot have another child? Is she ambivalent and anxious about her employment? Might there be stress as a result of role strain and conflict?

3. **Life Cycle Development**

It appears that, at age 34, Mrs. Chase may be in the middle of the adulthood phase of the human life cycle. She has expended much energy over the past 12 years in child-rearing and homemaking activities. Relatively recently, she took a full-time job outside the family home. At this point, it is not certain that this work is or will be as satisfying to her as child-rearing and homemaking have been. There may be role strain or conflict between the family and work roles. She and her husband had wanted more children, but her medical condition (the cyst or the surgery to remove it) appears to prevent that from happening.

Questions: What led her to seek employment outside the home? How well does she really like the work? Is it congruent with her long-term, personal life goals? What thoughts and feelings does she have about her 12-year-old son in relation to her employment? How does her husband feel about her working? Has she successfully resolved the disappointment concerning her inability to have more children?

4. **Competence**

Based on the first interview, I believe that Mrs. Chase shows a high level of competence. She has coped well with life transitions and problems. In spite of the current concerns, she continues to function well in several important social roles.

5. **Risk**

Although reporting feelings of depression, I do not believe that Mrs. Chase currently represents any danger to herself or others. In response to a question concerning suicidal thoughts and actions, she indicated that she has never taken any self-destructive action and does not have suicidal thoughts. Similarly, she reported that she has never experienced thoughts nor taken actions intended to hurt another person.

B. **Family/Household/Primary Social Systems**

1. **Identity and Structure**

Based on information gained in the first interview, it appears to me that the Chase family system is structured in such a way that Mrs. Chase is the primary executive or manager. She seems to have responsibility for the bulk of the family's activities. She relieves Mr. Chase of most household and parenting duties. She is the primary housekeeper and parent. She plans and prepares meals, does the shopping, coordinates transportation for Robert, and pays the bills. In several ways, Mrs. Chase seems to care for both the males in the family system. Until Mrs. Chase began full-time work outside the home, the family rules and role boundaries had been clear. Mrs. Chase sought ideas and input from Richard and Robert, but she made and implemented most decisions. Now that she is home less often and there are increased demands on her, some of the rules and roles may be in flux. At this point, it seems that Mrs. Chase is trying to maintain her previous family duties while adding additional occupational responsibilities.

Questions: If Mrs. Chase were forced to choose between the two, would she prefer to work outside the home or remain as the primary parent and manager of the home? If she were to continue to work outside the home, what changes would she, Richard, and Robert need to make in order to lessen the extent of her household and family responsibilities? Would they be willing to make such changes? What would it be like for her to decrease her responsibility for and control of family and household duties?

Members of the Chase family appear to have adopted many of the stereotypes of men, women, and children projected by the dominant North American culture. Mrs. Chase's adolescent experience and the shame she felt during the confession to a priest may continue to affect her today in relation to her son Robert. She may wonder about his unfolding sexuality and be concerned about how he will deal with adolescent changes. Should Mrs. Chase and her family desire to change their family rules, roles, and communication patterns, it may be useful to explore with them some of their gender- and age-based assumptions and expectations.

Generally speaking, it appears that communication patterns within the Chase family are relatively open. They seem to like each other. Sometimes, however, the male family members appear to "hint" at rather than clearly state their preferences. Mrs. Chase seems to respond to such indirect expressions by guessing what those wishes might be. For example, at a family dinner recently, Robert "made a face" when he was served his meal. Mrs. Chase then asked, "What's the matter?" Robert said, "Nothing." Mrs. Chase asked, "Don't you like the meal? I'll get you something else." Robert said, "Don't bother, this is okay." Mrs. Chase said, "No, I'll get you something else to eat." Robert said, "Oh, okay. Thanks." At this point, Mrs. Chase interrupted her own meal, got up, and prepared something Robert wanted to eat.

Questions: Are the communication patterns in the family such that the male family members tend to avoid full and direct expression? Does Mrs. Chase try to "read their minds" and subtly contribute to this process? Do Richard and Robert realize that they sometimes communicate indirectly through facial expressions and bodily gestures? What might be the consequence of more direct and full verbal expression within the family system? What would each family member stand to gain or lose?

Robert's adolescence and Mrs. Chase's full-time outside employment probably represent the most significant stressors the family system now faces. Although the family system appears capable of making adaptive changes, it remains uncertain whether the members will choose to do so. If not, I think it unlikely that the family can tolerate Mrs. Chase's full-time employment outside the home for too much longer.

Questions: Would Mrs. Chase be willing to let her husband and son assume greater responsibility for household and family tasks? Would they be willing to do so? How would the family members anticipate coping with the inevitable stress that accompanies change? What stress-reducing mechanisms do the family members have that might be applied during transitional periods such as this one?

2. **Mood and Emotion**

Mrs. Chase appears to have the affection and support of her husband and son. Her mother, father, and siblings do not appear to provide much in the way of interest, understanding, or support. She does have several friends who care a great deal about her. In these relationships as in most others, however, she seems to "give more than she receives" and "knows more about others than others know about her." Nonetheless, she believes strongly that both her husband and son would be willing to do anything they could to help her.

3. **Life Cycle Development**

As a system, the Chase family is moving into a phase when an adolescent child stimulates a number of issues and decisions for the youth, the parents, and the family system as a whole. According to Mrs. Chase, Robert is beginning to experience bodily changes and has become more self-conscious and self-centered. These changes may be affecting the nature of the relationship between Robert and Mrs. Chase and perhaps that with his father as well. Mrs. Chase, directly or indirectly, may be uneasy and unclear concerning her parenting role during this time. It is not certain how Mr. Chase is responding to Robert's adolescence.

Questions: What specific issues and dilemmas, if any, is Robert confronting? Is Mrs. Chase comfortable with an increase in her son's autonomy and personal responsibility? How is Mr. Chase relating to his son during this time? What hopes and dreams do Mr. and Mrs. Chase have for Robert's future? What doubts and fears do they have about him? What were the adolescent years like for Mr. and Mrs. Chase? Are they experiencing feelings reminiscent of their own adolescence?

C. **Environment**

1. **Resources**

There are sufficient resources within the environment of the Chase family. They have adequate opportunities to meet their needs and aspirations. They have not been subject to oppression or discrimination.

Mrs. Chase does report being concerned about "teenage boys" in the neighborhood. She wonders whether Robert might be influenced by "bad boys" and get into some trouble.

Questions: Might Mrs. Chase believe that she is less able to protect Robert from the influence of the neighborhood boys now that she works outside the home? Does she feel an obligation to keep Robert entirely away from negative influences? Does she suspect that Robert might be especially susceptible to such influences and that he might be unable to make responsible decisions? Might she be associating Robert's adolescence with her own teenage experience?

2. **Sociocultural**

There appears to be a favorable match between the sociocultural affiliation and traditions of the Chase family and the surrounding community. They are well accepted within the community.

D. **Summary Assessment**

Mrs. Chase and her family have a lengthy history of competent functioning. The family members individually and as a system appear to be coherent and stable. However, Mr. Chase, Robert, and especially Mrs. Chase have begun to experience strain associated with changing demands upon them. These demands were initiated by two important events. First, about six months ago Mrs. Chase began to work full-time outside the home. This has significantly increased the extent of her responsibilities and has caused her considerable stress. It appears that she has tried to continue to "do it all." The other family members are reacting to her increased stress and perhaps anticipate that they may have to change themselves. Second, Robert is beginning to undergo early adolescent changes. The family system has yet to accommodate to the implications of the "boy-becoming-man" process.

There are several factors that may have relevance to the identified problems. First, Mrs. Chase comes from a family of origin where she assumed adult responsibilities from an early age. She reports that her mother abused alcohol and her father was a workaholic. It is possible that Mrs. Chase tends to assume substantial responsibility for others—perhaps especially family members—because she was socialized to do so from an early age. Working full-time outside the home may represent a major psychosocial conflict for her. One part of her, perhaps like her father, may be strongly tempted to invest a great deal of time and energy in her employment. Another part may feel much anxiety and uncertainty when she is away from the home. She is so familiar with the role of caretaker for her husband and son that she may sometimes feel anxious when she is working and unable to meet their needs. Second, Mrs. Chase wanted to have more children, but a medical condition has prevented that. She may not, as yet, have fully explored and grieved for the loss of her hopes for additional children. She may also invest greater energy in her son Robert, since "he's my only child." Third, Robert, as an early adolescent, may be troubled by physical, psychological, and social changes he is undergoing. This, along with Mrs. Chase's employment, is probably causing considerable systemic stress within the family. As a person emotionally attuned to the family, Mrs. Chase is understandably affected during this transition period. She may be confronting the limitations of her family-centered role identification.

If the problems of sadness, anxiety, and irritation were magically to disappear, it is likely that Mrs. Chase would continue to work outside the home while maintaining responsibility for most of the child and home care. The symptoms may be a signal that she's trying to do or be too many things. Perhaps it's time to reconsider her primary role identifications and her attitudes concerning family, employment, and leisure.

Questions: Are the needs of Robert such that, working full-time outside the home, Mrs. Chase believes that she is not providing him what he needs to develop into healthy adolescence and adulthood? Has he had special needs that she feels she is neglecting? Has her husband expressed concerns or indicated discomfort with her employment? What is her view of the ideal way to spend free time? If the family system were to regain its previous level of equilibrium by Mrs. Chase terminating her outside employment and returning to her traditional family and household roles, what would be the advantages and disadvantages to her, to Mr. Chase, to Robert, to the family system as a whole? If she maintains her employment, what might be other means through which the family could regain a sense of reasonable equilibrium?

◆ EXERCISE 8-2: FORMULATING A TENTATIVE ASSESSMENT

For this exercise, please review the information that you organized into the description section of your own case record as part of Exercise 8-1. Based upon what you know about yourself and what you included in the description, proceed to formulate a tentative assessment through analysis and synthesis of the available data. Record it in your course notebook. In conducting your assessment, however, remember that much of what you determine remains tentative and speculative—even in this case, where you are assessing yourself. These are ideas or hypotheses that await later support and confirmation. Formulate your ideas in accord with the format provided above in the assessment section of the Description, Assessment, and Contract.

Summary

During the assessment phase of social work practice, you and the client attempt to make sense of the data gathered during the exploration phase. The assessment gives the parties involved a perspective from which to initiate the process of contracting. Two skills are especially pertinent to the assessment phase: organizing information and formulating a tentative assessment.

◆ **EXERCISE 8-3: SUMMARY**

Building on the first interview you had with your colleague (see Exercise 7-9), conduct a second interview. Ensure that the interview setting is private, and again tape-record the meeting. Using the exploring and other relevant skills addressed thus far, interview your colleague with a view toward formulating an assessment. At the conclusion of the meeting, arrange for another meeting in about one week.

1. At the conclusion of the interview, ask your partner for feedback concerning his or her thoughts and feelings about the experience. Ask your colleague for a frank reaction to the following questions. (a) Did you feel comfortable and safe with me serving as a social worker? (b) Did you feel that I was sincerely interested in you and in what you had to say? (c) Did you feel that I understood what you were trying to communicate? If so, what contributed to this? If not, what led you to believe that I did not understand? (d) What information did we discuss that helped you to better understand or assess those factors that contribute to the problems or issues of concern? (e) What material was neglected that might have contributed to a more complete and accurate assessment? (f) In general, was the experience satisfying? If so, what factors helped to make it so? If not, what contributed to that? (g) What would you suggest that I do in the future in order to improve the quality of my interviewing skills? Summarize your partner's feedback in the space below.

2. In the space below, record your own reaction to the conversation. How did you feel about the interview? What did you like and what did you dislike about it? Do you believe that you used all of the relevant skills during the interaction? Which skills do you seem to perform well? Which skills need more practice? What information did you gain that will contribute to the formulation of an assessment? What additional information would be useful? What would you do differently if you were to redo the interview?

3. In your notebook, organize the relevant information from both the first meeting (review your earlier transcript) and this second interview according to the format provided in the description section of the Description, Assessment, and Contract.

4. Using the information that you organized into a description, proceed to formulate a tentative assessment through analysis and synthesis of the available data. Record it in a separate notebook. Remember to continue to disguise the identity of your colleague. Also, recall that much of what you determine remains tentative and speculative. These are ideas or hypotheses that await further support and confirmation. Formulate your observations and ideas in accordance with the format provided above in the assessment section of the Description, Assessment, and Contract.

5. After you have completed the description and assessment portions of the case record, play the audiotape or videotape. Study the tape for two purposes. First, make note of significant information that you neglected to include in your description and assessment. Add it to the appropriate sections of your DAC. Second, based on your performance in the interview, use the rating scales provided (where 0 = no proficiency and 10 = complete proficiency) to assess your current level of proficiency in the individual social work skills.

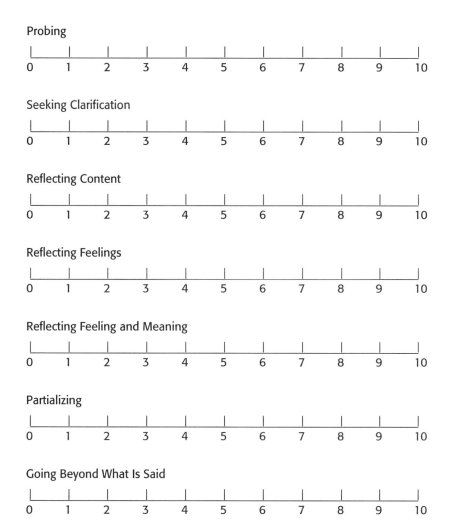

Probing

0	1	2	3	4	5	6	7	8	9	10

Seeking Clarification

0	1	2	3	4	5	6	7	8	9	10

Reflecting Content

0	1	2	3	4	5	6	7	8	9	10

Reflecting Feelings

0	1	2	3	4	5	6	7	8	9	10

Reflecting Feeling and Meaning

0	1	2	3	4	5	6	7	8	9	10

Partializing

0	1	2	3	4	5	6	7	8	9	10

Going Beyond What Is Said

0	1	2	3	4	5	6	7	8	9	10

6. Review your ratings to identify those individual skills in which you remain less proficient (e.g., a score of 7 or less). Then, in the space below, outline the steps you might take to improve your skill in those areas.

7. Now that you have completed these exercises, use the following rating scales (where 0 = no proficiency and 10 = complete proficiency) to conduct a summary evaluation of your proficiency in the assessing skills.

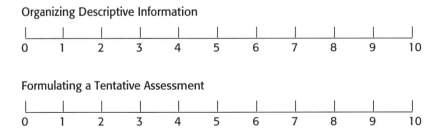

Organizing Descriptive Information

| | | | | | | | | | | |
|0|1|2|3|4|5|6|7|8|9|10|

Formulating a Tentative Assessment

| | | | | | | | | | | |
|0|1|2|3|4|5|6|7|8|9|10|

8. Finally, review your ratings to identify those assessing skills in which you remain less proficient (e.g., a score of 7 or less). Then, in the space below, outline the steps you might take to improve your skill in those areas.

Chapter 9

Contracting

Contracting follows integrally from the assessment process. It yields clearly identified problems, specific goals for work, a change program for pursuing the goals, and, often, one or more discrete action steps. Usually, you and the client also determine a means to evaluate progress toward goal achievement.

These processes typically begin during or shortly after the assessment process. Skills especially applicable to this phase of practice include: (1) reflecting a problem, (2) sharing your view of a problem, (3) specifying problems for work, (4) establishing goals, (5) developing an approach, (6) identifying action steps, (7) planning for evaluation, and (8) summarizing the contract.

Reflecting a Problem

By using the skill of *reflecting a problem*, you demonstrate to clients that you understand their view of an identified problem. Reflecting a problem is an important form of active, empathic listening; it constitutes the beginning of the contracting process.

Clients, especially adults who voluntarily seek social services, are usually quite ready to share their views about the problems of concern, but some clients may need support, guidance, and encouragement to do so. In other circumstances, you may have to assume the major responsibility for both problem specification and goal determination.

Regardless of the context, do not assume that the problems clients first identify will necessarily remain the focus for work. They may do so, but as a result of exploration with an attentive social worker, clients often identify concerns that are more pressing or more fundamental than those they initially mentioned. Some clients test workers by trying out a near problem first. Based on your competence in responding to it, they may then move on to identify a real problem of much greater significance.

As you begin to practice the skill of reflecting a problem, please use the format outlined below. Later, when you gain greater proficiency, experiment with alternate formats.

SUGGESTED FORMAT FOR REFLECTING A PROBLEM

As you see it, one of the problems you'd like to
address in our work together is _____.

Example

CLIENT: My wife left me—sure, for very good reasons—but I'm really down about it. She has left me before but always came back. This time I know she won't. She's gone for good, and I don't know what to do. I can't go on the way things are. I'm so sad and lost without her.

WORKER: (reflecting problems) As you see it, there are two major problems you'd like to address in our work together. First, you feel terrible. You're lonely and depressed, and you find it hard to function well when you feel that way. Second, you're unsure of how to get on with your life without your wife.

Reflecting a problem is, of course, a form of active listening. If you accurately paraphrase the problem as experienced by clients, they are likely to respond, "Yeah, that's right," or something similar, to verify your reflection. Nonetheless, it is often useful to precede problem reflections with reflections of feeling, content, or feeling and meaning, to show you understand clients' experience. Also, it may be helpful to follow your problem reflection by applying the skill of seeking feedback. For instance, following the worker's response in the example shown above, the client might be asked, "Are these the major problems you'd like to work on?"

It is very important to communicate your understanding of the nature of the problems of concern as the clients themselves see them. In effect, you show clients that you intend to help them address the problems *they* wish to address. By confirming that their view of the problems is legitimate, you communicate respect for them as persons and for their right to self-determination.

◆ **EXERCISE 9-1: REFLECTING A PROBLEM**

For these exercises, assume that you are a social worker with a family counseling center. In the spaces provided, write the words you would say to reflect a problem as the client sees it.

1. You are interviewing Mrs. O., a 77-year-old widow who lives alone in a small apartment. She says, "Most of the time, I feel all right. But I'm really beginning to worry that these spells might be a sign of a serious illness." Write the words you would use in reflecting a problem as Mrs. O. sees it.

2. You are in the midst of an interview with the blended S. family. Mr. S. says, "I guess I can say this in front of the children—they know so much already. Anyway, today at work, I learned that there will soon be massive layoffs. It's likely that I will lose my job within the next three or four weeks. Just what we need, to top off the rest of our problems." Write the words you would say in reflecting a problem as Mr. S. sees it.

3. You are conducting an interview with Mrs. F., the Latina woman who is concerned that her children are mistreated. She says, "I guess I've never felt we really belong here in this town. Nobody really seems to like us or want us here. I guess we just don't fit." Write the words you might say in reflecting a problem as Mrs. F. sees it.

Sharing Your View of a Problem

Based on your exploration and assessment of the person-problem-situation, you may identify one or more problem areas that the client has not mentioned. Or you may take a somewhat different perspective on a problem the client has identified. For example, a client may identify his wife's nagging as a problem. After gaining some insight into what the client views as nagging, you might ask, "I wonder, might what you call *nagging* be a sign of a more basic problem? Could it be that the two of you have trouble communicating so that you really understand one another?"

Sometimes, you must assume primary responsibility for problem and goal definition. For example, when the situation is immediately life-threatening (e.g., a client is suicidal, psychotic, or heavily intoxicated) or the client is involuntary (e.g., required to seek counseling or face felony charges for child abuse), you may define the problem for the client. Then the client decides whether or not to participate in the process.

Even when the situation is neither life-threatening nor involuntary, you may legitimately share your view of possible problems. Based on the tentative assessment, you may suggest that additional problems be considered, or that an identified problem be defined differently. You may have professional knowledge or previous experience that leads you to consider a problem area not previously discussed. For example, suppose a client describes feelings of constant fatigue, difficulty sleeping, loss of appetite, decreased interest in pleasurable activities, and diminished social involvement. You would probably wonder whether the client might be mourning the loss of someone or something of value, be physically ill, or perhaps be significantly depressed.

You will naturally form opinions as to what factors may be relevant to the clients' present situation. Often, you will share these ideas with clients—but this must be done in the same way you share all your professional opinions. That is, you communicate them as opinions or ideas to consider, not as indisputable facts, and you allow clients the freedom to agree or disagree. As a part of this process, you routinely seek feedback from the client concerning these newly identified or redefined problems.

In practicing this skill, follow the format outlined below.

SUGGESTED FORMAT FOR REFLECTING A PROBLEM

As we have talked about you and your situation, I have been wondering about _____. What do you think? Is that a problem we should consider too?

Example

CLIENT: (Lisa, partner in a lesbian relationship) We fight all the time. Virtually every single day we have a knock-down, drag-out fight. Ever since we moved in together, two months ago, we have fought like cats and dogs. We were so great together before we decided to share the apartment. We don't hit each other, but there sure is a lot of yelling and screaming.

WORKER: (sharing her view of a problem) As we've talked about your relationship and how moving in together has affected it, I've been wondering about the question of roles and expectations. It seems to me that moving from a dating relationship to a live-in relationship represents a very significant change—one that might leave each of you uncertain about what the other wants and needs in this new form of relationship. What do you think? Might the uncertainty about expectations now that you live together be an issue we should address too?

◆ EXERCISE 9-2: SHARING YOUR VIEW OF A PROBLEM

For these exercises, assume that you are a social worker with a family counseling center. In the spaces provided, write the words you would say in sharing your view of a problem.

1. You have spent nearly a full hour talking with Mrs. O., the 77-year-old widow who lives alone in a small apartment. She has expressed disappointment that her grown children no longer visit her. She worries about her spells and the possibility that she might be seriously ill; she is concerned that she might soon lose her independence and autonomy. Based on this summary of concerns and a review of exchanges that occurred earlier (Exercises 7-1.2, 7-2.2, 7-3.2, 7-4.2, 7-5.2, 7-6.2, 7-7.2, 9-1.1), write the words you would use in sharing your view

of a problem. Experiment with one or two other forms of sharing your view of a problem as it might apply to Mrs. O.

2. You have spent approximately 75 minutes talking with the seven-member, blended S. family. Several problem areas have emerged, including strain and conflict between Mr. S.'s children and Mrs. S., financial difficulties, marital distress, and most recently the threat to Mr. S.'s job. Based on this summary of concerns and a review of exchanges that occurred earlier (Exercises 7-1.3, 7-2.3, 7-3.3, 7-4.3, 7-5.3, 7-6.3, 7-7.3, 9-1.2), write the words you would use in sharing your view of a problem. Experiment with one or two other forms of sharing your view of a problem as it might apply to the S. family.

3. You have now talked with Mrs. F. for about 45 minutes. You've explored several problem areas, including her feelings that she and her family do not fit in this community, her children's apparently increasing disrespect for her and their Latino heritage, and most importantly, the concern for her children's safety at school. Based on this summary of concerns and a review of exchanges that occurred earlier (Exercises 7-1.4, 7-2.4, 7-3.4, 7-4.4, 7-5.4, 7-6.4, 7-7.4, 9-1.3), write the words you would use in sharing your view of a problem. Experiment with one or two other forms of sharing your view of a problem as it might apply to Mrs. F. and her family.

Specifying Problems for Work

Specifying problems for work constitutes the first definitive indication that you and the client have agreed to work together toward resolving certain problems. It is a fundamental component of the social work contract. Usually, the specified problems for work are derived from problems the client has identified, those you have contributed, or some negotiated combination or compromise of the two. Whatever their source, the specified problems for work provide you with a guide for all your subsequent professional activities. Whenever possible, the problems for work should be stated in clear and specific terms. They may be recorded within the contract portion of the Description, Assessment, and Contract (DAC).

Specification of problems for work follows naturally from the processes of exploring and assessing the person-problem-situation. Typically, you use the skills of reflecting problems and sharing your view of problems before you specify actual problems for work. Specification of problems results in an agreement—a contract—that these problem areas will be the primary focus of the work that you and the client will undertake together. In practicing this skill, consider the format outlined below.

SUGGESTED FORMAT FOR SPECIFYING PROBLEMS FOR WORK

I think we agree about the problems to address in our work together. Let's review them and I'll write them down so that we can refer to them as we go along. First, there is the problem of _____. Second, the problem of _____. Third, _____. Does this seem to be an accurate list of the problems of concern?

Example

CLIENT: (who has identified and explored two major problems for which she sought help from your agency; you have contributed a third problem about which the client concurs) Well, that's my story. I hope you can help with the mess I'm in.

WORKER: (specifying problems for work) I hope so too. It seems to me that we have identified three major problem areas to address during our work together. Let's review them once more and I'll jot them down so that we can refer to them as we go along. First, there is the problem of housing. You have been living on the street now for three weeks and the weather is beginning to turn cold. Second, there is the problem of diabetes. You have been without medicine for a week now and you have no insurance or money to pay for it. Third, you lost your job two months ago and need to find work in order to make some money. What do you think? Is this an accurate list of the problems of concern?

◆ EXERCISE 9-3: SPECIFYING PROBLEMS FOR WORK

For these exercises, assume that you are a social worker with a family counseling center. Review your responses to Exercises 9-1 and 9-2 and then, in the spaces provided, write the words you would say in specifying problems for work with each of the clients identified below. Use the format suggested above, but feel free to be somewhat creative in preparing your response. Since you cannot actually interact with these clients, you need a certain amount of flexibility.

1. Refer to Exercises 9-1.1 and 9-2.1 and then write the words you would us to specify problems for work as they might apply to 77-year-old Mrs. O.

2. Refer to Exercises 9-1.2 and 9-2.2 and then write the words you would us to specify problems for work as they might apply to the seven-member S. family.

3. Refer to Exercises 9-1.3 and 9-2.3 and then write the words you would use to specify problems for work as they might apply to Mrs. F.

Establishing Goals

Following the specification of problems, you encourage clients to participate in the process of establishing goals. Setting final or outcome goals is the second critical element of the contracting process. It is a vital step toward change. Final goals are envisioned aims toward which cognitive, emotional, behavioral, and situational actions are directed. Consider the title of a book by David Campbell: *If You Don't Know Where You're Going, You'll End Up Somewhere Else* (1974). Without clear goals, you and your clients are indeed likely to end up somewhere other than where you intend.

Gerard Egan (1982b, pp. 212–218) suggests that effective goals

- ◆ should be stated as accomplishments
- ◆ should be stated in clear and specific terms
- ◆ should be stated in measurable or verifiable terms
- ◆ should have a realistic chance of success
- ◆ would, if achieved, be adequate to improve the situation
- ◆ are congruent with clients' value and cultural systems
- ◆ should include a time frame for achievement

According to Egan, effective goals meet the criteria outlined above. First, well-formed goals are described as accomplishments rather than processes. "To lose weight" is a process. "To achieve a weight of 125 pounds and maintain that weight for six months" is an accomplishment. Second, effective goals are clear and specific. They are not vague resolutions or general mission statements. "Securing employment" is unspecific. "Within six months of today, to secure employment as a short-order cook in a restaurant" is much more clear and specific. Third, well-stated goals are described in measurable or verifiable terms. The criteria for successful accomplishment of the goals are understood by both client and worker. "To feel better" is not sufficiently measurable. "To feel better as indicated by sleeping the night through (at least seven hours per night on at least five nights per week), completely eating three meals daily, and by scoring at least 15% higher on the Beck Depression Inventory" is much more measurable. Fourth, goals should be realistic. Given the motivations, opportunities, strengths, resources, and capacities of the person-problem-situation systems, the established goals should have a reasonably high probability of attainment. A goal "to get all straight As" would not be realistic for a student who has never before received a single A. Fifth, effective goals are adequate. A goal is adequate to the degree that its accomplishment would significantly improve the problem situation. Goals that would not contribute to a resolution of the problems are therefore inadequate. Sixth, effective goals are congruent with the client's value and cultural systems. Unless a life-threatening situation exists, you should generally neither ask nor expect clients to forsake their fundamental personal or cultural values. Seventh, effective goals are described in terms of a time frame. Both you and your clients need to know *when* the goals are to be achieved.

Although specifying goals in a manner consistent with Egan's criteria represents an ideal, it is not always desirable or feasible to define goals as rigorously as Egan suggests. Do not become so fanatical in your attempt to define goals in a precise manner that you lose touch with the client's reality. Some clients are in such a state of uncertainty and confusion that pushing them too hard toward specificity would exacerbate their state of distress. Therefore, on occasion, you should postpone goal specification, outlining a more general goal or direction for the time being. Later, when the confusion and ambiguity subside, you may appropriately return to encourage identification of clear and precise goals that conform more closely to Egan's ideal.

Whether stated in specific or general terms, goals should follow logically from and relate directly to the specified problems for work. Accomplishment of the goals should have the effect of resolving the identified problems for work. Consistent with the values of the profession, goals are jointly established with clients and have their consent. When you and your client establish final goals, you agree to work toward accomplishing them. Since, quite often, the accomplishment of one goal resolves more than one problem, it may not always be necessary to have a separate goal for each and every problem.

Most of the time, clients are quite capable of active participation in goal identification. As part of that process, you request that they indicate a goal for one or more problems for work. However, you should ask them to do so in a special way.

Clients often respond to direct questions such as "What is your goal for resolving this problem?" in vague and general terms. You can often encourage clearer goal descriptions by using probes that require clients to describe specifically *how they will know* when a particular problem is resolved. In addition to furthering the purposes of goal establishment identified above, these probes serve another extremely important function. They encourage clients to envision, in considerable detail, a future in which the problem has indeed been resolved. In so doing, clients often begin to feel better, more energized, and more motivated to work toward goal attainment. To yield such results, however, these probes must be phrased in a certain way.

For this purpose, the exploring skill of *seeking clarification* is adapted so as to encourage clients to both establish a goal and to imagine a future in which the problem has been resolved. Clarification-seeking questions, phrased in the format suggested below, tend to yield these dual results.

SUGGESTED FORMAT FOR ENCOURAGING GOAL IDENTIFICATION

In specific terms, how will you know when the
problem of _____ is truly resolved?

or

What would indicate to you that this problem is truly a thing
of the past?

Example

WORKER: Now that we have a pretty clear list of the problems, let's try to establish specific goals for each one. The first problem we've identified is that your 14-year-old son skips school two or three days each week. Let's imagine that it is now some point in the future and the problem has been completely resolved. What would indicate to you that your son's truancy problem is truly a thing of the past?

CLIENT: Well, I guess I'll know when Johnny goes to school every day and his grades are better.

WORKER: (reflecting goal; seeking feedback) When Johnny goes to school daily and improves his grades, you will feel that it's no longer a problem. Is that right?

CLIENT: Yes.

WORKER: (seeking specificity) Okay, now let's try to be even more specific. When you say "Johnny will go to school every day" do you also mean that he will attend all his classes when he's there?

CLIENT: Yes.

WORKER: (seeking specificity) What do you think would be a reasonable time frame for accomplishing this goal?

CLIENT: Well, I don't know. I'd like him to start now.

WORKER: (sharing opinion; seeking feedback) That would be great progress! But I wonder if that might be expecting too much. Let's see, it's now one month into the school year. As I understand it, Johnny skipped school some last year too and this year he is skipping even more. What do you think about a two-month time frame for accomplishing the goal?

CLIENT: That sounds really good.

WORKER: (establishing goal) Okay, How does this sound as our first goal: "Within two months from today's date, Johnny will go to school every day and attend all his classes, except when he's sick enough to go to a doctor"? Let me take a moment to write that down for us. . . . Now about the grades. As I understand, he is currently failing most of his courses. How will you know when that is no longer a problem?

As should be apparent from the above example, you often need to be quite active in encouraging goal identification. These probes reflect implicit optimism: They require clients to envision a future in which the problem is indeed a thing of the past. Therefore, in seeking goal identification, try to avoid phrases such as, "*If* the problems *were* gone...." This could imply that the problem might not be resolved.

Sometimes, in response to your probes, clients formulate clear goals with which you can readily concur. When this happens, you may simply reflect the goal by paraphrasing the client's words. You may use a format such as the following.

SUGGESTED FORMAT FOR REFLECTING A GOAL

As you see it, one goal for our work together is _____.

Example

CLIENT: (responding to worker's request to state a goal) Well, I guess I'd like to improve the quality of the communication between us.

WORKER: (reflecting goal; seeking feedback) As you see it then, one goal for our work together is for the two of you to become better at talking pleasantly and respectfully with one another. Is that right?

CLIENT: Yes.

Reflecting a goal involves communicating your empathic understanding of a client's view of a goal that he or she would like to pursue in your work together. As are all reflecting skills, it is a specific form of active listening. Reflecting a goal demonstrates that you have heard and understood a goal as the client expressed it. When reflecting goals, you may paraphrase or mirror the client's words even if the goal is stated in a general way. Alternately, you can go somewhat beyond what the client has said, phrasing your response so that the goal is stated in more clear and specific terms.

Sometimes, in spite of your active encouragement, a client cannot or will not identify a goal. In such instances, you may simply postpone the goal-setting process and engage in additional exploration of the person-problem-situation. Alternately, you may propose a tentative goal, which the client may accept, reject, or modify. In *sharing your view of a goal*, you may adopt a format such as the following.

SUGGESTED FORMAT FOR SHARING YOUR VIEW OF A GOAL

I wonder, would it make sense to establish as one goal for our work together _____?

Example

WORKER: Now that we have a pretty clear understanding of the problems and a sense of the direction we'd like to go, let's establish goals for our

---

work together. We've agreed that your pattern of alcohol consumption is a significant problem. I wonder, would it make sense to establish as a goal for our work together to limit the amount of daily alcohol intake to one 12-ounce can of beer each day?

Example

CLIENT: Yes. It does feel like I've lost everything I had hoped for. I guess it's normal to feel sad when a marriage fails.

WORKER: (reflecting feeling and meaning) Your dreams for the future of your marriage have been shattered, and you feel a powerful sense of loss and sadness.

CLIENT: Yes, my marriage meant a lot to me.

WORKER: (encouraging goal identification) I wonder if it might be possible for us to identify a goal in relation to these feelings of sadness and loss. Let's imagine that it's now some time in the future when these feelings are long since past. What will you be thinking, feeling, and doing when these feelings of depression are no longer a problem for you?

CLIENT: Gee, I don't know exactly. I guess when I'm finally over her I'll feel a lot better.

WORKER: (reflecting content; encouraging goal specificity) So it will be a positive sign when you begin to feel better. And what will indicate to you that you're feeling better?

CLIENT: I guess once I'm over this, I'll be able to sleep and eat again and not think about her so much, and I might even be dating someone else.

WORKER: (reflecting content; sharing your view of a goal; seeking feedback) So when you begin to eat and sleep better, and you think about her less, we'll know that things have taken a positive turn. Let's make the goals even more specific so that we will know when you have completely achieved them. How does this sound to you? "Within six months, to (1) sleep six or more hours per night at least five nights per week, (2) regain the weight that you lost, (3) at least 75% of the time, think about things other than your wife, and (4) go out on at least one date." What do you think?

CLIENT: Real good. Right now I probably think about her 95% of the time, and the idea of going on a date sounds just awful. If I were thinking about other things, doing other things, and dating someone else, I'd know that I'd finally be over her.

WORKER: (establishing goal) Okay. Let me jot that down so we can remember it.

◆ EXERCISE 9-4: ESTABLISHING GOALS

For these exercises, assume that you are continuing in your role as a social worker with a family counseling center. In the spaces provided for each case situation below, complete three tasks. First, write the words you would say in *encouraging the client to identify a goal*. Second, prepare a *general goal statement* that reasonably follows from one or more of the problems that you specified in Exercise 9-3. Third, prepare a *specific goal statement* that reasonably follows from one or more of the problems that you specified in Exercise 9-3. Try to write it so that it meets Egan's ideal criteria for effective goal statements.

Of course, the nature of this exercise does not allow you to interact with clients in negotiating goals. Therefore, simply formulate appropriate probes and then share your view of goals that might match the problems. The primary purpose here is to practice probes that encourage goal identification and to practice preparing two forms of goal statements.

1.a. Write the words you would say in asking a probe that encourages Mrs. O., the 77-year-old widow, to identify a goal that relates to one or more of the problems specified in Exercise 9-3.1.

b. On behalf of Mrs. O., write a general goal statement that relates to one or more of the problems specified in Exercise 9-3.1.

c. Now write a specific goal statement that relates to one or more of the problems specified in Exercise 9-3.1.

2.a. Write the words you would say in asking a probe that encourages members of the S. family to identify a goal that relates to one or more of the problems specified in Exercise 9-3.2.

b. On behalf of the S. family, write a general goal statement that relates to one or more of the problems specified in Exercise 9-3.2.

c. Now write a specific goal statement that relates to one or more of the problems specified in Exercise 9-3.2.

3.a. Write the words you would say in asking a probe that encourages Mrs. F., the Latina mother who is concerned about her children, to identify a goal that relates to one or more of the problems specified in Exercise 9-3.3.

b. On behalf of Mrs. F., write a general goal statement that relates to one or more of the problems specified in Exercise 9-3.3.

c. Now write a specific goal statement that relates to one or more of the problems specified in Exercise 9-3.3.

4. When you have completed the above exercises, review the specific goal statements that you wrote and then ask yourself the following questions. Are the goals described as accomplishments rather than processes? Are the goals clear and specific? Are they measurable or verifiable in some way? Are they realistic, given the circumstances? Are they adequate? Do they appear to be consistent with the fundamental values and cultural preferences that you might expect of these clients? Finally, are the goals congruent with the specified problems identified in Exercise 9-3? If your answer to any of these questions is No, revise your specific goal statements so that they do meet Egan's ideal form.

Developing an Approach

Once goals have been established, you engage the client in the process of developing an approach for pursuing them. In developing an approach, you and the client must identify who will meet with you, and who or what will be the target for change. Together, you and the client must also determine who will be involved in the change efforts and how those efforts might affect others. For example, consider a case in which the mother of an 8-year-old boy expresses concern about his disobedience and aggression. You and the client would determine who will meet with you and in what context. Will it be the mother and boy together; the mother separately; the boy separately; sometimes one, sometimes the other, sometimes both; the boy in a group with other boys; or the mother in a group with other mothers? There are numerous possibilities, and many decisions are required. You must also determine what social work role or roles you will play (e.g., advocate, mediator, broker, educator, or counselor) and what method, approach, or strategy to adopt in relation to the established goals. For example, should you serve as counselor? If so, should your perspective be task-centered, family systems, ecological, behavior modification, or some combination thereof? You and the client must also determine how to implement the change efforts. How active should you be? How direct should you be? Should you encourage the client to take the initiative, or should you assume primary leadership responsibility? You and the client must decide how fast to proceed with change efforts and how to approach other persons who could or should be involved. You and the client must decide where to hold your meetings and where the change efforts will occur. Sometimes it is easier for clients, or more likely to yield positive results, to meet in their homes rather than in your agency office. On other occasions, an entirely neutral location may be the best choice. You and the client must also determine when you will meet (morning, afternoon, evening), how often (once per week, once per month), and how long (30 minutes, one hour). Typically, you and the client will establish a time frame for your work together. Will you plan to work together toward these goals for six weeks, three months, six months? In addition, you and the client should identify possible obstacles as well as potential resources that might affect the outcome of your plan.

In developing an approach, you and the client consider a number of factors and develop a scheme or program to guide your work together. The following is an example of how an approach might be succinctly recorded as part of the contract portion of the DAC. (See Summarizing the Contract later in this chapter for more discussion of this part of the DAC.)

Example

1. Approach

   We, Carol Johnson and Susan Holder, agree to meet together for weekly one-hour sessions over the course of the next eight weeks. Our purpose is to accomplish the goals identified above. We will approach this work as a cooperative, problem-solving effort, with each of us contributing ideas and suggestions, and each of us taking steps toward goal achievement. Sometimes we will meet in the agency and sometimes in Ms. Johnson's home. If agreeable to Ms. Johnson, we may ask her husband to join us for one or two meetings. Throughout the eight-week period, we will monitor the rate and degree of progress toward goal achievement. At the end of that time, we will determine whether to conclude our work, consult with or refer to someone else, or contract with each other for further work together.

◆ EXERCISE 9-5: DEVELOPING AN APPROACH

For these exercises, assume that you are continuing your work with the clients described in the previous exercises (Mrs. O., the S. family, and Mrs. F.). Review your responses to Exercises 9-3 (specifying problems for work) and 9-4 (establishing goals). Then, in the spaces provided below each vignette, develop an approach for your work with each client. Of course, it should be congruent with the identified problems and goals and consistent with the dimensions discussed above.

1. Develop an approach for your work with Mrs. O. Write it so it could be included as part of the Contract portion of a DAC.

2. Develop an approach for your work with the S. family. Write it so it could be included as part of the Contract portion of a DAC.

3. Develop an approach for your work with Mrs. F. Write it so it could be included as part of the Contract portion of a DAC.

4. When you have completed the above exercises, review the approaches you have formulated. Ask yourself whether each approach adequately describes who is to be involved in meeting with you; who or what are the targets of change; where, when, and how long the meetings are to occur; how active you are to be; what role or roles you are going to assume; what strategy or approach is to be used; and what the time frame is to be. In addition, ask whether the approach in any way infringes on the personal values and the cultural preferences you might expect of these particular clients. Finally, determine whether the approach is logically congruent with the specified problems identified in Exercise 9-3 and the final goals identified in Exercise 9-4. In the space below, summarize the results of your review and specify those aspects of the approach development process that you need to strengthen.

Identifying Action Steps

Often, the goals that you and the client formulate are too large to accomplish in a single action, and it would be unrealistic and impractical to try to accomplish all of them at once. When this is the case, you engage the client in identifying small action steps or tasks (Reid, 1992) that are consistent with the approach and likely to contribute to goal accomplishment. These tasks or action steps are a form of subordinate goals. They may be recorded within the Plans section of the Contract portion of the DAC.

In identifying action steps, you and the client use the information gained and the hypotheses generated during the description and assessment phases. You attempt to foster a flexible, creative, brainstorming atmosphere in which all sorts of ideas are identified and examined. Several skills are applicable during this process. The exploring skills of probing, reflecting, and going beyond what is said are three of the more pertinent.

There are many ways to resolve problems and achieve goals. Some approaches require changes in the person; others involve changes in the situation; and many entail changes in both dimensions. Changes such as increasing one's knowledge about parenting or increasing one's skill in communicating assertively are examples of *person-focused* change. Securing adequate food and shelter or organizing a tenants' union to lobby for improved building conditions exemplify *situation-focused* change. In social work practice, changes are rarely limited to the individual person. Changes in the situation are often necessary. Whenever you serve as an advocate, broker, or mediator, you are working toward situational change. For example, an unemployed client's situation is likely to be dramatically improved when you intercede with a prospective employer to help the client secure a new job. Or consider the example of a female client living with a man who periodically beats her. With your help, several situational changes might be possible. Her male companion could be encouraged to join in a process of relationship counseling designed to enhance direct verbal communication and decrease the risk of future violence. Or he might be asked to participate in a program for abusive men. The client might file a criminal complaint with the police and courts, or she might leave the household for a safe shelter. All these involve changes in the situation, and all would affect the person as well. Although an action step in any given case may be primarily person-focused or primarily situation-focused, you should be aware of the following systemic principle. *Changes in one aspect of the person-situation system nearly always result in changes in other aspects.*

Completion of tasks or action steps contribute to the achievement of larger, final goals. Because they usually involve relatively small steps, they have a higher probability of success than would be the case if the final goal were attempted in a single action. For example, suppose you were 50 pounds overweight and wanted to lose that much in order to improve your health. Except by surgery, it is physically impossible to lose 50 pounds at one time. Reducing by one pound, then another, and then another, however, is conceivable. It is similar to the "one day at a time" principle of Alcoholics Anonymous. Abstaining from alcohol for the rest of one's life is indeed a large order for anyone who has drunk large quantities of alcohol every day for many years. Abstaining for one day, for one hour, or even for one minute is much more manageable and certainly more probable. By putting together and accomplishing several tasks or action steps (subordinate goals), a large goal that otherwise would seem insurmountable may be successfully achieved.

The skill of identifying action steps involves establishing subordinate goals that include *doing something*. These actions constitute steps, tasks, or activities that you or the client take in your efforts toward goal accomplishment. Various action steps may be referred to as client tasks, worker tasks, or in-session tasks (Tolson, Reid, & Garvin, 1994). *Client tasks* are action steps that clients take during the intervals between your meetings. *Worker tasks* are those that you, the social worker, agree to complete before you meet again with a client. *In-session tasks* are procedures, activities, or intervention techniques that you or the client undertake during your meetings together.

In attempting to specify these tasks or action steps, you and the client first engage one another in generating a first, small step toward the final goal. You may initiate this process by asking questions such as "What would represent a first step toward achieving this goal?" or "What needs to change in order for you to be able to make a small step toward achieving this goal?"

Questions such as the following often yield useful information in the identification of action steps. "What will be the first sign that you are beginning to make progress toward this goal?" "What will be the very first indication that there is progress in this matter?" "What will be the very first sign that you are taking steps to reach your goal?" Such questions tend to increase clients' optimism and motivation, as do those used in establishing goals. They do so by bringing the near future into their present thinking. You ask clients to imagine or visualize the situation being somewhat improved and to identify signs of that improvement. These signs often indicate the kinds of specific action steps that might be taken in order to progress toward goal attainment.

Notice the emphasis on identifying an action that might be taken. Your focus is on doing something that represents movement toward goal achievement. Depending on the nature of the agreed-upon goals, you may encourage clients to identify steps leading to changes in themselves (thoughts, feelings, or behaviors) or in their situations that might help to resolve the identified problems.

During this phase, you ask questions that will yield small and manageable tasks or actions. As you and the client come to consensus concerning initial action steps, reflect them in clear terms.

In identifying action steps, you might use a format such as the following.

SUGGESTED FORMAT FOR IDENTIFYING AN ACTION STEP

So, the (first or next) step that (you, I, or we) are going to take is _____. (You, I, or we) will complete this task by (*insert date*) and talk about it at our next meeting.

Example

CLIENT: *(identifying an action step)* I'll go ahead and talk with her to see if she'd be interested in the idea of joint counseling.

WORKER: *(identifying an action step)* Okay, the next step that you will take is to talk with your partner and ask her if she might be interested in joining us for a few meetings. You'll talk with her within the next few days in order to give her a chance to think about it and give you her response before our next meeting. How does that sound? Fine, let me jot that down so we can keep it in mind.

By identifying an action step, you firmly cement the contract for your work with the client. The following are some examples of typical processes by which a worker might engage a client in establishing action steps.

Example

WORKER: *(reflecting a goal; seeking an action step)* Your first goal is to improve your sleeping patterns. Right now, you sleep the night through only about one day per week and you want to be able to do so at least five days per week. Going from one to five nights is a pretty large jump. It might be helpful to start with something a bit smaller. What would represent a good first step toward achieving the goal?

Example

WORKER: *(reflecting a goal; seeking an action step)* We have established as your first goal the improvement of your sleeping patterns. Right now, you sleep the night through about one day per week and you want to be able to do so at least five days per week. What will be the first signs that you are beginning to sleep better?

___

If the client cannot or will not respond to your encouragement by identifying a small action step, you may tentatively propose one for consideration. Of course, as always, be sure to seek the client's reactions to the idea. In proposing a task, you might use a format such as the following.

___

SUGGESTED FORMAT FOR PROPOSING AN ACTION STEP

As a first step toward the goal of _____, what do you think about (*insert client task, worker task, or in-session task as needed*)?

Example

WORKER: *(proposing a client task)* We have identified the goal of graduating from high school by completing your General Education Diploma within the next 12 months. As a first step toward that goal, what do you think about contacting the school that you attended through the ninth grade in order to ask for your academic records?

___

Example

WORKER: *(proposing a worker task)* We have identified the goal of graduating from high school by completing your General Education Diploma (GED) within the next 12 months. As a first step toward that goal, I'd like to contact the department of education and ask for information about local GED programs. How does that sound to you?

___

Example

WORKER: *(proposing an in-session task)* Here's a copy of the application form for the GED program. I thought we might try to complete it together during our meeting today. What do you think?

___

♦ **EXERCISE 9-6: IDENTIFYING ACTION STEPS**

Continuing with the cases described above, review your responses to Exercises 9-4 (establishing goals) and 9-5 (developing an approach). Then, in the spaces provided below, use the suggested format to write the words you might use to encourage each client to identify an initial, small task or action step. Then, write three action steps (client tasks, worker tasks, and in-session tasks) that you might propose to each client. Of course, they should be congruent with the identified problems and goals and, if completed, clearly represent a contribution to goal achievement.

1.a. Write the words you might say in encouraging Mrs. O. to identify an action step.

b. Write the words you might say in proposing a client task to Mrs. O.

c. Write the words you might say in proposing a worker task to Mrs. O.

d. Write the words you might say in proposing an in-session task to Mrs. O.

2.a. Write the words you might say in encouraging members of the S. family to identify an action step.

b. Write the words you might say in proposing a client task to the S. family.

c. Write the words you might say in proposing a worker task to the S. family.

d. Write the words you might say in proposing an in-session task to the S. family.

3.a. Write the words you might say in encouraging Mrs. F. to identify an action step.

b. Write the words you might say in proposing a client task to Mrs. F.

c. Write the words you might say in proposing a worker task to Mrs. F.

d. Write the words you might say in proposing an in-session task to Mrs. F.

4. When you have completed the above exercises, review the tasks or action steps identified and ask yourself the following questions. Are the steps described so that they involve actually doing something? Are the steps clear and specific? Would they in any way infringe on the personal values and the cultural preferences that you might expect of these clients? Finally, are the action steps congruent with the specified problems, the final goals, and the approaches identified in Exercises 9-3, 9-4, and 9-5? In particular, what is the probability that, if completed, the action steps would indeed contribute to the achievement of the identified goals? In the space below, summarize the results of your review and specify aspects of action step identification you need to develop further.

Planning for Evaluation

As a professional social worker, you are responsible for evaluating progress toward problem resolution and goal achievement. Regardless of the nature of the agency setting, the presenting problems, or the client's circumstances, it is possible to create some method for measuring progress toward goal attainment. Sometimes, such evaluation can be quite objective; at other times, more subjective. In any case, you must evaluate progress somehow. In many practice contexts, failure to do so would constitute negligence.

There are several means of measuring progress toward goal attainment. One of the more applicable methods is called *goal attainment scaling* (Kiresuk & Sherman, 1968). Goal attainment scaling (GAS) is particularly well suited to social work practice because the dimensions for measurement are not predetermined (as is the case with standardized tests). In goal attainment scaling, the dimensions for assessment evolve from the goals negotiated by you and the client, so they are specific to each person-problem-situation. Compton and Galaway (1989, pp. 671–674) and Kagle (1984, pp. 74–76) provide useful summaries of goal attainment scaling procedures. To develop a goal attainment scale, you generate a series of five predictions concerning the possible outcomes of work toward achievement of each goal. The predictions provide you and your client with markers on which to base your evaluation of progress. The possible outcomes range from worst to best and are classified (Compton & Galaway, 1994, p. 551) as shown in Table 9.1.

TABLE 9.1
Goal Attainment Scale[1]

	Goal #1	Goal #2	Goal #3	Goal #4	Goal #5
1. most unfavorable results thought likely					
2. less than expected success					
3. expected level of of success					
4. more than expected success					
5. most favorable results thought likely					

Among the other means for evaluating progress toward goal achievement are counting and subjective rating. In *counting*, you, the client, or another person in the client's environment keeps track of the frequency of a particular phenomenon that is integrally related to the final goal. For example, consider self-esteem; people with low self-esteem often think disparaging and critical thoughts about themselves. You and such a client might identify as a final goal to increase the frequency of self-approving thoughts. You might provide the client with a small notepad in which to keep track of the number of self-approving thoughts during a given period (e.g., each day for one week). The frequency counts are then transferred to graph paper, with the expectation that the change program will lead the client to increase the frequency of self-approving thoughts per day. Counting is often used to establish a *baseline* for the targeted phenomenon, prior to the implementation of intervention plans. The baseline then is used as a measure to gauge the effectiveness of your approach. Counting can be applied to many different phenomena in the dimensions of person and situation.

Subjective rating requires that you, the client, or another person make a relative judgment concerning the extent, duration, frequency, or intensity of a targeted phenomenon. For example, you might ask a client to form an imaginary ten-point scale that runs from "worst" or "least" (number 1) to "best" or "most" (number 10). Then the client is asked to rate the phenomenon on the scale. For example, suppose a client is concerned about the quality of the relationship with her partner. You could make a request in this fashion: "Would you please imagine a scale that runs from 1 to 10, with 1 being the lowest possible and 10 being the highest possible? Now, on the basis of your best judgment, please rate the quality of the relationship as it has been today."

---

[1]Adapted from *Social Work Processes*, Fifth Edition, by B. R. Compton and B. Galaway, p. 551. Copyright © 1994 Brooks/Cole Publishing Company.

Suppose that the client rates the day's quality of the relationship as 4. You could then ask the client (her partner might be invited to participate as well) to conduct such a subjective rating once each evening. The request might be phrased in this manner: "Each evening just before going to bed, please record in a notebook your subjective rating of the quality of the relationship during that day. Please do not share your ratings with your partner until we meet together again. We'll transfer your ratings onto a graph in order to determine how your views change as we work toward improving the quality of the relationship. How does that sound?"

Subjective ratings can be used in relation to virtually all human psychological and social phenomena. Of course, since they are by definition subjective, they are quite susceptible to individual bias and other forms of human error. Nonetheless, where more objective means are inappropriate or impractical, subjective ratings may be extremely useful.

As a social worker, you may also select from a vast array of paper-and-pencil instruments that are widely available. For example, Walter Hudson, a distinguished social worker, has produced *The Clinical Measurement Package: A Field Manual* (1982). The Clinical Measurement Package (CMP) contains nine scales that are of great utility to social workers. These scales assess phenomena that often apply to the problems and goals clients identify when they meet with social workers. The CMP scales address dimensions such as self-esteem, generalized contentment, marital satisfaction, sexual satisfaction, parental attitudes, child attitudes toward mother, child attitudes toward father, family relations, and peer relations. Each of the scales may be completed and scored quickly.

Two other social workers, Kevin Corcoran and Joel Fischer, have published *Measures for Clinical Practice: A Sourcebook* (Corcoran & Fischer, 1987; Fischer & Corcoran, 1994). Their most recent edition includes two volumes of Rapid Assessment Instruments (RAIs) relevant for many aspects of social work practice. Volume 1 contains more than 100 measures relevant for assessing various dimensions of couples, families, and children. Volume 2 reviews more than 200 instruments relevant for adults. Included among the measures are instruments for assessing spouse abuse, alcoholism, marital happiness, family adaptability and cohesion, depression, self-concept, and dozens of other dimensions of human experience. *Measures for Clinical Practice* is a rich resource of easily administered and rapidly scored instruments.

◆ **EXERCISE 9-7: PLANNING FOR EVALUATION**

Review your responses to Exercises 9-3, 9-4, 9-5, and 9-6 as they relate to the case situations described. Then, in the spaces provided, write the words you would say to identify two means for evaluating progress toward goal achievement in each of those case situations. First, plan an evaluation process that is more objective in nature. Then plan a subjective method to measure progress. The primary purpose is to encourage you to consider various means for measuring progress in your work with clients. Whatever evaluation plans you generate should, of course, relate directly to the identified problems and goals, so that progress can be determined.

1.a. Prepare a brief subjective plan by which you might evaluate progress toward problem resolution or goal achievement in your work with Mrs. O.

b. Prepare an objective plan by which you might evaluate progress toward problem resolution or goal achievement in your work with Mrs. O.

2.a. Prepare a brief subjective plan by which you might evaluate progress toward problem resolution or goal achievement in your work with the S. family.

b. Prepare an objective plan by which you might evaluate progress toward problem resolution or goal achievement in your work with the S. family.

3.a. Prepare a brief subjective plan by which you might evaluate progress toward problem resolution or goal achievement in your work with Mrs. F.

b. Prepare an objective plan by which you might evaluate progress toward problem resolution or goal achievement in your work with Mrs. F.

4. When you have completed the above exercises, please consider the means of evaluation you have identified and ask yourself the following questions. How subject to evaluator bias and error are the means you have selected? What are the ethical implications of these forms of evaluation? Do the means appear to be respectful of the personal values and the cultural preferences you might expect of these clients? Finally, are the means likely to be accurate in measuring changes on the dimensions specified in Exercises 9-3 and 9-4? In the space below, summarize the results of your review and specify those aspects of evaluation planning you need to develop further.

Summarizing the Contract

Summarizing the contract involves a concise review of the essential elements of the understanding that you and the client have reached. It covers problems for work, final goals, the approach, tasks or action steps, and the means by which progress is to be evaluated.

When written, the contract may be organized in accordance with the framework shown below and incorporated into the DAC. Alternately, it may be prepared separately as a formal contract, using letterhead paper, with spaces for you and the client to sign. In both written forms, the contract provides for descriptions of problems, goals, and plans. The contract represents your basic agreement with the client to work together toward the resolution of problems and the achievement of goals. You will probably find such contracts extremely applicable in your social work practice. Of course, the specific dimensions of the format shown here may not be relevant for practice in all social work settings or with all clients, all problems, or all situations. As a professional social worker, you must assume responsibility for adopting contract guidelines that best match the needs and functions of your agency and your own practice.

SUGGESTED FORMAT

Contract Section of the
Description, Assessment, and Contract

III. Contract
    A. Problems
        1. Client-Defined Problems
           In this section, you clearly outline the problems that the client identifies.

2. **Worker-Identified Problems**

   In this section, you outline the problems that you identify.

3. **Problems for Work**

   In this section, you outline the problems that both parties agree to address. These are the problems that remain the focus for work unless or until they are renegotiated by you and the client. Of course, either party may request that the problems for work be reconsidered or revised.

B. **Final Goals**

   In this section, outline the final or outcome goals that you and the client have identified. They should, of course, relate to the problems for work. Ideally, final goals are defined in clear and specific terms so that progress toward their attainment can be measured. Sometimes, of course, only general goal statements are possible or advisable. Whether specific or general, record the goal statements in this section.

C. **Plans**

   1. **Approach**

      In this section, summarize the approach that you and your client have planned. You usually make note of factors such as who will be involved; where, when, and how often the work will occur, and for how long; and how the process will unfold. You should also identify, where applicable, the theoretical perspective or social work model that has been selected for use in work with this particular client.

   2. **Client's Tasks or Action Steps**

      In this section, outline the initial tasks or action steps that the client agrees to undertake in his or her attempt to achieve the agreed-upon goals.

   3. **Worker's Tasks or Action Steps**

      In this section, outline the initial tasks or activities that you agree to undertake in your effort to help achieve the agreed-upon goals.

   4. **In-Session Tasks or Action Steps**

      In this section, outline the initial tasks or activities that you and the client agree to undertake during your meetings together.

   5. **Plans to Evaluate Progress**

      In this section, outline the means and processes by which progress toward goal accomplishment is to be evaluated.

The following is an example of the contract portion of a social worker's Description, Assessment, and Contract. Notice that it is a continuation of the Lynn B. Chase case presented earlier.

Example
Lynn B. Chase

III. Contract
A. Problems
1. Client-Defined Problems
Mrs. Chase identified the following problems:
   a. Frequent arguments with her son Robert and, less often, with her husband Richard
   b. Increased irritability, criticism, and anger toward Robert and, to a lesser degree, toward Richard
   c. Unplanned weight loss (ten pounds) over the past six months
   d. Sleep disturbance
   e. Resumption of cigarette smoking after five years' abstinence
   f. Fatigue
   g. Headaches

2. Worker-Identified Problems
On the basis of our first interview, I tentatively identified the following as potential problems (tentative hypotheses only; they may be inaccurate).
   a. Ambivalence about job at Fox Manufacturing
   b. Feelings of depression
   c. Ambivalence about Robert's adolescence
   d. Feelings of loss, disappointment, and grief because client probably cannot have another child
   e. Stress and tension; anxiety
   f. Thoughts and feelings of excessive responsibility and possibly of control
   g. Role strain and possibly role conflict among roles of mother, wife, homemaker, and employee
   h. Issues related to childhood experiences (i.e., growing up in a family system with a parent who reportedly abused alcohol; largely absent and possibly workaholic father; unhappy incidents with childhood peers; feeling overweight and unattractive; church-related issues; reported episodes of attempted molestation by maternal uncle)
   i. Interactional styles that may be classified as predominantly nonassertive with occasional periods of aggressive verbal expression

3. Problems for Work
Mrs. Chase and I agreed on the following problems for work. These will provide us with a focus for our work together:

a. Frequent arguments with her son Robert and, less often, with her husband Richard

b. Irritability, criticism, and anger toward Robert and, to a lesser degree, toward Richard

c. Sleep disturbance

d. Ambivalence regarding job at Fox Manufacturing

e. Stress and tension; anxiety

f. Thoughts and feelings of excessive responsibility and possibly of control

g. Role strain and possibly role conflict among roles of mother, wife, homemaker, and employee

B. **Final Goals**

Mrs. Chase and I agreed on the following goals for work:

1. Within six weeks, decrease by 50% the frequency of unwarranted arguments with Robert and Richard and increase the frequency of satisfying interactions with them by 50%.

2. Within six weeks, decrease by 50% the frequency and intensity of inappropriate feelings of irritability, criticism, and anger toward Robert and Richard and increase appropriate feelings of comfort, understanding, and acceptance of them by 50%.

3. Within six weeks, sleep eight full hours per night and awaken feeling refreshed at least four of seven mornings a week.

4. Within six weeks, decrease the ambivalence about the job at Fox Manufacturing by deciding whether or not Lynn Chase really wants to keep the job.

5. Within six weeks, decrease the stress, tension, and anxiety and increase feelings of personal comfort and calmness by 50%.

6. Within two weeks, explore in greater depth the issue of excessive responsibility and control; by the end of that time, decide whether maintaining or lessening the current level of responsibility and control is desirable

C. **Plans**

1. **Approach**

In order to achieve the final goals, Mrs. Chase and I agreed on the following approach:

Mrs. Lynn Chase and I (Susan Holder, social worker) will meet for eight one-hour sessions during the next two months. Our purpose is to work together toward achievement of the final goals identified above. We will approach this work as a cooperative effort, with each party contributing ideas and suggestions. On occasion, we may ask Mrs. Chase's husband or son to join us. Throughout the two-month period, we will monitor the rate and degree of progress. At the end of that time, we will determine whether to conclude our work, consult with or refer to someone else, or contract with each other for further work together.

2. **Client's Tasks or Action Steps**

   Mrs. Chase and I agreed that she would undertake the following steps during the first week of our work together. Other tasks will be identified and implemented later in the program.

   a. As a first step toward decreasing the stress, tension, and anxiety and increasing feelings of personal comfort and calmness, Mrs. Chase agreed to spend 15 minutes each day during the next week planning for or working in her garden.

   b. As a first step toward decreasing the frequency of inappropriate feelings of irritability, criticism, and anger toward Robert and Richard and increasing appropriate feelings of comfort, understanding, and acceptance of them by 50%, Mrs. Chase agreed to do two things during the course of the next week. First, she agreed to resist "stuffing" her feelings. Whether by writing them down on paper, verbally expressing them in a place where no one can hear, or expressing them directly to the relevant person or persons, she agreed to express whatever feelings she experiences within a few minutes of the time that she first becomes aware of them. Second, she agreed to take five minutes every day to engage Robert and Richard pleasantly by inquiring about their thoughts, feelings, and activities.

   c. As a first step toward addressing the goal of determining whether a lessening of responsibility and control in some areas might be helpful, Mrs. Chase agreed to identify and write down as many reasons as she can why she should continue to maintain her current level of responsibility and control. Following that, Mrs. Chase agreed to identify as many reasons as she can why a lessening of her responsibility and control might be beneficial to her, her husband, and her son at this time. We agreed to review the two lists of reasons in our next meeting.

3. **Worker's Tasks or Action Steps**

   a. I, Susan Holder, agreed to prepare this contract or agreement in written form and provide a copy to Mrs. Chase.

   b. I agreed to assume responsibility for planning tentative agendas for our meetings together and to consult with Mrs. Chase concerning the implementation of the action steps and their effects.

    c. I agreed to provide Mrs. Chase with a notebook and related materials for completing written tasks and monitoring progress.

4. **In-Session Tasks or Action Steps**

Mrs. Chase and I agreed that during our meetings together, we would undertake some or all the following activities (additional in-session tasks will be identified and implemented later in the program):

    a. Value-clarification exercises intended to aid Mrs. Chase in addressing various issues about which she experiences ambivalence.

    b. Self-talk analysis to help Mrs. Chase identify the "things she says to herself" that seem associated with the feelings of irritability, criticism, anger, depression, stress, and tension.

    c. Strength-oriented, "bragging" exercises to help Mrs. Chase heighten her feelings of calmness.

5. **Plans to Evaluate Progress**

Progress toward goal achievement will be evaluated in several ways. First, Mrs. Chase agreed to keep a daily log in her notebook, where she intends to record the time and date of all "arguments" and all "satisfying interactions." Second, Mrs. Chase also agreed to log the time and date of all inappropriate feelings of "irritability, anger, and criticism" toward Richard or Robert, as well as all feelings of "comfort, understanding, and acceptance" of them. Third, Mrs. Chase agreed to use the log book to record the number of hours slept each night and to rate, on a subjective scale of 1–10, how refreshed she feels upon awakening. Fourth, Mrs. Chase agreed to register completion of her daily 15 minutes of "gardening." Evaluation of progress toward other goals will occur by asking Mrs. Chase for self-reports. In regard to the issues of excessive responsibility and ambivalence about her job at Fox Manufacturing, progress will be indicated when Mrs. Chase reports that she has decided whether to lessen responsibility and control and whether she wants to keep her job. A decision in either direction will be considered progress.

◆ **EXERCISE 9-8: SUMMARIZING THE CONTRACT**

For this exercise, please review the information you organized into the description and assessment sections of your own DAC in Exercises 8-1 and 8-2. Based on what you know about yourself and what you included in the description and assessment sections, proceed to formulate a contract in your course notebook as if you were your own social worker. In creating your contract, be aware that you too, in spite of your considerable self-understanding, are still likely to miss some of the problems or issues that a professional social worker might help you to identify. Therefore, even though it concerns you, the contract you develop should be viewed as tentative. Prepare the contract in accordance with the format provided above in the contract section of the Description, Assessment, and Contract.

Summary

During the contracting phase of social work practice, you, on the basis of the assessment and in conjunction with the client, attempt to define clearly the problems and goals for work and to develop plans likely to resolve the identified problems and achieve the final goals. Skills that are especially applicable to this phase of practice include (1) reflecting a problem, (2) sharing your view of a problem, (3) specifying problems for work, (4) establishing goals, (5) developing an approach, (6) identifying action steps, (7) planning for evaluation, and (8) summarizing the contract.

◆ **EXERCISE 9-9: SUMMARY**

Building on the earlier two interviews that you had with your student colleague, conduct a third interview for the purpose of developing a contract for work. Ensure that the interview setting is private and again tape-record the meeting. Using the skills of exploring and contracting and other relevant social work skills, interview your colleague with a view toward negotiating a contract. At the conclusion of the meeting, arrange for another meeting in about one week.

1. Following the interview, ask your partner for candid feedback concerning his or her thoughts and feelings about the experience. Ask for a totally honest reaction to the following questions. (a) Did you feel comfortable and safe with me? Did you feel that I seemed like a person you could trust? (b) Did you feel that I was sincerely interested in you and in what you had to say? (c) Did you feel that I understood what you were trying to communicate? If so, what contributed to that? If not, what indicated to you that I did not understand? (d) Does the contract as I summarized it really match your views of the problems that concern you? (e) Do the goals we've established fit your needs and preferences? (f) What is your reaction to the first action steps we've planned? (g) What do you think about our plans for evaluating progress? (h) Did you find the experience productive? (i) What could I do better or differently in order to improve the quality of this interview? (j) How could the interview have been better or more satisfying for you? Summarize your colleague's feedback in the space provided.

2. Review your own reaction to the conversation. How did you feel about the interview? What did you like and what did you dislike about it? Do you believe that you used relevant skills during the interaction? Were you able to develop the essential elements of a contract? If so, what helped you to do that? If not, what hindered you in that effort? What additional information would be useful? What would you do differently if you were to redo the interview? Summarize the results of your review in the space provided.

3. In your course notebook, prepare a record according to the format provided in the contract section of the Description, Assessment, and Contract.
4. After you have completed the contract, play the audiotape or videotape. Identify the specific social work skills that you used. Make notes of significant exchanges that affect the way in which you drafted the contract, and revise the contract accordingly.
5. At some point during the week, share the contract section of the case record with your student colleague. Ask for your colleague's thoughts and feelings about the written contract. Ask about its accuracy and correct any errors in fact or differences in interpretation concerning the contract. Request that your colleague respond specifically to the goals and action steps reflected in the contract section. Summarize your colleague's feedback and your own reactions in the space provided.

6. Now that you have completed these exercises, use the following rating scales (where 0 = no proficiency and 10 = complete proficiency) to conduct a summary evaluation of your proficiency in the contracting skills.

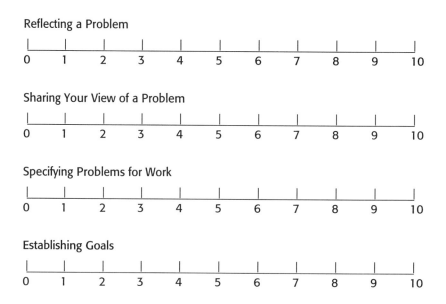

Reflecting a Problem

| | | | | | | | | | | |
0   1   2   3   4   5   6   7   8   9   10

Sharing Your View of a Problem

| | | | | | | | | | | |
0   1   2   3   4   5   6   7   8   9   10

Specifying Problems for Work

| | | | | | | | | | | |
0   1   2   3   4   5   6   7   8   9   10

Establishing Goals

| | | | | | | | | | | |
0   1   2   3   4   5   6   7   8   9   10

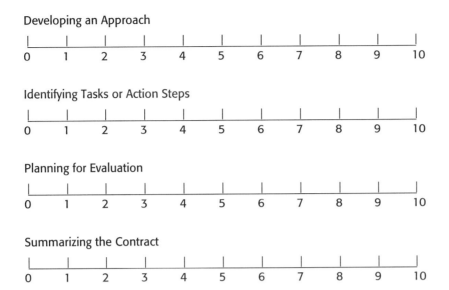

Developing an Approach

| | | | | | | | | | | |
0   1   2   3   4   5   6   7   8   9   10

Identifying Tasks or Action Steps

| | | | | | | | | | | |
0   1   2   3   4   5   6   7   8   9   10

Planning for Evaluation

| | | | | | | | | | | |
0   1   2   3   4   5   6   7   8   9   10

Summarizing the Contract

| | | | | | | | | | | |
0   1   2   3   4   5   6   7   8   9   10

7. Finally, review your ratings to identify those contracting skills in which you remain less proficient (e.g., a score of 7 or less). Then, in the space below, outline the steps you might take to improve your skill in those areas.

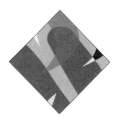

Chapter 10

Working and Evaluating

As you engage clients in the process of working toward the goals you have jointly agreed on, you make a transition. You move from those social work skills that are used primarily for collecting information, developing a relationship, formulating an assessment, and negotiating the contract to those skills that are used to promote change. These *working and evaluating skills* build on the clients' experience and frame of reference by introducing, in a much more expressive fashion, your own professional knowledge and expertise.

The skills covered in earlier chapters are primarily empathic, exploratory, and contractual in nature. You use them to clarify policies under which you will operate; to explore factors associated with the origin, development, and maintenance of the problems of concern; to learn about and understand the client's experience of the person-problem-situation from the client's own perspective; to develop an assessment; and to agree on a plan or approach for pursuing the goals toward which you will work. Throughout these processes, you listen actively, probe, and seek feedback. In empathic fashion, you regularly reflect understanding back to the client. This encourages further self-expression and self-exploration on the part of the client, while strengthening your relationship. You may go slightly beyond the literal statements of the client, but your primary focus is on the client's experience and frame of reference.

The working and evaluating skills are significantly different. Here, you may appropriately proceed from and express your social work frame of reference—your own professional knowledge and experience. These tend to be more expressive than empathic in nature. Through the working and evaluating skills, you express your professional agenda—your thoughts, feelings, beliefs, opinions, hypotheses, deductions, and conclusions. You first use such an expressive skill during the beginning phase of practice, when you suggest a tentative purpose for meeting and outline relevant policy and ethical factors. You also express your knowledge and experience when you share your view of a problem or propose a goal during the assessing and contracting processes.

Occasionally, the expressive skills bear little obvious relationship to the words or actions of the clients. Most of the time, however, they reflect your attempt to expand on the client's experience. You use what you have learned from the client in order to process it from your own professional perspective. Then you express yourself in a fashion you believe will be useful to the client in progressing toward the final goals.

Because the working and evaluating skills tend to be expressive rather than empathic, you must be especially clear about your rationale for using them at a particular time. Your motivations must be professional, not personal. You should not share your knowledge, feelings, or opinions simply because they occur to you at the moment. Rather, the working skill you select must relate to the contract for work. To help you determine whether an expressive working skill is indeed appropriate and applicable, ask yourself questions such as the following. "Have we adequately explored the person, problem, and situation? Have I sufficiently communicated empathic understanding of the client's experience that I may now reasonably consider using a work-phase expressive skill? Do we have a clear contract for work? What is my objective in using this skill at this time? Will the use of this skill now help the client with our agreed-upon work toward problem resolution and goal attainment? Does the use of this skill convey respect for the client's personal values and cultural preferences? How will the client react to my expression? What is the risk that using this skill now might endanger the client's individual or social well-being? How do I personally think and feel about this client at this time? Am I tempted to use a working skill now in order to express a personal view or satisfy my own impulse?"

Such an analysis should help you to determine the appropriateness and applicability of a work-phase expressive skill. If there is doubt, simply return to an empathic, exploring skill.

During the work and evaluation phase, of course, you continue to use many of the empathic skills previously discussed. Reflective communications, probing, and seeking clarification are needed throughout the entire helping process. During this phase, however, working skills such as rehearsing, reviewing, focusing, reframing, and advising are increasingly used. In using expressive working skills, you maintain your focus on the assessment and contract for work. In particular, your efforts are shaped by the established goals. Each application of a working skill should, in some way, relate to one or more of the goals.

The skills especially applicable to this phase include (1) rehearsing action steps, (2) reviewing action steps, (3) evaluating, (4) focusing, (5) educating, (6) advising, (7) representing, (8) responding with immediacy, (9) reframing, (10) confronting, (11) pointing out endings, and (12) progress recording.

Rehearsing Action Steps

Often, as part of the contracting process, clients have agreed to attempt a task or action step. In the work phase, the worker prepares and motivates them to carry out the task. Unfortunately, commitments made by clients during an interview frequently do not translate into action outside the context of your meeting together. This is one of the major challenges you and clients must confront if your work together is to be more than a palliative. Some means must be incorporated into the working process to facilitate the transfer of learning into the real world of the client. Several things may be done within the context of the interview itself; these may be conceptualized as in-session tasks. Procedures such as role-play, guided practice, and visualization serve to bridge the gap between the special circumstances of the social work interview and the more common environment of everyday life. Rehearsal activities incorporate aspects of doing with thinking and feeling. Involving more than talk alone, these activities constitute action-step practice. Engaging several dimensions of experience (thinking, feeling, doing) in the rehearsal activity, the client moves closer to what is necessary in the real-world context.

Rehearsing an action step decreases anxiety associated with the idea of taking the action, enhances motivation, and increases the probability that the step will be taken. It also improves the chance that the action step will be successful. In using this skill, you review the action step with the client and then consider probable scenarios. Of course, many clients are quite capable of generating alternate courses of action, but some are not. When a client needs such help, you may appropriately assume a more active role in identifying options. You might propose a few different ways to undertake the step or present examples of how other people do so. As part of the rehearsal process, you might *model* the action step for the client by saying or doing what is needed. Or, in a *role-play,* you may assume the role of a person who will be involved in the client's enactment of the action step. During or following the role-play, you give the client guidance, feedback, support, and encouragement.

Another form of rehearsal involves clients *visualizing* themselves undertaking an agreed-upon action step (Lazarus, 1984). Before using visualization, you must first determine whether a particular client has the capacity to create mental pictures. You might probe for this by asking, "If I were to ask you to imagine in your mind's eye the kitchen in the place where you live, could you do so?" If the client says "Yes," you could then say, "Good, some people aren't able to imagine as well as you do. Your mental capacity in this area will help us a great deal in our work together." You might then say, "Please assume a relaxed position and take a few slow, deep breaths. You may close your eyes if you wish but closing your eyes is not essential—many people can visualize just as well with their eyes open." Then you might go on to ask, "Please imagine a movie screen on which you can see the context where the step you'll take will occur. Now see yourself actually taking the action we have discussed." You might pause briefly and then ask the client to study the visualized scene in great detail, noticing all aspects of the action step.

Visualization can be used for the purpose of identifying client fears and anticipating potential obstacles to successful action, as well as for the purpose of rehearsal. When you and a client clearly understand what needs to be done, you may ask him or her to imagine successfully completing the action step. Following that, you may also ask the client to identify the positive thoughts and feelings that accompany imaginary completion of the action step.

Returning to the Chase case, the following is an excerpt from an interview in which Susan Holder helps the client rehearse an action step through role-play.

Example

WORKER: (identifying an action step; seeking feedback) One of the steps we identified is to express your affection for both Robert and Richard at least once each day. If I understand the usual patterns correctly, this would represent a change from the way you have recently related. Is that right?

CLIENT (MRS. CHASE): Yes, it would be a big change.

WORKER: It's been my experience that accomplishing changes such as this takes quite a bit of planning and preparation. Unless the step is practiced ahead of time, there is a tendency for things to stay the same. With that in mind, I wonder if you would be willing to practice with me what you are going to say and do each day?

CLIENT: Okay.

WORKER: Thanks. When you think of where and when you might make your first caring statement to Robert, what comes to mind?

CLIENT: Well, I think that I'd like to start off the day with something positive.

WORKER: Good idea! Where do you think you will be when you make your first affectionate statement?

CLIENT: Well, I think it will probably be in the kitchen.

WORKER: In the kitchen. . . . Let me assume the role of Robert. And, if you would, please let's imagine that it's tomorrow morning and we are now in the kitchen. What will you say to him tomorrow?

CLIENT: Well, I think I'll say something like, "Robert, I know that we have been on each other's nerves lately. I know that a lot of it has been my fault. I guess I've been more stressed out than I realized. Anyway, I want to say I'm sorry and I want you to know that I have never loved you more than I do now."

WORKER (AS ROBERT): Geez. Thanks, Mom. I love you too.

WORKER (AS HERSELF): Thanks Lynn. When you say those words to Robert, I can really feel your love for him. How does it feel to you?

CLIENT: It feels really good. I feel warm inside. Loving toward him and also better about myself.

WORKER: How do you think Robert will respond to your words?

CLIENT: I'm not sure. But I do think he'll like it, and it should bring us closer.

WORKER: That's exactly what you want to happen, isn't it?

CLIENT: Yes, it sure is.

WORKER: How do you feel when you realize that Robert will probably appreciate your comments and feel very loved?

CLIENT: Really good. I can't wait until tomorrow morning!

The following excerpt illustrates how Ms. Holder, the social worker, helps Mrs. Chase rehearse an action step through the use of visualization.

Example

WORKER: *(identifying the step; exploring probability of action; seeking feedback)* One of the steps we identified as a means to decrease stress and increase feelings of personal comfort is to spend 15 minutes each day planning for or working in your garden. I must admit to wondering about your ability to actually do that. You are very busy. You do so many things that I wonder whether you will really take the time to do the 15 minutes of gardening each day. What do you think?

CLIENT (MRS. CHASE): Well, to be honest, I have known for some time that I need to get back to gardening and I just haven't done it. I keep on making promises to myself and I keep on breaking them.

WORKER: Thanks for being frank with me. If we're going to get anywhere with these problems, honesty and openness is the best policy. If you don't think you will actually take a step that we identify, please tell me.

CLIENT: Okay, I will.

WORKER: Thanks Lynn. Making changes such as this takes a good deal of planning and preparation. Unless we practice ahead of time, things tend to stay the same. With that in mind, I wonder if you would be willing to try a little experiment that may make it a little easier to actually do the gardening that you'd like to do?

CLIENT: Well, I guess so. What kind of experiment?

WORKER: I'm sure that you've heard the old saying, "Practice makes perfect." Well, for many people, practicing in one's imagination is nearly as effective as practicing for real. If you happen to be one of the people who can form mental pictures, then we can use that capacity to increase the likelihood that you will actually begin to garden for real. Is that description clear?

CLIENT: Yes, I think so. How do I do it?

WORKER: First, let's find out about your picture-making ability. Please try now to imagine your garden as it used to be when it was in full bloom. Can you picture it?

CLIENT: Yes. I can see it now.

WORKER: Can you see it in color or is it black and white?

CLIENT: It's in color.

WORKER: Now please imagine yourself in the garden tilling the soil around the growing plants. Is that the sort of thing you might be doing?

CLIENT: Yes. I'd be down on my knees, working the soil.

WORKER: Can you visualize that in your mind's eye?

CLIENT: Yes.

WORKER: Now, please describe what you are feeling, what you are experiencing, as you work the garden.

CLIENT: Well, I feel warm and relaxed. I feel content. I feel happy. Working the soil is, well, it's pleasurable.

WORKER: Now please picture yourself in the garden this very evening. Can you do that?

CLIENT: Yes.

WORKER: And does that feel as good as the other picture did?

CLIENT: Yes.

WORKER: Now, let's shift to a different picture. Suppose it rains. Can you imagine planning or preparing for the garden in a way that would also be relaxing or pleasurable?

CLIENT: Yes. I can work on my drawings of the garden. I kind of draft out what plants, what fruits, what vegetables go where in the garden. I also work out what to plant when, and the approximate date they should be harvested.

WORKER: And what do you feel in this picture?

CLIENT: I feel just as relaxed and content as when I'm in the garden itself.

WORKER: Let's create a picture of you actually doing that on rainy days when you cannot go out into the garden.

CLIENT: Okay.

As a result of rehearsing, whether through role-play, guided practice, visualization, or some combination, clients are more likely to carry out the activity in their own world.

◆ EXERCISE 10-1: REHEARSING ACTION STEPS

For these exercises, assume that you are a social worker with a family counseling center. Respond in the spaces provided by describing what you would do and say in using the skill of rehearsing the action steps you identified as part of Exercise 9-6.

1. You are in the midst of an interview with Mrs. O., the 77-year-old widow who lives alone. You have agreed on the problems and goals for work and have identified an action step. In the space below, describe what you would do and say in using the skill of rehearsing the action step with this client. In formulating your description, anticipate what the client might say or do in response to your statements and actions.

2. You are in the midst of an interview with the seven-member, blended S. family. You have agreed on the problems and goals for work and have identified an action step. In the space below, describe what you would do and say in using the skill of rehearsing the action step with this client system. In formulating your description, anticipate what the clients might say or do in response to your statements and actions.

3. You are interviewing Mrs. F. You have agreed on the problems and goals for work and have identified an action step. In the space below, describe what you would do and say in using the skill of rehearsing the action step with this client. In formulating your description, anticipate what the client might say or do in response to your statements and actions.

Reviewing Action Steps

There are three possible outcomes when a client agrees to undertake an action step: (1) the client may complete it; (2) the client may partially complete it; or (3) the client may not attempt any portion of the action step. The first two outcomes almost always represent progress; the third does not. Even the third outcome, however, may be useful if the process is carefully reviewed in order to improve the chance of success in the future. In working with clients, try to increase the probability that they will attempt and complete agreed-upon action steps. If clients rehearse an action step before attempting it for real, they are more likely to try it. Motivation is also enhanced when clients understand that they will have a chance to *review the action step* after attempting it. For most clients, when you demonstrate your interest in the process and outcome of their action steps by asking about them, you help to increase the probability that further action steps will be attempted. By reviewing what happened following the attempt, you also gather information that can be used in the evaluation of progress toward goal achievement and in identifying subsequent action steps.

In reviewing action steps, adopt an attitude of supportive curiosity. If the client has partly or completely undertaken the activity, express your pleasure. If a client has not attempted the action step, on the other hand, it is usually unwise to express disapproval or criticism. Rather, convey your interest by questions such as "What do you think got in the way of your attempt?" In such circumstances, explore with the client the thinking and feeling experiences that led him or her to defer taking the action step. Also inquire about situational factors that may have contributed to a change in plans. Often, it will become clear that unanticipated obstacles interfered with completion of the action step. Alternate plans can then be devised, and you and the client can proceed to rehearse the revised action step. When a client has completed an action step, you may appropriately express both pleasure and curiosity as you inquire about the factors contributing to the accomplishment. "What was different this time that enabled you to take this step?" For clients who have partly completed the activity, inquire with pleasure and interest about those differences that made it possible to take this "step in the right direction." Later, you may explore what factors blocked a more complete attempt and then, with the client, formulate a slightly revised plan. If clients have partially or completely undertaken the action step, encourage them to identify and express the satisfying thoughts and feelings that accompany action toward goal achievement. In many circumstances, you may also appropriately share your positive impressions about the client's efforts. Following such encouragement, you and the client may then proceed to identify and rehearse additional action steps.

Example
Reviewing a Completed Action Step

WORKER (MS. HOLDER): Last time we talked, you agreed to spend 15 minutes each day in gardening activities. If you recall, we went through the process of visualizing those activities in your mind's eye. How did that work out?

CLIENT (MRS. CHASE): It was great! I gardened every day, sometimes more than 15 minutes, and I enjoyed it enormously. It spread out into other parts of my life too. I felt more calm and content throughout the day.

WORKER: Wonderful! So, it was truly effective in increasing your feelings of contentment?

CLIENT: Yes. It really worked. I had only one headache all week, and I felt much better.

WORKER: Terrific! Now is there anything about the gardening activity that we should change in order to make it better?

CLIENT: No. It's working just fine. Let's not change anything about it.

WORKER: Agreed. Let's keep the gardening activity just the same. That is, each day you will spend 15 minutes in a gardening activity. Is that right?

CLIENT: Yes.

Example
Reviewing a Partially Completed Action Step

WORKER (MS. HOLDER): Last time we talked, you agreed to spend 15 minutes each day in gardening activities. If you recall, we went through the process of visualizing those activities in your mind's eye. How did that work out?

CLIENT (MRS. CHASE): Well, I gardened on two days this week but I couldn't find the time to do any more than that. I was just too busy.

WORKER: You were able to find time to do the gardening on two of the seven days. That's a very good beginning. On the two days that you gardened, what was it like?

CLIENT: Well, I guess at the beginning of the week I was just determined to do the gardening. I did it and I liked it. It's a lot to do, to start up a garden when you haven't worked on it for a long time. But I enjoyed it a lot and I felt good on those two days. On the third day, I just couldn't find the time.

WORKER: It sounds like the two days that you did the gardening were very good days for you. You enjoyed those days at lot. On the third day when you did not garden you didn't feel as well. Would I be correct in saying that the gardening is definitely a helpful activity?

CLIENT: Oh, yes! If only I would do it!

WORKER: Let's see if we can figure out some way to make it easier for you to do the gardening and gain the benefits from it. What was different about the days that you did garden from the days that you didn't?

CLIENT: Well, I was really motivated on the first two days. On the third day, I had a tough time at work, and I was exhausted when I got home. I just slumped onto the sofa and went to sleep. I guess I was tired every night after that.

WORKER: Let's assume then that when you come home from work really tired, it's much harder for you to do the gardening, even though it leads to relaxing and contented feelings. I wonder, when you fall asleep on the sofa after work, do you awaken feeling as rested and relaxed as you do when you garden?

CLIENT: Actually, I feel much worse after dozing on the sofa. I'm kind of grouchy for the rest of the evening. And, I don't sleep very well at night. It's better when I garden.

WORKER: Now that we know that, let's see what we can do to help you garden even when you're tired and exhausted from work. Imagine that you have just come home from a stressful day at work. You're exhausted. Your usual pattern has been to crash on the sofa. This time, however, imagine yourself taking a drink of ice water and walking out to the garden. You sit in a chair and look at your garden while drinking the ice water. You don't do anything. You just sit there. After ten minutes or so, you can feel the stress and exhaustion begin to lessen. You decide to do just a little bit of gardening. After 15 minutes, you pause, and notice that you feel calm and relaxed. You're no longer tired. Instead, you're ready to go on with the rest of your evening . . . How about it, Mrs. Chase, could you imagine that pretty clearly?

CLIENT: Yes. And I can see myself really relaxing during the gardening. I don't relax as well when I sleep on the sofa.

WORKER: In that case, what do you think about trying the 15 minutes of gardening again during this next week—only, let's go for four days instead of all seven?

CLIENT: That sounds good. I think I'll do it this week.

Example
Reviewing an Unattempted Action Step

WORKER (MS. HOLDER): Last time we talked, you agreed to spend 15 minutes each day in gardening activities. If you recall, we went through the process of visualizing those activities in your mind's eye. How did that work out?

CLIENT (MRS. CHASE): Well, I thought about it but I couldn't find the time to do any gardening at all. I was just too busy.

WORKER: You were unable to find time to do the gardening at all during this past week. Tell me, during this week's time, have there been any signs that things are getting better?

CLIENT: Well, no. Things are about the same. I did feel a lot better after talking with you last time, but that lasted only a day or so.

WORKER: It sounds like there was some temporary relief from talking about the problems with me, but there hasn't been any real progress, is that right?

CLIENT: Yes, I'm afraid so.

WORKER: Let's talk some about the gardening activity itself. In our discussion last time, you were quite sure that if you began to garden again, even for a little bit, you would soon feel better. Do you think that still holds true, or have you reconsidered whether gardening would actually be helpful to you?

CLIENT: Well, I know it would help me, but I just can't find the time.

WORKER: If you still think the gardening would be helpful, let's see if we can identify what gets in the way of taking time to do it. During this past week, what did you end up doing instead of the gardening?

CLIENT: Well, on the first evening I planned to garden, Robert injured his knee playing basketball and I had to take him to the emergency room. He has been in bed all this week. I've been nursing him each evening after I get home from work.

WORKER: Your son's injury got in the way. How is his knee now?

CLIENT: Well, it's much better. He should be able to get out of bed about the middle of next week. Then he'll start walking around the house. By the first part of the following week, he should be able to return to school.

WORKER: It sounds as if your son is well on the way to recovery, and you will soon have more time once he can get around on his own. Do you think that when he does start to walk again, you will be more likely to do the gardening?

CLIENT: I think so. It depends upon how much help he needs.

WORKER: It sounds like you'll be nursing him at least for another several days. What is involved when you care for him in the evening?

CLIENT: Well, first I make him supper and then I take it to his room. Then we talk for a while. Then I clean up the kitchen and do the dishes. Then I check on Robert again. We usually talk some more. By that time, it's time for bed.

WORKER: Lynn, it seems to me that we have a choice to make here. First, if you really believe that once Robert is better you will begin the gardening, we can simply delay the starting date of the gardening activities. If you believe, however, that if it were not Robert's injury it would be something else that would prevent you from gardening, then perhaps we should take this opportunity to challenge the pattern of excessive caretaking. We have explored this before. If your decision not to garden is a matter of neglecting yourself rather than simply a matter of unusual circumstances, perhaps we might begin to change that right now while Robert is still injured. What do you think?

CLIENT: Well, honestly, I think it's some of both. Robert's injury gives me an opportunity to caretake him and it provides me with a reason not to take good care of myself by gardening.

WORKER: Then, what do you think? Should we delay the startup date for the gardening activities, or should we start now in order to challenge the tendency to avoid caring for yourself?

CLIENT: Well, I guess I'd like to start right now. Even with Robert's injury, I should be able to find 15 minutes at some point during the evening.

WORKER: All right. I wonder, though, because of the extra responsibilities due to Robert's injury, should we change the plan from 15 minutes every single day to 15 minutes three times during the next week? That might be more reasonable, given the current circumstances.

CLIENT: Yes, yes. I think that would be just about right. I know I can garden three times during the next seven days.

WORKER: Okay. We've changed the plan for gardening from once every day to three times during the next week. Now, what do you think about rehearsing this a little bit?

As a result of reviewing action steps, clients are more likely to believe that you are genuinely interested in them. Reviewing increases the probability that additional action steps will be attempted and successfully completed.

◆ EXERCISE 10-2: REVIEWING ACTION STEPS

For these exercises, assume that you are a social worker with a family counseling center. In the spaces provided, create simulated dialogues between yourself and the client that reflect how you might use the skill of reviewing action steps. Follow up on the case situations for which you identified action steps in Exercise 9-6.

1. You are in the midst of reviewing action steps with Mrs. O., a 77-year-old widow who lives alone. She reports that she has fully completed the agreed-upon action step. In the space below, write the words you might say in reviewing the action step with this client.

2. You are in the midst of reviewing action steps with the seven-member, blended S. family. The family indicates that they partly carried out the agreed-upon action step. In the space below, write the words you might say in reviewing the action step with them.

3. You are in the midst of reviewing action steps with Mrs. F. She reports that she did not attempt the agreed-upon action step. In the space below, write the words you might say in reviewing the action step with this client.

Evaluating

Evaluation of progress is crucial during the work and evaluation phase. It often occurs while reviewing action steps. Through the skill of *evaluating*, you engage the client in reviewing progress toward goal attainment. Progress may be indicated by changes in such indicators as goal attainment scales, frequency counts, subjective ratings, or paper-and-pencil instruments. The presence or absence of progress, as well as the rate of change, if any, can be recorded in case notes or presented graphically. When reviewed with clients, evidence of progress may improve self-esteem and increase motivation to undertake further action. Over time, if evaluation reveals no progress, or change in a negative direction, you and the client should reconsider the assessment, the contract, and the action steps that you have planned. Obviously, when progress toward goal achievement is not forthcoming, you must reexamine the approach to change.

Through the skill of evaluating, you engage the client in examining data that have been collected in accordance with your plan for evaluating progress. You and the client consider the information and determine whether it reflects progress toward goal attainment and problem alleviation, no change, or a change in the wrong direction. As you do when reviewing action steps, you may appropriately express your pleasure when there is clear evidence of progress and encourage clients to identify those factors that contributed to make the positive changes. When there is no evidence of progress, you may ask the client to help analyze why. You and the client then consider whether a major revision in the plan is needed or whether relatively minor adjustments might suffice. Frequently, the evaluation instruments provide useful information to supplement the client's experience and your own observations. When problems worsen, you and the client engage in an intensive reanalysis. Together, you need to determine if the planned action steps, rather than helping, have contributed to the deteriorating situation. Often, initial negative effects are an expected but temporary phenomenon, subsequently followed by positive results. Because of the systemic nature of many problems, it is not uncommon for "things to become worse before they get better." Also, negative effects are not always the result of your approach or the action steps undertaken. They may be effects of ongoing changes in the person-situation. Of course, sometimes they are indeed caused by the change program itself. When this occurs, a major revision to the contract is imperative.

As an example, consider Mrs. Chase's daily sleep log, in which she records the number of hours she sleeps each night. The social worker, Susan Holder, has reviewed these daily logs and converted the sleep data into the graph displayed in Figure 10.1.

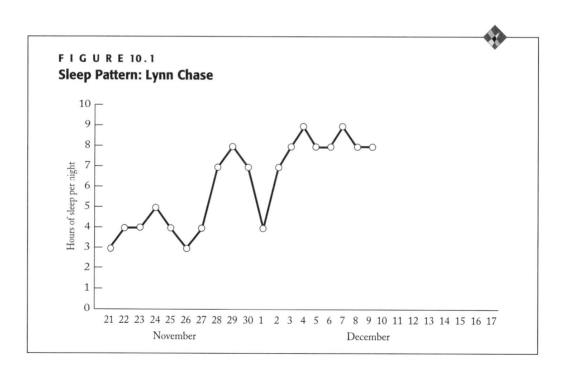

FIGURE 10.1
Sleep Pattern: Lynn Chase

As the graph shows, Mrs. Chase slept approximately four hours nightly during the period between November 21 and November 27. According to her, four hours has been the approximate amount she has slept each night over the last few months. On the evening of November 28, following the second interview with Susan Holder, Mrs. Chase implemented the change program they had jointly devised. Beginning on that night and continuing for the next 12 days, Mrs. Chase's daily log reflects general progress toward achieving the goal of sleeping eight hours nightly. There were only two nights when she did not sleep at least seven hours.

In evaluating progress, Mrs. Chase and Susan can reasonably infer that, with regard to the goal of sleeping more, the plan is working successfully. They should also review Mrs. Chase's subjective ratings concerning how refreshed she feels upon awakening in the morning. Those ratings may also be converted into graph form for ready review.

◆ EXERCISE 10-3: EVALUATING

For these exercises, assume that you are a social worker with a family counseling center. In the spaces provided, create simulated dialogues between yourself and the client, showing how you might use the skill of evaluating progress toward goal attainment.

1. You are in the midst of evaluating progress toward goal attainment with Mrs. O. The measurement data clearly indicate that progress toward goal achievement has not occurred; in fact, the problems have worsened. In the space below, create a simulated dialogue between yourself and the client as you review the data and discuss the implications.

2. You are in the midst of evaluating progress toward goal attainment with the S. family. The measurement data indicate that progress toward goal achievement has not occurred. There has been no change in either a positive or a negative direction. In the space below, create a simulated dialogue between yourself and the clients as you review the data and discuss the implications.

3. You are in the midst of evaluating progress toward goal attainment with Mrs. F. The measurement data clearly indicate that progress toward goal achievement has occurred. There is a definitive change in a positive direction. In the space below, create a simulated dialogue between yourself and the client as you review the data and discuss the implications.

Focusing

Focusing (Perlman, 1957, pp. 145–149) is a skill used to direct or maintain attention to the work at hand. Occasionally, both workers and clients wander away from the issues that are relevant to the agreed-upon purposes for work. These diversions are often productive, leading to greater understanding and improving the chances for effective change. Sometimes, however, these departures may be clearly unproductive. Through the skill of focusing, you redirect energy to relevant topics. Also, something of significance may occur that goes unnoticed by the client. By directing attention to it, you may heighten her or his awareness and understanding. For example, in working with a family, you may observe that just as plans for an action step are about to be finalized, one sibling interrupts with a complaint about another family member's past misbehavior. As a social worker, you might hypothesize that the interruption represents a defensive or self-protective act, a resistance to change, or perhaps an attempt to maintain family-system equilibrium. However you regard it theoretically, you may use the skill of focusing to respond to the interruption. You could say to the family member who interrupts, "Would you please hold on to that thought so that we can come back to it later? Let's complete our plans first. Thanks." Through such a form of focusing, you guide the family back to the work at hand. To accomplish a different purpose, that of enhancing process awareness, you might focus in a different way: "I noticed that just about the time we were reaching consensus on a step to address one of the problems, Johnny brought up his concern about Sheila's past behavior. I wonder, Johnny, what do you think led you to raise the topic at this particular time?"

◆ EXERCISE 10-4: FOCUSING

For these exercises, assume that you are a social worker with a family counseling center. In the spaces provided, write the words you would say in using the skill of focusing.

1. You are reviewing action steps with Mrs. O. In the midst of this process, Mrs. O. begins to reminisce about a childhood girlfriend. It is your judgment that Mrs. O. would be better served at this time if you were to complete the process of reviewing action steps. You intend to return later in the interview to her childhood memory. In the space provided, write the words you would say in using the skill of focusing with Mrs. O. Also, anticipate Mrs. O.'s response and your reaction to it.

2. You are in the midst of exploring a new topic of importance to the S. family. Only the parents and the teenage children are present for this meeting. The subject involves the emerging sexuality of one of the adolescents. As the discussion begins, you observe that Mrs. S. changes the subject to a less anxiety-provoking issue. This pattern seems to occur whenever the adolescent family members begin to express sexual concerns. Based on your professional judgment, you conclude that continuing with the topic of adolescent sexuality would be congruent with the values and cultural background of the family, helpful to the family, and would represent a step toward goal achievement. You therefore decide to use the skill of focusing. In the space provided, write the words you would say in demonstrating two forms of focusing with the S. family. First, show how you would focus in order to redirect the discussion back to the topic of adolescent sexuality. Second, indicate how you might refocus in order to enhance the family's awareness of the pattern of shifting away from difficult topics. Also, anticipate Mrs. S.'s response and your reaction to her statements.

3. You are in the midst of role-playing an action step with Mrs. F. She has assumed the role of her own daughter. A few moments after taking the part of her own daughter, Mrs. F.'s eyes begin to water, and then tears start to fall onto her cheeks. Mrs. F. shrugs and continues in the role of her daughter. You make a professional judgment that Mrs. F would benefit from a more complete expression of her feelings and an exploration of the meaning of the tears. You also realize that such steps would be entirely consistent with the contract for work. In the space provided, write the words you would say in using the skill of focusing to call attention to the tears as well as to the thoughts and feelings behind them. Also, anticipate Mrs. F.'s response and your reaction to it.

Educating

During the work phase, it may become apparent that a client lacks certain information or competency that might aid in the achievement of the agreed-upon goals for work. In such circumstances, you may appropriately assume the role of teacher or educator. The skill of *educating* involves several dimensions. Often, you share knowledge and educated opinions. For example, you might inform parents about major developmental milestones that are to be expected in an infant's first year of life. You could share your ideas about how parents might facilitate childhood development through, for instance, mutual play activities. In educating, the information should be conveyed in such a way that clients may freely consider its relevance for their particular situation and decide whether to accept it. This is particularly true when the information you express is opinion rather than fact. Even when factually correct information is presented, you continue to respect the right of clients to disagree and choose their own course of action.

In educating clients, realize that all people do not learn in the same way. There are several different learning styles; some of your clients are likely to have learning styles that differ from your own preferred manner of teaching or learning. Therefore, try to individualize your educational approach in order to reach each client. For example, some clients have an affinity for deductive thinking. They enjoy theoretical concepts and principles. Once an abstract principle is understood, they can apply it through deductive reasoning to everyday life. Other clients possess strength in inductive thinking: They can take a specific incident or situation and reach a clear understanding of it. Sometimes, this understanding can then be applied to similar circumstances in the future, but at other times these clients may have to go through the learning process all over again. Such clients frequently benefit more from examples, illustrations, and specific guidelines than from abstract presentations. Many clients also learn better when you tell a story, use a metaphor, or share an analogy. For example, in working with an adult male client who feels trapped by circumstances, you might—having thoroughly explored the situation with the client—realize that he is, in many ways, trapping himself. There are options, but the client has not really seen or seriously considered them. At such a time, you might tell a story in the following fashion.

Example

I remember a comic strip I once saw. In the first frame, there is a desperate-looking man, staring out between the iron bars of a jail. His eyes and head are absolutely still. He looks only through the bars and nowhere else. He seems to be highly anxious, afraid, and depressed all at the same time. In the second frame, we see the scene from a more distant perspective. Again we notice the desperate man looking out between the bars. But then we notice that there are iron bars on one side of the room only. The other three sides don't have bars at all; there aren't even any walls. It's completely open. The prisoner, if he would only move his head out from between the bars and look in another direction, could easily see that he could walk away any time he wanted.

In addition, some clients learn best by hearing, others by seeing, and others through a multisensory learning approach (a combination of hearing, seeing, and physically experiencing). Some people learn best by working independently; others by working cooperatively with others, receiving guidance and feedback throughout the process. Certain individuals are more receptive to learning during the morning, others during the afternoon, and still others during the evening hours. Some people enjoy moving around while learning, whereas others prefer stillness. Some prefer to have stimulation in the form of music or background noise, while others learn best when it is absolutely quiet. As you try to educate clients, discover their preferred learning styles and adapt your teaching approach accordingly.

Sometimes, you can serve important educational functions by sharing personal feelings and experiences. It is very much like telling a story, but it is a story about yourself. In self-disclosing, you almost always become a more genuine human being to the client. Additionally, the personal experience may carry special meaning to the client, who might attribute considerable significance to the message or moral of your personal story. In sharing your personal feelings and experiences, however, be careful not to become the client's client. There should be a clear relationship between your own self-disclosures and the established goals for work. Also, you should not take so much time in sharing your experiences and feelings that it detracts significantly from the client's opportunity for self-expression. If you share too much of yourself, especially personal difficulties or tragedies, the client may begin to view you as troubled or needy rather than as competent. If your client does begin to see you in this light, it could seriously diminish your effectiveness. The client might abruptly end the relationship with you and look for a healthier professional. Alternately, your client may start to take care of you, assuming the role of caretaker or surrogate parent. In addition, your client might begin to protect you from the full impact of the truth about the situation. Therefore, be cautious about speaking of yourself too often or to too great an extent. Remember, social work services are primarily for the client, not for you.

◆ **EXERCISE 10-5: EDUCATING**

For these exercises, assume that you are a social worker with a family counseling center. In the spaces provided, write the words you would say in using the skill of educating.

1. You are in the midst of discussing Mrs. O.'s eating patterns with her. You discover that she almost never has a hot meal and rarely eats vegetables. Her most typical meal is a bologna sandwich. You and Mrs. O. agree that more balanced meals are desirable. You then begin to educate Mrs. O. about the meals-on-wheels program available in your community. Through this program, Mrs. O. could have delivered to her apartment one or two hot, nutritionally balanced meals per day. In the space provided, outline the major elements of the information you would like to communicate to her. Then write the words

you would say as you begin to educate Mrs. O. about the meals-on-wheels program.

2. You are in the midst of an individual meeting with a teenage member of the S. family. She reports to you in confidence that she is sexually active and "will continue to have sex with my boyfriend no matter what my mother says!" She reports that she and her boyfriend do not practice birth control but that she would like to have some protection. She also mentions that she has recently begun to feel some unusual itching and discomfort "down there" (in her vaginal area). In the space provided, outline the major elements of the information you would like to communicate to her. Then write the words you would say in beginning to educate the teenager about birth control possibilities and about medical care.

3. You are role-playing an action step with Mrs. F. She plays the role of her daughter while you play the part of Mrs. F. Through this experience, Mrs. F. becomes aware of her feelings of extreme guilt about the way she has reared her children. She sobs and says, "I tried not to repeat the bad things my parents did to me, but it looks like I did so anyway." In the space provided, outline the major elements of the information you might communicate to Mrs. F. in educating her about the human tendency to repeat intergenerational family patterns even when trying not to. Then, write the words you would say in telling a story or disclosing a personal experience of your own, so as to begin to educate the Mrs. F. about this human tendency.

Advising

In working with clients, it is sometimes proper for you to provide advice. Making a suggestion or recommendation can be a perfectly appropriate action by a social worker. In using the skill of *advising*, you should almost always convey that the client may freely accept or reject your advice. As Maluccio (1979) has observed, many clients very much value and appreciate professional advice. Nonetheless, particularly during the early stages of your professional development, you may experience conflict about advising. You may be tempted to give too much advice or perhaps too little. As a social worker, you are probably keenly aware of the values of self-determination and respect for the uniqueness of each person. In interpreting these values, you might conclude that you should never offer any advice at all. Or you might decide that clients are entitled to all the knowledge you possess; you might therefore provide a great deal of advice, whether or not it is requested or needed. These two positions represent the extremes of a continuum. Most likely, you will take a more moderate stance, giving advice in certain circumstances but not in all. Some advising is usually appropriate and helpful; the key is knowing when to, when not to, and especially how to give advice.

In general, resist the temptation to offer advice based on your own personal feelings, attitudes, and preferences. This can be difficult in situations when a client asks, "What should I do?" or "What would you do if you were in my place?" For example, suppose you have worked for several weeks with a 19-year-old man who is gay. As a result of your exploration together, the young man has become much more self-accepting and comfortable with his sexual orientation. Recently, he raised the issue of whether to tell his tradition-bound parents the truth about his sexual orientation. He asks you, "Should I tell them?"

You could, of course, deftly avoid answering his question by responding with a question of your own: "What do you think?" Or you might respond directly and share your personal opinion: "Of course. Tell them. You have nothing to be ashamed about." Or, not knowing what to do or say, you might become confused and uncertain. On the one hand, you might expect that the client would probably feel less distressed and more personally integrated if he were to tell his parents about his sexual orientation. On the other hand, you might also anticipate that such an encounter between the young man and his parents could be extremely stressful. It could conceivably lead to the loss of his parents' approval and support; he might even lose all contact with them. You might come to the conclusion that this decision is ultimately his and his alone to make. Following that line of thinking, you might respond directly to his question, but without advising him what to do: "I'd be more than glad to explore this issue with you and help you make a decision. But I cannot simply give you an easy, direct answer to that question. I cannot advise you what to do. The final decision is yours and yours alone to make."

Of course, there are also many occasions when you clearly should offer direct and specific advice. For example, suppose that you have been helping an adult female client become more assertive with her lover. You and the client have rehearsed assertive communication during your meetings together. The client is about to take a step toward greater assertion in her intimate relationship. You believe that soft or caring expressions tend to strengthen relationships and provide a basis for moving toward hard or confrontational assertions. You therefore advise the client to begin with affectionate, caring assertions and later, after some experience, to initiate assertive expressions that involve requests that her partner make changes.

Usually, it is preferable to provide advice in such a way that the client may freely accept or reject it. On some occasions, however, you may actually need to direct the actions of clients or other persons. For example, in an emergency where an injured child is in life-threatening danger, you might direct another by saying, "We must get this child to the hospital now!"

Advising is involved in many aspects of practice. You might, for example, advise an adult male client who grew up in a family where his father was regularly intoxicated and abusive to read selected books on the topic of children of alcoholic families. You might suggest that the client consider attending Adult Children of Alcoholics (ACOA) or Al-Anon meetings as an adjunct to your work together. You might advise another client concerning how best to complete a job application or how to request a raise. You might advise a client to seek medical care. You might appropriately give advice concerning a variety of life circumstances. In so doing, you would phrase the advice in slightly different ways to accomplish different objectives. Unless life-threatening circumstances exist, however, you should nearly always express advice in the form of a suggestion or perhaps a strong recommendation. Avoid communicating advice as commands or directives, such as an authoritarian boss might deliver to a subordinate employee or an angry parent might say to a disobedient child.

As you begin to practice the skill of advising, please use the format outlined below. As you become more proficient in using the skill, experiment with alternate formats.

SUGGESTED FORMAT FOR ADVISING

I have a suggestion that I'd like you to consider.

I suggest (or recommend) that you _____.

◆ EXERCISE 10-6: ADVISING

For these exercises, assume that you are a social worker with a family counseling center. In the spaces provided, write the words you would say in using the skill of advising.

1. You have now provided Mrs. O. with information about the meals-on-wheels program available in your community. However, Mrs. O. seems uncertain and ambivalent about the service. In the space provided, write the words you would say in advising Mrs. O. to participate in the meals-on-wheels program.

2. During an individual meeting with a teenage member of the S. family, she describes clear symptoms that suggest she has contracted a sexually transmitted disease (STD). In the space provided, write the words you would say in advising the teenager to seek medical care.

3. As you and Mrs. F. have explored more about the relationship between her parenting patterns and the childhood experiences in her own family of origin, you conclude that she might benefit from the construction of a family genogram. In the space provided, write the words you would say in advising Mrs. F. to help you complete her family genogram.

Representing

The skill of *representing* includes those actions you take on behalf of clients in pursuit of agreed-upon goals. Representational activities are usually intended to facilitate clients' interaction with members of various social systems. Representing incorporates the interventive roles of *brokering*, *advocating*, and *mediating* (Compton & Galaway, 1994, pp. 427–438). Therefore, representing is a complex process indeed. It builds on many of the skills of the preparing, beginning, and exploring phases, as well as those of assessing, contracting, and working. Instead of working for and with the client, however, you work for the client but with others. For example, suppose an unemployed adult woman is currently homeless and desperately needs immediate shelter, food, clean clothes, and financial support. Based on your joint assessment, you and the client concur that if she were to apply directly to a certain resource agency for help, she would probably be denied. Therefore, the client asks you to represent her in this matter. You agree to make an initial contact with the appropriate agency. Then, with the support of the client, you sketch out several action steps. As in the process of preparing for a first meeting with a client, you carefully prepare for the contact with the agency in order to improve your chances of effectively representing the client.

During the course of your social work career, collect the names and phone numbers of other social workers and representatives of various community resources. Get to know people at churches, community centers, hospitals, neighborhood associations, government welfare organizations, and other systems that might serve as resources for clients. Make notes about such people and keep them in a card file or computerized database for easy access. Periodically send them friendly thank-you notes and mail letters of praise to their supervisors and agency administrators. Such actions tend to enhance your value within the helping community and improve the chances that your clients will receive the high-quality service they deserve.

In the instance of the woman in need of food and shelter, you might decide that a good first step would be to contact a social work colleague at the agency in question. Once you make telephone contact, proceed in much the same manner as if you were beginning with a client. Introduce yourself and secure an introduction in return. Depending on the circumstances, you might make a few informal, friendly remarks to put your colleague at ease. Then outline the purpose for the contact: "I have a client here with me who is in need of assistance. She is unemployed, without money. She hasn't eaten for two days and has no place to stay tonight. I'm calling in order to determine whether she might be eligible to receive some help from your agency." Following this description of purpose, you may seek feedback to confirm that your message has been understood. At this point in the process, you could invite your colleague to provide information about eligibility requirements or to inquire further about your client's circumstances.

Representing clients in such cases is often extremely satisfying. Interactions with resource persons may be both pleasant and productive. Clients may receive what they need and be treated well. If you cultivate positive relationships with resource persons and know something about the mission and programs of various service organizations, you are more likely to be effective in representing your clients.

However, representing clients is not always enjoyable or satisfying. Sometimes, you must be an assertive advocate on behalf of clients who are not being treated fairly. It can be frustrating. For example, consider the situation of a client who seeks your help in dealing with a landlord. In the middle of a cold winter, heat, which is supposed to be provided to all tenants as part of their rent, is not reaching into the client's apartment. In spite of several complaints, the landlord has taken no action to correct the situation. The client then asks you to represent her by contacting the landlord on her behalf.

First, you would use the preparing skills to formulate a preliminary plan. You explore the situation more fully with the client, securing detailed facts about the heating problem and learning about her experience as a tenant there. You might then consult city officials who are knowledgeable about housing regulations and landlord-tenant laws, expanding your own knowledge base. You also prepare for the initial contact with the landlord. In this instance, suppose you decide to telephone first. You might call, give your name, and say, "I am a social worker with the tenants' advocacy program of the city social services agency. One of your tenants, Mrs. Wicker, has contacted us about a problem with the heating system. It seems that the family has been without heat for five days. Could you tell me what's being done to repair the problem and how much longer it will be before their apartment is warm enough for them to live there?"

If the landlord does not acknowledge the problem and, for example, begins to denigrate the client, you might respond, "Regardless of the complaints you have about Mrs. Wicker and her family, they still need heat. As you know, it's dangerously cold, and the lives of the family members could be in serious jeopardy if heat is not restored soon." If the landlord remains unresponsive, you might outline the steps you could take should the heating system remain unrepaired and the family continue to be in danger. In several respects, your comments are similar to those you might share in beginning with a client. You state your purpose, describe your role as client advocate, and discuss the actions you could take should your client continue to be in need or at risk (i.e., your policies and procedures). You also make a specific request for action from the landlord (i.e., you outline the landlord's role).

If the landlord acknowledges the problem, outlines a plan and a timetable for repair, and makes a commitment to provide the family with sufficient heat, you may appropriately express your thanks and credit him for being responsive to your request. You would then apprise the client of the landlord's plan and request that she notify you about the outcome. If the landlord follows through with the plan, you might again communicate appreciation for the positive action. If the landlord does not follow through, however, you would probably contact him again, report that the apartment is still dangerously cold, and inform him specifically about the steps you will now take to ensure the safety and well-being of your client.

You will probably represent clients quite frequently as a regular part of social work practice, in order to link clients with needed community resources and to secure fair and equitable treatment, as part of the processes of mediation and conflict resolution. In representing, ensure that you have clients' informed consent to act on their behalf, and always keep their best interests in mind.

◆ EXERCISE 10-7: REPRESENTING

For these exercises, assume that you are a social worker with a family counseling center. In the spaces provided, outline the action steps you might take in representing the clients in the following situations. Describe how you would prepare to represent the client, and then write the words you would say in beginning with the person contacted on behalf of the client.

1. With her consent, you are representing Mrs. O., an elderly person who almost never has hot or nutritionally balanced meals. You are about to contact the community meals-on-wheels program in order to seek their help in providing Mrs. O. with at least one sound meal daily. In the space provided, outline the steps you would take prior to making contact, and then write the words you would say as you begin to represent Mrs. O. with the resource agency.

2. With her consent and that of her parents, you are representing Gloria, a teenage member of the S. family, in relation to some sexual issues. You have jointly decided that you will contact the office of her family physician, to arrange for a prompt appointment to deal with a sexually transmitted disease. (When Gloria called for an appointment, she was too embarrassed to say why she needed one right away. An appointment was scheduled for a month later.) In the space provided, outline the steps you would take prior to making contact with the physician's office, and then write the words you would say in beginning to represent Gloria in this matter.

3. With the informed consent of Mrs. F., you are representing her during interactions with the principal of the school, where her daughters report that they have often been harassed by several teenage boys. According to the girls, the boys spit on them and used ethnic epithets in referring to their Latino heritage. In the space provided, outline the steps you would take in preparing for contact with the principal, and then write the words you would say as you begin to represent Mrs. F.

Responding with Immediacy

The skill of *responding with immediacy* (Carkhuff & Anthony, 1979, pp. 114–116) involves exploration of the client's experiences and feelings about you, your relationship, or the work you are engaged in, *as they occur*. In responding with immediacy, you focus on the client's experience of what is occurring here and now between the two of you. These thoughts and feelings become the subject for immediate exploration. Responding with immediacy makes things real. It intensifies the relationship and encourages the client to explore relational concerns as they emerge. When you respond in an immediate manner, you also demonstrate or model an open communication style. Such openness may promote greater honesty and authenticity on the part of clients, increase their understanding of interpersonal patterns, and reduce any hesitation to address problems and goals. One format for responding with immediacy is as follows.

SUGGESTED FORMAT FOR RESPONDING WITH IMMEDIACY

Right here and now with me you seem to be
(thinking/feeling/doing/experiencing) _____.

Usually, the skill is applied directly to the client's immediate feelings about you, your relationship, or the nature and utility of your work together. Your response becomes less immediate and less powerful as you move away from the context of "right here and right now with me." Responding with immediacy occurs in the present tense. Whenever the discussion shifts into the past or future tense, the interaction becomes less immediate. For example, if you comment about something that happened between you and the client a week or two ago, he or she may recall it differently or not at all, or the client may intellectually process the information without feeling its full impact. Although it may still be a useful comment to make, exploring a previous exchange rarely has the powerful effect of responding immediately to something that is occurring right now.

In many cases, the manner in which clients relate to you is representative of their general pattern of relating with people. Clients sometime recreate in the working relationship the same problematic conditions that emerge in other relationships. By responding immediately to such relational patterns as they come up, you can help clients learn to recognize them and to develop new, more useful styles of interaction.

Responding with immediacy is not appropriate for use with all clients. It depends on the nature of your contract, including the goals for work, and your theoretical approach. In general, you would not respond with immediacy unless the client's reactions are clearly relevant to the problems and goals for work. Also, social workers differ in the degree to which they emphasize and attend to immediate interactions in their relationships with clients. Some social work practice approaches regard worker-client relational factors as extremely important, while others consider them less so. Nonetheless, most social workers recognize that client reactions within the working relationship are often relevant to the helping process. Responding with immediacy is a skill for addressing client experiences as they occur.

For example, suppose that you have begun to work with an adult female client who identifies as a problem the fact that her spouse does not like her company. Indeed, her spouse has confirmed this: "It's true. I'm sorry to say that I don't much like her company. Every time we start to talk, she drifts off into the ozone—into some daydream world." During your meetings with this client, you notice that her attention frequently does seem to wander, in a fashion similar to her spouse's description. She seems to focus on her own thoughts and listens just enough to your comments to stay distantly aware of the conversation. You begin to observe, and to feel, that when you talk, she essentially tunes you out. Since this pattern relates to the agreed-upon contract, you might appropriately respond with immediacy: "Right here and now as I'm talking, I notice that your eyes are turned away from me. You seem to be looking off into the distance and thinking about something else. What are you experiencing right now?"

The use of responding with immediacy often results in a significant increase in energy between you and your client. Both of you are likely to become much more oriented to the present moment and more engaged with one another. Because immediate responses often heighten intensity and interpersonal intimacy within the professional relationship, use the skill only after rapport is well established and, of course, a contract agreed upon. Your clients should know that you genuinely have their interest at heart before you move into the intimate realm of immediacy.

◆ EXERCISE 10-8: RESPONDING WITH IMMEDIACY

For these exercises, assume that you are a social worker with a family counseling center. In the spaces provided, write the words you would say in using the skill of responding with immediacy.

1. During a discussion with Mrs. O. about her eating patterns, you advise her to enroll in a meals-on-wheels program so she can get at least one hot meal per day. As you share your recommendation, you notice Mrs. O. turn her body away from you and subtly shake her head. You conclude that her nonverbal behavior may be saying No to your advice. In the space provided, write the words you would say in responding with immediacy to Mrs. O.'s nonverbal reaction. Also note what you anticipate her response to your comments would be.

2.	You are in the midst of an individual meeting with Gloria, a teenage member of the S. family. She confides to you that although she is sexually active with her boyfriend, she often fantasizes about another person. As she says that, she looks deeply into your eyes, blushes, and then looks away in what appears to be an embarrassed reaction. You suspect that she has had sexual fantasies about you. You know that it would be quite consistent with your contract to discuss this directly. In the space provided, write the words you would say in responding with immediacy to the teenager's expression. How do you think she would react to your immediate response?

3.	As Mrs. F. talks with you about her own parenting practices and those that she experienced as a child in her own family of origin, you observe that she sits back in her chair, crosses her arms in front of her, and appears to frown. You're not entirely certain what this reaction means, but you suspect that she may be feeling ashamed and vulnerable. You think she is afraid that you might be critical of her. In the space provided, write the words you would say in responding with immediacy to Mrs. F. How do you think she would respond to your comments?

Reframing

The term *reframing* (Bandler & Grinder, 1982; Hartman & Laird, 1983) refers to the words you say and the actions you take when introducing clients to a new way of looking at some aspect of themselves, the problem, or the situation. Usually, it involves sharing a different perspective from that which clients have previously adopted. Clients sometimes embrace a point of view in such a determined fashion that the perspective itself constitutes an obstacle to goal achievement. Of course, fixed views are not necessarily problematic, and you should not indiscriminately attempt to challenge or reframe all of them. Reframing is applicable when the fixed attitude constitutes a fundamental part of the problem for work. It is similar to the skill of educating, but it differs in that the overall purpose of reframing is to liberate the client from a dogmatic perspective. As a result of reframing, clients may reconsider strongly held beliefs. This may, in turn, affect their feelings and behavior as well.

There are several forms of reframing. One of the more common is *reframing a negative into a positive.*

Example
Reframing a Negative into a Positive

When you say that you're "stupid" and "indecisive" because you have difficulty choosing from among various courses of action, I feel confused. I mean, what you refer to as indecisive appears to me to be the ability to see different points of view. It sounds like you're open-minded and willing to consider many perspectives and options. To me, this sounds like flexibility—not indecisiveness. And what you call stupidity sounds a great deal to me like carefulness, thoroughness, and patience. These are attributes that I find extremely appealing and functional. Are you sure they are so bad?

Another form of reframing is *personalizing meaning* (Carkhuff & Anthony, 1979, pp. 95–131), through which you encourage clients to shift the attribution of responsibility away from other people, organizations, or external forces (i.e., the situation) and toward themselves. Personalizing meaning can help people assume greater responsibility for effecting change. It can be liberating, even empowering. Personalizing meaning can help clients see a relationship between their own beliefs, values, attitudes, and expectations, on the one hand, and the feelings they experience or the behavior they enact on the other. This form of reframing involves going beyond the communication directly expressed by the client. You slightly alter the client's expression so as to shift an externalized meaning toward a more internalized or personalized meaning, for which the client is likely to feel greater responsibility, personal power, and control. In personalizing meaning, you may use a format such as the following.

SUGGESTED FORMAT FOR PERSONALIZING MEANING

You feel (do or experience) _____ because

you think (believe/value/perceive/expect) _____.

Because the skill of personalizing meaning is derived from your frame of reference rather than the client's, it constitutes an expressive rather than an empathic skill. Therefore, you should phrase your comments in a tentative manner. Personalizing meaning suggests that the client's thoughts, feelings, or actions are more associated with conscious individual processes than with external or situational factors. Occasionally, it may leave clients feeling more guilty or more burdened with responsibility. It also may convey a sense of considerable optimism, because such feelings are a result of one's own values, beliefs, or thoughts. These are aspects of a person that are not necessarily permanent—one's beliefs and attitudes can and do change. Notice how much more positive such an explanation is than the view that one feels a certain way because one is jinxed, has a deficient superego structure, had a lousy childhood, suffers from a personality disorder, or because "That's just the way I am."

Here is an example of a social worker talking with a client who is a master of social work student.

Example
Personalizing Meaning

CLIENT: I'm devastated! I got a C+ in my social work field placement. I'll never make it through the program. I'm a total failure.

WORKER: You're disappointed in yourself because you believe you should do better than C+ work, and you think that getting a C+ means that you won't be able to graduate?

Situationalizing meaning is another form of reframing through which you change the meaning suggested by clients' expressions. Although there is certainly an empathic element, in this form of reframing you also begin to alter slightly the meaning as presented by the client. In the case of situationalizing meaning, you reflect understanding of the client's feelings or behavior but then suggest that they may also be viewed as a result of external, societal, systemic, situational, or other factors beyond the client's individual control or responsibility.

Frequently, situationalizing meaning results in an expansion of clients' perspectives and a lessening of their sense of guilt, self-blame, or personal responsibility.

Example
Situationalizing Meaning

CLIENT: I'm a wreck. I can't sleep or eat; I can't concentrate. I know my head is really messed up. I've always been kind of crazy.

WORKER: You feel awful; you're anxious and depressed and you have lots of problems. I wonder, though, might these feelings be an understandable reaction to the recent changes in your life? Wouldn't even the most well-adjusted person feel out of sorts and have some difficulty sleeping after being laid off from a good job and not having any immediate prospects for another?

◆ EXERCISE 10-9: REFRAMING

For these exercises, assume that you are a social worker with a family counseling center. In the spaces provided, write the words you would say in using the skill of reframing.

1. You are in the midst of discussing Mrs. O.'s eating patterns. She says that she has not been eating balanced meals because "I cannot get anyone to drive me

to the grocery, it's too far to walk, and when I telephone to have it delivered they always get it wrong." In the space provided, write the words you would say in reframing Mrs. O.'s statement so that it reflects a personalized meaning. How do you think she might react?

2. You are in the midst of an individual meeting with Gloria, a teenage member of the S. family. She says, "My mother is always on my case. She's a wild woman. She's so controlling. I can't do anything I want to do. She thinks that I'm five years old." In the space provided, write the words you would say in reframing her statement from a negative to a positive. Anticipate her reaction. Also, experiment by reframing her statement so that it has a personalized meaning.

3. During a meeting with Mrs. F., she confirms that she is indeed feeling guilty and ashamed that she may have harmed her children. She says, "I feel so ashamed. I've done just what I've always criticized my parents for." In the space provided, write the words you would say in reframing Mrs. F.'s statement so that it reflects a situationalized meaning. Also, record how you might reframe her statement so that it has a personalized meaning. Finally, respond to her words with the skill of reframing a negative into a positive. How do you think she might react to these forms of reframing?

Confronting

In *confronting* (Carkhuff & Anthony, 1979, pp. 116–119), you point out to clients—directly and without disapproval—discrepancies, inconsistencies, or contradictions in their words, feelings, and actions. In confronting, you challenge clients to examine themselves in terms of congruence. For example, suppose an adult male client has requested help from you in regard to a troubled marriage. The client says, "I am willing to do whatever is necessary to improve this relationship." Following a joint meeting with you and his spouse, during which he promised "to go out for a date with my spouse this week," he voluntarily worked overtime at his job and arrived home three hours late—too late for the date. After the client subsequently missed another planned date night, you might confront him by saying, "You said you want to improve the relationship and you agreed to two dates with your spouse. However, you worked late on the nights you had planned to go out with your wife. What do you think this might mean?"

In confronting, you may use the following format (Carkhuff & Anthony, 1979, p. 117).

SUGGESTED FORMAT FOR CONFRONTING

On the one hand you say (feel, think, or do) _____ but (and/yet) on the other hand you say (feel, think, or do) _____.

Confrontation can have a powerful effect on clients. It has the potential to cause severe disequilibrium in people who are highly stressed or have fragile coping skills. Therefore, before using the skill of confronting with a particular client, be certain that person has the psychological and social resources to endure the impact. Certainly, the relationship between you and the client should be well established prior to any confrontation. In confronting, try to be descriptive about the incongruities or discrepancies that you observe. Avoid judgmental or evaluative speculations and conclusions. Finally, it is usually wise to "precede and follow confrontations with empathic" responses (Hammond, Hepworth, & Smith, 1977, p. 280).

◆ **EXERCISE 10-10: CONFRONTING**

For these exercises, assume that you are a social worker with a family counseling center. In the spaces provided, write the words you would say in using the skill of confronting.

1. You are in the midst of an interview with Mrs. O., approximately two weeks after she has begun to receive daily hot meals through the meals-on-wheels program. Prior to that, she had agreed that more balanced meals would be desirable and said that she would eat the food when it was delivered. During the course of this meeting, you notice that the day's meal remains untouched. There is also evidence that Mrs. O. has not eaten the delivered meals for the past two days. In the space provided, write the words you would say in confronting Mrs. O. about the uneaten meals. How do you think she might respond to your confrontation?

2. You are in the midst of an individual meeting with Gloria, a teenage member of the S. family. She reports that her physician had prescribed medication for treating the sexually transmitted disease. The doctor told her to abstain from sexual intercourse during the two-week period she is to take the medication. She was also told to inform her boyfriend that he should see his doctor and be treated before he resumed any sexual relations. Otherwise, they would continue to infect each other. The girl says that her boyfriend will not go to the doctor and continues to want to have sex with her. She says, "I'll probably just let him have what he wants because if I don't, he'll go somewhere else." In the space provided, write the words you would say in confronting the girl about this situation. How do you think she might respond to your confrontation?

3. During the course of your interaction with the principal of the school where Mrs. F.'s daughters have apparently been harassed by several teenage boys, the principal says, "There is no racism at this school. The F. girls are simply too sensitive. They are the only Latino students we have in the school, and they will just have to learn to deal with the boys. We never had any trouble before they enrolled here." In the space provided, write the words you would say in confronting the principal. How do you think he might respond to your confrontation?

Pointing Out Endings

In *pointing out endings* (Shulman, 1992, p. 206), you remind the client "some time before the last sessions that the working relationship is coming to a close." In most cases where a contract has been established, a time frame for working together has also been determined. This occurs as a significant part of planning an approach to your work together (see Chapter 9). Periodically during the work phase, you make reference to this time frame for work. Of course, the timetable may be renegotiated when the situation warrants. Ideally, however, any such revision should be considered carefully and discussed openly with your client. Extending a time frame does not necessarily increase the probability of goal achievement. On occasion, additional time may imply that the goals are just too difficult to accomplish. Also, time extensions may leave an impression that your working relationship can go on indefinitely.

By pointing out endings, you may help motivate clients to work hard on the action steps so as to complete them within the established time frame. As Perlman has suggested (1979, pp. 48–77), the social work relationship is limited in time. After all, as a social worker you are not marrying or adopting your clients. You are a professional helper, not a member of their family. By establishing time limits and pointing out endings, you help clients to prepare psychologically for the process of concluding the working relationship. If the topic of the forthcoming conclusion to the relationship is avoided, you and your clients can deny the immediacy of the feelings. Such denial may allow temporary emotional respite from strong feelings, but it also prevents the parties from psychologically anticipating and preparing themselves for ending. Therefore, in spite of feelings of discomfort, you should occasionally refer to the upcoming conclusion to the relationship.

The skill of pointing out endings may be undertaken in several ways. Regardless of the specific form it takes, the skill leads the client to consider consciously and emotionally the fact that the relationship will end. Whether it involves a transfer, a referral, or a termination, you gently remind the client that there will soon be an ending and that there may very well be some thoughts and feelings triggered by the change.

For example, suppose you and a family have agreed to meet for eight sessions, with a goal of improving communication among the members. The work has proceeded quite well. By the fourth meeting, the family members have progressed to such an extent that they are able to express differences of opinion without feeling devalued or rejected. There has also been a noticeable decrease in tension and an increase in humor. Toward the end of the session, you say, "We're now finishing up our fourth session. There are four meetings left. We're halfway there."

Following such a reminder, you might probe for and explore thoughts and feelings associated with the idea of ending. You might ask, "As we think about concluding our relationship, some thoughts or feelings may come up. I wonder, would you want to talk some about them?" Or you might ask, "How will things be different once we have concluded our work together?" Although a specific format is not universally applicable, the primary element in pointing out endings is the reminder. Statements such as "We have ___ meetings left" or "We will be meeting for another ___ weeks" serve this function. In the case of transfers or referrals, clarify what will happen following your ending with the client. You might say, "We have ___ meetings left before you begin to work with _____," or "We will be meeting for another ___ weeks before you begin the program at _____."

◆ EXERCISE 10-11: POINTING OUT ENDINGS

For these exercises, assume that you are a social worker with a family counseling center. In the spaces provided, write the words you would say in using the skill of pointing out endings.

1. You have been working with Mrs. O. for approximately two months. Her eating patterns have improved to the point where your services are no longer needed. She is now regularly receiving and eating meals delivered by the meals-on-wheels program. Her weight has returned to normal, and her energy level has improved. Three weeks earlier, you and Mrs. O. had discussed the progress and decided that you would conclude your relationship in one month. The meeting next week will be your last. In the space provided, write the words you would say in pointing out endings to Mrs. O. Describe how she might react to your pointing out the upcoming ending of the relationship.

2. You are in the midst of the next-to-last meeting with the S. family. Over the course of several months, many productive changes have occurred. Two sessions before, the family members indicated that they were well on their way to accomplishing their goals. At that time, you had agreed to meet three more times. Next week you will have the concluding session. In the space provided, write the words you would say in pointing out endings with the S. family. Describe how they might react to your pointing out the upcoming ending of your working relationship with them.

3. Through a joint discussion two weeks earlier, you and Mrs. F. concluded that she could best complete work toward goal attainment by participating in a ten-week assertiveness training group sponsored by another community agency. The group begins in three weeks. Next week will be your last meeting together. In the space provided, write the words you would say in pointing out endings to Mrs. F. Describe how she might respond to your pointing out the upcoming ending of your working relationship.

Progress Recording

As a professional social worker, you are obligated to keep records throughout all phases of practice. During the work phase, you should keep track of any revisions to the initial assessment and contract. You incorporate within the case record notes about progress toward goal achievement and include the results of evaluation procedures such as goal attainment scaling, subjective ratings, test scores, or graphs. You also record additional action steps and make note of changes to those previously established. Particularly, you record events, issues, or themes that might relate to the process of working toward goal accomplishment. In some instances, you should provide a rationale for an action you are taking or a recommendation you are making. For example, suppose you were to learn from an adult male client that he sometimes sexually molests his infant son. You are, of course, required by law to report this information to relevant authorities. Usually, this means a telephone call to the child-protection services division of the department of welfare or human services. Because the information has been acquired during a meeting protected by your client-worker confidentiality, you should meticulously record the data (i.e., the words the client said) that led you to conclude that the child may be at risk of abuse. You should also record what you said to the client in response. For example, you may have informed him that you, as a professional social worker, are required by law to report this information to child-protection authorities. You should note this. You may also have indicated that you would like to continue to serve as his social worker during this time; you should record this as well. When you make the phone call to the relevant authorities, you should record the date and time, the person contacted, and what was said. Of course, unless the client provides informed consent to do so, you must refrain from sharing information about the client beyond what is needed to initiate the investigation into the possibility of child abuse.

In many settings, social workers use a problem-oriented approach to recordkeeping during the work phase (Burrill, 1976, pp. 67–68; Johnson, 1978, pp. 71–77; Martens & Holmstrup, 1974, pp. 554–561). Often, a SOAIGP format is adopted (Kagle, 1991, pp. 101–104). Derived from the original SOAP format (subjective, objective, assessment, and plan), SOAIGP stands for:

- ◆ *S—supplemental* information from clients or family members
- ◆ *O*—your *observations* and those of other agency staff
- ◆ *A—activities* that you, the client, or others undertake
- ◆ *I*—your *impressions*, hypotheses, assessments, or evaluations
- ◆ *G*—current *goals*
- ◆ *P—plan* for additional activities or action steps

Within the *supplemental* category, you may include new or revised information provided by clients, family members, or other persons within the client's primary social systems. Within the *observation* section, you may describe your own observations of the person, problem, and situation. If applicable, observations of other agency staff members may also be reported. Within the *activities* category, you may summarize client tasks, worker tasks, and in-session tasks that have occurred. Within *impressions*, you may summarize your current evaluation of progress toward goal achievement and make note of your tentative impressions and hypotheses. You may also summarize results of frequency counts, subjective ratings, and test results within this section. Under *goals*, you may record goals that are the current focus of work or make revisions to original goals. Within the *plan* section, you may make note of changes in your approach and identify additional action steps that you or your client intend to take.

For example, following an interview with Mrs. Chase, Susan Holder might prepare a SOAIGP entry for the case file as follows.

Example
SOAIGP Entry for Meeting with Lynn Chase
December 19, 1994

S. Mrs. Chase indicated that she had accomplished the action step we had identified for this week. She reported that it was a great help. She stated that she has felt in better spirits than she has for months.

Prior to the meeting, Mr. Chase had telephoned to report that things are much better at home. He said, "Everybody has begun to help out at home, and we're all much happier. Thanks a lot."

O. Mrs. Chase does indeed appear to be in much better spirits. She speaks with energy and expressiveness. Her face is animated when she talks about her family life and her gardening. When she discusses work, there is a slight change to a more "businesslike" quality.

A. During today's meeting, Mrs. Chase and I talked at length about her childhood. On several occasions, she referred to her mother's drinking and the mixed feelings she experienced as a child when she dealt with her intoxicated mother. She sobbed when she talked of the embarrassment and rage she felt when a friend had visited while her mother was drunk and verbally abusive. She also revealed that she felt "somehow to blame" for her mother's drinking. She said, "I used to feel that if I were somehow better or less of a problem, then Mother wouldn't need to drink so much."

I reminded Mrs. Chase that we had three more meetings together. She said that "she would miss me," but already "things were much better."

I. Mrs. Chase's daily logs reflect progress toward two of the goals: sleeping better and arguing less with Robert and Richard. It is my impression that the change program continues to be viable. There is no need to change it at this time.

G. The previously established goals remain in effect.

P. We identified a new action step. In addition to those already identified last week, Mrs. Chase has agreed to read Janet Woititz's book, *Adult Children of Alcoholics*, within three weeks of today's date.

Susan Holder, BSW, MSW

◆ **EXERCISE 10-12: PROGRESS RECORDING**

For these exercises, assume that you are a social worker with a family counseling center. In the spaces provided, prepare SOAIGP entries for case records concerning the following client interviews.

1. On Monday of this week, you completed an interview with Mrs. O. The meeting occurred a few weeks after she had begun to receive daily hot meals

through the meals-on-wheels program. For the first two weeks, she appeared to eat each of the meals that had been delivered. During the course of this meeting, however, you realized that the day's meal remained untouched. There was also evidence that she had not eaten the meals for the previous two days. You asked her about the uneaten food and she said that she hadn't been hungry. You asked whether she would eat the meal that would be delivered tomorrow. She said, "Oh, I don't know." In the space provided, prepare a progress note regarding the interview. Use the SOAIGP format.

2. Earlier today, you completed an interview with Gloria, a teenage member of the S. family. She reported that following your last meeting together, she had told her boyfriend that he would have to see his doctor and receive treatment before she would again have sex with him. She appeared to be pleased that she could report this to you. You praised her for taking that action and asked about her boyfriend's response. She said that he had left in a huff, but she thought that he might be back.

In the space provided, prepare a progress note regarding the interview. Use the SOAIGP format.

3. Earlier today, you completed a meeting with Mrs. F., her daughters, and the principal of their school. During the course of the meeting, the girls described in detail what the teenage boys had said and done to them. They talked of the boys spitting at them and calling them names that made reference to their Latino heritage. The girls were able to identify the boys by name. The principal appeared to be quite taken aback by what the girls had to say. He apparently believed the girls because he said that he was indeed sorry that this had happened. Furthermore, he said that he would have a talk with the boys the very next day. He also asked the girls to tell him right away if anything like this were ever to happen again.

In the space provided, prepare a progress note regarding the interview. Use the SOAIGP format.

Summary

During the work and evaluation phase of social work practice, you and the client take action toward resolving the identified problems and achieving the established goals. In this process, you use both empathic skills and work phase expressive skills. Skills pertinent to the work phase include (1) rehearsing action steps, (2) reviewing action steps, (3) evaluating, (4) focusing, (5) educating, (6) advising, (7) representing, (8) responding with immediacy, (9) reframing, (10) confronting, (11) pointing out endings, and (12) progress recording.

◆ **EXERCISE 10-13: SUMMARY**

Building on the earlier meetings you had with your student colleague, conduct another interview, primarily for the purpose of working toward the goals identified through the contracting process. As you did previously, ensure that the interview setting is private, and once again tape-record the meeting. Using empathic and especially work-phase expressive skills, interview your colleague with a view toward helping him or her take steps toward goal attainment. Toward the conclusion of the meeting, arrange for another interview in about one week. Be sure to point out that the next meeting will be your last.

1. At the conclusion of the interview, ask your partner for feedback concerning thoughts and feelings about the experience. Ask for a candid reaction to the following questions. (a) Did you feel that I conveyed understanding and respect to you during this interview? (b) Did you think that the meeting was productive in helping you progress toward goal attainment? (c) What feedback do you have for me concerning the quality of my performance of various working and evaluating skills? (d) Did you find the experience satisfying? (e) Do you believe that you have made progress toward goal attainment? If so, what do you identify as having been most helpful to that progress? If not, what were the obstacles? Did I do anything that was not helpful to you? (f) What suggestions do you have for me concerning how the interview could have been better or more helpful for you? Summarize your partner's feedback in the space below.

2. In the following space, summarize your own reaction to the interview. How did you feel about the interview? What did you like and what did you dislike about it? Do you believe that you used all of the relevant empathic and expressive skills during the interaction? What would you do differently if you were to redo the interview? What working and evaluating skills require further practice?

3. In your course notebook, prepare a progress note regarding the meeting you had with your student colleague. Use the SOAIGP format described above.
4. After you have completed the SOAIGP recording, play the audiotape or videotape. Make notes of significant exchanges that affected the way in which you prepared your SOAIGP record. Revise the record accordingly.

    At some point during the week, share the SOAIGP record with your student colleague. Ask your colleague to share his or her thoughts and feelings while reading the record. Ask for comments about the record's accuracy, and correct any errors or differences in interpretation. In the following space, summarize your colleague's comments and discuss what you have learned from the feedback.

5. Based on your performance in the interview, use the rating scales provided (where 0 = no proficiency and 10 = complete proficiency) to assess your current level of proficiency in the following social work skills. If you did not use a particular skill, you need not simulate a rating. Do, however, ask yourself whether there were points during the interview when you should have used one of these skills.

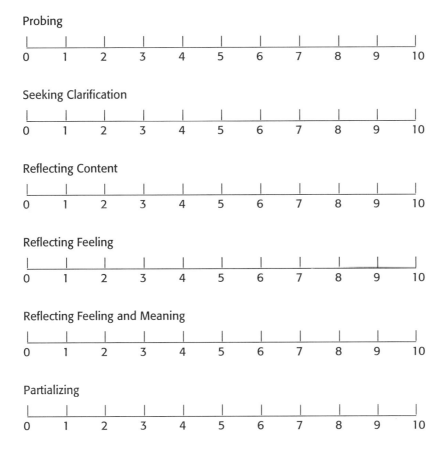

Probing

| | | | | | | | | | | |
0   1   2   3   4   5   6   7   8   9   10

Seeking Clarification

| | | | | | | | | | | |
0   1   2   3   4   5   6   7   8   9   10

Reflecting Content

| | | | | | | | | | | |
0   1   2   3   4   5   6   7   8   9   10

Reflecting Feeling

| | | | | | | | | | | |
0   1   2   3   4   5   6   7   8   9   10

Reflecting Feeling and Meaning

| | | | | | | | | | | |
0   1   2   3   4   5   6   7   8   9   10

Partializing

| | | | | | | | | | | |
0   1   2   3   4   5   6   7   8   9   10

Going Beyond What Is Said

6. Now that you have completed these exercises, use the rating scales provided (where 0 = no proficiency and 10 = complete proficiency) to conduct a summary evaluation of your proficiency in the working skills.

Rehearsing Action Steps

Reviewing Action Steps

Evaluating

Focusing

Educating

Advising

Representing

Responding with Immediacy

Reframing

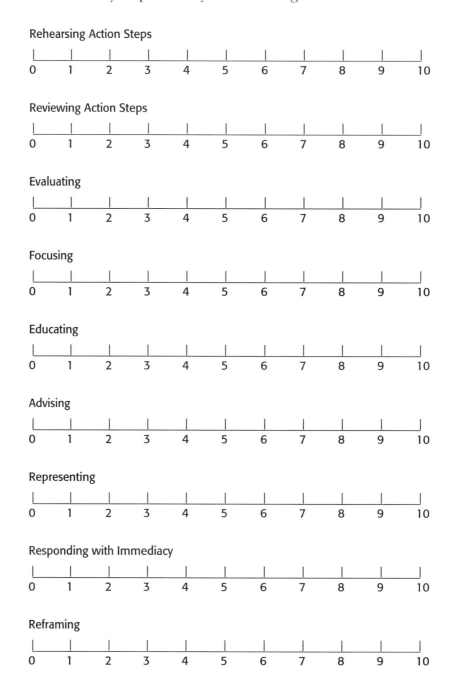

Confronting

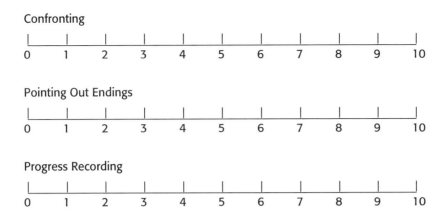

Pointing Out Endings

Progress Recording

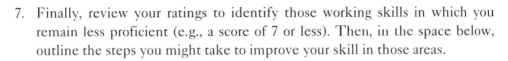

7. Finally, review your ratings to identify those working skills in which you remain less proficient (e.g., a score of 7 or less). Then, in the space below, outline the steps you might take to improve your skill in those areas.

Chapter 11

Ending

The four most common forms of concluding a relationship with a client are (1) transferral, (2) referral, (3) termination, and (4) client discontinuation. In the first three, you and the client openly discuss the ending process and jointly determine the best course of action given the circumstances. These are the preferred modes of concluding relationships with clients. The fourth form, quite common in many agency settings, is exclusively client-initiated. Often with good reason, clients may decide to stop meeting with you. They may do so by informing you during a meeting, in a telephone conversation, or even by letter. They may also discontinue without notifying you, by failing to attend a scheduled meeting. The ending message is communicated by their absence. In such cases (assuming you can make contact by phone or in person), it is often very useful to seek clarification from clients who have discontinued in this manner. However, you should be extremely sensitive to clients' indirect expressions during these contacts. Sometimes, in response to your inquiry, clients might say they will resume meeting with you "since you were so nice as to call," when in fact they have decided to discontinue. If you probe carefully during such contacts, you may learn something about the ways you presented yourself or how you intervened that played a role in the decision to discontinue. This information may be helpful with other clients in the future. Providing clients with an opportunity to express themselves about the service may also help them conclude the relationship in a more satisfactory manner. It may expand their view of you, the agency, and the experience enough to enable them to seek services again at some point in the future.

Clients are more likely to discontinue without notification at certain times. There is an increased probability of client discontinuation whenever changes occur. Changing from a customary meeting time or relocating from one meeting place to another may lead clients to discontinue. Transferring a client to another social worker within the same agency can also be a stressful transition, which the client may resolve through discontinuation. Perhaps the most difficult of all is referring a client to another professional in a different agency. This involves many changes—a new location; another agency with at least somewhat different policies, procedures, and mission; a new meeting schedule; and, of course, a different helping professional. Many clients, understandably, cope with these numerous changes by discontinuing. Although the dynamics of transfers and referrals are similar, transfers are generally easier to manage. Referrals involve more change, and the psychosocial demands on the client are greater. Nonetheless, transfers and referrals, like termination and discontinuation, bring about a conclusion to the relationship between you and the client.

Ending a significant relationship is often a difficult and painful experience. It is certainly challenging for social workers. Concluding a relationship with a client can stimulate strong feelings of sadness and loss, and perhaps other emotions as well. For clients, the process of ending may be even more intense. Usually, by the time of termination, clients will have come to view you as a kind, caring, and understanding person who listened well and had their best interests at heart. Often, clients have shared personally intimate thoughts and feelings. This may lead them to feel both safe and vulnerable. They may have entrusted their secrets to you, a person with whom they may never again have contact. They may have overcome a major problem, turned their lives around, or accomplished a significant goal. They may experience intense gratitude and want to express it to you—perhaps with a tangible or symbolic gift. The conclusion of the relationship may elicit a host of deep feelings. Some clients may feel intensely sad, as if they have lost a best friend, which may in fact be the case. They may feel frightened and dependent as they ask themselves, "How can I make it without you?" They may feel guilty that they did not work as hard as they might have or that they did not take as much advantage of the opportunities for change and growth as they could have. They may feel rejected by you or angry that the relationship is ending. They may think, "If you really cared about me, you wouldn't end the relationship—you must not care about me at all. You must be glad to be rid of me!" Clients may also deny or minimize feelings that lie beneath the surface of consciousness. They may present themselves as being quite ready to terminate, while actually struggling with strong feelings that they have not acknowledged or expressed. There are many manifestations of the psychological and social processes associated with ending—a transition that often provokes significant reactions from both you and your clients. Ideally, these responses are explored as part of the ending process.

Although the particular form of ending may vary, there are several skills that are important to the process. Drawing on the work of William Schwartz (1971) and Elizabeth Kubler-Ross (1969), Lawrence Shulman (1992) discusses the dynamics and describes several skills associated with the ending process. The skills presented here are derived in part from those he identifies. The social work ending skills include (1) reviewing the process, (2) final evaluating, (3) sharing ending feelings and saying goodbye, and (4) recording the closing summary.

Reviewing the Process

Reviewing the process is the skill of tracing what has occurred between you and the client over the time you have worked together. It is a cooperative process; each party shares in the retrospection. Usually, you begin by inviting the client to review the process from the time you first met up through the present. For example, you might say, "I've been thinking about the work we've done together over the course of these last several months. We've covered a lot of ground together, and there have been some substantial changes in you and your situation. As you think back over all that we've done together, what memories come to mind?"

Following the responses to your request, you might probe for additional thoughts and feelings and then share some of your own significant recollections. This often stimulates recall of other experiences.

◆ **EXERCISE 11-1: REVIEWING THE PROCESS**

For these exercises, assume that you are a social worker with a family counseling center. In the spaces provided, write the words you would say in reviewing the process with each client.

1. You have been working with Mrs. O. for approximately two months. She has accomplished the goal of improving her eating and nutritional patterns. She has seen a medical doctor, who prescribed medication that has effectively controlled the spells. You both seem quite pleased about the work you have done together. This is your last meeting. In the space provided, write the words you would say in reviewing the process with Mrs. O.

2. You are in the midst of the final meeting with the S. family. Over the course of several months, many productive changes have occurred. In the space provided, write the words you would say in reviewing the process with the S. family.

3. This is your concluding session with Mrs. F. The school situation has dramatically improved, and Mrs. F. and her daughters are communicating in a much more satisfying way. In two weeks, Mrs. F. will begin a ten-week assertiveness training group sponsored by another community agency. In the space provided, write the words you would say in reviewing the process with Mrs. F.

Final Evaluating

In addition to reviewing the process, you also engage the client in a final evaluation of progress toward problem resolution and goal attainment. For this discussion, you may draw on the results of measurement instruments such as before-and-after test scores, graphs, and various ratings. You may also share your own subjective impressions of progress. Whatever you do share in the form of a final evaluation, be sure to seek feedback from the client about it.

As part of this process, you express your pleasure concerning the positive changes that have occurred. You credit the client for all the work that entailed, and you also help the client identify problems that have not been completely resolved and goals that have been only partially achieved. Work toward such goals does not have to stop because you and your client are concluding your working relationship. The client alone, or with the support of friends and family members, may continue to take action steps toward desirable objectives. By the time they conclude the relationship with the social worker, many clients have become competent problem solvers in their own right. They are often quite capable of defining goals and identifying action steps on their own. This phenomenon, when it occurs, is enormously satisfying for social workers. When clients become effective problem solvers who are skilled at self-help, you may reasonably conclude that you have indeed helped them to help themselves. If, as a consequence of their association with you, clients acquire skills with which to address future problems, they have gained a great deal indeed.

Like most of the ending skills, *final evaluating* is a cooperative process. You and the client share your respective evaluations of progress and jointly identify areas that may require additional work. To initiate this final evaluation, you may say something such as "Let's now take a final look at where we stand in regard to progress toward the goals that we identified. One of our major goals was _____. How far do you think we have come toward achieving it?"

Goals that have been largely or completely accomplished are discussed with appropriate pleasure and satisfaction. You urge the client to experience and enjoy the sense of personal competence and self-approval that accompanies goal achievement. As areas requiring additional work are clarified, you encourage the client to plan additional action steps that can be taken after you conclude your relationship together. Of course, this discussion is not nearly as extensive or as detailed as when you and the client established action steps as part of the contracting and work processes. Rather, you encourage the client to look forward to future activities that can support continued growth and development. You may initiate this process by asking a question such as "What kinds of activities do you think might help you to continue the progress you've made so far?"

As part of the final evaluation, you may find it beneficial to seek feedback from the client about things you said or did that were helpful and things that were not. This kind of evaluation may be of help to clients in identifying behaviors they can adopt for their own future use. It may also provide an opportunity for clients to share their gratitude to you for your help. However, the primary purpose for seeking feedback about helpful and unhelpful factors is to aid you in your own professional growth and development. In a sense, you request that clients evaluate your performance as a social worker. By seeking such evaluative feedback, you may gain information about yourself that may prove useful in your work with other current and future clients. In asking for feedback, you might say, "I would appreciate it if you would tell me about those things I did that were particularly helpful to you during our work together. . . . And could you also identify things I did that were not helpful?"

◆ EXERCISE 11-2: FINAL EVALUATING

In the spaces provided, write the words you would say to engage each client in the process of final evaluating. Also, prepare statements to encourage each client to identify future action steps. Finally, write the words you might say in seeking evaluative feedback from each client concerning what has been helpful and what has not.

1. You have been working with Mrs. O. for approximately two months. She has accomplished virtually all of the goals that you identified together. This meeting is your last. In the space provided, write the words you would say to engage Mrs. O. in the three aspects of final evaluating.

2. You are meeting for the last time with the S. family. Over the course of several months, many productive changes have occurred. There is still strain among some of the family members, but they seem to be coping with it quite well. There are several indications that they are communicating much more directly and honestly with one another. All in all, the family has achieved more than half of the goals that were identified. In the space provided, write the words you would say to engage the S. family in the three aspects of final evaluating.

3. This is your concluding session with Mrs. F. She and her daughters have made quite remarkable gains. All three seem to be quite satisfied with the changes that have occurred. Mrs. F. is looking forward to the assertiveness training group she will join in a week or so. In the space provided, write the words you would say in initiating the three aspects of final evaluating with Mrs. F.

Sharing Ending Feelings and Saying Goodbye

The nature and intensity of the feelings clients experience as they conclude a relationship with you vary according to their personal characteristics, the duration of service, the problem and goals, the roles and functions you served, and the degree of progress (Hess & Hess, 1989). Because ending is a significant event in the lives of most clients, you should give them an opportunity to express feelings related to the ending process.

There are several emotional responses that clients may experience as they end their relationship with you: anger, sadness, loss, fear, guilt, dependency, ambivalence, gratitude, and affection. Clients may hesitate to express their emotions freely at this time. If they conclude the relationship without sharing some of these feelings, they may experience a sense of incompleteness. This "unfinished" quality may impede the appropriate process of psychological separation from you and inhibit the client's movement toward increased autonomy and independence. Therefore, you should encourage clients to express their ending feelings. You may say, "We've reviewed our work together and evaluated progress, but we haven't yet shared our feelings about ending the relationship with one another. As you realize that this is our final meeting together, what emotions do you experience?"

Of course, you will also experience various feelings as you conclude your working relationships with clients. You may have spent several weeks or months with a person, a couple, a family, or a group. During the course of your work together, a client may have shared painful emotions, discussed poignant issues, or made significant progress. Despite your professional status and commitment to an ethical code, you are also human. It is entirely understandable and appropriate that you also experience strong feelings as you end your relationships with clients. During the ending process, you may find yourself feeling guilty, inadequate, proud, satisfied, sad, angry, ambivalent, relieved, or affectionate. The kind and degree of your feelings may vary due to many factors. Like clients, you will almost always experience some kind of personal reaction during the ending phase. It is often useful to share some of these feelings. Unlike the client, however, you retain your professional responsibilities, even in ending. You cannot freely express whatever feelings you experience. You must consider the potential effects on the client. For example, suppose you feel annoyed at an adult male client because he did not work as hard toward change as you had hoped he would. You should not share these or any other such feelings unless to do so would help the client progress toward any remaining goals or aid him to conclude the relationship in a beneficial manner. Even during the final meeting, you make professional judgments about which feelings to express and how to express them. However, do not simply suppress feelings that are inappropriate to share with clients. Rather, engage in the skills of self-exploration and centering (see Chapter 5) in order to address them in a personally and professionally effective fashion.

When they are relevant and appropriate, you may share your personal feelings about ending the relationship. For example, you might say, "When I think about the fact that we will not meet together anymore, I feel a real sense of loss. I'm really going to miss you."

Often, when you do share your feelings, clients respond by sharing additional emotions of their own. You may then reflect their feelings and perhaps share more of your own. Finally, however, you and the client complete the ending process by saying goodbye.

◆ EXERCISE 11-3: SHARING ENDING FEELINGS AND SAYING GOODBYE

In the spaces provided, write the words you would say to encourage each client to share feelings about ending. Also, prepare statements in which you share your own ending feelings with each client. As part of your own sharing, please specify those feelings that you think you might experience had you actually worked with each client. Identify those that would be appropriate to share and those that would not. Finally, note the exact words you would use in saying goodbye.

1. After working with Mrs. O. for approximately two months, you have completed your review of the process and conducted a final evaluation. You have approximately fifteen minutes left in this very last meeting. In the space provided, write the words you would say to engage in sharing ending feelings and saying goodbye to Mrs. O.

2. You have reviewed the process and engaged in a final evaluation of progress with the S. family. In the last several minutes remaining in this final meeting, you would like to share ending feelings and say goodbye. In the space provided, write the words you would say in doing so with the S. family.

3. You are in the process of winding down your final session with Mrs. F. You have reviewed the process and engaged in a final evaluation of progress. Now it is time to move toward closure. In the space provided, write the words you would say in sharing ending feelings and saying goodbye to Mrs. F.

Recording the Closing Summary

Following your final meeting with a client, you condense what occurred into a written closing summary. This final entry is usually somewhat more extensive that the typical progress recording. When the ending session has included a review of the process, a final evaluation, and a sharing of ending feelings, you will probably have most of what you need to complete a closing summary. Include in the final recording the following information (Wilson, 1980, pp. 119–120): (1) date of final contact; (2) your name and title as well as the name of the client; (3) beginning date of service; (4) the reason contact between you and the client was initiated; (5) the agreed-upon problems and goals for work; (6) the approach taken, the nature of the services that you provided, and the activities that you and the client undertook; (7) a summary evaluation of progress and an identification of problems and goals that remain unresolved or unaccomplished; (8) a brief assessment of the person-problem-situation as it now exists; and (9) the reason for closing the case. For example, following the final interview with Mrs. Chase, Susan Holder might prepare a closing summary as follows.

Example
Closing Summary
Lynn B. Chase

Process and Problems

Today, January 12, 1995, Mrs. Lynn B. Chase and I, Susan Holder, MSW, met together for the eighth and final time. Mrs. Chase and I first met on November 21, 1994. At that time, we jointly specified the following problems for work: (1) frequent arguments with and feelings of irritability and anger toward son and husband; (2) stress, tension, and anxiety; (3) sleep disturbance; (4) ambivalence about job; (5) thoughts and feelings of excessive responsibility and possibly of control; and (6) role strain and possibly conflict among the roles of mother, wife, homemaker, and employee. Based on these problems, we established several related goals and developed an eight-week plan by which to approach our work together.

Evaluation

In reviewing the work process and evaluating progress, Mrs. Chase reported today that the feelings of stress and anger have decreased substantially since the time of the first contact. She also indicated that relations between her, her husband, and her son have greatly improved since the family redistributed housework responsibilities more evenly. She said that she assumes less of a caretaker role with them. She said that she now believes that they have actually benefited from the assumption of greater family and household responsibility. She stated that she now sleeps fine and rarely has a headache. Mrs. Chase reported that her job at Fox Manufacturing is now quite satisfying; she said she is glad she kept it. And she has been engaging in more playful and pleasurable activities, particularly gardening.

Mrs. Chase indicated that the single most helpful aspect of our work together was when I said to her that "doing for your husband and son may prevent them from developing their full potential."

Continuing Goals

Mrs. Chase indicated that she is still working on issues related to excessive caretaking and intends to do further reading. She reported that she might attend an ACOA meeting to see what it's like. She said that she is also considering taking an assertiveness training course.

Current Assessment

Based on the available evidence, Mrs. Chase, her son, and her husband are communicating more directly, sharing household responsibilities, and experiencing considerable satisfaction in their relationships with one another. Robert seems to be negotiating the demands of adolescence in a constructive fashion, and Mrs. Chase has made considerable progress in reversing her long-held patterns of excessive responsibility and control.

    Mrs. Chase and her family have many personal strengths that should serve them well in the future. I anticipate that Mrs. Chase will continue to grow and develop now that she has permitted herself to consider more expansive and more flexible personal and familial roles.

Ending Process

Mrs. Chase and I concluded our work together in a positive manner. She expressed her gratitude, and I shared my affection for her as well as my pleasure at the progress she has made. The case was closed in the eight-week time frame as contracted.

Susan Holder, BSW, MSW
January 12, 1995

◆ EXERCISE 11-4: RECORDING THE CLOSING SUMMARY

In the spaces provided, prepare brief closing summaries for each of the following clients. You may have to simulate some information, but your responses to earlier exercises contain most of the needed information related to problems, goals, action steps, and progress.

1. You have just completed your final meeting with Mrs. O. In the space provided, prepare a simulated closing-summary record of your work with Mrs. O.

2. You have completed the final meeting with the S. family. In the space provided, prepare a simulated closing-summary record of your work with the family.

3. You have concluded the last session with Mrs. F. In the space provided, prepare a simulated closing-summary record of your work with Mrs. F.

Summary

The ending phase of social work practice gives you and your clients opportunities to look back on your relationship and the work you undertook together. You have a chance to evaluate overall progress and to identify directions for future work. However, concluding these working relationships can be both a joyful and a painful experience for you and your clients. Each of you may experience satisfaction concerning the progress achieved, regret about actions that might have been but were not taken, and sadness at the departure of a person who has been important. In optimum circumstances, these feelings can be explored as part of the ending process.

The particular form of ending may be transferral, referral, termination, or discontinuation. Several skills are important to the process, including (1) reviewing the process, (2) final evaluating, (3) sharing ending feelings and saying goodbye, and (4) recording the closing summary.

◆ EXERCISE 11-5: SUMMARY

Conduct a final interview with the student colleague who has served as your client during these past several weeks. As you did previously, ensure that the interview setting is private, and once again tape-record the meeting. Using empathic, working, and especially ending skills, interview your colleague with a view toward concluding the relationship. This is your last meeting. Therefore, use the relevant ending skills of reviewing the work process, final evaluating, and sharing ending feelings and saying goodbye.

1. At the conclusion of the interview, ask your partner about his or her thoughts and feelings regarding this concluding interview. In particular, ask for feedback concerning your use of the ending skills. Since this is your last meeting together as part of this exercise, ask your partner to provide you with feedback concerning the entire five-session experience. Summarize your partner's feedback in the space below.

2. In the space below, record your own reaction to this final meeting. How did you feel about the interview? What did you like and what did you dislike about it? Do you believe that you used all the relevant empathic, expressive, and ending skills during the interaction? How well did you use the ending skills? What would you do differently if you were to redo this final interview? Which of the ending skills should you practice further?

Now reflect upon the entire series of interviews. Share your overall impressions and reactions about the experience in the space below.

3. In your course notebook, prepare a closing summary of your work with the student-client.
4. After you have completed the closing summary, play the audiotape or videotape. Make note of significant exchanges that affected the way in which you prepared your record. Revise the record accordingly.
5. Based on your performance in the final interview, use the rating scales provided (where 0 = no proficiency and 10 = complete proficiency) to assess your current level of proficiency in the various social work skills listed. If you did not use a particular skill, you need not simulate a rating, but do ask yourself whether there were points during the interview when you should have used that skill.

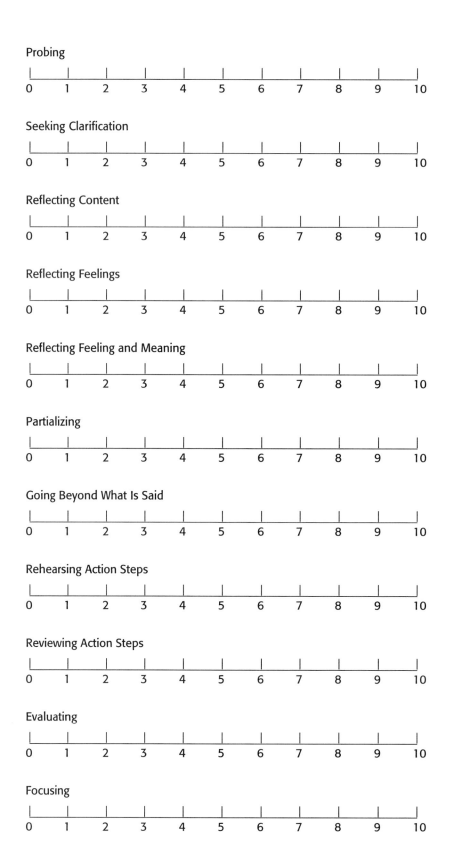

Probing

| 0 | 1 | 2 | 3 | 4 | 5 | 6 | 7 | 8 | 9 | 10 |

Seeking Clarification

| 0 | 1 | 2 | 3 | 4 | 5 | 6 | 7 | 8 | 9 | 10 |

Reflecting Content

| 0 | 1 | 2 | 3 | 4 | 5 | 6 | 7 | 8 | 9 | 10 |

Reflecting Feelings

| 0 | 1 | 2 | 3 | 4 | 5 | 6 | 7 | 8 | 9 | 10 |

Reflecting Feeling and Meaning

| 0 | 1 | 2 | 3 | 4 | 5 | 6 | 7 | 8 | 9 | 10 |

Partializing

| 0 | 1 | 2 | 3 | 4 | 5 | 6 | 7 | 8 | 9 | 10 |

Going Beyond What Is Said

| 0 | 1 | 2 | 3 | 4 | 5 | 6 | 7 | 8 | 9 | 10 |

Rehearsing Action Steps

| 0 | 1 | 2 | 3 | 4 | 5 | 6 | 7 | 8 | 9 | 10 |

Reviewing Action Steps

| 0 | 1 | 2 | 3 | 4 | 5 | 6 | 7 | 8 | 9 | 10 |

Evaluating

| 0 | 1 | 2 | 3 | 4 | 5 | 6 | 7 | 8 | 9 | 10 |

Focusing

| 0 | 1 | 2 | 3 | 4 | 5 | 6 | 7 | 8 | 9 | 10 |

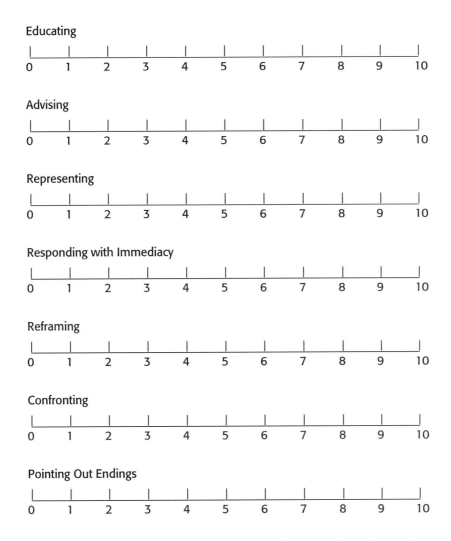

Educating

| | | | | | | | | | |
0   1   2   3   4   5   6   7   8   9   10

Advising

| | | | | | | | | | |
0   1   2   3   4   5   6   7   8   9   10

Representing

| | | | | | | | | | |
0   1   2   3   4   5   6   7   8   9   10

Responding with Immediacy

| | | | | | | | | | |
0   1   2   3   4   5   6   7   8   9   10

Reframing

| | | | | | | | | | |
0   1   2   3   4   5   6   7   8   9   10

Confronting

| | | | | | | | | | |
0   1   2   3   4   5   6   7   8   9   10

Pointing Out Endings

| | | | | | | | | | |
0   1   2   3   4   5   6   7   8   9   10

6. Now that you have completed these exercises, use the rating scales provided (where 0 = no proficiency and 10 = complete proficiency) to conduct a summary evaluation of your proficiency in the ending skills.

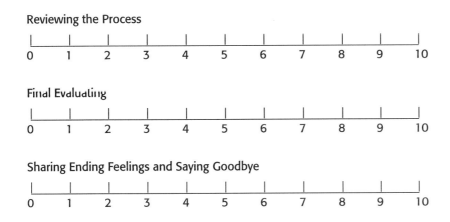

Reviewing the Process

| | | | | | | | | | |
0   1   2   3   4   5   6   7   8   9   10

Final Evaluating

| | | | | | | | | | |
0   1   2   3   4   5   6   7   8   9   10

Sharing Ending Feelings and Saying Goodbye

| | | | | | | | | | |
0   1   2   3   4   5   6   7   8   9   10

Recording the Closing Summary

7. Review your ratings to identify those ending skills in which you remain less proficient (e.g., a score of 7 or less). Then, in the space below, outline the steps you might take to improve your skill in those areas.

Appendix 1

The Social Work Skills Practice Test

Please take the following practice test as an aid in learning the social work skills. You might find it helpful to use the test in one of several ways: (a) as a pretest to measure the extent of your knowledge and skill prior to completing The Social Work Skills Workbook, *(b) as a general test by which to practice a large range of the social work skills at one time, and (c) as a posttest to evaluate your knowledge and skill following completion of the workbook.*

As you consider each of the following items, record your responses in a separate notebook.

You have been serving as a social worker in a counseling role with a voluntary client for about six months. The client has accomplished virtually all of the goals that you jointly identified during the contracting phase of work. You enjoy your visits with this client, and the client also appears to enjoy them. You have extended the time frame for work once already, and as a professional you realize that it would be unwise to do so again. You therefore suggest to the client that you meet for three more times and then conclude your working relationship. When you make this suggestion, the client pauses for a moment and then says, "That sounds about right. You have helped me a great deal, and I think I am ready to conclude this relationship with you. In gratitude for your help, however, I would very much like to invite you to join me in a terrific business opportunity. I have just bid on and won the right to open a McDonald's restaurant on that really busy highway near here. If you can come up with $500 I would like to give you a 5% share in the franchise. In one year, that share should be worth at least $20,000. Now, don't answer right away. Think about it for a week or so and then let me know when we meet next time."

1. Identify and discuss the social work values, the legal duties, and the ethical principles, if any, that might relate to this situation. If applicable, use a hierarchical ethical screen to resolve any conflicts. Then describe what you would do in this situation in order to behave in an ethical manner. Cite the values, ethics, and/or legal duties that support your action plan.

Yesterday, Mrs. Little telephoned the family service agency where you work to express her concerns that her husband (of six months) is too severe in his discipline of her 7-year-old daughter (from a previous relationship).

2. In your agency, you serve as a social worker specializing in helping couples and families. You will be talking with Mrs. Little when she visits the agency later today. In your separate notebook, demonstrate your knowledge of and ability to use the applicable preparing skills (*preparatory arranging, preparatory empathy, preliminary planning, preparatory self-exploration*, and *centering*) in advance of your first meeting with Mrs. Little. Be sure to label each of the skills by making a brief notation beside it.

After you have prepared for the initial meeting with Mrs. Little, the time for her appointment arrives. You walk up to her in the waiting room and escort her to your office.

3. Write the words you would say in beginning with Mrs. Little. If applicable, use the beginning skills of *introducing yourself, seeking introductions, describing the initial purpose and (possibly) role, outlining a client's role, discussing policy and ethical considerations*, and *seeking feedback*. Label each of the skills you choose to use by making a brief notation alongside your use of the skill. If you determine that a skill would not be applicable as you begin in this situation, provide a brief rationale for omitting it.

Client (spouse of one year): "We fight all the time about his teenage son—the one from his first marriage. My husband doesn't think I should discipline the boy at all. He doesn't want me to correct him or to punish him in any way. But, I'm around the boy much more than my husband is and I have to deal with the brat!"

4. Write the words you would say in using two forms of the skill of *probing* in your attempt to encourage further client exploration following the statement reported above. Make your first probe open-ended and the second, closed-ended.

Client (14-year-old boy): "Sometimes I wonder whether there is something wrong with me. Girls just turn me off. But boys . . . when I'm close to a good-looking boy, I can feel myself becoming excited. Does that mean I'm gay?"

5. Write the words you would say in using the skill of *reflecting content* in your attempt to encourage further client exploration following the statement reported above.

Client (14-year-old boy): "If I am gay, what will I do? If my mother finds out she'll be crushed. She'll feel that it's her fault somehow. I'm so scared and so worried. If my friends learn that I'm gay, what will they do?"

6. Write the words you would say in using the skill of *reflecting feelings* in your attempt to encourage further client exploration following the statement reported above.

Client (21-year-old male): "My father began to molest me when I was about 9 years old. When I think about it, I just shudder. It was so disgusting; so humiliating. Even today, whenever I think about it, I still feel dirty and damaged. My father kept doing it until I was 14. After that he'd try sometimes but I was too strong for him."

7. Write the words you would say in using the skill of *reflecting feeling and meaning* in your attempt to encourage further client exploration following the statement reported above.

Client (14-year-old female in foster care): "This family treats me like dirt. They call me names and don't let me do anything I want to do. Half the time they don't even feed me. I just hate it there!"

8. Write the words you would say in using the skill of *seeking clarification* in your attempt to encourage further client exploration following the statement reported above.

Client (adult male of African ancestry): "Sometimes it seems so phony. I grew up hearing whites call me 'boy' and 'nigger.' I was poor as dirt and sometimes I was beaten just because of the color of my skin. But I fought on through it all. I kept my pride and made it to college. I did really well too. When I graduated a lot of the big companies wanted to meet their minority quota so I was hired right away at a good salary. I've been at this company now for five years, and I have contributed a great deal. I've been promoted twice and received raises. But, so far not one white person in the company has ever asked me to his home. Now what does that say to you?"

9. Write the words you would say in using the skill of *going beyond what is said* in your attempt to encourage further client exploration following the statement reported above.

Client (17-year-old male): "I don't know what's wrong with me. I can't get a date to save my life. Nobody will go out with me. Every girl I ask out says 'no.' I don't have any real guy friends either. I am so lonely. Even my folks hate my guts! My mother and I fight all the time, and my stepdad will have nothing to do with me. I spend most of my time alone in my room listening to music. I know I'm real depressed, but I don't know what to do about it."

10. Write the words you would say in using the skill of *partializing* in your attempt to focus the client's exploration following the statement reported above.

Presume that you are a social worker in the Child Protective Services (CPS) unit of a Department of Child Welfare. Your job is to investigate allegations of child abuse and neglect and to determine if the child or children involved require protective service.

A county resident has telephoned CPS to report that she has observed severe bruises on the back and the legs of Paul S., an 8-year-old neighborhood child. The neighbor has heard loud arguments in the child's home and believes that the child has been beaten on several occasions. You are called to respond to the allegation. You drive to the neighborhood and go to the S. home, where the abuse is reported to have occurred. The door is answered by a woman who confirms that she is the child's mother, Mrs. S. After you introduce yourself by name and profession, you describe your purpose and role and outline the relevant policy and ethical factors.

Mrs. S. says, "I know why you're here—it's that damn nosy neighbor down the street. She's always butting into other people's business. She called you, didn't she?"

You respond to Mrs. S.'s expression by saying, "I'm not allowed to reveal how information regarding allegations of child abuse or neglect comes to us. My job is to investigate the reports however they occur and determine whether or not a child is in danger. Is that clear?"

Mrs. S. says, "Yeah. Come on in. I guess you want to see Paul." She loudly calls for Paul (who has been playing in another room).

Paul enters the room with a quizzical look on his face. Using terms he can easily understand, you introduce yourself and outline your purpose and role. You take Paul to a quiet area, well away from his mother (who abruptly goes to the kitchen). Then you say, "I'm here to make sure that you are safe from harm and to find out whether anyone might have hurt you in any way. Paul, do you understand what I am saying? Yes? Okay, then, I'd like to ask you some questions. First, who lives in this house with you?"

Paul says, "Well, my mom lives with me. And, uh uh, her boyfriend stays here a lot too." You ask, "What is he like?" Paul hesitates, looks questioningly toward the kitchen, then looks back into your eyes. It looks to you that he's afraid to say anything more. You respond by communicating your understanding about how difficult and frightening it is to be interviewed in this way.

Paul responds to your empathic feeling reflection by saying, "Yeah, it sure is." You follow that by asking, "Paul, does anyone ever hurt you?" Paul again hesitates, but then says, "Yeah. Charlie, that's my mom's boyfriend, sometimes hits me with his belt."

Paul responds to your empathic content reflection by saying, "Yeah. He and my mom get drunk and yell and hit each other. I get so scared. If I make any noise at all, Charlie starts yelling at me. Then he takes off his belt and beats me with it."

You communicate your understanding of the feeling and meaning inherent in his message. Then you ask an open-ended probe concerning the nature of the beatings and the location of any bruises that might exist.

Paul responds to your question by saying, "I have bruises all over my legs and back and my bottom. It hurts real bad. Sometimes when Charlie beats me, I start to bleed. I hate him! I hate him! I wish he'd just leave and never come back."

You then ask Paul to elaborate further. He responds by saying, "Things were fine until Charlie showed up. Mom and I got along great! See, my real dad was killed in a car wreck before I was born and so it has always been just Mom and me—that is, until Charlie moved in."

11. Respond to Paul's most recent statement by using the skill of *reflecting the problem*.

After you reflect the problem, Paul says, "Yeah, that's it all right." Following that exchange, you excuse yourself from Paul and join Mrs. S in the kitchen. You indicate that you have seen severe bruises on Paul's legs, back, and buttocks. You go on to say that you will take Paul into protective custody and place him in the local Children's Home until a more complete investigation can be conducted. You indicate that the final decision about Paul's custody is in the hands of Judge Dixon, who will conduct the hearing, but before leaving with Paul, you would like to share with her your view of the problem.

12. Record the words you would say in using the skill of *sharing your view of a problem* with Mrs. S.

After arranging for Paul to enter the Children's Home, you take time to write in the case record.

13. Outline the sections that might be useful to include in the description section of a Description, Assessment, and Contract (DAC) as you consider organizing information concerning the S. case.
14. Outline, in general, what you might include in the assessment section of a Description, Assessment, and Contract (DAC) as it relates to the S. case.
15. Identify the sections or categories that you would include in the contract section of a Description, Assessment, and Contract (DAC) as it relates to the S. case.
16. Based on your view of a problem as described above, formulate a final goal (any goal that reasonably follows from the problem you identified would be fine), in two ways. First, write a general goal statement. Then, write a specific goal statement.
17. Building on your view of a problem and a final goal as described above, identify a means to evaluate progress toward goal attainment.
18. Next, in a manner that is congruent with the problem, goal, and means to evaluate progress, plan an approach that might conceivably apply to this case and could enable the client to progress toward goal achievement.

Several weeks have passed. Charlie has been charged with various crimes associated with child abuse and left the S. household. [It appears he may have fled the area.] Mrs. S. has progressed from an initial state of confusion to a point where she actively participates in the counseling process with you. Indeed, she seems to find the sessions interesting and stimulating as well as helpful. Paul remains at the Children's Home, but he may be able to return home within this next week. Mrs. S. has visited him daily, and those visits have gone very well.

During one of your counseling sessions, Mrs. S. says to you (while tears stream down her cheeks), "You know, when I was a child, my stepfather used to beat me too.

He made me pull down my pants and he beat my butt with a razor strap. I used to cry and cry but he kept doing it and my mother never could or would stop him. They never listened to me and nobody ever protected me. In fact, and it's strange to think about it this way, but when you came to this house to make sure that Paul was all right, that was the first time I had ever seen anybody try to protect somebody else from harm. And you are the first and only person who has ever seemed interested in me and in what I think and feel. Thank you so much for that."

19. Record the words you would say in responding to Mrs. S.'s verbal and nonverbal expression with the skill of *responding with immediacy*.

Following that exchange, you continue to explore with Mrs. S. her history of relationships with alcoholic and abusive men. It's a pattern that seems remarkably similar to the relationship she observed between her own mother and her stepfather. In the midst of this discussion, she says, "I guess I must be masochistic. I must like to be beaten and degraded. Boy, am I ever sick!"

20. Respond to the client's statement with the skill of *reframing a negative into a positive*.
21. Respond to the client's statement with the form of reframing that *personalizes the meaning*.
22. Respond to the client's statement with the form of reframing that *situationalizes the meaning*.
23. Now shift gears and respond to Mrs. S.'s expression with the skill of *confronting*.
24. Following your reframing and confrontational responses, it seems appropriate that you use the skill of *educating* in an attempt to help Mrs. S. understand how adults who were abused as children tend to behave. Write the words you might use in educating her about this topic.
25. Following your attempt to educate Mrs. S., it appears that she might benefit from some specific advice on how to be a better parent to her son Paul. Record the words you might use in *advising* her in this area.

Approximately one week goes by. Paul has returned home, and both he and his mother are delighted. In a session with the two of them, you are discussing one of the goals Mrs. S. has identified for herself: becoming a more loving parent and a better listener. You ask Paul, "How would you like your mother to show you she loves you?" Instead of answering the question, Paul grabs a ball and begins to bounce it.

26. Respond to the situation described above by using the skill of *focusing*.

Later in the session, Paul, Mrs. S., and you are "playing a game" of drawing on large pieces of paper. With crayons, each of you draws a picture of the S. family. Interestingly, Paul's drawing reflects a mother and a child who are both large in size—that is, the child (Paul) is every bit as tall and as large as is the mother (Mrs. S.).

27. Please respond to your observation about the relative size of the mother and son by using whatever social work skill you believe to be the most applicable.

Record the words you might say in using the skill. Following that, discuss the rationale for your choice.

A few more weeks go by. Paul and Mrs. S. appear to be thriving. Paul is clearly no longer in danger. You have been authorized by the court to provide no more than four additional counseling sessions.

28. Write the words you might say to Paul and Mrs. S. in *pointing out endings*.

A month goes by. You, Paul, and Mrs. S. are meeting for the last time. Things are better than ever. They have achieved all of the identified goals and are extremely pleased with their progress. They are also grateful to you.

29. Write the words you might say in initiating a *review of the process*.
30. Write the words you might say in encouraging Paul and Mrs. S. to engage in a *final evaluation*.
31. Write the words you might say in *sharing ending feelings and saying goodbye*.

Appendix 2

Code of Ethics of the National Association of Social Workers*

I. The Social Worker's Conduct and Comportment as a Social Worker
  A. Propriety—The social worker should maintain high standards of personal conduct in the capacity or identity as social worker.
    1. The private conduct of the social worker is a personal matter to the same degree as is any other person's, except when such conduct compromises the fulfillment of professional responsibilities.
    2. The social worker should not participate in, condone, or be associated with dishonesty, fraud, deceit, or misrepresentation.
    3. The social worker should distinguish clearly between statements and actions made as a private individual and as a representative of the social work profession or an organization or group.
  B. Competence and Professional Development—The social worker should strive to become and remain proficient in professional practice and the performance of professional functions.

*From *The Code of Ethics of the National Association of Social Workers*, National Association of Social Workers, 1994. As adopted by the 1979 Delegate Assembly and revised by the 1990 and 1993 NASW Delegate Assemblies, effective July 1, 1994. Copyright 1994, National Association of Social Workers, Inc. Reprinted by permission.

1. The social worker should accept responsibility or employment only on the basis of existing competence or the intention to acquire the necessary competence.
2. The social worker should not misrepresent professional qualifications, education, experience, or affiliations.
3. The social worker should not allow his or her own personal problems, psychosocial distress, substance abuse, or mental health difficulties to interfere with professional judgment and performance or jeopardize the best interests of those for whom the social worker has a professional responsibility.
4. The social worker whose personal problems, psychosocial distress, substance abuse, or mental health difficulties interfere with professional judgment and performance should immediately seek consultation and take appropriate remedial action by seeking professional help, making adjustments in workload, terminating practice, or taking any other steps necessary to protect clients and others.
C. Service—The social worker should regard as primary the service obligation of the social work profession.
   1. The social worker should retain ultimate responsibility for the quality and extent of the service that individual assumes, assigns, or performs.
   2. The social worker should act to prevent practices that are inhumane or discriminatory against any person or group of persons.
D. Integrity—The social worker should act in accordance with the highest standards of professional integrity and impartiality.
   1. The social worker should be alert to and resist the influences and pressures that interfere with the exercise of professional discretion and impartial judgement required for the performance of professional functions.
   2. The social worker should not exploit professional relationships for personal gain.
E. Scholarship and Research—The social worker engaged in study and research should be guided by the conventions of scholarly inquiry.
   1. The social worker engaged in research should consider carefully its possible consequences for human beings.
   2. The social worker engaged in research should ascertain that the consent of participants in the research is voluntary and informed, without any implied deprivation or penalty for refusal to participate, and with due regard for participants' privacy and dignity.
   3. The social worker engaged in research should protect participants from unwarranted physical or mental discomfort, distress, harm, danger, or deprivation.
   4. The social worker who engages in the evaluation of services or cases should discuss them only for the professional purposes and

only with persons directly and professionally concerned with them.

5. Information obtained about participants in research should be treated as confidential.

6. The social worker should take credit only for work actually done in connection with scholarly and research endeavors and credit contributions made by others.

II. The Social Worker's Ethical Responsibility to Clients

   F. Primacy of Clients' Interests—The social worker's primary responsibility is to clients.

1. The social worker should serve clients with devotion, loyalty, determination, and the maximum application of professional skill and competence.

2. The social worker should not exploit relationships with clients for personal advantage.

3. The social worker should not practice, condone, facilitate or collaborate with any form of discrimination on the basis of race, color, sex, sexual orientation, age, religion, national origin, marital status, political belief, mental or physical handicap, or any other preference or personal characteristic, condition or status.

4. The social worker should not condone or engage in any dual or multiple relationships with clients or former clients in which there is a risk of exploitation of or potential harm to the client. The social worker is responsible for setting clear, appropriate, and culturally sensitive boundaries.

5. The social worker should under no circumstances engage in sexual activities with clients.

6. The social worker should provide clients with accurate and complete information regarding the extent and nature of the services available to them.

7. The social worker should apprise clients of their risks, rights, opportunities, and obligations associated with social service to them.

8. The social worker should seek advice and counsel of colleagues and supervisors whenever such consultation is in the best interest of clients.

9. The social worker should terminate service to clients, and professional relationships with them, when such service and relationships are no longer required or no longer serve the clients' needs or interests.

10. The social worker should withdraw services precipitously only under unusual circumstances, giving careful consideration to all factors in the situation and taking care to minimize possible adverse effects.

11. The social worker who anticipates the termination or interruption of service to clients should notify clients promptly and seek the transfer, referral, or continuation of service in relation to the clients' needs and preferences.

G. Rights and Prerogatives of Clients—The social worker should make every effort to foster maximum self-determination on the part of clients.

1. When the social worker must act on behalf of a client who has been adjudged legally incompetent, the social worker should safeguard the interests and rights of that client.

2. When another individual has been legally authorized to act in behalf of a client, the social worker should deal with that person always with the client's best interest in mind.

3. The social worker should not engage in any action that violates or diminishes the civil or legal rights of clients.

H. Confidentiality and Privacy—The social worker should respect the privacy of clients and hold in confidence all information obtained in the course of professional service.

1. The social worker should share with others confidences revealed by clients, without their consent, only for compelling professional reasons.

2. The social worker should inform clients fully about the limits of confidentiality in a given situation, the purposes for which information is obtained, and how it may be used.

3. The social worker should afford clients reasonable access to any official social work records concerning them.

4. When providing clients with access to records, the social worker should take due care to protect the confidences of others contained in those records.

5. The social worker should obtain informed consent of clients before taping, recording, or permitting third party observation of their activities.

I. Fees—When setting fees, the social worker should ensure that they are fair, reasonable, considerate, and commensurate with the service performed and with due regard for the clients' ability to pay.

1. The social worker should not accept anything of value for making a referral.

III. The Social Worker's Ethical Responsibility to Colleagues

J. Respect, Fairness, and Courtesy—The social worker should treat colleagues with respect, courtesy, fairness, and good faith.

1. The social worker should cooperate with colleagues to promote professional interest and concerns.

2. The social worker should respect confidences shared by colleagues in the course of their professional relationships and transactions.

3. The social worker should create and maintain conditions of practice that facilitate ethical and competent professional performance by colleagues.

4. The social worker should treat with respect, and represent accurately and fairly, the qualifications, views, and findings of colleagues and use appropriate channels to express judgements on these matters.

5. The social worker who replaces or is replaced by a colleague in professional practice should act with consideration for the interest, character, and reputation of that colleague.

6. The social worker should not exploit a dispute between a colleague and employers to obtain a position or otherwise advance the social worker's interest.

7. The social worker should seek arbitration or mediation when conflicts with colleagues require resolution for compelling professional reasons.

8. The social worker should extend to colleagues of other professions the same respect and cooperation that is extended to social work colleagues.

9. The social worker who serves as an employer, supervisor, or mentor to colleagues should make orderly and explicit arrangements regarding the conditions of their continuing professional relationship.

10. The social worker who has the responsibility for employing and evaluating the performance of other staff members should fulfill such responsibility in a fair, considerate, and equitable manner, on the basis of clearly enunciated criteria.

11. The social worker who has the responsibility for evaluating the performance of employees, supervisees, or students should share evaluations with them.

12. The social worker should not use a professional position vested with power, such as that of employer, supervisor, teacher, or consultant, to his or her advantage or to exploit others.

13. The social worker who has direct knowledge of a social work colleagues's impairment due to personal problems, psychosocial distress, substance abuse, or mental health difficulties, should consult with that colleague and assist the colleague in taking remedial action.

K. Dealing with Colleagues' Clients—The social worker has the responsibility to relate to the clients of colleagues with full professional consideration.

1. The social worker should not assume professional responsibility for the clients of another agency or a colleague without appropriate communication with that agency or colleague.

2. The social worker who serves the clients of colleagues, during a temporary absence or emergency, should serve those clients with the same consideration as that afforded any client.

IV. The Social Worker's Ethical Responsibility to Employers and Employing Organizations

    L. Commitments to Employing Organization—The social worker should adhere to commitments made to the employing organization.

        1. The social worker should work to improve the employing agency's policies and procedures, and the efficiency and effectiveness of its services.

        2. The social worker should not accept employment or arrange student field placements in an organization which is currently under public sanction by NASW for violating personnel standards, or imposing limitations on or penalties for professional actions on behalf of clients.

        3. The social worker should act to prevent and eliminate discrimination in the employing organization's work assignments and in its employment policies and practices.

        4. The social worker should use with scrupulous regard, and only for the purpose for which they are intended, the resources of the employing organization.

V. The Social Worker's Ethical Responsibility to the Social Work Profession

    M. Maintaining the Integrity of the Profession—The social worker should uphold and advance the values, ethics, knowledge, and mission of the profession.

        1. The social worker should protect and enhance the dignity and integrity of the profession and should be responsible and vigorous in discussion and criticism of the profession.

        2. The social worker should take action through appropriate channels against unethical conduct by any other member of the profession.

        3. The social worker should act to prevent the unauthorized and unqualified practice of social work.

        4. The social worker should make no misrepresentation in advertising as to qualifications, competence, service, or results to be achieved.

    N. Community Service—The social worker should assist the profession in making social services available to the general public.

        1. The social worker should contribute time and professional expertise to activities that promote respect for the utility, the integrity, and the competence of the social work profession.

        2. The social worker should support the formulation, development, enactment, and implementation of social policies of concern to the profession.

    O. Development of Knowledge—The social worker should take responsibility for identifying, developing, and fully utilizing knowledge for professional practice.

1. The social worker should base practice upon recognized knowledge relevant to social work.
2. The social worker should critically examine, and keep current with, emerging knowledge relevant to social work.
3. The social worker should contribute to the knowledge base of social work and share research knowledge and practice wisdom with colleagues.

VI. The Social Worker's Ethical Responsibility to Society
   P. Promoting the General Welfare—The social worker should promote the general welfare of society.
   1. The social worker should act to prevent and eliminate discrimination against any person or group on the basis of race, color, sex, sexual orientation, age, religion, national origin, marital status, political belief, mental or physical handicap, or any other preference or personal characteristic, condition, or status.
   2. The social worker should act to ensure that all persons have access to the resources, services, and opportunities which they require.
   3. The social worker should act to expand choice and opportunity for all persons, with special regard for disadvantaged or oppressed groups and persons.
   4. The social worker should promote conditions that encourage respect for the diversity of cultures which constitute American society.
   5. The social worker should provide appropriate professional services in public emergencies.
   6. The social worker should advocate changes in policy and legislation to improve social conditions and to promote social justice.
   7. The social worker should encourage informed participation by the public in shaping social policies and institutions.

Appendix 3

Canadian Association of Social Workers' Code of Ethics*

Definitions

In this Code,

Best interest of client means

(a)   that the wishes, desires, motivations, and plans of the client are taken by the social worker as the primary consideration in any intervention plan developed by the social worker subject to change only when the client's plans are documented to be unrealistic, unreasonable or potentially harmful to self or others or otherwise determined inappropriate when considered in relation to a mandated requirement.

(b)   that all actions and interventions of the social worker are taken subject to the reasonable belief that the client will benefit from the action, and

(c)   that the social worker will consider the client as an individual, a member of a family unit, a member of a community, a person with a distinct

---

*The Social Work Code of Ethics, adopted by the Board of Directors of the Canadian Association of Social Workers (CASW) is effective January 1, 1993 and replaces the CASW Code of Ethics (1983). This Code is reprinted here with the permission of CASW. The copyright in the document has been registered with Consumer and Corporate Affairs Canada, Registration No. 427837.

ancestry or culture and will consider those factors in any decision affecting the client.

Client[1] means
- (a) a person, family, group of persons, incorporated body, association or community on whose behalf a social worker provides or agrees to provide a service
  - (i) on request or with agreement[2] of the person, family, group of persons, incorporated body, associations or community, or
  - (ii) as a result of a legislated responsibility, or
- (b) a judge of a court of competent jurisdiction who orders the social worker to provide to the Court an assessment.[3]

Conduct unbecoming means behaviour or conduct that does not meet standard of care requirements and is therefore subject to discipline.[4]

Malpractice and negligence means behaviour that is included as "conduct unbecoming" and relates to social work practice behaviour within the parameters of the professional relationship that falls below the standard of practice and results in or aggravates an injury to a client. Without limiting the generality of the above,[5] it includes behaviour which results in assault, deceit, fraudulent misrepresentations, defamation of character, breach of contract, violation of human rights, malicious prosecution, false imprisonment or criminal conviction.

Practice of social work includes the assessment, remediation and prevention of social problems, and the enhancement of social functioning of individuals, families, groups and communities by means of
- (a) the provision of direct counselling services within an established relationship between a social worker and client;
- (b) the development, promotion and delivery of human service programs, including that done in collaboration with other professionals;
- (c) the development and promotion of social policies aimed at improving social conditions and equality; and[6]
- (d) any other activities approved by CASW.[7]

Social worker means a person who is duly registered to practice social work in a province or territory or, where mandatory registration does not exist, a person practising social work who voluntarily agrees to be subject to this Code.

Standard of practice means the standard of care ordinarily expected of a competent social worker. It means that the public is assured that a social worker has the training, the skill and the diligence to provide them with professional social work services.

Preamble

Philosophy

The profession of social work is founded on humanitarian and egalitarian ideas. Social workers believe in the intrinsic worth and dignity of every human being and are committed to the values of acceptance, self-determination and respect of individuality. They believe in the obligation of all people, individually and collectively, to provide resources, services and opportunities for the overall benefit of humanity. The culture of individuals, families, groups, communities and nations has to be respected without prejudice.[8]

Social workers are dedicated to the welfare and self-realization of human beings; to the development and disciplined use of scientific knowledge regarding human and social behaviours; to the development of resources to meet individual, group, national and international needs and aspirations; and to the achievement of social justice for all.

Professional Practice Conflicts

If a conflict arises in professional practice, the standards declared in this Code take precedence. Conflicts of interest may occur because of demands from the general public, workplace, organizations or clients. In all cases, if the ethical duties and obligations or ethical responsibilities of this Code would be compromised, the social worker must act in a manner consistent with this Code.

Nature of This Code

The first seven statements in this code establish ethical duties and obligations. These statements provide the basis of a social worker's relationship with a client and are based on the values of social work. A breach of any of these statements forms the basis of a disciplinary action. The remaining three statements are characterized as ethical responsibilities and are seen as being different from the ethical duties and obligations. These ethical responsibilities are not likely to form the basis of any disciplinary action if breached. However, these sections may form the basis of inquiry. These ethical responsibilities may be used in conjunction with breaches of other sections of this code and may form the basis of necessary background information in any action for discipline. Of equal importance, these ethical responsibilities are desirable goals to be achieved by the social work profession which by its nature is driven by an adherence to the values that form the basis of these desirable ethical behaviours.

Social Work Code of Ethics

Ethical Duties and Obligations

1. A social worker shall maintain the best interest of the client as the primary professional obligation.
2. A social worker shall carry out her or his professional duties and obligations with integrity and objectivity.
3. A social worker shall have and maintain competence in the provision of a social work service to a client.
4. A social worker shall not exploit the relationship with a client for personal benefit, gain or gratification.
5. A social worker shall protect the confidentiality of all information acquired from the client or others regarding the client and the client's family during the professional relationship unless
   (a) the client authorizes in writing the release of specified information
   (b) the information is released under the authority of a statute or an order of a court of competent jurisdiction, or
   (c) otherwise authorized by this Code.
6. A social worker who engages in another profession, occupation, affiliation or calling shall not allow these outside interests to affect the social work relationship with the client.
7. A social worker in private practice shall not conduct the business of provision of social work services for a fee in a manner that discredits the profession or diminishes the public's trust in the profession.

Ethical Responsibilities

8. A social worker shall advocate for workplace conditions and policies that are consistent with the Code.
9. A social worker shall promote excellence in the social work profession.
10. A social worker shall advocate change
    (a) in the best interest of the client, and
    (b) for the overall benefit of society, the environment and the global community.

Primary Professional Obligation

1. A social worker shall maintain the best interest of the client as the primary professional obligation.

1.1 The social worker is to be guided primarily by this obligation. Any action which is substantially inconsistent with this obligation is an unethical action.

1.2 A social worker in the practice of social work shall not discriminate against any person on the basis of race, ethnic background, language, religion, marital status, sex, sexual orientation, age, abilities, socio-economic status, political affiliation or national ancestry.[9]

1.3 A social worker shall inform a client of the client's right to consult another professional at any time during the provision of social work services.

1.4 A social worker shall immediately inform the client of any factor, condition[10] or pressure that affects the social worker's ability to perform an acceptable level of service.

1.5 A social worker shall not become involved in a client's personal affairs that are not relevant to the service being provided.

1.6 A social worker shall not state an opinion, judgment or use a clinical diagnosis unless there is a documented assessment, observation or diagnosis to support the opinion, judgment or diagnosis.

1.7 Where possible, a social worker shall provide or secure social work services in the language chosen by the client.

Integrity and Objectivity

2. A social worker shall carry out his or her professional duties and obligations with integrity and objectivity.[11]

2.1 The social worker shall identify and describe education, training, experience, professional affiliations, competence, and nature of service in an honest and accurate manner.

2.2 The social worker shall explain to the client her or his education, experience, training, competence, nature of service and action at the request of the client.

2.3 A social worker shall cite an educational degree only after it has been received from the institution.

2.4 A social worker shall not claim formal social work education in an area of expertise or training solely by attending a lecture demonstration, conference, panel discussion, workshop, seminar or other similar teaching presentation.[12]

2.5 The social worker shall not make a false, misleading or exaggerated claim of efficacy regarding past or anticipated achievement with respect to clients.

2.6 The social worker shall distinguish between actions and statements made as a private citizen and actions and statements made as a social worker.[13]

Competence in the Provision of Social Work Services

3.   A social worker shall have and maintain competence in the provision of a social work service to a client.

3.1   The social worker shall not undertake a social work service unless the social worker has the competence to provide the service or the social worker can reasonably acquire the necessary competence without undue delay, risk or expense to the client.

3.2   Where a social worker cannot reasonably acquire the necessary competence in the provision of a service to a client, the social worker shall decline to provide the service to the client, advising the client of the reason and ensuring that the client is referred to another professional person if the client agrees to the referral.

3.3   The social worker, with the agreement of the client, may obtain advice from other professionals in the provision of service to a client.

3.4   A social worker shall maintain an acceptable level of health and well-being in order to provide a competent level of service to a client.[14]

3.5   Where the social worker has a physical or mental health problem, disability, or illness that affects the ability of the social worker to provide competent service or that would threaten the health or well-being of the client, the social worker shall discontinue the provision of social work service to a client

     (a)   advising the client of the reason and,[15]

     (b)   ensuring that the client is referred to another professional person if the client agrees to the referral.

3.6   The social worker shall have, maintain and endeavor periodically to update an acceptable level of knowledge and skills to meet the standards of practice of the profession.

Limit on Professional Relationship

4.   A social worker shall not exploit the relationship with a client for personal benefit, gain or gratification.

4.1   The social worker shall respect the client and act so that the dignity, individuality and rights of the person are protected.

4.2   The social worker shall assess and consider a client's motivation and physical and mental capacity in arranging for the provision of an appropriate service.

4.3   The social worker shall not have a sexual relationship with a client.

4.4   The social worker shall not have a business relationship with a client, borrow money from a client, or loan money to a client.[16]

4.5   The social worker shall not have a sexual relationship with a social work student assigned to the social worker.

4.6   The social worker shall not sexually harass any person.

Confidential Information

5. A social worker shall protect the confidentiality[17] of all information required from the client or others regarding the client and the client's family during the professional relationship[18] unless

    (a) the client authorizes in writing the release of specified information,[19]

    (b) the information is released under the authority of a statute or an order of a court of relevant jurisdiction, or

    (c) otherwise authorized under this Code.

5.1 The requirement of confidentiality also applies to social workers who work as

    (a) supervisors,

    (b) managers,

    (c) educators,

    (d) administrators.

5.2 A social worker who works as a supervisor, manager or administrator shall establish policies and practices that protect the confidentiality of client information.

5.3 The social worker may disclose confidential information to other persons in the workplace who, by virtue of their responsibilities, have an identified need to know as determined by the social worker.

5.4 Clients shall be the initial or primary source of information about themselves and their problems unless the client is incapable or unwilling to give information or when corroborative reporting is required.

5.5 The social worker has the obligation to ensure that the client understands what is being asked, why and to what purpose the information will be used, and to understand the confidentiality policies and practices of the workplace setting.

5.6 Where information is required by law, the social worker shall explain to the client the consequences of refusing to provide the requested information.

5.7 Where information is required from other sources, the social worker

    (a) shall explain the requirement to the client, and

    (b) shall attempt to involve the client in selecting the sources to be used.

5.8 The social worker shall take reasonable care to safeguard the client's personal papers or property if the social worker agrees to keep the property at the request of the client.

Recording Information

5.9 The social worker shall maintain only one master file on each client.[20]

5.10 The social worker shall record all relevant information, and keep all relevant documents in the file.

5.11 The social worker shall not record in a client's file any characterization that is not based on clinical assessment or fact.

Accessibility of Records

5.12   The social worker who contracts for the delivery of social work services with a client is responsible to the client for maintaining the client record.

5.13   The social worker who is employed by a social agency that delivers social work services to clients is responsible

      (a)   to the client for the maintaining of a client record, and

      (b)   to the agency to maintain the records to facilitate the objectives of the agency.

5.14   A social worker is obligated to follow the provision of a statute that allows access to records by clients.

5.15   The social worker shall respect the client's right of access to a client record subject to the social worker's right to refuse access for just and reasonable cause.

5.16   Where a social worker refuses a client the right to access a file or part of a file, the social worker shall advise the client of the right to request a review of the decision in accordance with the relevant statute, workplace policy or other relevant procedure.

Disclosure

5.17   The social worker shall not disclose the identity of persons who have sought a social work service or disclose sources of information about clients unless compelled legally to do so.[21]

5.18   The obligation to maintain confidentiality continues indefinitely after the social worker has ceased contact with the client.

5.19   The social worker shall avoid unnecessary conversation regarding clients.

5.20   The social worker may divulge confidential information with consent of the client, preferably expressed in writing, where this is essential to a plan of care or treatment.

5.21   The social worker shall transfer information to another agency or individual, only with the informed consent of the client or guardian of the client and then only with the reasonable assurance that the receiving agency provides the same guarantee of confidentiality and respect for the right of privileged communication as provided by the sending agency.

5.22   The social worker shall explain to the client the disclosure of information requirements of the law or of the agency before the commencement of the provision of social work services.

5.23   The social worker in practice with groups and communities shall notify the participants of the likelihood that aspects of their private lives may be revealed in the course of their work together, and therefore require a commitment from each member to respect the privileged and confidential nature of the communication between and among members of the client group.

5.24   Subject to section 5.26, the social worker shall not disclose information acquired from one client to a member of the client's family without the informed consent of the client who provided the information.

5.25   A social worker shall disclose information acquired from one client to a member of the client's family where
   (a)   the information involves a threat of harm to self or others,[22]
   (b)   the information was acquired from a child of tender years and the social worker determines that its disclosure is in the best interests of the child.[23]

5.26   A social worker shall disclose information acquired from a client to a person or a police officer where the information involves a threat of harm to that person.

5.27   A social worker may release confidential information as part of a discipline hearing of a social worker as directed by the tribunal or disciplinary body.

5.28   When disclosure is required by order of a court, the social worker shall not divulge more information than is reasonably required and shall where possible notify the client of this requirement.

5.29   The social worker shall not use confidential information for the purpose of teaching, public education or research except with the informed consent of the client.

5.30   The social worker may use non-identifying information for the purpose of teaching, public education or research.

Retention and Disposition of Information

5.31   Where the social worker's documentation is stored in a place or computer maintained and operated by an employer, the social worker shall advocate for the responsible retention and disposition of information contained in the file.

Outside Interest

6.   A social worker who engages in another profession, occupation, affiliation or calling shall not allow these outside interests to affect the social work relationship with the client.

6.1   A social worker shall declare to the client any outside interests that would affect the social work relationship with the client.

6.2   A social worker shall not allow an outside interest:
   (a)   to affect the social worker's ability to practise social work;
   (b)   to present to the client or to the community that the social worker's ability to practise social work is affected; or
   (c)   to bring the profession of social work into disrepute.[24]

Limit on Private Practice

7.   A social worker in private practice shall not conduct the business of provision of social work services for a fee in a manner that discredits the profession or diminishes the public's trust in the profession.

7.1   A social worker shall not use the social work relationship within an agency to obtain clients for his or her private practice.

7.2   Subject to section 7.3, a social worker who enters into a contract for service with a client
    (a)   shall disclose at the outset of the relationship, the fee schedule for the social work services,
    (b)   shall not charge a fee that is greater than that agreed to and disclosed to the client, and
    (c)   shall not charge for hours of service other than the reasonable hours of client service, research, consultation and administrative work directly connected to the case.

7.3   A social worker in private practice may charge differential fees for services except where an increased fee is charged based on race, ethnic background, language, religion, marital status, sex, sexual orientation, age, abilities, socio-economic status, political affiliation or national ancestry.

7.4   A social worker in private practice shall maintain adequate malpractice, defamation and liability insurance.

7.5   A social worker in private practice may charge a rate of interest on delinquent accounts as is allowed by law.[25]

7.6   Notwithstanding section 5.17 a social worker in private practice may pursue civil remedies to ensure payment for services to a client where the social worker has advised the client of this possibility at the outset of the social work service.

Ethical Responsibilities to the Workplace

8.   A social worker shall advocate for workplace conditions and policies that are consistent with the Code.

8.1   Where the responsibilities to an employer are in conflict with the social worker's obligations to the client, the social worker shall document the issue in writing and shall bring the situation to the attention of the employer.

8.2   Where a serious ethical conflict continues to exist after the issue has been brought to the attention of the employer, the social worker shall bring the issue to the attention of the association or regulatory body.[26]

8.3   A social worker shall follow the principles in the Code when dealing with
    (a)   a social worker under the supervision of the social worker,
    (b)   an employee under the supervision of the social worker, and
    (c)   a social work student under the supervision of the social worker.

Ethical Responsibilities to the Profession

9.   A social worker shall promote excellence in the social work profession.

9.1   A social worker shall report to the appropriate association or regulatory body any breach of this Code by another social worker which adversely affects or harms a client or prevents the effective delivery of a social service.

9.2   A social worker shall report to the association or regulatory body any unqualified or unlicensed person who is practising social work.

9.3   A social worker shall not intervene in the professional relationship of a social worker and client unless requested to do so by the client and unless convinced that the best interests and well-being of the client require such intervention.

9.4   Where a conflict arises between a social worker and other professionals, the social worker shall attempt to resolve the professional differences in ways that uphold the principles of this Code and the honour of the social work profession.

9.5   A social worker engaged in research shall ensure that the involvement of clients in the research is a result of informed consent.

Ethical Responsibilities for Social Change

10.   A social worker shall advocate change
   (a)   in the best interest of the client, and
   (b)   for the overall benefit of society, the environment and the global community.

10.1   A social worker shall identify, document and advocate for the elimination of discrimination.

10.2   A social worker shall advocate for the equal distribution of services to all persons.

10.3   A social worker shall advocate for the equal access of all persons to resources, services and opportunities.

10.4   A social worker shall advocate for a clean and healthy environment and shall advocate the development of environmental strategies consistent with social work principles.

10.5   A social worker shall provide reasonable professional services in a state of emergency.

10.6   A social worker shall promote social justice.

Notes

1. A client ceases to be a client 2 years after the termination of a social work service. It is advisable for this termination to be clearly documented on the case file.

2. This sub-paragraph identifies two situations where a person may be considered a voluntary client. The person who requests a social work service is clearly a voluntary client. A person also may originally be receiving services as a result of the actions of a court or other legally mandated entity. This person may receive a service beyond that originally mandated and therefore be able to terminate voluntarily that aspect of the service. A situation where a person is referred by another professional or family member clearly falls into this "voluntary service" relationship when that person agrees with the service to be provided. This type of social work relationship is clearly distinguishable from the relationship in sub-paragraph (ii) where the social worker does not seek or have agreement for the service to be provided.

3. In this situation, the social worker is providing an assessment, information or a professional opinion to a judge of competent jurisdiction to assist the judge in making a ruling or determination. In this situation, the relationship is with the judge and the person on whom the information, assessment or opinion is provided is not the client. The social worker still has some professional obligations towards that person, for example: competence and dignity.

4. In reaching a decision in *Re Matthews and the Board of Directors of Psychotherapy* (1986)54, O.R. (2nd) 375, Saunders, J. makes three important statements regarding standards of practice and by implication the Code of Ethics:

   (i)   Standards of practice are inherent characteristics of any profession.
   (ii) Standards of practice may be written or unwritten.
   (iii) Some conduct is clearly regarded as misconduct and need not be written down whereas other conduct may be the subject of dispute within a profession.

5. The importance of the collective opinion of the profession in establishing and ultimately modifying the Code of Ethics was established in an 1884 case involving the medical profession. Lord Esher, M. R. stated:

   > "If it is shown that a medical man, in the pursuit of his profession, has done something with regard to it which would be reasonably regarded as disgraceful or dishonourable by his professional brethren of good repute and competency," then it is open to the General Medical Council to say that he has been guilty of "infamous conduct in a professional respect."

6. This definition except paragraph (d) has been taken from *An Act to Incorporate the New Brunswick Association of Social Workers*, chapter 78 of the Statutes of New Brunswick, 1988, section 2.

7. The procedure for adding activities under this paragraph will be established by a bylaw by the CASW Board of Directors.

8. Taken from: *Teaching and Learning about Human Rights: A Manual for Schools of Social Work and the Social Work Profession*; U.N. Centre for Human Rights, Co-operation with International Federation of Social Workers and International Association of Schools of Social Workers, United Nations, New York, 1992.

9. This obligation goes beyond grounds of discrimination stated in most Human Rights Legislation and therefore there is a greater professional obligation than that stated in provincial legislation.

10. The term *condition* means a physical, mental or psychological condition. There is an implied obligation that the social worker shall actively seek diagnosis and treatment for any signs or warnings of a condition. A disclosure under this section may be of a general nature. See also 3.4.

11. The term *objectivity* is taken from the Quebec Code of Professional Conduct. See Division 2: Integrity and Objectivity (6.0 Quebec) November 5, 1979 Vol. 2 No. 30. The term *objectivity* is stated in the following: 3.02.01. A social worker must discharge his professional duties with integrity and objectivity.

12. The provincial associations may regulate the areas of expertise to be stated or advertised by a social worker. This will vary in each province according to its enabling legislation. Where there is not sufficient legislative base for this regulation, the claim of an expertise without sufficient training may form the basis of a determination of unprofessional conduct.

13. Even with a distinction made under this section, a social worker's private actions or statements may be of such a nature that the social worker cannot avoid the responsibilities under this Code. See also 6.2(c).

14. This section should be considered in relation to section 1.4 and involves proper maintenance, prevention and treatment of any type of risk to the health or well-being of the social worker.

15. It is not necessary in all circumstances to explain specifically the nature of the problem.

16. Where a social worker does keep money or assets belonging to a client, the social worker should hold this money or asset in a trust account or hold the money or asset in conjunction with an additional professional person.

17. Confidentiality means that information received or observed about a client by a social worker will be held in confidence and disclosed only when the social worker is properly authorized or obligated legally or professionally to do so. This also means that professionally acquired information may be treated as privileged communication and ordinarily only the client has the right to waive privilege.

Privileged communication means statements made within a protected relationship (i.e., husband-wife, professional-client) which the law protects against disclosure. The extent of the privilege is governed by law and not by this Code.

Maintaining confidentiality of privileged communication means that information about clients does not have to be transmitted in any oral, written or recorded form. Such information, for example, does not have to be disclosed to a supervisor, written into a workplace record, stored in a computer or microfilm database, held or on audio or videotape or discussed orally. The right of privileged communication is respected by the social worker in the practice of social work notwithstanding that this right is not ordinarily granted in law.

The disclosure of confidential information in social work practice involves the obligation to share information professionally with others in the workplace of the social worker as part of a reasonable service to the client. Social workers recognize the need to obtain permission from clients before releasing information about them to sources outside their workplace, and to inform clients at the outset of their relationship that some information acquired may be shared with the officers and personnel of the agency who maintain the case record and who have a reasonable need for the information in the performance of their duties.

18. The social worker's relationship with a client can be characterized as a fiduciary relationship.

In *Fiduciary Duties in Canada* by Ellis, fiduciary duty is described as follows: . . . where one party has placed its "trust and confidence" in another and the latter has accepted—expressly or by operation of law—to act in a manner consistent with the reposing of such "trust and confidence," a fiduciary relationship has been established.

19. The "obligation of secrecy" was discussed by the Supreme Court of Canada in *Halls v. Mitchell*, (1928) S. C. R. 125, an action brought by a disabled CNR worker against a company doctor who had disclosed the employee's medical history, to the latter's detriment, Mr. Justice Duff reviewed the duty of confidentiality:

> We are not required, for the purposes of this appeal, to attempt to state with any sort of precision the limits of the obligation of secrecy which rests upon the medical practitioner in relation to the professional secrets acquired by him in the course of his practice. Nobody would dispute that a secret so acquired is the secret of the patient, and, normally, is under his control, and not under that of the doctor. Prima facie, the patient has the right to require that the secret shall not be divulged; and that right is absolute, unless there is some paramount reason which overrides it.

Thus the right of secrecy/confidentiality rests squarely with the patient; the Court carefully provided that there is an "ownership" extant in the confidentiality of the personal information. Duff, J. continued by allowing for "paramount" criteria which vitiates from the right:

> Some reasons may arise, no doubt, from the existence of facts which bring into play overpowering consideration connected with public justice; and there may be cases in which reasons connected with the safety of individuals or of the public, physical or moral, would be sufficiently cogent to supersede or qualify the obligations prima facie imposed by the confidential relation.

Duff, J. continued:

> The general duty of medical men to observe secrecy, in relation to information acquired by them confidentially from their patients is subject, no doubt, to some exceptions, which have no operation in the case of solicitors; but the grounds of the legal, social or moral imperatives affecting physicians and surgeons, touching the inviolability of professional confidences, are not, any more than those affecting legal advisers, based exclusively upon the relationships between the parties as individuals.

20. The master file refers to all relevant documents pertaining to the client consisting of such information as demographics, case recordings, court documents, assessments, correspondence, treatment plans, bills, etc. This information is often collected through various means including electronic and computer driven sources. However, the client master file exists as one unit, inclusive of all information pertaining to the client, despite the various sources of the recording process. The description and ownership of the master file is most often defined by workplace standards or policies. The client's master file should be prepared keeping in mind that it may have to be revealed to the client or disclosed in legal proceedings.

21. A social worker may be compelled to reveal information under the section when directly ordered by the court to do so. Before disclosing the information, the social worker shall advise the court of the professional obligations that exist under this section of the Code and where reasonably possible inform the client.

22. The case of *Tarasoff v. The Regents of the University of California et al.* (1976), 551 P.2d 334 (Cal. Supreme Court) focused on the obligation of a psychiatrist to maintain the confidentiality of his patients' statements in their discussions. In that case the patient told the psychiatrist that the patient had an intention to kill a certain woman. When the patient actu-

ally did kill this woman, her parents brought suit alleging that the psychiatrist owed a duty to tell the woman of the danger to her.

It was held that the psychiatrist did have a duty to tell the woman of the threat. The court recognized that the psychiatrist owed a duty to the patient to keep in confidence the statements the patient made in therapy sessions, but held there was also a duty of care to anyone whom the psychiatrist knew might be endangered by the patient. At a certain point the obligation of confidentiality would be overridden by the obligation to this third person. The psychiatrist's knowledge itself gave rise to a duty of care. What conduct would be sufficient to fulfill the duty to this third person would depend on the circumstances, but it might be necessary to give a warning that would reveal what the patient had said about the third party. The court in this case held that the psychiatrist had a duty to warn the woman about the patient's stated intention to kill her and failing to warn her the psychiatrist was liable in negligence. Moreover, the court stated that the principle of this duty of care belonged to not just a psychiatrist but also to a psychologist performing therapy. It would follow that the principle would also apply to social workers performing therapy.

23. For the purpose of this Code, a child of tender years shall usually be determined to be a child under the age of seven years subject to a determination by a social worker considering the child's social, physical, intellectual, emotional or psychological development.

24. This section brings the social worker's outside interest and personal actions in line with the professional duties and obligations as set out in this Code.

25. This rate shall be stated on all invoices or bills sent to the client.

26. In this situation the professional obligations outweigh any obligations to a workplace.

Appendix 4

Alphabetized Vocabulary of Standard English Feeling Words

Feelings and emotions are extremely complicated human experiences. They are extraordinarily difficult to define. Some theorists consider feelings to be the subjective experience of physical sensations; others view emotions as the physiological experiences that accompany thoughts and actions. Still others consider emotions to be discrete experiences unrelated to thoughts, physical sensations, actions, or circumstances. Consensus concerning the definition of feelings does not exist. Perhaps it never will. It is clear, however, that individual human beings define and experience feelings and emotions in unique ways. Therefore, a broad range of words—some nouns, some verbs, some adjectives—are presented below in order to account for just a small amount of the wonderful diversity that occurs in the human experience of feelings.

abandoned	achieved	adverse	agony
abased	acknowledged	advocated	agonized
abashed	acquiesced	affected	agreeable
abdicated	acrimonious	affectionate	aimless
abducted	adamant	affinity	alarmed
abhor	adapted	afraid	alarming
abominable	adept	aggravated	alienated
abrasive	adjusted	aggressive	alive
abrupt	admired	aggrieved	alleviate
accepted	admonished	aghast	alluring
acclaimed	adored	agile	alone
accused	adrift	agitate	aloof
accustomed	adventurous	aglow	altruistic

amazed
ambiguous
ambitious
ambivalent
ameliorate
amicable
amused
anemic
angelic
angry
angst
anguish
animosity
annoyed
anomie
anonymous
antagonistic
antagonized
anticipation
antsy
anxious
apathetic
apocalyptic
apologetic
appalling
appetizing
apprehensive
approachable
approving
arbitrary
arcane
archaic
ardent
ardor
arduous
argumentative
arresting
arrogant
artificial
ashamed
assailed
assaulted
assertive
assuaged
assured

astonished
astounding
attuned
attached
attentive
attracted
audacious
auspicious
aversive
awarded
awful
back-sided
backstabbed
bad
balanced
balked
bamboozled
banking
barrage
bashful
basic
battered
bawdy
beaming
beaten
beautiful
beckoning
becoming
bedazzled
bedeviled
bedraggled
befuddled
begrudging
beguiling
beholden
belittled
bellicose
belligerent
belonging
bemoan
beneficent
benign
berated
bereaved
bereft

bested
betrayed
beware
bewildered
bewitched
biased
bidden
bigoted
bitter
blah
blamed
bleary
blessed
blissful
blocked
blue
blunted
blushed
bogged-down
boggled
bolstered
bonded
bored
botched
bothered
boundless
bountiful
boxed-in
braced
branded
brave
brazen
breached
bright
brilliant
brisk
broached
broken
browbeaten
bruised
brushed-off
brutalized
bucking
buck-passing
bugged

bulldozed
bullied
buoyant
burdened
burned
burned-out
busted
butchered
cakewalk
calculating
calling
callous
callow
calm
cancerous
candid
canned
capitulated
capricious
capsulated
captivated
captive
care
carefree
careful
careless
caring
caretaking
caroused
carping
cast-off
cataclysmic
catalyst
catapulted
catastrophic
catharsis
caught
caustic
cautious
celibate
cemented
censored
censured
certain
challenged

chancy
changeable
charismatic
charitable
charmed
charming
chased
chaste
cheap
cheapened
cheeky
cheered
cheerful
cheesy
cherished
chivalrous
chummy
chump
civil
clammy
clandestine
clean
cocksure
coherent
cohesive
coincidental
cold
cold-blooded
cold-shouldered
collared
collusive
combative
combustible
comfortable
come-on
coming-out
commanded
committed
compartmentalized
compassionate
compelling
compensated
competent
complacent
complete

compliant
complicated
complementary
complimented
composed
comprehensible
comprehensive
compressed
compromised
concentrating
concerned
conciliatory
conclusive
concocted
condemned
condescending
condoned
conducive
confident
confined
conflicted
congenial
congratulated
congruent
connected
conquered
conscientious
considerate
considered
consoled
consoling
conspiratorial
constant
consternation
constrained
constricted
constructive
contaminated
contemplative
contented
contentious
contributory
convenient
convinced
convincing

cool
corrected
corroborate
corrosive
cosmetic
counted
countered
courageous
courteous
covered
cowardly
cozy
crabby
crafty
craggy
crappy
credible
creepy
crestfallen
cried
cringe
critical
criticize
crooked
cross
crossed
crucified
cruddy
crummy
crushed
crystallized
curative
curious
cursed
cut
dangerous
debased
dejected
demeaned
demure
denigrated
depressed
detached
determined
devoted

disappointed
disapproval
disbelief
disgust
dismal
dismayed
displeased
distant
distasteful
distrust
disturbed
doubtful
dubious
ecstatic
elated
elevated
embarrassed
empty
enamored
energetic
enervated
enraged
enriched
enthusiastic
entrusted
envious
euphoric
exasperated
excited
exhausted
fantastic
fearful
fearless
ferocious
flighty
flustered
fondness
forgiveness
forgotten
forsaken
frazzled
friendly
frightened
frustrated
gagged

galvanized	hapless	hung up	intolerable
gamey	happy	hurried	intolerant
garrulous	hard	hurt	intoxicated
gawky	hardboiled	hyped	intrusive
generous	hardheaded	hysterical	invincible
genial	hard-edged	ice-cold	irate
gentle	hardy	idiotic	irritable
genuine	harmful	idyllic	irritated
glad	harmless	ignominious	itchy
glee	harried	ill at ease	jaded
glib	harassed	indifferent	jagged
gloomy	hate	impatient	jaundiced
glow	hated	impersonal	jaunty
glum	haunting	impetuous	jealous
golden	hazardous	impotent	jerky
good	hazy	impressive	jolly
graceful	healthful	impulsive	joyful
graceless	healthy	inadequate	joyless
gracious	heartache	incoherent	joyous
grand	heartbroken	incompetent	jubilant
great	heartless	incomplete	judged
greedy	heartsick	inconsiderate	judgmental
green	heartwarming	indebted	just
gregarious	helpful	indecisive	keen
grief	helpless	independent	kind
grim	hesitant	indestructible	kindhearted
gross	high-spirited	indifferent	kinky
gruesome	hoggish	indignant	kooky
gruff	hog-tied	indiscreet	laborious
grubby	homesick	indispensable	lenient
grumpy	honorable	indulgent	lightheaded
grungy	hope	inept	lighthearted
guarded	hopeful	infantile	limited
gullible	hopeless	infatuated	lonely
guilty	horny	inferior	lonesome
guiltless	horrendous	inhibited	loss
gutsy	horrible	injurious	lost
gutted	horrified	innocent	lousy
haggard	hostile	insane	lovable
hammered	hot	insatiable	love
hamstrung	hotblooded	insolent	lovely
handcuffed	hotheaded	inspirational	lovesick
handicapped	huffy	intense	lovestruck
handy	humble	interested	low
hangdogged	hungry	intimate	loyal

luckless	motivated	passionate	quandary
lucky	mournful	passive	quarrelsome
ludicrous	muddled	patchy	queasy
lukewarm	murky	patient	quizzical
mad	mushy	peaceful	radiant
maddening	mysterious	penalized	radiate
magical	nasty	permissive	radical
magnanimous	natural	perplexed	rage
magnetic	naughty	persecuted	ragged
magnificent	nauseous	persistent	rancor
majestic	necessary	personable	raped
maladjusted	needful	pessimistic	rapture
malaise	needy	petty	rash
malicious	negative	petulant	raucous
malignant	neglected	phobic	raunchy
manic	neglectful	phoney	rebellious
manipulated	nervous	picky	rebuffed
manipulative	nice	pitiful	recalcitrant
martyred	noble	pivotal	reckless
masterful	normal	pleasing	reclusive
mature	nostalgic	pleasurable	refreshed
mean	nosey	plentiful	regretful
meaningful	noteworthy	poetic	reinvigorate
meaningless	notorious	poignant	rejected
mean-spirited	oafish	poisonous	rejoice
mediocre	obdurate	polluted	rejuvenated
meditative	obedient	pout	relaxed
melancholy	object	praised	released
mellow	obligated	praiseworthy	relentless
melodramatic	obnoxious	prejudicial	relieved
mercurial	obscene	pressure	relish
methodical	obstinate	presumptuous	reluctant
mind-boggling	obstructionist	prickly	remorse
mindful	odd	pride	remorseful
mindless	odious	prideful	remorseless
mischievous	offensive	protective	remote
miserable	onerous	proud	renewed
mistrust	optimistic	prudish	repellent
misty	ornery	pulled	repentant
misunderstood	outrage	pushed	reprehensible
monotonous	outrageous	putoff	reprimanded
monstrous	pained	puzzled	reproached
monumental	panic	quake	repugnant
moody	panic-stricken	qualified	repulsive
mortified	paranoid	qualm	resentful

resentment	scapegoated	slick	taken-in
reserved	scarce	smug	tangled
resigned	scared	soiled	tattered
resilient	scarred	solemn	teased
resistant	scattered	solid	tedious
resolute	scrambled	sordid	teed-off
resolved	scrapped	sorrow	tempted
resourceful	scrawny	spacey	tempting
respectful	searching	spellbound	tenacious
responsible	seasoned	spiritual	tender
responsive	secure	spiteful	tension
restful	sedated	splendid	tenuous
restless	seductive	split	terminal
restricted	seedy	spoiled	terrible
reticent	seeking	spooky	terrific
retiring	sensational	squeamish	terrified
revolting	sensitive	stable	terrorized
revulsion	sensual	stalked	testy
rewarding	sentimental	steady	thankful
ridiculed	serious	stern	therapeutic
risky	settled	stilted	thickskinned
rosy	severe	stodgy	thinskinned
rotten	sexual	stressed	thoughtful
rough	shady	stretched	thoughtless
rude	shaggy	strong	thrashed
rueful	shaken	strung-out	threatened
rugged	shaky	stuck	threatening
ruined	shame	stumped	thrifty
rundown	shameful	stunned	thrilled
rush	shameless	sullen	thrilling
rushed	sheepish	sunk	thunderstruck
sacked	shifty	super	ticked
sacred	shocked	supported	ticked-off
sacrificial	shortchanged	supportive	timid
sacrilegious	shunned	surly	tingle
sacrosanct	sick	surprised	tingling
sad	sickening	suspicious	tired
saddled	sincere	sympathetic	tireless
safe	sinful	taboo	tiresome
sanctimonious	singled-out	taciturn	tolerate
sanctified	sinister	tacky	torment
sanguine	skeptical	tactful	torpid
satisfied	sleazy	tactless	touched
scandalized	sleepless	tainted	tough
scandalous	sleepy	taken	toxic

tragic
tranquil
transcendent
transformed
trapped
trashed
traumatic
treacherous
tricked
tricky
triggered
tripped
triumphant
trivial
troubled
troubling
trust
tuckered
turbulent
turned-off
turned-on
twinkling
tyrannized
ubiquitous
ugly
umbrage
unabashed
unaccepted
unaccustomed
unacknowledged
unappealing
unappreciated

unashamed
unbearable
uncared-for
uncertain
unclean
uncomfortable
undaunted
undecided
understood
undesirable
undisturbed
unequal
unfaithful
unfavorable
unglued
unimportant
unified
united
unjust
unkind
unlucky
unpleasant
unproductive
unreasonable
unrelenting
unrelentless
unrepentant
unresponsive
unsafe
unselfconscious
unselfish
unstable

upbeat
uprooted
upstaged
uptight
urgent
vacant
vain
valiant
valued
vandalized
vengeful
victimized
victorious
vigilant
vigorous
vindicated
virtuous
violated
violent
vital
vitriolic
vituperative
vulnerable
wacky
wane
wanted
wanting
washed-out
washed-up
wasted
weak
weakened

well-adjusted
well-balanced
well-intentioned
well-meaning
well-rounded
wicked
wide-awake
wide-eyed
wild
wild-eyed
wily
winced
winded
wiped-out
wired
wishful
withdrawn
wobbly
wonderful
wondrous
worried
worthless
worthwhile
worthy
wounded
wretched
wrought-up
xenophobic
yielded
yielding
zealous
zestful

Appendix 5

Summary Self-Evaluation: Social Work Skills Proficiency

Please use this instrument to conduct a summary self-evaluation of your proficiency in the social work skills. Proficiency requires the following: First, you should understand the skill and be able to describe how it might be used. Ability to recall the recommended practice format, suggested for many of the skills, reflects such an understanding. Second, you should be able to associate the skill with the phase of social work practice in which it is commonly used. Third, you should be able to demonstrate an ability to use the skill at a time and in a context that is professionally appropriate. Fourth, you should be able to demonstrate expertise in the use of the skill. Finally, you should be able to adapt the skill or combine it with others in order to meet the particular needs or demands of a unique social work situation.

Based on your self-evaluation of the dimensions described above, rate your estimated proficiency in each of the skills identified below according to a scale where 0 = no proficiency and 10 = complete proficiency.

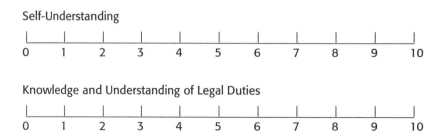

Self-Understanding

| 0 | 1 | 2 | 3 | 4 | 5 | 6 | 7 | 8 | 9 | 10 |

Knowledge and Understanding of Legal Duties

| 0 | 1 | 2 | 3 | 4 | 5 | 6 | 7 | 8 | 9 | 10 |

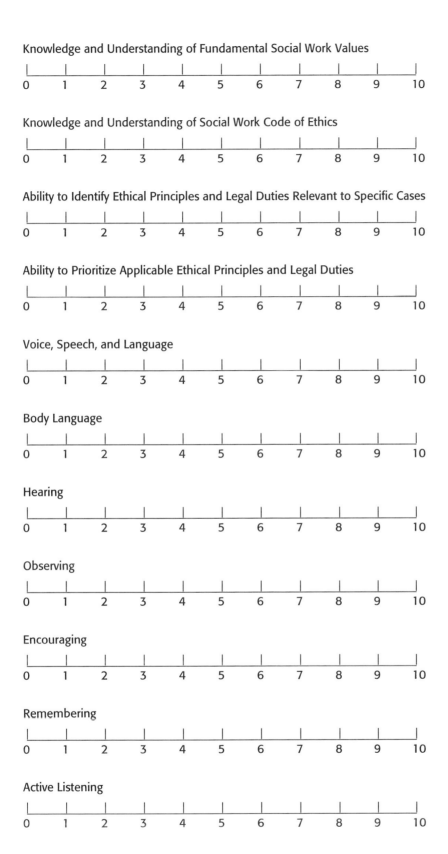

Knowledge and Understanding of Fundamental Social Work Values

0	1	2	3	4	5	6	7	8	9	10

Knowledge and Understanding of Social Work Code of Ethics

0	1	2	3	4	5	6	7	8	9	10

Ability to Identify Ethical Principles and Legal Duties Relevant to Specific Cases

0	1	2	3	4	5	6	7	8	9	10

Ability to Prioritize Applicable Ethical Principles and Legal Duties

0	1	2	3	4	5	6	7	8	9	10

Voice, Speech, and Language

0	1	2	3	4	5	6	7	8	9	10

Body Language

0	1	2	3	4	5	6	7	8	9	10

Hearing

0	1	2	3	4	5	6	7	8	9	10

Observing

0	1	2	3	4	5	6	7	8	9	10

Encouraging

0	1	2	3	4	5	6	7	8	9	10

Remembering

0	1	2	3	4	5	6	7	8	9	10

Active Listening

0	1	2	3	4	5	6	7	8	9	10

Preparatory Reviewing

0	1	2	3	4	5	6	7	8	9	10

Preparatory Exploring

0	1	2	3	4	5	6	7	8	9	10

Preparatory Consulting

0	1	2	3	4	5	6	7	8	9	10

Preparatory Arranging

0	1	2	3	4	5	6	7	8	9	10

Preparatory Empathy

0	1	2	3	4	5	6	7	8	9	10

Preparatory Self-Exploration

0	1	2	3	4	5	6	7	8	9	10

Centering

0	1	2	3	4	5	6	7	8	9	10

Preliminary Planning and Recording

0	1	2	3	4	5	6	7	8	9	10

Introducing Yourself

0	1	2	3	4	5	6	7	8	9	10

Seeking Introductions

0	1	2	3	4	5	6	7	8	9	10

Describing Initial Purpose

0	1	2	3	4	5	6	7	8	9	10

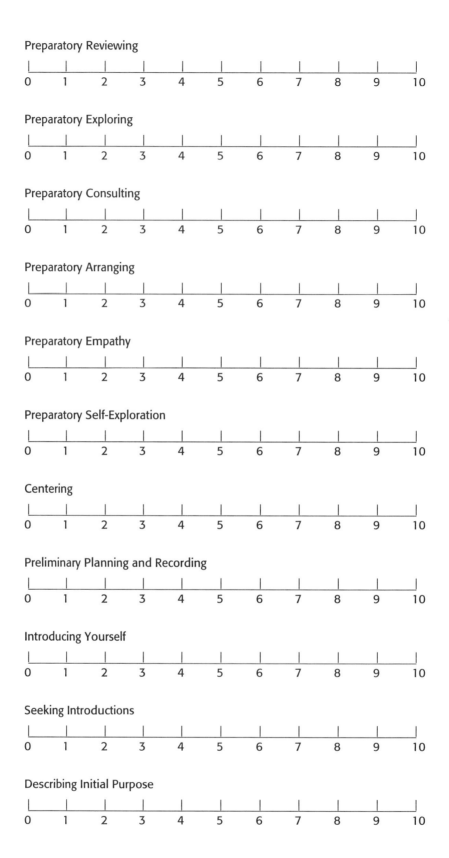

Outlining the Client's Role

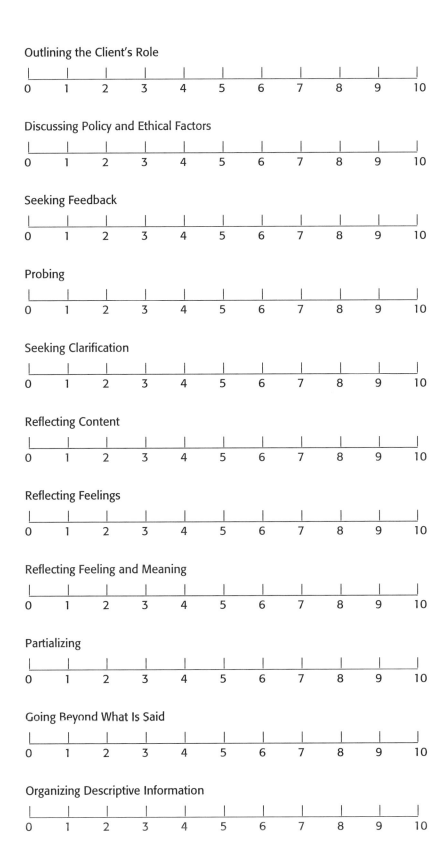

0	1	2	3	4	5	6	7	8	9	10

Discussing Policy and Ethical Factors

0	1	2	3	4	5	6	7	8	9	10

Seeking Feedback

0	1	2	3	4	5	6	7	8	9	10

Probing

0	1	2	3	4	5	6	7	8	9	10

Seeking Clarification

0	1	2	3	4	5	6	7	8	9	10

Reflecting Content

0	1	2	3	4	5	6	7	8	9	10

Reflecting Feelings

0	1	2	3	4	5	6	7	8	9	10

Reflecting Feeling and Meaning

0	1	2	3	4	5	6	7	8	9	10

Partializing

0	1	2	3	4	5	6	7	8	9	10

Going Beyond What Is Said

0	1	2	3	4	5	6	7	8	9	10

Organizing Descriptive Information

0	1	2	3	4	5	6	7	8	9	10

Formulating a Tentative Assessment

| | | | | | | | | | | |
0   1   2   3   4   5   6   7   8   9   10

Reflecting a Problem

| | | | | | | | | | | |
0   1   2   3   4   5   6   7   8   9   10

Sharing Your View of a Problem

| | | | | | | | | | | |
0   1   2   3   4   5   6   7   8   9   10

Specifying Problems for Work

| | | | | | | | | | | |
0   1   2   3   4   5   6   7   8   9   10

Establishing Goals

| | | | | | | | | | | |
0   1   2   3   4   5   6   7   8   9   10

Developing an Approach

| | | | | | | | | | | |
0   1   2   3   4   5   6   7   8   9   10

Identifying Action Steps

| | | | | | | | | | | |
0   1   2   3   4   5   6   7   8   9   10

Planning for Evaluation

| | | | | | | | | | | |
0   1   2   3   4   5   6   7   8   9   10

Summarizing the Contract

| | | | | | | | | | | |
0   1   2   3   4   5   6   7   8   9   10

Rehearsing Action Steps

| | | | | | | | | | | |
0   1   2   3   4   5   6   7   8   9   10

Reviewing Action Steps

| | | | | | | | | | | |
0   1   2   3   4   5   6   7   8   9   10

Evaluating

0	1	2	3	4	5	6	7	8	9	10

Focusing

0	1	2	3	4	5	6	7	8	9	10

Educating

0	1	2	3	4	5	6	7	8	9	10

Advising

0	1	2	3	4	5	6	7	8	9	10

Representing

0	1	2	3	4	5	6	7	8	9	10

Responding with Immediacy

0	1	2	3	4	5	6	7	8	9	10

Reframing

0	1	2	3	4	5	6	7	8	9	10

Confronting

0	1	2	3	4	5	6	7	8	9	10

Pointing Out Endings

0	1	2	3	4	5	6	7	8	9	10

Progress Recording

0	1	2	3	4	5	6	7	8	9	10

Reviewing the Process

0	1	2	3	4	5	6	7	8	9	10

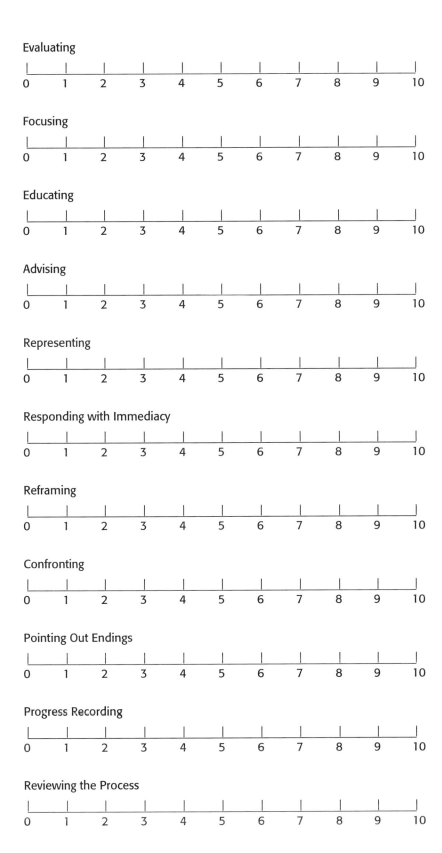

Final Evaluating

| | | | | | | | | | | | | |
0   1   2   3   4   5   6   7   8   9   10

Sharing Ending Feelings and Saying Goodbye

| | | | | | | | | | | | | |
0   1   2   3   4   5   6   7   8   9   10

Recording the Closing Summary

| | | | | | | | | | | | | |
0   1   2   3   4   5   6   7   8   9   10

Appendix 6

Social Work Skills Interview Rating Form*

You may use this rating form as part of the process of evaluating your own or others' performance of the social work skills during interviews with clients. You may use it, for example, in rating your performance during an interview with an individual, a couple, a family, or a small group. You may also use the form in order to provide evaluative feedback to a colleague who is attempting to improve the quality of his or her performance.

In using the form, please use the following rating system:

N/A   During the course of the interview, the skill in question was not appropriate or necessary and was therefore not used, having no effect on the interview.

-3   During the course of the interview, the skill in question was used at an inappropriate time or in an unsuitable context, seriously detracting from the interview.

-2   During the course of the interview, the skill in question was attempted at an appropriate time and in a suitable context but was done so in an incompetent manner, significantly detracting from the interview.

-1   During the course of the interview, the skill in question was not used at times or in contexts when it should have been, detracting from the interview.

---

*Note: Because this rating form is intended for the purpose of evaluating social work skills used during face-to-face interviews, skills related to ethical decision-making, assessing, and recording are not included.

0   During the course of the interview, the skill in question was used and demonstrated at a minimal level of competence. Its use did not detract from or contribute to the interview.

+1   During the course of the interview, the skill in question was attempted at an appropriate time and in a suitable context and was generally demonstrated at a fair level of competence. Its use represented a modest contribution to the interview.

+2   During the course of the interview, the skill in question was attempted at an appropriate time and in a suitable context and was generally demonstrated at a moderate level of competence. Its use represented a significant contribution to the interview.

+3   During the course of the interview, the skill in question was attempted at an appropriate time and in a suitable context and was generally demonstrated at a good level of competence. Its use represented a substantial contribution to the interview.

+4   During the course of the interview, the skill in question was attempted at an appropriate time and in a suitable context and was generally demonstrated at superior level of performance. Its use represented a major contribution to the interview.

Talking and Listening—The Basic Interpersonal Skills

1. **Voice, Speech, and Language**   N/A -3 -2 -1 0 +1 +2 +3 +4
Comments:

2. **Body Language**   N/A -3 -2 -1 0 +1 +2 +3 +4
Comments:

3. **Hearing**   N/A -3 -2 -1 0 +1 +2 +3 +4
Comments:

4. **Observing**   N/A -3 -2 -1 0 +1 +2 +3 +4
Comments:

5. **Encouraging**   N/A -3 -2 -1 0 +1 +2 +3 +4
Comments:

6. **Remembering**   N/A -3 -2 -1 0 +1 +2 +3 +4
Comments:

7. **Active Listening**   N/A -3 -2 -1 0 +1 +2 +3 +4
Comments:

Beginning

8. **Introducing Yourself**
   Comments:

   N/A -3 -2 -1 0 +1 +2 +3 +4

9. **Seeking Introductions**
   Comments:

   N/A -3 -2 -1 0 +1 +2 +3 +4

10. **Describing Initial Purpose**
    Comments:

    N/A -3 -2 -1 0 +1 +2 +3 +4

11. **Outlining the Client's Role**
    Comments:

    N/A -3 -2 -1 0 +1 +2 +3 +4

12. **Discussing Policy
    and Ethical Factors**
    Comments:

    N/A -3 -2 -1 0 +1 +2 +3 +4

13. **Seeking Feedback**
    Comments:

    N/A -3 -2 -1 0 +1 +2 +3 +4

Exploring

14. **Probing**
    Comments:

    N/A -3 -2 -1 0 +1 +2 +3 +4

15. **Seeking Clarification**
    Comments:

    N/A -3 -2 -1 0 +1 +2 +3 +4

16. **Reflecting Content**
    Comments:

    N/A -3 -2 -1 0 +1 +2 +3 +4

17. **Reflecting Feelings**
    Comments:

    N/A -3 -2 -1 0 +1 +2 +3 +4

18. **Reflecting Feeling and Meaning**
    Comments:

    N/A -3 -2 -1 0 +1 +2 +3 +4

19. **Partializing**
    Comments:

    N/A -3 -2 -1 0 +1 +2 +3 +4

20. **Going Beyond What Is Said**
    Comments:

    N/A -3 -2 -1 0 +1 +2 +3 +4

Contracting

21. **Reflecting a Problem**   N/A -3 -2 -1   0 +1 +2 +3 +4
    Comments:

22. **Sharing Your View of a Problem**   N/A -3 -2 -1   0 +1 +2 +3 +4
    Comments:

23. **Specifying Problems for Work**   N/A -3 -2 -1   0 +1 +2 +3 +4
    Comments:

24. **Establishing Goals**   N/A -3 -2 -1   0 +1 +2 +3 +4
    Comments:

25. **Developing an Approach**   N/A -3 -2 -1   0 +1 +2 +3 +4
    Comments:

26. **Identifying Action Steps**   N/A -3 -2 -1   0 +1 +2 +3 +4
    Comments:

27. **Planning for Evaluation**   N/A -3 -2 -1   0 +1 +2 +3 +4
    Comments:

28. **Summarizing the Contract**   N/A -3 -2 -1   0 +1 +2 +3 +4
    Comments:

Working and Evaluating

29. **Rehearsing Action Steps**   N/A -3 -2 -1   0 +1 +2 +3 +4
    Comments:

30. **Reviewing Action Steps**   N/A -3 -2 -1   0 +1 +2 +3 +4
    Comments:

31. **Evaluating**   N/A -3 -2 -1   0 +1 +2 +3 +4
    Comments:

32. **Focusing**   N/A -3 -2 -1   0 +1 +2 +3 +4
    Comments:

33. **Educating**   N/A -3 -2 -1   0 +1 +2 +3 +4
    Comments:

34. Advising   N/A -3 -2 -1 0 +1 +2 +3 +4
    Comments:

35. Representing   N/A -3 -2 -1 0 +1 +2 +3 +4
    Comments:

36. Responding with Immediacy   N/A -3 -2 -1 0 +1 +2 +3 +4
    Comments:

37. Reframing   N/A -3 -2 -1 0 +1 +2 +3 +4
    Comments:

38. Confronting   N/A -3 -2 -1 0 +1 +2 +3 +4
    Comments:

39. Pointing Out Endings   N/A -3 -2 -1 0 +1 +2 +3 +4
    Comments:

Ending

40. Reviewing the Process   N/A -3 -2 -1 0 +1 +2 +3 +4
    Comments:

41. Final Evaluating   N/A -3 -2 -1 0 +1 +2 +3 +4
    Comments:

42. Sharing Ending Feelings   N/A -3 -2 -1 0 +1 +2 +3 +4
    and Saying Goodbye
    Comments:

Overall Impressions:

References and Bibliography

Acosta, F. X., Yamamoto, J., & Evans, L. A. (1982). *Effective psychotherapy for low-income and minority patients.* New York: Plenum.

Aguilar, I. (1972). Initial contacts with Mexican American families. *Social Work, 17,* 66–70.

Albert, R. (1986). *Law and social work practice.* New York: Springer.

Alberti, R. E., & Emmons, M. L. (1970). *Stand up, speak out, talk back.* San Luis Obispo, CA: Impact.

Altmann, H. (1973). Effects of empathy, warmth and genuineness in the initial counseling interview. *Counselor Education and Supervision, 12,* 225–229.

Anderson, J. (1988). *Foundations of social work practice.* New York: Springer.

Aronson, H., & Overall, B. (1966). Treatment expectations of patients in two social classes. *Social Work, 11,* 35–41.

Baer, B., & Federico, R. (1978). *Educating the baccalaureate social worker.* Cambridge, MA: Ballinger.

Baker, F., & Northman, J. E. (1981). *Helping: Human services for the 80s.* St. Louis, MO: C. V. Mosby.

Bandler, R., & Grinder, J. (1979). *Frogs into princes: Neuro-linguistic programming.* Moab, UT: Real People.

Bandler, R., & Grinder, J. (1982). *Reframing: Neuro-linguistic programming and the transformation of meaning* (pp. 5–78). Moab, UT: Real People.

Banks, G. (1971). The effects of race on one-to-one helping interviews. *Social Service Review, 45,* 137–144.

Banville, T. G. (1978). *How to listen—how to be heard.* Chicago: Nelson/Hall.

Barker, R. L. (1991). *The social work dictionary* (2nd ed.). Silver Spring, MD: National Association of Social Workers.

Bartlett, H. (1970). *The common base of social work practice.* New York: National Association of Social Workers.

Bates, M. (1983). Using the environment to help the male skid row alcoholic. *Social Casework, 64*, 276–282.

Bernstein, B. (1977). Privileged communications to the social worker. *Social Work, 22*, 264–268.

Bernstein, B. (1978). Malpractice, an ogre on the horizon. *Social Work, 23*, 106–111.

Bernstein, S. (1960). Self-determination: King or citizen in the realm of values. *Social Work, 5*(1), 3–8.

Bertcher, H. J. (1979). *Group participation: Techniques for leaders and members.* Newbury Park, CA: Sage.

Besharov, D. J. (1985). *The vulnerable social worker: Liability for serving children and families.* Silver Spring, MD: National Association of Social Workers.

Besharov, D. J., & Besharov, S. H. (1987). Teaching about liability. *Social Work, 32*(6), 517–522.

Biagi, E. (1977). The social work stake in problem-oriented recording. *Social Work in Health Care, 3*(2), 211–222.

Biestek, F. (1957). *The casework relationship.* Chicago: Loyola University Press.

Block, C. (1979). Black Americans and the cross-cultural counseling and psychotherapy experience. In A. Marsella & P. Pederson (Eds.), *Cross-cultural counseling and psychotherapy* (pp. 177–194). New York: Pergamon.

Bloom, M. (1981). *Primary prevention: The possible science.* Englewood Cliffs, NJ: Prentice-Hall.

Bloom, M., & Fischer, J. (1982). *Evaluating practice: Guidelines for the accountable professional.* Englewood Cliffs, NJ: Prentice-Hall.

Boehm, W. (1958). The nature of social work. *Social Work, 3*, 10–19.

Bolton, R. (1979). *People skills: How to assert yourself, listen to others, and resolve conflicts.* Englewood Cliffs, NJ: Prentice-Hall.

Brill, N. I. (1985). *Working with people: The helping process* (3rd ed.). New York: Longman.

Brown, C., & Hellinger, M. (1975). Therapists' attitudes toward women. *Social Work, 20*, 266–270.

Brown, L., & Levitt, J. (1979). A methodology for problem-system identification. *Social Casework, 60*, 408–415.

Burrill, G. (1976). The problem-oriented log in social casework. *Social Work, 21*(1), 67–68.

Cameron, J., & Talavera, E. (1976). An advocacy program for Spanish-speaking people. *Social Casework, 57*, 427–431.

Campbell, D. (1974). *If you don't know where you're going, you'll probably end up somewhere else.* Niles, IL: Argus Communications.

Canadian Association of Social Workers. (1994). *Social work code of ethics.* Ottawa: Author.

Canda, E. (1983). General implications of Shamanism for clinical social work. *International Social Work, 26*, 14–22.

Carkhuff, R. R. (1969). *Helping and human relations* (Vols. 1 & 2). New York: Holt, Rinehart and Winston.

Carkhuff, R. R. (1984). *Helping and human relations* (2nd ed., Vols. 1 & 2). Amherst, MA: Human Resource Development.

Carkhuff, R. R. (1987). *The art of helping VI* (6th ed.). Amherst, MA: Human Resource Development.

Carkhuff, R. R., & Anthony, W. A. (1979). *The skills of helping.* Amherst, MA: Human Resource Development.

Carkhuff, R. R., & Pierce, R. (1967). Differential effects of therapist race and social class upon patient depth of self-exploration in the initial clinical interview. *Journal of Consulting Psychology, 31*, 632–634.

Carkhuff, R. R., & Truax, C. B. (1965). Training in counseling and psychotherapy. *Journal of Consulting Psychology, 29*, 333–336.

Cautela, J. R., & Kearney, A. J. (1986). *The covert conditioning handbook.* New York: Springer.

Chafetz, J. (1972). Women in social work. *Social Work, 17*, 12–18.

Compton, B., & Galaway, B. (1984). *Social work processes* (3rd ed.). Homewood, IL: Dorsey.

Compton, B., & Galaway, B. (1989). *Social work processes* (4th ed.). Belmont, CA: Wadsworth.

Compton, B., & Galaway, B. (1994). *Social work processes* (5th ed.). Pacific Grove, CA: Brooks/Cole.

Cooper, S. (1978). A look at the effect of racism on clinical work. *Social Casework, 54*, 78.

Corcoran, K., & Fischer, J. (1987). *Measures for clinical practice: A sourcebook.* New York: Free Press.

Cormier, W. H., & Cormier, L. S. (1985). *Interviewing strategies for helpers: Fundamental skills and cognitive behavioral interventions* (2nd ed.). Pacific Grove, CA: Brooks/Cole.

Council on Social Work Education. (1976). *Teaching for competence in the delivery of direct services.* New York: Author.

Council on Social Work Education. (1992). *Curriculum policy statement.* Alexandria, VA: Author.

Cournoyer, B. R. (1983). Assertiveness among MSW students. *Journal of Social Work Education, 19*(1), 24–30.

Cournoyer, B. R. (1988). Personal and professional distress among social caseworkers: A developmental-interactional perspective. *Social Casework, 69*(5), 259–264.

Cournoyer, B. R. (1994a). A study of self-esteem, acceptance of others, self-control, and assertiveness in beginning MSW students. Indianapolis, IN: Author.

Cournoyer, B. R. (1994b). Basic communication skills for work with groups. In B. Compton & B. Galaway, *Social work processes* (5th ed., pp. 328–335). Pacific Grove, CA: Brooks/Cole.

Cowger, C., & Atherton, C. (1974). Social control: A rationale for social welfare. *Social Work, 19*, 456–462.

Cumming, J., & Cumming, E. (1969). *Ego and milieu: Theory and practice of environmental therapy.* New York: Atherton.

Danish, S. J., & Hauer, A. L. (1973a). *Helping skills: A basic training program—leader's manual.* New York: Behavioral Publications.

Danish, S. J., & Hauer, A. L. (1973b). *Helping skills: A basic training program—trainee's workbook.* New York: Behavioral Publications.

Dauw, D. C. (1980). *Increasing your self-esteem: How to feel better about yourself.* Prospect Heights, IL: Waveland.

Davenport, J., & Reims, N. (1978). Theoretical orientation and attitudes toward women. *Social Work, 23,* 306–311.

Devore, W., & Schlesinger, E. (1981). *Ethnic-sensitive social work practice.* St. Louis, MO: C. V. Mosby.

Dorfman, R. A. (Ed.). (1988). *Paradigms of clinical social work.* New York: Brunner/Mazel.

Draper, B. (1979). Black language as an adaptive response to a hostile environment. In C. Germain (Ed.), *Social work practices: People and environment* (pp. 267–281). New York: Columbia University Press.

Edleson, J. L., & Rose, S. D. (1981). Developing skills for the interview. In S. P. Schinke (Ed.), *Behavioral methods in social welfare* (pp. 257–268). New York: Aldine.

Egan, G. (1982a). *Exercises in helping skills: A training manual to accompany the skilled helper* (2nd ed.). Pacific Grove, CA: Brooks/Cole.

Egan, G. (1982b). *The skilled helper: Model, skills, and methods for effective helping* (2nd ed.). Pacific Grove, CA: Brooks/Cole.

Elson, M. (1986). *Self psychology in clinical social work.* New York: Norton.

Epstein, L. (1980). *Helping people: The task-centered approach.* St. Louis, MO: C. V. Mosby.

Eriksen, K. (1979). *Communications skills for the human services.* Reston, VA: Reston.

Evans, D. R., Hearn, M. T., Uhlemann, M. R., & Ivey, A. E. (1979). *Essential interviewing: A programmed approach to effective communication.* Pacific Grove, CA: Brooks/Cole.

Everstine, D. S., & Everstine, L. (1983). *People in crisis: Strategic therapeutic interventions.* New York: Brunner/Mazel.

Everstine, L., Everstine, D. S., Heymann, G. M., True, D. H., Johnson, H. G., & Seiden, R. H. (1980). Privacy and confidentiality in psychotherapy. *American Psychologist, 35,* 828–840.

Fey, W. F. (1955). Acceptance by others and its relation to acceptance of self and others: A revaluation. *Journal of Abnormal and Social Psychology, 30,* 274–276.

Fischer, J. (1978) *Effective casework practice: An eclectic approach.* New York: McGraw-Hill.

Fischer, J., & Corcoran, K. (1994). *Measures for clinical practice: A sourcebook* (Vols. 1 & 2, 2nd ed.). New York: Free Press.

Fischer, J., Dulaney, D., Fazio, R. T., Hudak, M. T., & Zivototsky, E. (1976). Are social workers sexists? *Social Work, 21,* 428–433.

Fischler, R. (1980). Protecting American Indian children. *Social Work, 25,* 341–349.

Fortune, A. E. (Ed.). (1985). *Task-centered practice with families and groups.* New York: Springer.

Fox, E., Nelson, M., & Bolman, W. (1963). The termination process: A neglected dimension in social work. *Social Work, 14*(4), 53–63.

Fredman, N., & Sherman, N. (1987). *Handbook of measurements for marriage and family therapy.* New York: Brunner/Mazel.

Gambrill, E. (1983). *Casework: A competency-based approach.* Englewood Cliffs, NJ: Prentice-Hall.

Garvin, C. (1987). *Contemporary group work* (2nd ed.). Englewood Cliffs, NJ: Prentice-Hall.

Garvin, C., & Seabury, B. (1984). *Interpersonal practice in social work: Processes and procedures.* Englewood Cliffs, NJ: Prentice-Hall.

Gaylin, W. (1976). *Caring.* New York: Alfred A. Knopf.

Gaylin, W. (1979). *Feelings: Our vital signs.* New York: Harper & Row.

Germain, C. B. (Ed.). (1979). *Social work practice: People and environments—an ecological perspective.* New York: Columbia University Press.

Ghali, S. (1982). Understanding Puerto Rican traditions. *Social Work, 27,* 98–102.

Gilgun, J. F. (1989). An ecosystemic approach to assessment. In B. Compton & B. Galaway, *Social work processes* (4th ed., pp. 455–470). Belmont, CA: Wadsworth.

Gillespie, D. F. (1987). Ethical issues in research. In National Association of Social Workers, *Encyclopedia of Social Work* (pp. 503–512). Washington, DC: Author.

Giordano, J. (1974). Ethnics and minorities. A review of the literature. *Clinical Social Work Journal, 2,* 207–220.

Gitterman, A., & Schaeffer, A. (1972). The white professional and the black client. *Social Casework, 53,* 280–291.

Golan, N. (1981). *Passing through transitions.* New York: Free Press.

Goldstein, E. G. (1984). *Ego psychology and social work practice.* New York: Free Press.

Goodman, G., & Esterly, G. (1988). *The talk book: The intimate science of communicating in close relationships.* Emmaus, PA: Rodale.

Good Tracks, J. (1973). Native American noninterference. *Social Work, 18,* 30–34.

Gottesfeld, M. L., & Pharis, M. E. (1977). *Profiles in social work.* New York: Human Sciences.

Green, J. (Ed.). (1982). *Cultural awareness in the human services.* Englewood Cliffs, NJ: Prentice-Hall.

Green, R., & Cox, G. (1978). Social work and malpractice: A converging course. *Social Work, 23,* 100–104.

Haley, J. (1978). *Problem solving therapy.* San Francisco: Jossey-Bass.

Halleck, S. (1963). The impact of professional dishonesty on behavior of disturbed adolescents. *Social Work, 8,* 48–56.

Hamilton, G. (1951). *Theory and practice of social case work* (2nd ed., rev.). New York: Columbia University Press.

Hammond, D., Hepworth, D., & Smith, V. (1977). *Improving therapeutic communication.* San Francisco: Jossey-Bass.

Harris, L., & Lucas, M. (1976). Sex-role stereotyping. *Social Work, 21,* 390–395.

Hartman, A. (1978). Diagrammatic assessment of family relationships. *Social Casework, 59,* 465–476.

Hartman, A., & Laird, J. (1983). *Family-centered social work practice.* New York: Free Press.

Hartman, B. L., & Wickey, J. M. (1978). The person-oriented record in treatment. *Social Work, 23*(4), 296–299.

Hedlund, B. L., & Lindquist, C. U. (1984). The development of an inventory for distinguishing among passive, aggressive, and assertive behavior. *Behavioral Assessment, 6,* 379–390.

Henley, N. M. (1972). *Body politics: Power, sex, and nonverbal communication.* Englewood Cliffs, NJ: Prentice-Hall.

Henry, S. (1981). *Group skills in social work.* Itasca, IL: F. E. Peacock.

Henry, S. (1992). *Group skills in social work* (2nd ed.). Pacific Grove, CA: Brooks/Cole.

Hepworth, D., & Larsen, J. (1986). *Direct social work practice: Theory and skills* (2nd ed.). Chicago: Dorsey.

Hepworth, D., & Larsen, J. (1990). *Direct social work practice: Theory and skills* (3rd ed.). Belmont, CA: Wadsworth.

Hess, H., & Hess, P. M. (1989). Termination in context. In B. Compton & B. Galaway, *Social work processes* (4th ed., pp. 646–657). Belmont, CA: Wadsworth.

Ho, M. (1976). Social work with Asian Americans. *Social Casework, 57,* 195–201.

Hollis, F., & Woods, M. E. (1981). *Casework: A psychosocial therapy* (3rd ed.). New York: Random House.

Howe, E. (1980). Public professions and the private model of professionalism. *Social Work, 25,* 179–191.

Hudson, W. (1982). *The clinical measurement package: A field manual.* Homewood, IL: Dorsey.

Ivey, A. E. (1971). *Microcounseling: Innovations in interview training.* Springfield, IL: Thomas.

Ivey, A. E. (1976). The counselor as teacher. *Personnel and Guidance Journal, 54,* 431–434.

Ivey, A. E. (1988). *Intentional interviewing and counseling: Facilitating client development* (2nd ed.). Pacific Grove, CA: Brooks/Cole.

Ivey, A. E., & Authier, J. (1978). *Microcounseling: Innovations in interviewing, counseling, psychotherapy, and psychoeducation.* Springfield, IL: Thomas.

Ivey, A. E., & Simek-Downing, L. (1980). *Counseling and psychotherapy: Skills, theories, and practice.* Englewood Cliffs, NJ: Prentice-Hall.

Jakubowski, P., & Lange, A. J. (1978). *The assertive option: Your rights and responsibilities.* Champaign, IL: Research Press.

Johnson, D. W. (1981). *Reaching out: Interpersonal effectiveness and self-actualization* (2nd ed.). Englewood Cliffs, NJ: Prentice-Hall.

Johnson, H. C. (1978). Integrating the problem-oriented record with a systems approach to case assessment. *Journal of Education for Social Work, 14*(3), 71–77.

Johnson, L. C. (1986). *Social work practice: A generalist approach* (2nd ed.). Newton, MA: Allyn and Bacon.

Johnson, L. C. (1995). *Social work practice: A generalist approach* (5th ed.). Newton, MA: Allyn and Bacon.

Joseph, M. V. (1985). A model for ethical decision making in clinical practice. In C. B. Germain (Ed.), *Advances in clinical social work practice: Selected papers, 1982 NASW national conference on clinical social work* (pp. 207–217). Silver Spring, MD: National Association of Social Workers.

Kadushin, A. (1972). The racial factor in the interview. *Social Work, 17,* 88–99.

Kadushin, A. (1983). *The social work interview* (2nd ed.). New York: Columbia University Press.

Kadushin, A. (1990). *The social work interview* (3rd ed.). New York: Columbia University Press.

Kagle, J. D. (1984). *Social work records.* Homewood, IL: Dorsey.

Kagle, J. D. (1991). *Social work records* (2nd ed.). Belmont, CA: Wadsworth.

Kane, R. A. (1974). Look to the record. *Social Work, 19*(4), 412–419.

Keefe, T. (1976). Empathy: The critical skill. *Social Work, 21,* 10–14.

Keith-Lucas, A. (1971). Ethics in social work. In National Association of Social Workers, *Encyclopedia of Social Work* (pp. 324–329). Washington, DC: Author.

Keith-Lucas, A. (1972) *The giving and taking of help.* Chapel Hill: University of North Carolina Press.

Keith-Lucas, A. (1977). Ethics in social work. In National Association of Social Workers, *Encyclopedia of Social Work* (pp. 350–355). Washington, DC: Author.

Kiresuk, T. & Sherman, R. E. (1968). Goal attainment scaling: A general method for evaluating comprehensive community health programs. *Community Mental Health Journal, 4,* 443–453.

Kirst-Ashman, K. K., & Hull, Jr., G. H. (1993). *Understanding generalist practice.* Chicago: Nelson-Hall.

Kitano, H. (Ed.). (1971). *Asians in America.* New York: Council on Social Work Education.

Knapp, M. L. (1972). *Nonverbal communication in human interaction.* New York: Holt, Rinehart and Winston.

Knoll, F. (1971). Casework services for Mexican Americans. *Social Casework, 52,* 279–284.

Kosberg, J. (1973). The nursing home: A social work paradox. *Social Work, 18,* 104–110.

Kosberg, J., & Harris, A. (1978). Attitudes toward elderly clients. *Health and Social Work, 3,* 67–90.

Krill, D. F. (1978). *Existential social work.* New York: Free Press.

Krill, D. F. (1986). *The beat worker: Humanizing social work & psychotherapy practice.* Lanham, MD: University Press of America.

Kubler-Ross, E. (1969). *On death and dying.* New York: Macmillan.

Lambert, M. J. (1982). Relation of helping skills to treatment outcome. In E. K. Marshall & P. D. Kurtz (Eds.), *Interpersonal helping skills: A guide to training methods, programs, and resources* (pp. 26–53). San Francisco: Jossey-Bass.

Lange, A. J., & Jakubowski, P. (1976). *Responsible assertive behavior: Cognitive/behavioral procedures for trainers.* Champaign, IL: Research Press.

Lazarus, A. (1984). *In the mind's eye: The power of imagery for personal enrichment.* New York: Guilford.

Levinson, H. (1977). Termination of psychotherapy: Some salient issues. *Social Casework, 58*(8), 480–498.

Levy, C. (1976a). Personal vs. professional values: The practitioner's dilemma. *Clinical Social Work Journal, 4,* 110–120.

Levy, C. (1976b). *Social work ethics.* New York: Human Sciences Press.

Lewinsohn, P. M., Munoz, R. F., Youngren, M. A., & Zeiss, A. M. (1978). *Control your depression.* Englewood Cliffs, NJ: Prentice-Hall, 175–177.

Lewis, H. (1984). Ethical assessment. *Social Casework, 65,* 203–211.

Lewis, R., & Ho, M. (1975). Social work with Native Americans. *Social Work, 20,* 379–382.

Lieberman, F. (Ed). (1982). *Clinical social workers as psychotherapists.* New York: Gardner.

Loewenberg, F., & Dolgoff, R. (1988). *Ethical decisions for social work practice* (3rd ed.). Itasca, IL: F. E. Peacock.

Loewenberg, F., & Dolgoff, R. (1992). *Ethical decisions for social work practice* (4th ed.). Itasca, IL: F. E. Peacock.

Maduro, R., & Martinez, C. (1974). Latino dream analysis: Opportunity for confrontation. *Social Casework, 55,* 461–469.

Mahaffey, M. (1976). Sexism in social work. *Social Work, 2,* 419.

Maldonado, D. (1975). The Chicano aged. *Social Work, 20,* 213–216.

Maluccio, A. (1979). *Learning from clients: Interpersonal helping as viewed by clients and social workers.* New York: Free Press.

Maluccio, A. (Ed.). (1981). *Promoting competence in clients: A new/old approach to social work practice.* New York: Free Press.

Maluccio, A., & Marlow, W. (1974). The case for contract. *Social Work, 19,* 28–36.

Marsh, P. (Ed.). (1988). *Eye to eye: How people interact.* Topsfield, MA: Salem House.

Marshall, E. K., Charping, J. W., & Bell, W. J. (1979). Interpersonal skills training: A review of the research. *Social Work Research and Abstracts, 15,* 10–16.

Marshall, E. K., Kurtz, P. D., and associates. (1982). *Interpersonal helping skills: A guide to training methods, programs, and resources.* San Francisco: Jossey-Bass.

Martens, W. M., & Holmstrup, E. (1974). Problem-oriented recording. *Social Casework, 55*(9), 554–561.

Matarazzo, R. G. (1978). Research on the teaching and learning of psychotherapeutic skills. In S. L. Garfield & A. E. Bergin (Eds.), *Handbook of psychotherapy and behavior change* (2nd ed., pp. 941–966). New York: Wiley.

Mayadas, N. S., & O'Brien, D. E. (1976). Teaching casework skills in the laboratory: Methods and techniques. In Council on Social Work Education, *Teaching for competence in the delivery of direct services* (pp. 72–82). New York: Author.

Mayer, J., & Timms, N. (1969). Clash in perspective between worker and client. *Social Casework, 50,* 32–40.

Mayfield, W. (1972). Mental health in the black community. *Social Work, 17,* 106–110.

Mays, D. T., & Franks, C. M. (1985). *Negative outcome in psychotherapy and what to do about it.* New York: Springer.

McCann, C. W. (1979). Ethics and the alleged unethical. *Social Work, 24,* 5–8.

McGoldrick, M., & Gerson, R. (1985). *Genograms in family assessment.* New York: Norton.

McIntosh, J. (1985). Suicide among the elderly: Levels and trends. *American Journal of Orthopsychiatry, 55,* 288–293.

McKay, M., Davis, M., & Fanning, P. (1983). *Messages: The communications skills book.* Oakland, CA: New Harbinger.

Medina, C., & Neyes, M. (1976). Dilemmas of Chicano counselors. *Social Work, 21,* 515–517.

Meichenbaum, D., & Turk, D. C. (1987). *Facilitating treatment adherence.* New York: Plenum.

Meyer, C. (1970). *Social work practice: A response to the urban crisis.* New York: Free Press.

Meyer, C. (1979). What directions for direct practice? *Social Work, 24,* 267–272.

Middleman, R., & Goldberg, G. (1974). *Social service delivery: A structural approach to social work practice.* New York: Columbia University Press.

Middleman, R. R., & Wood, G. G. (1990). *Skills for direct practice in social work.* New York: Columbia University Press.

Miller, D. (1974). The influence of the patient's sex on clinical judgment. *Smith College Studies in Social Work, 44,* 89–100.

Miller, H. (1968). Value dilemmas in social casework. *Social Casework, 13,* 27–33.

Minahan, A. (1981). Social workers and oppressed people. *Social Work, 26,* 183–184.

Montagu, A., & Matson, F. (1979). *The human connection.* New York: McGraw-Hill.

Montiel, M. (1973). The Chicano family: A review of research. *Social Work, 18,* 21–23.

Morales, A. (1971). The collective preconscious and racism. *Social Casework, 52,* 285–293.

Morales, A. (1977). Beyond traditional conceptual frameworks. *Social Work, 22,* 387–393.

Morales, A. (1978). Institutional racism in mental health and criminal justice. *Social Casework, 59,* 387–395.

Morales, A. (1981). Social work with third-world people. *Social Work, 26,* 45–51.

Morales, A. (1984). Substance abuse and Mexican American youth: An overview. *Journal of Drug Issues, 14,* 297–311.

Morales, A., & Salcido, R. (1986). Social work with Mexican Americans. In A. Morales & B. Sheafor, *Social work: A profession of many faces* (4th ed., pp. 475–498). Boston: Allyn and Bacon.

Morales, A., & Sheafor, B. (1986). *Social work: A profession of many faces* (4th ed.). Boston: Allyn and Bacon.

Morales, A., & Sheafor, B. (1992). *Social work: A profession of many faces* (6th ed.). Boston: Allyn and Bacon.

Morrison, B. J., Rehr, H., & Rosenberg, G. (1985). How well are you doing? Evaluation strategies for practice. In C. B. Germain (Ed.), *Advances in clinical social work practice: Selected papers, 1982 NASW national conference on clinical social work* (pp. 218–231). Silver Spring, MD: National Association of Social Workers.

Mosko, M. (1976). Feminist theory and casework practice. In B. Ross & S. Khinduka (Eds.), *Social work in practice* (pp. 181–190). Washington, DC: National Association of Social Workers.

Moss, S., & Moss, M. (1967). When a caseworker leaves an agency: The impact on worker and client. *Social Casework, 48*(7), 433–437.

Munson, C. E. (Ed.). (1980). *Social work with families: Theory and practice.* New York: Free Press.

Murase, K. (1977). Minorities: Asian Americans. In National Association of Social Workers, *Encyclopedia of Social Work* (pp. 953–960). Washington, DC: Author.

Myers, J. E. B. (1992). *Legal issues in child abuse and neglect.* Newbury Park, CA: Sage.

National Association of Social Workers. (1980). *Code of ethics of the National Association of Social Workers.* Silver Spring, MD: Author.

National Association of Social Workers. (1981). *NASW standards for the classification of social work practice.* Silver Spring, MD: Author.

Nelsen, J. C. (1975). Social work's fields of practice, methods, and models: The choice to act. *Social Service Review, 49*, 264–270.

Nelson, J. C. (1980). *Communication theory and social work practice.* Chicago: University of Chicago Press.

Northen, H. (1982). *Clinical social work.* New York: Columbia University Press.

Norton, D. (1978). *The dual perspective: Inclusion of ethnic minority content in the social work curriculum.* New York: Council on Social Work Education.

Nugent, W. R., & Thomas, J. W. (1993). Validation of a clinical measure of self-esteem. *Research on Social Work Practice, 3*(2), 191–207.

Ortego, P. (1971). The Chicano renaissance. *Social Casework, 52*, 294–307.

Parad, H. J. (Ed.). (1958). *Ego psychology and dynamic casework: Papers from the Smith College School for Social Work.* New York: Family Service Association of America.

Pease, A. (1981). *Signals: How to use body language for power, success and love.* New York: Bantam.

Pedersen, P. B., & Ivey, A. (1993). *Culture-centered counseling and interviewing skills: A practical guide.* Westport, CT: Praeger.

Perlman, H. H. (1957). *Social casework: A problem-solving process.* Chicago: University of Chicago Press.

Perlman, H. H. (1968). *Persona: Social role and personality.* Chicago: University of Chicago Press.

Perlman, H. H. (Ed.). (1969). *Helping: Charlotte Towle on social work and social casework.* Chicago: University of Chicago Press.

Perlman, H. H. (1971). *Perspectives on social casework*. Philadelphia: Temple University Press.

Perlman, H. H. (1979). *Relationship: The heart of helping people*. Chicago: University of Chicago Press.

Phillips, H. (1957). *Essentials of social group work skill*. New York: Association Press.

Pilseker, C. (1978). Values: A problem for everyone. *Social Work, 23*, 54–57.

Pincus, A., & Minahan, A. (1973). *Social work practice: Model and method*. Itasca, IL: F. E. Peacock.

Pinderhughes, E. (1979). Teaching empathy in cross-cultural social work. *Social Work, 24*, 312–316.

Pinkston, E. M., Levitt, J. L., Green, G. R., Linsk, N. L., & Rzepnicki, T. L. (1982). *Effective social work practice: Advanced techniques for behavioral intervention with individuals, families, and institutional staff*. San Francisco: Jossey-Bass.

Polansky, N. (1971). *Ego psychology and communication: Theory for the interview*. New York: Atherton.

Powell, G., Yamamoto, J., Romero, A., & Morales, A. (Eds.). (1983). *The psychosocial development of minority group children*. New York: Brunner/Mazel.

Priestley, P., & McGuire, J. (1983). *Learning to help: Basic skill exercises*. London: Tavistock.

Rauch, J. (1978). Gender as a factor in practice. *Social Work, 23*, 388–395.

Reamer, F. G. (1979). Fundamental ethical issues in social work. *Social Service Review, 53*, 229–243.

Reamer, F. G. (1980). Ethical content in social work. *Social Casework, 61*, 531–540.

Reamer, F. G. (1982). *Ethical dilemmas in social service*. New York: Columbia University Press.

Reamer, F. G. (1983). Ethical dilemmas in social work practice. *Social Work, 28*, 31–35.

Reamer, F. G. (1987). Values and ethics. In National Association of Social Workers, *Encyclopedia of Social Work* (pp. 801–809). Washington, DC: Author.

Reamer, F. G. (1994). *Social work malpractice and liability*. New York: Columbia University Press.

Reid, W. J. (1978). *The task-centered system*. New York: Columbia University Press.

Reid, W. J. (1992). *Task strategies: An empirical approach to social work*. New York: Columbia University Press.

Reid, W. J., & Epstein, L. (1972). *Task-centered casework*. New York: Columbia University Press.

Reid, W. J., & Epstein, L. (1977). *Task-centered practice*. New York: Columbia University Press.

Reid, W. J., & Shyne, A. W. (1969). *Brief and extended casework*. New York: Columbia University Press.

Richmond, M. E. (1944). *Social diagnosis*. New York: Free Press. (First published in 1917.)

Riley, R. (1975). Family advocacy: Case to cause and back to case. *Child Welfare, 50*, 374–383.

Ripple, L. (1955). Motivation, capacity, and opportunity as related to the use of casework service: Plan of study. *Social Service Review, 29*, 172–193.

Ripple, L., & Alexander, E. (1956). Motivation, capacity, and opportunity as related to the use of casework service: Nature of client's problem. *Social Service Review, 30*, 38–54.

Roberts, R. W., & Nee, R. H. (Eds.). (1970). *Theories of social casework.* Chicago: University of Chicago Press.

Rogers, C. R. (1957). The necessary and sufficient conditions of psychotherapeutic personality change. *Journal of Consulting Psychology, 21*, 95–103.

Rogers, C. R. (1961). *On becoming a person.* Boston: Houghton Mifflin.

Rogers, C. R. (1975). Empathic: An unappreciated way of being. *Counseling Psychologist, 5*, 2–10.

Rosenbaum, M. (1980). A schedule for assessing self-control behaviors: Preliminary findings. *Behavior Therapy, 11*, 109–121.

Rosenthal, P. (1984). *Words and values: Some leading words and where they lead us.* New York: Oxford University Press.

Rothman, J., Gant, L., & Hnat, S. (1985). Mexican American family culture. *Social Service Review, 59*, 197–215.

Rubenstein, H., & Bloch, M. H. (Eds). (1982). *Things that matter: Influences on helping relationships.* New York: Macmillan.

Saari, C. (1986). *Clinical social work treatment: How does it work?* New York: Gardner.

Salcido, R. (1979a). Problems of the Mexican American elderly in an urban setting. *Social Casework, 60*, 609–615.

Salcido, R. (1979b). Undocumented aliens: A study of Mexican families. *Social Work, 24*, 306–311.

Saltzman, A., & Proch, K. (1990). *Law in social work practice.* Chicago: Nelson-Hall.

Santa Cruz, L., & Hepworth, D. (1975). News and views: Effects of cultural orientation on casework. *Social Casework, 56*, 52–57.

Satir, V. (1972). *Peoplemaking.* Palo Alto, CA: Science and Behavior Books.

Scheflen, A. E., with Scheflen, A. (1972). *Body language and social order: Communication as behavioral control.* Englewood Cliffs, NJ: Prentice-Hall.

Schinke, S. P. (Ed.). (1981a). *Behavioral methods in social welfare.* New York: Aldine.

Schinke, S. P. (1981b). Individual case evaluation. In S. P. Schinke (Ed.), *Behavioral methods in social welfare* (pp. 303–314). New York: Aldine.

Schubert, M. (1971). *Interviewing in social work practice: An introduction.* New York: Council on Social Work Education.

Schulman, E. D. (1982). *Intervention in human services: A guide to skills and knowledge* (3rd ed.). St. Louis, MO: C. V. Mosby.

Schwartz, M. (1973). Sexism in the social work curriculum. *Journal of Education for Social Work, 9*, 65–70.

Schwartz, M. (1974). Importance of sex of worker and client. *Social Work, 19*, 177–186.

Schwartz, M. (1975). Casework implications of a worker's pregnancy. *Social Casework, 56,* 27–34.

Schwartz, W. (1971). On the use of groups in social work practice. In W. Schwartz & S. Zalba (Eds.), *The practice of group work* (pp. 3–24). New York: Columbia University Press.

Schwartz, W. (1976). Between client and system: The mediating function. In R. R. Roberts & H. Northen (Eds.), *Theories of social work with groups* (pp. 188–190). New York: Columbia University Press.

Seabury, B. (1975). Negotiating sound contracts with clients. *Public Welfare, 37,* 33–39.

Seabury, B. (1976). The contract: Uses, abuses and limitations. *Social Work, 21,* 16–21.

Shelton, J. L., & Levy, R. L. *Behavioral assignments and treatment compliance.* Champaign, IL: Research Press.

Shulman, L. (1978). A study of practice skill. *Social Work, 23,* 274–280.

Shulman, L. (1981). *Identifying, measuring, and teaching helping skills.* New York: Council on Social Work Education.

Shulman, L. (1982). *Skills of supervision and staff management.* Itasca, IL: F. E. Peacock.

Shulman, L. (1984). *The skills of helping individuals and groups* (2nd ed.). Itasca, IL: F. E. Peacock.

Shulman, L. (1991). *Interactional social work practice: Toward an empirical theory.* Itasca, IL: F. E. Peacock.

Shulman, L. (1992). *The skills of helping individuals and groups* (3rd ed.). Itasca, IL: F. E. Peacock.

Siporin, M. (1975). *Introduction to social work practice.* New York: Macmillan.

Skidmore, R., & Thackeray, M. G. (1982). *Introduction to social work* (3rd ed.). Englewood Cliffs, NJ: Prentice-Hall.

Smalley, R. E. (1967). *Theory for social work practice.* New York: Columbia University Press.

Sobey, F. (Ed.). (1977). *Changing roles in social work practice.* Philadelphia: Temple University Press.

Solis, F. (1971). Socioeconomic and cultural conditions of migrant workers. *Social Casework, 52,* 308–315.

Solomon, B. (1976a). *Black empowerment: Social work in oppressed communities.* New York: Columbia University Press.

Solomon, B. (1976b). Is it sex, race or class? *Social Work, 21,* 421–426.

Solomon, B. (1986). Social work with Afro-Americans. In A. Morales & B. Sheafor, *Social work: A profession of many faces* (4th ed., pp. 501–521). Boston: Allyn and Bacon.

Sorrels, B. D. (1983). *The nonsexist communicator.* Englewood Cliffs, NJ: Prentice-Hall.

Souflee, F., & Schmitt, G. (1974). Education for practice in the Chicano community. *Journal of Education for Social Work, 10,* 75–84.

Spiegel, J. P., & Machotka, P. (1974). *Messages of the body.* New York: Free Press.

Stein, T. J. (1981). *Social work practice in child welfare.* Englewood Cliffs, NJ: Prentice-Hall.

Strayhorn, J. M. (1977). *Talking it out: A guide to effective communication and problem solving.* Champaign, IL: Research Press.

Sue, D. W. (1977). Counseling the culturally different: A conceptual analysis. *Personnel and Guidance Journal, 55,* 422–425.

Sue, D. W., & Sue, D. (1990). *Counseling the culturally different: Theory and practice.* New York: Wiley.

Sundel, S. S., & Sundel, M. (1980). *Be assertive: A practical guide for human service workers.* Newbury Park, CA: Sage.

Sydnor, G. L., Akridge, R. L., & Parkhill, N. L. (1972). *Human relations training: A programmed manual.* Minden, LA: Human Resources Development Training Institute.

Tannen, D. (1990). *You just don't understand: Women and men in conversation.* New York: Morrow.

Tannen, D. (1994). *Talking from 9 to 5: How women's and men's conversational styles affect who gets heard, who gets credit, and what gets done at work.* New York: Morrow.

Tanner, B. A., & Parrino, J. J. (1975). *Helping others: Behavioral procedures for mental health workers.* Eugene, OR: E-B Press.

Tolson, E. R., Reid, W. J., & Garvin, C. D. (1994). *Generalist practice: A task-centered approach.* New York: Columbia University Press.

Truax, D. B., & Carkhuff, R. R. (1967). *Toward effective counseling and psychotherapy: Training and practice.* Chicago & New York: Aldine Atherton.

Turner, F. J. (Ed.). (1983). *Differential diagnosis and treatment in social work* (3rd ed.). New York: Free Press.

Turner, F. J. (Ed.). (1986). *Social work treatment: Interlocking theoretical approaches* (3rd ed.). New York: Free Press.

Underwood, M., & Underwood, E. (1976). Clinical observations of a pregnant therapist. *Social Work, 21,* 512–514.

VandeCreek, L., & Knapp, S. (1993). *Tarasoff and beyond: Legal and clinical considerations in the treatment of life-endangering patients* (Rev. ed.). Sarasota, FL: Professional Resource Press.

Van Hoose, W. H., & Kottler, J. A. (1985). *Ethical and legal issues in counseling and psychotherapy* (2nd ed.). San Francisco: Jossey-Bass.

Velasquez, J., McClure, M., & Benavides, E. (1984). A framework for establishing social work relationships across racial/ethnic lines. In B. Compton & B. Galaway, *Social work processes* (3rd ed., pp. 260–267). Homewood, IL: Dorsey Press.

Walz, T., Willenbring, G., & deMoll, L. (1974). Environmental design. *Social Work, 19,* 38–48.

Webbink, P. (1986). *The power of the eyes.* New York: Springer.

Wegscheider-Cruse, S. (1985). *Choice-making.* Pompano Beach, FL: Health Communications.

Weil, M., & Sanchez, E. (1983). The impact of the Tarasoff decision on clinical social work practice. *Social Service Review, 57,* 112–124.

Wells, C. C., with Masch, M. K. (1986). *Social work ethics day to day.* New York: Longman.

Whittaker, J. K. (1974). *Social treatment: An approach to interpersonal helping.* Chicago: Aldine.

Whittaker, J. K., & Garbarino, J. (1983). *Social support networks: informal helping in the human services*. New York: Aldine.

Wicks, R. J. (1984). *Counseling strategies and intervention techniques for the human services* (2nd ed.). New York: Longman.

Wilson, S. J. (1978). *Confidentiality in social work*. New York: Free Press.

Wilson, S. J. (1980). *Recording: Guidelines for social workers*. New York: Free Press.

Wodarski, J., & Bagarozzi, D. A. (1979). *Behavioral social work*. New York: Human Sciences.

Woititz, J. G. (1983). *Adult children of alcoholics*. Pompano Beach, FL: Health Communications.

Woititz, J. G. (1985). *Struggle for intimacy*. Pompano Beach, FL: Health Communications.

Wolman, B. B. (Ed.). (1973). *Dictionary of behavioral science*. New York: Van Nostrand Reinhold.

Wood, G. G., & Middleman, R. R. (1989). *The structural approach to direct practice in social work*. New York: Columbia University Press.

Woody, R. H. (1988). *Fifty ways to avoid malpractice: A guidebook for mental health professionals*. Sarasota, FL: Professional Resource Press.

Yalom, I. D. (1975). *The theory and practice of group psychotherapy* (2nd ed.). New York: Basic Books.

Yelaja, S. A. (1982). *Ethical issues in social work*. Springfield, IL: Charles C Thomas.

Zastrow, C. (1989). *The practice of social work* (3rd ed.). Chicago: Dorsey.

Zastrow, C. (1992). *The practice of social work* (4th ed.). Belmont, CA: Wadsworth.

Zastrow, C. (1995). *The practice of social work* (5th ed.). Pacific Grove, CA: Brooks/Cole.

Zunin, L. (1972). *Contact: The first four minutes*. Los Angeles: Nash.

TO THE OWNER OF THIS BOOK:

I hope that you have enjoyed *Social Work Skills Workbook*, Second Edition, as much as I have enjoyed writing it. I'd like to know as much about your experiences with the book as you care to offer. Only through your comments and the comments of others can I learn how to make *Social Work Skills Workbook* a better book for future readers.

School: _____

Your instructor's name: _____

1. For what course was this book assigned?_____

_____

_____

2. What did you like most about Social Work Skills Workbook? _____

_____

_____

3. What did you like least about the book? _____

_____

_____

4. Were all of the chapters of the book assigned for you to read? _____

   If not, which ones weren't? _____

5. In the space below, or in a separate letter, please let me know what other comments about the book you'd like to make. (For example, were any chapters or concepts particularly difficult?) I'd be delighted to hear from you!

_____

_____

_____

_____

_____

_____

_____

_____

Optional:

Your name: _____ Date: _____

May Brooks/Cole quote you, either in promotion for *Social Work Skills Workbook,*
Second Edition, or in future publishing ventures?

Yes: _____ No: _____

Sincerely,

Barry Cournoyer

FOLD HERE

FOLD HERE

Brooks/Cole is dedicated to publishing quality publications for education in the human services fields. If you are interested in learning more about our publications, please fill in your name and address and request our latest catalogue, using this prepaid mailer.

Name: _____

Street Address: _____

City, State, and Zip: _____

FOLD HERE

FOLD HERE

PHASE-SPECIFIC SKILLS
(most applicable during specific phases or processes)

Assessing

Organizing Descriptive
Formulating a Tentativ

Exploring

Probing
Seeking Clarification
Reflecting Content
Reflecting Feelings
Reflecting Feeling and Meaning
Partializing
Going Beyond What Is Said

Beginning

Introducing Yourself
Seeking Introductions
Describing Initial Purpose
Outlining the Client's Role
Discussing Policy and Ethical Factors
Seeking Feedback

Preparing

Preparatory Reviewing
Preparatory Exploring
Preparatory Consulting
Preparatory Arranging
Preparatory Empathy
Preparatory Self-Exploration
Centering
Preliminary Planning and Recording